NEW ECONOMIC CONSTITUTIC

New Economic Constitutionalism in Europe focuses on the institutional mutation of constitutionalism following the major economic crisis in the Eurozone and globally. The main axis is that a new economic constitutionalism has arisen which trespasses on the conventional conceptual foundations and needs to be addressed with novel institutional vehicles. The author proposes an original and searching analysis of the significant constitutional evolutions that have taken place in member states in response to the global financial crisis. The book combines a sophisticated theoretical model of a new form of economic constitutionalism with detailed practical argumentation. This important new work provides a valuable addition to the understanding of this hugely important topic.

Volume 27: Studies of the Oxford Institute of European and Comparative Law

Recent titles in this Series

New Economic Constitutionalism in Europe

George Gerapetritis

·HART·

OXFORD · LONDON · NEW YORK · NEW DELHI · SYDNEY

HART PUBLISHING

Bloomsbury Publishing Plc

Kemp House, Chawley Park, Cumnor Hill, Oxford, OX2 9PH, UK

1385 Broadway, New York, NY 10018, USA

29 Earlsfort Terrace, Dublin 2, Ireland

HART PUBLISHING, the Hart/Stag logo, BLOOMSBURY and the Diana logo are
trademarks of Bloomsbury Publishing Plc

First published in Great Britain 2019

First published in hardback, 2019
Paperback edition, 2021

A catalogue record for this book is available from the British Library.

Library of Congress Cataloging-in-Publication Data

Names: Gerapetritis, George, author.

Title: New economic constitutionalism in Europe / George Gerapetritis.

Description: Oxford ; New York : Hart. 2019. | Series: Studies of the Oxford Institute of European
and Comparative law; volume 27 | Includes bibliographical references and index.

Identifiers: LCCN 2019029556 (print) | LCCN 2019029557 (ebook) |
ISBN 9781509909629 (hardback) | ISBN 9781509909650 (Epub)

Subjects: LCSH: Constitutional law—Economic aspects—European Union countries.

Classification: LCC KJC4445 .G468 2019 (print) | LCC KJC4445 (ebook) | DDC 342.24—dc23

LC record available at https://lccn.loc.gov/2019029556

LC ebook record available at https://lccn.loc.gov/2019029557

ISBN: HB: 978-1-50990-962-9
PB: 978-1-50995-211-3
ePDF: 978-1-50990-963-6
ePub: 978-1-50990-965-0

Typeset by Compuscript Ltd, Shannon

To find out more about our authors and books visit www.hartpublishing.co.uk. Here you will find
extracts, author information, details of forthcoming events and the option to sign up for our newsletters.

Στη μνήμη των γονέων μου

FOREWORD

Among all the challenges that have beset the European integration project since its inception, the global financial crisis of 2008 and the ensuing Eurozone crisis are distinct. They came closer than any other event to posing an existentialist threat to one of the fundamental pillars of the integration compact, namely Economic and Monetary Union, and even to the EU itself. They also led to far-reaching mutations of the integration paradigm, mostly through informal rather than formal Treaty revisions.

The financial crisis led to the expansion of European Union competence in multiple ways. EU law colonised more areas of financial regulation, spearheading the introduction of normative standards in areas hitherto unregulated, such as credit rating agencies and derivatives. EU law became more detailed, more intense, and spread from the realm of regulation to the realm of monitoring and enforcement. Direct regulation by EU institutions and agencies, for example in the field of Banking Union, challenges the model of home country control and mutual recognition leading to a post-internal market regulatory model. It is not inaccurate to talk about the federalisation of financial regulation in the EU. Furthermore, the introduction of a plethora of economic governance measures has essentially led to the birth of a new area of law: the law of public finances, superimposing disciplines and normative standards in an area which until now government discretion reigned.

Most of these changes have been introduced in an attempt to make up for failures at Member State level but under shaky EU legal bases and in the absence of express Treaty revision. Crisis management led to law reform and constitutional convulsions led to a new regulatory framework driven by expediency, necessity and an instinct for institutional survival which left little room for coherence and strict adherence to accepted narratives of the rule of law. The crisis highlighted the mismatch between constitutional constraints and the need for extensive decision-making powers – both legislative and executive – at EU level. Crisis management has led EU institutions to an apologetic narrative of justification making a virtue out of necessity.

There is here a paradox. Since the establishment of the European Communities, successive treaty amendments and legislative developments have led to the increasing formalisation of EU law through the express recognition of constitutional rights, the adoption of detailed rules in several spheres, and the concretisation of norms and processes through administrative rule-making. EU law has become more specific, more rule-bound, and more process-bound. Nevertheless, as a result of reforms or reactions to successive crises, especially the financial crisis, it has also become more uncertain and is characterised by a higher level of constitutional fluidity and normative indeterminacy. Judged by reference to pre-crisis constitutional benchmarks, the governance clock has been reset.

This monograph examines the effects of the financial crisis on constitutional law. It posits that, in the aftermath of the crisis, a new economic constitutionalism has emerged which elevates the economy to a *sine qua non* for the harmonious functioning of the constitutional state and attributes it the same normative status as politics and law. New economic constitutionalism entails a new identity, namely fiscalism, which asserts that the constitution not only protects the economy by abstaining from intrusions but also grants priority to economic provisions over other constitutional commands. This entails a departure from ordoliberalism, a recalibration of our prevailing understanding of the rule of law, and a process of interpretative transformation of key constitutional notions, such as authority, property rights, and access to justice.

The book skillfully navigates the reader through the evolution of constitutional perceptions of the economy since the nineteenth century. It provides a comprehensive assessment of the measures introduced by the EU in the field of economic governance, financial assistance and Banking Union. It offers reflections on the way Member State constitutions view the economy, and an engaging account of national and EU case law pertaining to the crisis, illustrating, among others, the shifting judicial perceptions of the right to property, emphasising its social function. The analysis of judgments of, inter alia, the Court of Justice, the General Court, the European Court of Human Rights, and German, Polish, Greek, Hungarian, Portuguese and Latvian courts enables the author to assess the implications of the crisis on constitutionalism from the vantage point of several legal traditions. The author also assesses the institutional and political implications of the crisis. The latter has led, inter alia, to the dominance of the executive vis-a-vis the legislature, the weakening of deliberative and participatory democracy, and the growing delegitimisation of politics. The author's analysis does not stop in presenting an insightful critique. He puts forward recommendations for orthosis, seeking to determine the type of constitutionalism the EU should pursue.

This book provides thoughtful and perceptive reflections on a contemporary event that has had defining consequences for law, politics and governance. It offers both a doctrinal account and an analysis borrowing from sociology and economics. It is, without a doubt, a primary point of reference in the scholarship pertaining to the Eurozone crisis. Its importance, however, transcends that specific field. The depth of the narrative invites the reader to revisit the evolution of the European integration paradigm and, more broadly, reflect on the forces that shape constitutional commands at nation-state and supra-national levels.

The narrative is rich, the critique original, and the author's proposals daring, making this an accomplished monograph that adds much to our understanding of the EU as a construct and, more generally, contemporary constitutional law.

Takis Tridimas
London, March 2019

PREFACE

Another book focusing on the institutional aspects and implications of the economic crisis. One might reasonably question the usefulness of such an experiment given the existence of a sufficient bulk of literature on that matter. I consider that the added value of the monograph at hand lies in its holistic approach and its specific research goal: it includes a wide range of crisis regulation and case law from a significant number of national and international legal orders, in a rather multi-disciplinary approach, aiming at proving that a new constitutional era has emerged – one that changes in many respects the pre-crisis constitutional paradigm. This research effort presumably goes beyond most of the existing works that remain largely insulated within a particular cognitive framework, be it economy, or politics, or law, thus to some extent jeopardising the articulation of valid research results, especially when it comes to legal research: we lawyers, more often than not, try to suggest institutional solutions to allow for the maintenance of some degree of community stability in fields that we do not fully comprehend.

In order to properly assess complicated phenomena of social subsystems, such as economy, claiming a high-level of self-reliance, and to articulate a comprehensive and sustainable set of institutional solutions, law is necessary but does not suffice. This is especially true for the macroeconomic constitution, ie the making of fiscal policies, monetary issues, which is the main focus of this book, and, less so, for the microeconomic constitution, ie right to property, freedom of profession, freedom to establish an enterprise. The book, thus, aspires to be a complete manual on the crisis, of a mainly but not exclusively legal nature, where facts (legislation, case law and literature), assessment and proposed solutions interface and each part complements the others.

This monograph has benefited from input by a great number of people – academics, judges, politicians and citizens – with whom I have discussed the topic in many countries. I thank them all anonymously. I owe special thanks to the Institute of European and Comparative Law of the Faculty of Law of the University of Oxford and the Hellenic Observatory of the London School of Economics, and their academic and administrative staff, for hosting me as Visiting Professor in the course of my research and for the opportunity to test key concepts of the book in workshops and seminars. Indeed, I could not imagine a most appropriate hosting than the high quality *Studies of the Oxford Institute of European and Comparative Law*; I am truly obliged to the editors of the series. Special debt of appreciation is owned to Professor Christos Gortsos, Professor George Pagoulatos, Professor Dimitri Sotiropoulos, Dr Michalis Ioannidis and Mr Alexandros Kyriakidis for their tolerance and insightful comments when reading earlier drafts of my work, and to my students, who have always been the most critical audience. I also wish to thank Ms Mary Orfanou for her subtle linguistic overview and Hart Publishing for the excellent cooperation in the publication of the book. Finally, my deep gratitude to Takis Tridimas, Professor of European Law at King's College London, a highly distinguished scholar in the field of European Law and a person of very wide culture, for his foreword to the book. The mistakes of the book obviously burden only me.

Translations in English of legal instruments and judgments have been drawn from the official governmental and judicial authorities respectively. Where such an official translation was not available, a translation has been provided by me from French, Italian, German and Greek, and by professional translators from other languages.

The law and jurisprudence is stated as at 1 January 2019.

George Gerapetritis

CONTENTS

ABBREVIATIONS

APP	Asset Purchase Programmes
BoP	Balance of Payments assistance facility
BRRD	Bank Recovery and Resolution Directive
BVerfG	*Bundesverfassungsgericht*
ChFR	Charter of Fundamental Rights of the European Union
CRD	Capital Requirements Directive
EBA	Euro Banking Association
ECB	European Central Bank
ECHR	European Convention on Human Rights
ECtHR	European Court of Human Rights
CJEU	Court of Justice of the European Union
EC	European Community
ECOFIN	Economic and Financial Affairs Council
EDIS	European Deposit Insurance Scheme
EFSF	European Financial Stability Facility
EFSM	European Financial Stabilisation Mechanism
ELA	Emergency Liquidity Assistance
EMU	Economic and Monetary Union
ESCB	European System of Central Banks
ESM	European Stability Mechanism
EU	European Union
FIFA	Fédération Internationale de Football Association
GATT	General Agreement on Trades and Tariffs
GCEU	General Court of the European Union
GDP	Gross Domestic Product

ILO	International Labour Organization
IMF	International Monetary Fund
IMO	International Maritime Organisation
MoU	Memorandum of Understanding
MP	Member of Parliament
NATO	North Atlantic Treaty Organization
NEC	New economic constitutionalism
OECD	Organisation for Economic Co-operation and Development
OMTs	Outright Monetary Transactions
PSI	Private Sector Involvement agreement
QE	Quantitative Easing Programme
PSPP	Public Sector Purchase Programme
RIAA	Reports of International Arbitral Awards
SRB	Single Resolution Board
SRF	Single Resolution Fund
SRM	Single Resolution Mechanism
SSM	Single Supervisory Mechanism
TEU	Treaty on European Union
TFEU	Treaty on the Functioning of the European Union
TSCG	Treaty on Stability, Coordination and Governance in the Economic and Monetary Union
UK	United Kingdom
UN	United Nations
UNFCCC	United Nations Framework Convention on Climate Change
US	United States
USSR	Union of Soviet Socialist Republics
VAT	Value Added Tax
WTO	World Trade Organization

Injustice anywhere is a threat to justice everywhere

Martin Luther King Jr.
Letter from the Birmingham Jail (1963)

TABLE OF CASES

Estonia/Supreme Court

EU/CJEU

EU/GEU

France/Conseil d'Etat

France/Constitutional Council

Germany/Constitutional Court

Greece/Council of State

Greece/Areios Pagos

Hungary/Constitutional Court

Hungary/Administrative and Labour Court

Ireland/Supreme Court

Ireland/High Court

Latvia/Constitutional Court

Permanent Court of International Justice

Poland/Constitutional Tribunal

Portugal/Constitutional Court

Portugal/Supreme Administrative Court

Portugal/Employment Court of Lisbon

Portugal/Employment Court of Porto

Romania/Constitutional Court

Slovenia/Constitutional Court

Spain/Constitutional Court

UK/Supreme Court

UK/Court of Common Pleas

US/Federal Supreme Court

Introduction

The major theme of this book is the global economic crisis triggered in 2007[1] and its overall implications upon the Constitution, both as a concept and as the applied supreme law of States and, *mutatis mutandis*, of international organisations. Although a large part is devoted to the narrative aspects of the economic crisis, ie law and case law stemming thereof, the effort is to discern whether changes produced as – direct or less direct – consequences of the crisis can qualify as a new era of constitutionalism vis-à-vis economy. Naturally, such a mental enquiry remains largely at the realm of subjective judgements and presumptions that determine to some extent the research premises. Still, the extensive literature and case law provide a very solid research background to build a historical case of change of the constitutional paradigm.

The argument set forth in the monograph at hand suggests that in the aftermath of the crisis an era of 'new economic constitutionalism' has emerged. As happens in all such historical classifications in humanities and social sciences, the identification of a new period in time is mostly assessed through its implications as compared to the standard and consolidated features of prior periods. Accordingly, it is the aim of this research to identify a multi-layer and deep change in the implementation and conceptualisation of law in the aftermath of the crisis against prior doctrines and case law. Obviously, there is not a single mathematical way to prove that this change can be, altogether or partly, attributed to the economic crisis. However, numerous indications suggest that the change of the constitutional perception is directly linked to the crisis: new economic regulation is tailor-made to treat malfunctions evidenced during the crisis concerning prudent and sound administration of finances; judicial decisions refer to the economic crisis as a relevant consideration – eventually a legitimising factor – for measures interfering with human rights; political agendas have been adjusted to the ways their respective ideological side perceives the crisis. Economy has proved particularly resilient, whereas Constitutions, albeit not suffering overall collapse, have been subject to significant adjustments, most of them occurring outside formal amendment procedures. One might argue that such adjustments are welcome because they reflect the intrinsic quality of Constitutions to be flexible and adaptable at all times. Although the broad and sometimes all-embracing wording of Constitutions

---

[1] The term 'economic crisis' is used hereinafter to refer collectively to both the banking crisis (2007–09) and the sovereign debt / financial crisis (2009 onwards) in Europe.

facilitates such adaptability indeed, the question remains: what is the extent of permissible constitutional adaptation? Obviously, in order for Constitutions to retain their fundamental normative quality there must be a red line that cannot be crossed, even at times of crisis; an area of non-permissible constitutional interpretation is for obvious reasons imperative incumbent.

Constitutional adjustments have essentially upgraded economy within the institutional structures, not merely as a relevant consideration when drafting, implementing and interpreting rules, but also as a key factor when assessed against other constitutional values. This upgrade has been beset by the economic constitutional identity of financialism that appears to be a salient feature of contemporary constitutionalism. However, the transformation of the constitutional perception of economy through financialism has not been accompanied by a more enhanced set of institutional defence mechanisms. Although extensive economic regulation has been invariably introduced during the crisis period on both national and international level, there has not been a systematic effort to strengthen the fundamental structures of the constitutional state, the lapses of which are partly to blame for the outburst of the crisis. The basic tools used to treat the crisis have been almost exclusively economic (eg balanced budget rules, prudency regulation, financial assistance mechanisms and wide financial surveillance) whereas fundamental aspects of constitutionalism (eg representation, accountability, separation of powers, or the rule of law) have been overshadowed. The thesis put forward in this book is that the economic crisis triggered an era of new economic constitutionalism, having financialism as its forefront identity, that modified the economic drafting and reading of the Constitution, changed the constitutional balance of the branches of government and overturned the way politics was perceived in the pre-crisis period, without nonetheless proper attention attributed to the essentials of constitutionalism in order to mitigate the possibility of future turbulence and to render the constitutional architecture in Europe sounder and more resilient.

In order to substantiate the above basic thesis, the book adheres to a comparative multi-disciplinary and a narrative methodology. The *comparative* methodology refers horizontally to the different endorsement of the crisis by European national and international legal systems and vertically to the relationship developed between the European supranational/international structures, ie the European Union (EU) and the European Convention on Human Rights (ECHR), towards their respective Member/Contracting States. Given that the economic crisis has been a salient feature of regulation and case law throughout Europe, this book places emphasis on the EU, which has been the main regulatory actor in the course of the crisis, the ECHR that dealt with the consequences of the crisis on the rule of law and the social state, the domestic legal orders of the States that received financial assistance prior to the establishment of financial assistance mechanisms (Hungary, Latvia, Romania) and after this (Greece, Portugal, Ireland, Cyprus, Spain) and the legal orders of the lender States where national courts rendered significant judgments on the relevant matters (Germany, Poland, France, Belgium, Estonia, Slovenia). The *multi-disciplinary* methodology aims at employing research elements of more scientific fields. Obviously, law remains the basic root of the book; yet, economic considerations transcend its pages for obvious reasons relating to its main topic, whereas aspects of politics, history, sociology or psychology are applied considerably, irrespective of cognitive and space limitations that have not allowed me to explore them to such extent probably needed or as I might have desired. The *narrative* methodology means that the facts of the economic crisis (the narrative of the crisis) are not assessed against a value position. For the purposes of the book at hand, there is not a single value position, be that either the mainstream/prevailing view of law and economy or the author's personal appreciation and, thus, a subjective perception on the matter. Indeed, the phase of new economic constitutionalism, which constitutes the axis of the book, does not use pre-crisis constitutionalism as a normative benchmarking; the monograph merely uses legal and factual evidence to demonstrate the shift towards a new discernable constitutional era with different and measurable characteristics. The experiment, thus, leans predominantly towards realism rather than a deontological criticism vis-a-vis the new situation. The book develops in six chapters followed by the conclusions.

Chapter one presents the concept of new economic constitutionalism, which is the main axis of the book. The chapter first discerns the essential features of the relationship between the Constitution and the economy in a historical perspective. Three historical phases are identified in the respective sections:

(a) The era of constitutionalism, which was shaped and developed in the seventeenth- and eighteenth-century Europe as an element of modernity and persisted until the mid-war economic crisis. In this period, the Constitution was conceptually deemed as a privileged, if not necessary, means of community organisation, and was largely indifferent to economic matters.

(b) The era of economic constitutionalism, which lasted approximately until the 2007-onwards economic crisis. In this period, Constitutions embraced economy as a standard feature of interpretation in a context of global economy and constitutional pluralism. Yet, they did not actively give priority to economic provisions, but merely abstained from inhibiting the operation of economy within the permissible constitutional framework.

(c) New economic constitutionalism, triggered by the latest economic crisis and still in the process of shaping. In this period, Constitution and economy, both on domestic and international level, converge to financialism as an economic constitutional identity that gives priority to economic provisions though the transformation of conventional constitutional notions.

This chapter presents the context, the process and the causes of new economic constitutionalism, with an emphasis on the distinct characteristics substantiating the argument that the economic crisis mobilised a distinct historical period of constitutionalism.

Chapter two presents the impact of new economic constitutionalism on the economic drafting of the Constitution in order to identify the substantial bulk of regulation introduced to allow for a better understanding of the change of interpretation that follows. It includes three sections:

(a) European economic governance, including a concise presentation of the Economic and Monetary Union, the temporary (emergency) and the permanent financial assistance vehicles, the rules on enhanced EU economic governance, the Treaty on Stability, Coordination and Governance in the Economic and Monetary Union, the Two-Pack and Six-Pack, the European Semester, the European Central Bank asset purchase programmes and the banking union and bank resolution tools.

(b) Economic governance in EU Member States, including state economic models, economic liberty, state ownership, state economic institutions and rules of economic governance.

(c) Financial assistance to EU Member States prior and in the course of the economic crisis, presenting the facts resulting in the crisis and an outline of the corresponding resolution agreements.

Chapter three presents the impact of new economic constitutionalism on constitutional interpretation. It aims at proving the mutation of case law on all European layers in the post-crisis period. It includes two sections:

(a) Economic crisis case law, roughly presenting major judgments of the EU courts, the European Court of Human Rights and the domestic courts of most European States that were involved in the crisis either as lenders or debtors, with reference to specific categories, ie EU and euro-area institution building, social state decrease, salary/pension cuts, haircut of government bonds, bank deposit cuts and shareholders' rights.

(b) Human rights case law revisited, where the respective cases in question focus on serious decrease of the level of protection of property, arguably the right that has suffered the most from the abrupt constitutional adjustment, on the level of the scope of protection, of the intensity of judicial review and of the instruments of review, ie non-discrimination, public interest, proportionality and legitimate expectations.

Chapter four presents the institutional impact of new economic constitutionalism on governance. It aims at substantiating that the mix of government, both internally within the European legal orders (with the supremacy of the executive over the legislature and the upgrading of judicial policies), as well as between the legal systems themselves (with the relative submission of, at least debtor, Member States) has been altered, not only because of the new regulation introduced in the post-crisis period but also as a matter of – explicit or implicit – political struggle of domination. It includes three sections, two horizontal and one vertical: (a) parliamentary default and executive empowerment in the EU and Member States; (b) judicial responsiveness (Jureconomy) in the EU, ECHR and Member States; and (c) enhanced EU competences, which delineate EU dominance and sovereign withdrawal.

Chapter five presents the factual impact of new economic constitutionalism on politics. It aims at demonstrating the change on the political agenda and the political attitude in Europe as a result of the crisis. It includes four sections:

(a) Power politics, in the sense that there is an extensive use of command in politics as a coercive force, rather than on morality or legitimacy; this makes political actors significantly variable in terms of their relative power.

(b) Divisive politics, meaning the dominance of non-deliberative politics with artificial dilemmas and large-scale condemnation of the political opposite.

(c) Cross-border politics, intimating the involvement in domestic politics of external actors from other States or from international organisations, all becoming stakeholders because of their financial involvement.

(d) Delegitimised politics, evidenced in technocratic governments, manipulation of popular referenda and overall disassociation of the people with politics.

Chapter six presents a proposal for a recalibration of EU constitutionalism. It aims at subjecting the outcomes of the first five chapters of the book to a concise scheme of solution in order to produce some applied research results. It includes four sections:

(a) The principle section sets the basic question as to what type of constitution-alism should be targeted for the EU for the day after the economic crisis. A model of resilient institutional constitutionalism is promoted with specific proposals presented in the following sections.

(b) Multi-level representative governance suggests direct election of the European Commission en bloc and an EU second chamber equally representing the Member States and the European territories.

(c) Holistic deliberativism in decision-making process entails opinion conver-gence through wide and equal participation and reasoned and elaborate exchange of arguments so as to produce legitimate outcomes.

(d) Intergenerational sustainability and global solidarity reflect, respectively, the basic considerations that decision-making ought to enhance and demand the solidarity owed by everyone towards the globe and to provide for the ability to continue a behaviour for an indefinite period of time by introducing the rights of future generations as a consideration of equal value to the rights of the present generation.

The Conclusions of the book summarise research results considering that the reality of new economic constitutionalism calls for a different constitutional approach in search for a readjustment of constitutional mechanics to address the needs of classical constitutionalism.

1

New Economic Constitutionalism: The Concept

There are many links between Constitutions and the economy. Richard Posner identified as many as eight distinct, though somewhat overlapping, points of interaction between the two: economic properties; economics of constitutional design (eg separation of powers and federalism); economic effects of existing constitutional doctrines (eg media defamation); interpretation of economically collateral constitutional provisions (eg freedom of speech); constitutional clauses for the protection of free markets (eg a balanced-budget rule); judicial attitude towards liberty in the economic sphere; relationship between the Constitution and economic growth; and the use of economic analysis as an overarching guide to constitutional interpretation.[1]

There have been various phases in the relationship between the Constitution and the economy. Given the great number of economic milestones that could possibly trigger a new phase in this relationship, various typologies could be equally sustainable. This book employs a three-period distinction:

(1) *Constitutionalism*, where the Constitution is indifferent to economy, a phase extending from the seventeenth century until the mid-war period in the twentieth century.

(2) *Economic constitutionalism*, where the Constitution becomes interested in economy through the incorporation of economic provisions and of a corresponding constitutional interpretation of those provisions, a phase extending from the mid-war years until the eruption of the economic crisis, broadly until 2009.

(3) *New economic constitutionalism*, where the Constitution subsumes the economy and the economic constitutional clause as key instruments for drafting and interpreting the Constitution overall. This last phase is signalled by the economic crisis and is currently undergone.

The basic characteristics of those three phases will be presented hereinafter, with a special emphasis on the current state of new economic constitutionalism.

---

[1] RA Posner, 'The Constitution as an Economic Document' (1987) 56 *George Washington Law Review* 4.

I. Constitutionalism

Constitutionalism is a driving national ideology advocating the Constitution as the supreme and privileged means for the protection of individual freedoms from abuse in the exercise of public powers through limited government. Constitutionalism goes beyond the basic idea of the constitutional state. The constitutional state is a narrative reflection of a State which is organised through rules conferring competences; yet such rules do not necessarily place restrictions upon state agencies and do not necessarily divide powers among various state authorities but could conceivably operate in a state of Hobbesian constitutionally unlimited sovereignty, whereby unlimited sovereignty resides in a single supreme governmental person or body also exercising government power.[2] Constitutionalism, on the other hand, is conceptually based on three premises:

(a) It presupposes a perception of supreme law that provides for both procedural and substantive limitations upon state agencies, thus rendering the Constitution not merely a salient feature of the State but rather the key element in determining the relationship between the State and society, in a way that government can and should be legally limited in its powers in a Weberian legal-rational type of legitimacy and, accordingly, rendering legitimate authority dependent on adherence by the limited government. Although technically speaking there is no requirement that state powers be divided in more state agencies, the institutional mix containing separation of powers and checks and balances or any other relevant variation is considered to better serve the idea of limited government, as Aristotle and Montesquieu have argued.
(b) It safeguards the supremacy of the Constitution through its proper entrenchment and prohibition of amendment at the absolute discretion of the rulers in a given instance of time, thus requiring a more complicated process of revision, because otherwise the constitutional limits placed upon state authorities could be easily bypassed.
(c) It conveys a general belief that the Constitution is in a position to effectively prevent state arbitrariness and to act as a protecting mechanism in favour of the people. Since constitutionalism disallows unlimited state power, sovereignty must reside outside the State. As Austin first presented, constitutionalism is beset by the idea of limited government vested upon government authorities coupled with unlimited sovereignty, which lies primarily with the people in the form of popular sovereignty.[3]

[2] Th Hobbes, *De Cive* (1642).
[3] JL Austin, *The Province of Jurisprudence Determined* (Cambridge, Cambridge University Press, 1995).

Contemporary constitutionalism, as elaborated in diverse form by great scholars such as Carl Schmitt, John Elster, Charles H McIlwain and Bruce Ackerman,
is a reflection of modernity, which is in turn beset by Aristotelian reason free of
passion or Weberian reason based on cognitive processes. Still, reason acquires
a rather formal content, in that it is reflected on general and abstract norms, as
opposed to more substantive formulations of law prior to the constitutionalism
era and to modernity. Such norms purport to protect human liberty against
arbitrary action of the State, ie the police state *(Polizeistaat)*. Constitutionalism took its form in the seventeenth century in England, especially through the
1610 Dr Bonham's case[4] and the 1688 Glorious Revolution and in the rest of the
western world from the end of the eighteenth century through the great revolutions and the formation of nation-states.[5]

Vis-a-vis the economy, the first phase of constitutionalism arguably lasted
until the mid-war period, when the first major financial crisis of 1929 in the
US and its domino effect for the rest of the world entirely changed the constitutional recognition of the value and power of the economy upon the political/legal
system. During this era, economics, as any other form of science, started developing as a distinct subsystem through formation and evolution of idiosyncratic
cognitive structures, in parallel with the development of constitutionalism as a
key notion of governance. According to Polanyi, this epistemic differentiation was
produced in the early nineteenth century and resulted in the great transformation
of European civilisation from the pre-industrial world to the era of industrialisation and all corresponding effects of such transformation in social and economic
ideologies and policies.[6]

Constitutionalism is par excellence the field where legal and political subsystems converge. The two subsystems developed a common understanding that the
political system initiates normative propositions, ie the law, which in turn enjoys
the monopoly of coercion and is set, implemented and interpreted by the legal
system. On the highest level of law, political and legal systems converge on the
idea of political constitution. The recognition of the political constitution as the
cornerstone of state governance, as well as the recognition of both the review of
legality of executive acts and the constitutional review of legislation as major tools
of limited government (presumptions that apply equally to the political as well
as the legal subsystem), essentially reflect the convergence of the two subsystems
and their joint predominance over other social subsystems. Yet, there is a fundamental difference in the perception of legal against political constitutionalism.

---

[4] 8 Co Rep 107; 77 Eng Rep 638 (Court of Common Pleas [1610]).

[5] LD Kramer, *The People Themselves: Popular Constitutionalism and Judicial Review* (Oxford, Oxford University Press, 2004) 15.

[6] K Polanyi, 'Our Obsolete Market Mentality. Civilization Must Find a New Thought Pattern' (1947) 3 *Commentary* 109; K Polanyi, 'The Economy as Instituted Process' in K Polanyi, CM Arensberg And HW Pearson (Eds), *Trade and Market in the Early Empires: Economies In History And Theory* (New York, The Free Press, 1957) 243.

Legal constitutionalism, beset by the idea of legality, suggests that law and the judiciary are the means to control excesses of the political branches of government. Political constitutionalism stresses the lack of effectiveness and legitimacy of judicial review as a means to protect individual rights at national and transnational level.[7]

Irrespective of this internal differentiation in the conceptual approach of constitutionalism, when seen together in the context of contemporary constitutionalism, law/politics allow the stability of society and treats all other subsystems as merely coexisting social subsystems. Those other subsystems cannot challenge the exclusive power of the political/legal system to set and impose norms. This is not to suggest that subsystems are prevented from claiming more intense penetration into politics and law through legitimate pressure groups to advance their respective interests. In fact, modernity led to material constitutionalism through development of autonomous or semi-autonomous social fractions, basically established on a national level, such as economy or sports, with distinct structures and the actual power to influence decision-making processes of the political/legal subsystems, depending on time or region. Especially with regard to economy, financial efficiency and sustainability constitute basic values in the drafting and implementation of constitutional norms, among other important facets of constitutionalism, such as pluralism, representation through participation, rationality, accountability and advancement of the public interest. Nonetheless, law persists and supersedes as a normative phenomenon over all subordinate social systems, including the economy.

Constitutionalism is not committed to a specific economic view of the State, therefore it may well accommodate any sort of economic model. It views economy mostly as subsumed within the basic structure of a democratic regime, thus its limits are essentially to be found in the constitutional restrictions set upon the political power, either through the protection of human rights or through structural limitations in the exercise of economic activity. Yet, in the phase of constitutionalism, although a relevant consideration, economy does not enjoy any privileged status either as a social subsystem or as a criterion of setting standards of constitutional value.

II. Economic Constitutionalism

Economic constitutionalism upgrades economy to a privileged status in that it conceptually views that distinctions between politics and economy are determined

---

[7] A Tomkins, *Our Republican Constitution* (Oxford, Hart Publishing, 2005); R Bellamy, *Political Constitutionalism. A Republican Defence of the Constitutionality of Democracy* (Cambridge, Cambridge University Press, 2009); G Gee and GCN Webber, What is a Political Constitution? (2010) 30 *Oxford Journal of Legal Studies* 273.

through normative propositions of law. Accordingly, the Constitution acknowledges economy as a system with its own dynamics and incorporates structural stipulations that uphold economy as an activity of constitutional value. This becomes particularly evident in the context of globalisation which sets significant challenges concerning the operation of economic actors that transcends the conventional boundaries of constitutionalism.[8] This institutional upgrade occurs both directly and indirectly. Direct upgrade lies in the incorporation of structural economic provisions, including individual or collective economic rights, into constitutional charters. Indirect upgrade suggests that economic indicators should apply as yardsticks to interpret constitutional clauses (not only those relating to economy or economic rights) and concretise abstract constitutional concepts, such as public interest, exceptional circumstances, general welfare, social state and the like. Usually, the basic tool for such transformation of abstract norms into concrete rulings is balancing through the modules of law and economy as methodologically applying through the principle of proportionality, which, thus, operates both as a balancing vehicle and as a validating factor for the balancing outcome. Within the proportionality test, economy is subsumed in two stages: in the prior stage of assessing the goal pursued by the impugned measure, where economy finds a place as a legitimate public interest alongside other public goods; and in the subsequent application of the test itself, ie the suitability, necessity and *stricto sensu* proportionality.

Economic constitutionalism obviously transcends the original concept of constitutionalism, since the Constitution is no longer indifferent vis-a-vis economy. In that, it goes beyond the Westfalian-type state in that it seems to accept concessions to the conventional version of sovereignty.[9] Although in the context of economic constitutionalism it is not necessary for a constitution to establish an exclusive economic model and, correspondingly, reject all others (although it could well do so), economy permeates the Constitution. Irrespective of whether a constitution is open-ended or partisan with regard to the economic model, economy plays a vital role in drafting and interpreting the Constitution in the case of possible alternative readings of law. Furthermore, it becomes a constitutional prescription that policy-makers ought to take into consideration economic factors when drafting any kind of policy, not merely strictly monetary or budgetary, since every policy has by definition an economic impact and, potentially, there are no economically zero-sum policies. At any rate, economic constitutionalism is at contemporary times mostly associated to the ordoliberal perceptions of economy. Accordingly, economy still stands against politics and law as a distinctive subsystem which, nevertheless, enjoys a privileged status in the normative drafting

---

[8] DJ Gerber, 'Economic Constitutionalism and the Challenge of Globalization: The Enemy is Gone? Long Live the Enemy: Comment' (2001) 157 *Journal of Institutional and Theoretical Economics* 14.

[9] K Jayasuriya, 'Globalization, Sovereignty, and the Rule of Law: From Political to Economic Constitutionalism?' (2001) 8 *Constellations* 442.

and reading, also at a higher institutional level. In his extraordinary analysis of the constitutional upgrade of economy in the phase of economic constitutionalism while at the same time remaining against law/politics, with the latter being rather indifferent to the former, Posner argued that the upsurge of interest in remaking the Constitution into a charter of economic liberties has brought to the fore the fascinating paradox of dualism in constitutional interpretation: commitment to liberty in the personal sphere and almost indifference to liberty in the economic sphere, such as the right not to have one's property taken without just compensation, the right to occupational liberty, and the right to transact interstate business without discrimination by reason of being a non-resident, persists.[10]

Economic constitutionalism is better understood in the context of a sociological perception of law. Accordingly, functional differentiation in society establishes function systems that legitimately claim primacy in their respective domain, such as families or education. Although all function systems develop their own communicative channels, codes of conduct and attributes, not all of them develop the level of autonomy to be considered as disassociated from politics/law subsystem. The most fitted such theory is Niklas Luhmann's, which develops in three main theoretical pillars: a systems theory; a theory of social evolution; and a theory of social differentiation.[11] In Luhmann's perception, structural differentiation is beset by segmentation, stratification and specialisation through functional differentiation. Society cannot be explained in terms of a single unity but mostly as an all-embracing system composed of and motivated by its functionally differentiated parts. These subsystems are distinguishable from other societal groupings in that they are essentially self-guided and, therefore, contribute to the complexity of societal relationships. System differentiation is, thus, a replication, within a system, of the difference between a system and its environment, basically caused by complexity issues situated at the boundaries of functional systems. The more a subsystem presents a complexity gap between internal structures and the environment the more it claims autonomy. Economy emerged precisely as a distinct subsystem due to its complexity gap against its context. In the course of time, such complexity became more elaborate and sophisticated: economic activities, products and transactions become highly sophisticated and develop, as an autopoietic system, a structured complexity through reproductive mechanisms. This is indeed the key argument for autonomy of functionally differentiated subsystems within social structures, since factual autonomy is expected to result in regulatory autonomy so as to produce better results.

Economy falls par excellence within the ambit of this analysis because of its cognitive specificities and its self-motivated inclination to develop independently within social structures. As Renner puts it, the interaction of the legal with the economic and the political system in the post-globalisation era is marked by a shift

---

[10] Posner, 'The Constitution' (1987) 24–27.
[11] N Luhmann, *The Differentiation of Society* (New York, Columbia University Press, 1982).

from normative to cognitive expectation structures which produces a simultaneous over-complexity and under-complexity of the legal system: an over-complexity
of the cognitive expectations that the legal system has to process, and an under-
complexity of its internal normative structures. Yet, differentiation and claim for
autonomy does not suggest that there is no interaction between the systems. This
is particularly illustrated in the field of law and economy: economy may build
on cognitive expectations but also depends on normative expectation structures;
economy is commonly considered to be based on key liberal notions such as
private property, bindingness of contracts and free competition (albeit not always
explicitly), although economy by itself, ie as an autonomous subsystem, cannot
guarantee their acknowledgment nor their enforcement.[12] Therefore, a structural
coupling of politics/law and economy is vital in order to produce a set of viable
and effective rules between the centre and the periphery of one another, for the
purpose of maintaining their stability and simultaneous growth in their respective
environments. This is because economy, in the process of its functional differentiation, must effectively couple with positive law, which reflects the legitimacy of
the powerholders (political subsystem) and the predominance of legality (legal
subsystem).

   In order for the political/legal system to comply with the mandate of economic
constitutionalism and at the same time maintain its regulatory predominance,
it resorts to economic cognition. In this way, there is a merge of cognitive and
normative expectations that, by definition, require a structural coupling with
law/economy. It is this tendency of the economy as a cognitive subsystem to structurally couple with politics/law as normative expectations that essentially led to
economic constitutionalism. The concretisation of such structural coupling is evident
in most of the tools that have been used both on a domestic and on an international
European level. As an example among others such as contracts and corporations,
Renner uses the regulatory legislation on liability in the field of economy. After
rightly asserting that liability has originally been developed as a concept of representation, he identifies a fundamental paradox in economic constitutionalism:
liability is not determined through external standards but basically through self-
reference, ie its market value is ultimately controlled by the liable entity itself.
This is why States can devalue their currencies, in cases where domestic currency
sovereignty still exists, and corporations can buy their own shares. What solves
the paradox according to Renner is the distinction between equity (ie assets after
all obligations have been paid) and debt (obligations themselves). The stability
of the concept of liability is, thus, dependent upon the debt/equity ratio.[13] The
upholding of economic constitutionalism as a key notion and evolutionary phase

---

[12] M Renner, 'Death by Complexity. The Financial Crisis and the Crisis of Law in World Society' in
PF Kjaer, G Teubner and A Febbrajo (eds), *The Financial Crisis in Constitutional Perspective. The Dark
Side of Functional Differentiation* (Oxford, Hart Publishing, 2011) 93.
[13] ibid, 101–04.

of constitutionalism itself reveals that economy was eventually subject to structural differentiation and accepted as a privileged subsystem with which politics/law are in a constant dialogue. This dialectic set a higher standard of penetration of economy into the higher source of law. The cognitive processes of economy are expected to become the basis of the political subsystem when establishing relevant principles and, eventually, the legal subsystem is expected to incorporate these principles as normative propositions, not in any ordinary statute or executive decision but within the Constitution itself.

The mid-war era is considered to be the symbolic period of emergence of economic constitutionalism, as part of the political/judicial reaction to the immense financial crisis. The end of Word War I created a very positive constitutional momentum. New Constitutions were drafted in almost every European State; liberal socialism as fundamentally expressed in the Weimar Constitution and the social legislation produced therefrom seemed to further strengthen democracy, while at the same time the socialist experiment was developing in the Soviet Union. On the other hand, a flourishing economy marked the industrial 1920s with a high level of prosperity, illustratively reflected in *The Great Gatsby*, the development of a strong urban civil class with a sparkling culture, the improvement of living standards for the working class and an over-consumption based on artificial needs to satisfy high production levels. Furthermore, technology made life much easier, and the development of transport and communications in particular enabled a much more comfortable circulation of ideals and mobility of human capital. However, the whole scenery changed abruptly in the 1930s with the economic turn that caused the great depression, followed by a current of authoritarian regimes in Europe (Germany, Spain, Greece, Poland, Romania, Bulgaria and, earlier as of 1922, Italy).

At the same period in the US, in the middle of the New Deal turmoil, with judicial decisions striking down Roosevelt's recovery legislation and the Court packing scheme ahead, Albertsworth identified a gradual and slow weakening of constitutional safeguards by a process of judicial erosion, not as a planned judicial evasion of constitutional principles, but rather as a result of the constitutional difficulties that were inherent to their application to laws in court proceedings. In descriptive terms, he argued that there were certain constitutional mirages about the American Constitution and its control of human activities, which disappeared in view of facts and practices.[14] Accordingly, the Constitution was farther and farther removed into the background: 'we Americans take comfort in the belief that we live under iron-clad constitutional protections against invasion by the State of our rights of liberty and property'.[15] Holding this perception of the contrast between theory and fact 'for only in this fashion can we conserve and improve the heritage of constitutional government as we know it', he suggested that further

---

[14] EF Albertsworth, 'The New Constitutionalism' (1940) 26 *American Bar Association Journal* 865.
[15] EF Albertsworth, 'The Mirage of Constitutionalism' (1935) 29 *Illinois Law Review* 608, 612.

constitutional protection was needed and that industrial recovery in the long run depended upon such increased protection, because eventually the Constitution reigns, but does not always govern.[16] After the change of constitutional paradigm with the shift in case law in 1937, Albertsworth made a post-mortem of the institutional adjustment and spoke for the first time about a 'new constitutionalism'. He identified a certain weakening of monitoring constitutional principles against governmental action in certain spheres of human conduct, making possible an authoritarian form of government:

> As constitutional democracies are but modern developments in contrast with thousands of years of rule by monarchies, oligarchies, and theocracies, the questions have arisen, will Constitutionalism in the United States disappear and is Constitutionalism as important today in the struggle for economic power and survival as it was in the past? Have we instead created a New Constitutionalism unlike that of the past?[17]

Narratively, he revealed five basic attitudes in both popular thinking and in judicial decisions, which constituted the ingredients of the new Constitutionalism, as reflected in Supreme Court decisions over the New Deal era. First, because of the industrialism and of the change in the world order, people faced new problems and new needs, different in nature than those of the economy of agriculture at the time of the drafting of the US Constitution. Second, there was a triumph of majoritarianism, in the sense that the majority ought to govern despite the objections of minorities, especially in economic and social matters, and no restraints, such as natural law, could limit the power of the majority. Third, groups have stronger claim of recognition by law than unorganised and solitude individuals, because industrialism produced an 'age of associations and combination'. Group activity, therefore, was a concomitant of necessary protection even though governmental power had been exercised, for it might have been inefficient. Fourth, there was a supremacy of the political branches of federal government (the legislature and the executive), as true representatives of the majority will, over the judiciary. The rationale was that, once a law has been enacted, it should not lightly be disapplied by the judiciary merely because the latter may have different views on policy compared to the other two branches. And, fifth, a powerful State was necessary, with only few restraints upon its borrowing and taxing power, in order to fulfil the need for economic security and to plan for the economic welfare of the people.

In economic terms, Arbertsworth saw the rise of *state* capitalism in new constitutionalism at the expense of the pre-existing *private* capitalism. He claimed that for centuries, before the nineteenth century, private capitalism based on individual initiative had survived as the most ideal and beneficial system as regards the creation of high standards. Private capitalism's machine economy was producing

[16] ibid, 608–09, 630.
[17] Albertsworth, 'The New Constitutionalism' (1940) 865.

more than could possibly be consumed and, given the popular reluctance to lower the corresponding and ever-growing standards of living, Government was merely asked to provide the purchasing power necessary to maintain a balance between production and consumption, through deflation control, currency devaluation policies, production control, buying of commodity surpluses, extension of subsidies, pensions and doles to low-income citizens and through state engagement in productive enterprise itself. Twentieth-century industrialism saw the weakening of private capitalism, while the 1930s economic depression witnessed what almost amounted to its overthrow. State undertakings could not be financed through taxation under private capitalism; as a result, a policy of governmental credit was inaugurated. Increased government borrowing became necessary to keep up with state obligations and prevent weakening of governmental credit. Finally, rising unemployment substantiated the idea that private capitalism had to be continually supplemented by state support, which eventually resulted in a shift towards state industrialism and state capitalism. In his view, 'new constitutionalism' abandoned the absolute, fixed and static philosophical notion of conceptualism in the interpretation and application of the legislation, whereby the Constitution was an embodiment of natural law, preventing the State from interfering with individual (economic) activities, and emphasised the pragmatic character of both legislation and Constitutional doctrine, entailing a philosophy of judicial cooperation with the processes of democracy to render the latter adequate to address present-day national needs and aspirations. Accordingly, whatever laws have been enacted by the legislature towards the solution of economic and social problems are regarded with apparent sympathy by the Court, for they constitute the tangible expressions of a national urge towards a workable national economy during a period of economic maladjustment and transition.[18] In fact, what Albertsworth expressed was presumably the move from conventional to economic constitutionalism with the particular characteristics described hereinafter.

At the same time, in the UK, industrialisation seemed to exercise pressure upon the conventional political constitution based on parliamentary sovereignty. Historian Strong, in his work *A history of modern political Constitutions*, noticed in 1930 that, although the ancient Constitution in Britain had been democratised in the previous 50 years and had shown a capacity for adaptation to changing times and circumstances (basically through political equality), an obvious weakness of parliamentarianism was the overload of the state machinery and the new demands raised basically by economics, as envisaged in the programme of most social reformers at the time. In that regard, he considered the raise of the collective power of industrial workers as a potential danger for a schism in policy, one that constitutionalism ought to address proactively.[19] Interestingly, in the sixth edition of his book in 1963, Strong insisted on this eminent danger that political democracy

[18] ibid, 867–68.
[19] CF Strong, *A History of Modern Political Constitutions* (London, Sidgwick and Jackson, 1930) 349–50.

ought to deal with, considering that national democratic constitutionalism was still on trial.[20] This persistence exactly reflects the durability of the economic constitutionalism that appeared in the first quarter of the twentieth century and the accumulation of problems in the treatment of a rather conflicting relationship between political/legal and economic subsystems.

Economic constitutionalism is listed into post-modernity, in the sense that it devaluated material constitutionalism due to two key phenomena that transcended the conventional classifications world/State/peripheries: economic globalisation; and constitutional pluralism. The common core of the two concepts is the idea that territoriality is not the crucial or, on some occasions, even a relevant, factor in determining the economic and legal space respectively and, in turn, the establishment of hybrid spaces, where multiple actors operate at the same time in the same fields. Although there are many other concrete aspects of globalisation (mostly social and cultural), for the purposes of the present analysis it suffices to refer to economic globalisation, which indeed enhances to a great extent other forms of globalisation. This sort of globalisation presents an inherent tendency to contradict, in some ways, nation-state Constitutions, a crisis in modern constitutionalism that Teubner refers to as 'the new constitutional question'.[21]

Economic globalisation stands for the creation of a universal, albeit not always harmonised, economic space broadly disassociated from a specific territory. Universal economic space is facilitated by the high level of economic mobility of working forces (either as a matter of right, as in the EU, or as a matter of fact, as in the case of economic migration), transnational capital flow and the establishment of multinational enterprises with a great number of territorial affiliations. The above direct economic indicators are accompanied by further evolution in a wider perspective, and they support economic activities and bridge economy with society. From the consumers' point of view, industrialism brought over-production and over-consumption through the establishment of artificial needs, a model characterised as 'Fordism', after Henry Ford, the founder of the Ford Motor Company, and a pioneer in the relevant line of economy. The principle suggested standardisation of the product manufactured entirely by machinery and requiring no skilled workers, employment of assembly lines through tailor-made but easy to use tools and equipment and increase of the workers' salaries to afford over-consumption of their products. From the markets' point of view, industrialism needed to find getaways both to new production territories, in order to minimise production costs, and to new markets, in order to promote the products. Economic globalisation was greatly facilitated by the technological revolution, which virtually minimised distances through transport and communication, enabled distant transactions and ensured a very easy flow of information. This new economic

---

[20] ibid 358–59.
[21] G Teubner, *Constitutional Fragments. Societal Constitutionalism and gGlobalization* (Oxford, Oxford University Press, 2012) 1–2.

landscape rendered the conventional idea of dispute resolution, previously treated as a merely domestic issue, outdated and called for multi-faceted international and/or transnational legal solutions. Given that the phenomenon of withdrawal of territoriality involved issues of national sovereignty, substantially linked to the modern nation-state, the traditional tools of public and private international law were insufficient to deal with such complex issues of interconnectivity efficiently. Inevitably, since the issue of sovereignty was at stake, a reshaping of the orthodox Kelsenian constitutional theology needed to be revisited.

Constitutional pluralism stands for the phenomenon that more constitutional structures claim legitimacy and applicability in a hybrid legal space on the same subject-matter, especially activities associated with the economy. Constitutional pluralism is a more specific term than legal pluralism, in that it reflects the accumulation of more actors at the highest level of the hierarchy of norms in the same territory. Many other terms may be equally used to describe constitutional pluralism, such as plural or hybrid constitutionalism; yet the emphasis should be placed upon the idea of pluralism that reflects its multiplicity and complexity.[22] This complexity is reflected in most areas of economic activity nowadays: investments, the internet, the environment, tax and customs, intellectual property, but also in less obvious fields such as security, personal data and justice. Accordingly, the term constitutional pluralism is normally used in a narrative manner to reflect the reality of contemporary legal landscapes where domestic constitution and international law cohabitate. In federal States, state laws also constitute a column of pluralism, although they are broadly subsumed to the basic pillar of domestic constitution, from which they draw their legitimacy. Of course, other sources of authority may also claim participation in the plural legal environment, basically transnational or non-state rules and the structural stipulations of subsystems. This is particularly so because people, on many occasions, belong to sub-social fractions to which they pay conscious obedience, which may at times be even tantamount to the psychological adherence to state law: for many people, the conscious level of regular obedience towards religious canons or trade union ordinances, applies *opinio juris sive necessitatis* and is no different to that of a statute or even the Constitution.[23]

Broadly speaking, however, the main actors of contemporary legal pluralism are domestic Constitutions and international law. This is so because other norm-generating social subsystems cannot be equated with the horizontally applying and generally coercive law. Wherever a rule-instigated community exists, such as religion or sport, self-regulation by definition ends up adding further elements of complexity in the debate on constitutional pluralism because of overlapping

---

[22] For instance, J Bengoetxea, 'Rethinking EU Law in the Light of Pluralism and Practical Reason' in M Maduro, K Tuori and S Sankari (eds), *Transnational Law: Rethinking European Law and Legal Thinking* (Cambridge, Cambridge University Press, 2014) 145, suggests the use of 'legal plurality' or cultural plurality' for the EU as empirical reflections.

[23] ibid, 35–41.

legal authorities.[24] There are two ways to perceive the main legal actors of constitutional pluralism, ie constitution and transnational law, one being synthetic and the other antithetic. The synthetic approach suggests that both domestic constitution and international law ought to be seen as part of a legal osmosis that broadly reflects the evolution of modern State, through denationalisation and internationalisation. This approach searches for tools to address conflicts on the level of various pillars of law, more often than not on a more technical basis. The antithetic approach suggests that there is an inherent internal rivalry between domestic constitution and international law, with each one of them claiming dominance against the other. This approach usually has recourse to more conceptual arguments in order to seek the response as to which pillar should prevail, given that their inherent rivalry cannot be resolved in an effective manner and that only one legal set should apply altogether at the expense of the other. Thus, this approach searches, as the case might be, for suitable instruments to eliminate one or more pillars so as to award full predominance to the other. The argument in favour of domestic constitution normally lies with sovereigntist territorialism theories, whereas the argument in favour of international law normally refers to universalism, as a factual or utilitarian finding connected to the necessity of international cooperation and global governance and aiming at perpetual peace through Kant's third definitive article: since a violation of rights in one place is felt throughout the world irrespective of a narrower or wider community, the idea of a law of world citizenship is no 'high-flown or exaggerated' notion; it is a supplement to the unwritten code of the civil and international law, indispensable for the maintenance of public human rights and hence of perpetual peace also.[25] Yet, the realist approach, advocated by Petersmann, suggests that state Constitutions have become at contemporary times 'partial Constitutions' that can effectively protect 'aggregate public goods' only in cooperation with international (economic) law.[26]

Economic constitutionalism does not suggest a monopoly or even oligopoly of economic systems. It can conceivably embrace economic liberalism or interventionism or any of their multiple variations. What is essentially proclaimed by this concept is that there are principles and processes of a normative nature, established by law, which absorb the perplexities of politics/law. It says nothing, or very little, about the actual content of specific normative expectations attributed to economy within a specific constitutional environment. These normative expectations are developed through the ordinary regulatory processes, after having incorporated the cognitive expectations of the economic subsystem. Eventually, it is the

---

[24] For constitutional pluralism, see M Avbelj and J Komarek, *Constitutional Pluralism in the European Union and Beyond* (Oxford, Hart Publishing, 2012); K Jaklic, *Constitutional Pluralism in the EU* (Oxford, Oxford University Press, 2014).

[25] I Kant, *Perpetual Peace: A Philosophical Essay 1795* (Charleston, Nabu Press, 2013).

[26] E-U Petersmann, *International Economic Law in the 21st century. Constitutional Pluralism and Multilevel Governance of Interdependent Public Goods* (Oxford, Hart Publishing, 2012) 171–72.

judge who is called upon to decide how potential conflicts between political/legal expectations and economic aspirations ought to be moderated.

The elasticity of the economic constitution was seriously challenged in the context of the European Communities, that later became the Union, which essentially claimed overriding authority on monetary matters. Thus, EU law claimed its own legitimacy and persuasion outside the broader category of international law and essentially challenged the orthodox perception of state sovereignty, leading to a post-sovereign status where the Union, albeit not formally enjoying a sovereign status, in practice exercises its attributed powers in a sovereign manner.[27] The principle of supremacy – a cornerstone of the establishment of the Union establishment – and the actual political power vested to the Union which is, in turn, transformed into coercion vis-a-vis the Member States, jointly resulted in a tendency of EU law to essentially absorb, at least, all other sources of international law within the scope of powers conferred to the Union. Yet, in the period prior to the crisis, EU law did not arguably go as far as to essentially substitute domestic Constitutions, in spite of the consecutive expansion of the competences resulting from amendments of the Treaty. The failure to adopt a fully-fledged Union Constitution, which would have necessarily upgraded the legal status of the EU, especially vis-a-vis its Member States, seriously hampered the perspective of a more federal political structure that would produce a new high-level source of legitimacy. Thus, the procedural and substantive constraints embodied in the Treaties or established through case law, such as the principles of conferred powers, subsidiarity and proportionality and the doctrine of respect for the constitutional identity of the Member States, continued to draw a red line that the Union could not cross in determining its powers and implementing its policies. Those constraints arguably constituted a last line of defence of domestic Constitutions against possible expansionist policies by the EU. Although the constitutional identity factor applies, according to the case law of the Court of Justice, mostly in matters of a lesser economic impact, it constitutes a key doctrine in shaping the relationship between the Union and the Member States and, presumably, the most indicative confession on the part of EU law that domestic Constitutions are still the basic source of legitimacy and that there is a core in them that appears to be inviolable and sacrosanct. In the light of the above, economic constitutionalism prior to the banking and financial crisis was a balanced mix of domestic Constitutions and EU law. One might also include in this hybrid legal space the European Convention on Human Rights, as interpreted by the Court of Strasbourg, especially with regard to the right to property that is by all means the more relevant stipulation to economic constitutionalism, which therefore, renders economic governance genuinely polycentric.

---

[27] N MacCormick, *Questioning Sovereignty: Law, State, and Nation in the European Commonwealth,* Law, State, and Practical Reason Series (Oxford, Oxford University Press, 1997) 137–56.

In this institutionally complicated context, the idea of constitutional pluralism has played a key role both as a narrative explanation and as an expedition to
furnish a new version of constitutionalism and legitimacy in Europe. The fact that
traditionally constitutionalism was doctrinally associated to sovereignty constituted a significant impediment in establishing a coherent theory of European
constitutionalism in the absence of an orthodox sovereign body. Late positivist
Neil MacCormick, the founding father of the conceptual doctrine of constitutional
pluralism in Europe, first spoke of pluralist novelty of constitutionalism, as early as
1993, and of post-sovereignty in Europe based on the assumption that the complicated European structures, with wide overlapping and co-ordinated relations of
broadly autonomous legal orders, could not fall within a single sovereign power in a
conventional perception of constitutionalism based on his own classical doctrine
of law as an 'institutional normative order'. In his view, in Europe there is an undeniable abstract narrative of coexisting and heterarchical constitutional authorities,
none of which can legitimately claim dominance over others.[28] In his report
to the *Convention on the Future of Europe Democracy at many levels: European
Constitutional Reform*, MacCormick suggested that Europe constituted a supranational union of a unique kind that acknowledged shared and divided sovereignty
rather than its concentration, and that accommodated at least four significant
levels of government, ie Union level, Member State level, internal territorial
level and local authorities, themselves very varied in kind and scope of action.[29]
Expanding on MacCormick's work, his successor at the University of Edinburgh
Neil Walker characterised contemporary supranational legal orders as forms of
'late sovereignty', a downgraded perception of sovereignty in a more limited epistemic sense, ie an epistemic constitutional pluralism. This is so because the Union
consisted of a plurality of autonomous institutional normative orders, none of
which nevertheless could plausibly claim overall sovereignty.[30] Such heterarchy
reflects substantive constitutionalism that ought to rely on constitutional tolerance
of authority actors, as Weiler claims.[31] Joerges' 'conflicts-law constitutionalism'
suggests a law-mediated legitimacy through resolution of conflicts arising out of
Europe's diversity rather than the establishment of a unitary legal regime, reflecting a 'three-dimensional' differentiation, ie the emergence of legal frameworks
for regulatory politics and governance arrangements, the need for transnational
regulatory politics and the establishment of transnational co-operative and

---

[28] N MacCormick, 'Beyond the Sovereign State' (1993) 56 *The Modern Law Review* 1; MacCormick, *Questioning Sovereignty* (1997).

[29] Conv 298/02 of 24 September 2002, available at http://european-convention.europa.eu/pdf/reg/en/02/cv00/cv00298.en02.pdf.

[30] N Walker, 'The Idea of Constitutional Pluralism' (2002) 65 *The Modern Law Review* 317; N Walker, 'Late Sovereignty in the European Union' in N Walker (ed), *Sovereignty in Transition* (Oxford, Hart Publishing, 2003) 3.

[31] JHH Weiler, *The Constitution of Europe: 'Do the New Clothes have an Emperor?' and other Essays on European Integration* (Cambridge, Cambridge University Press, 1999) 93.

participatory arrangements.[32] Ernst-Ulrich Petersmann's multi-level constitutional pluralism calls for the collective supply of supplementary international
public goods and for enhancing partial constitutional regimes through cosmopolitan public reason.[33] Kalypso Nicolaïdes envisages an interdependent
constitutionalism among sovereign States in Europe, where citizenship needs to
be conceptually severed from nationality thus leading from a common identity to
the sharing of identities, from a community of identity to a community of projects
and from multi-level governance to multi-centred governance.[34] All in all, as
Nathan Gibbs rightly put it, the largely symbolic notion of a unified sovereignty
is no longer a self-sufficient basis for thinking of polity legitimacy in this broader
space in Europe.[35]

   From the point of view of substantive economic policies within the EU,
although economic constitutionalism does not necessarily convey a specific
economic model, ordoliberalism constituted the economic identity of the EU. This
is a model of social market economy advanced in post-war Germany (doctrinally
established by the Freiburg school), advocating free competition through state
regulation securing market principles, establishment of a strong and independent central bank to conduct monetary policy (which altogether aims at stability
and low inflation), low taxation, privatisation of public services and, as a coun-
ter-weight, through substantive social welfare and minimum wage. In that,
ordoliberalism pre-supposes a significant degree of autonomy in favour of the
economy through the central bank's essential competence to monitor the economy and, to a certain level, establish normative propositions enhancing monetary
policy. Accordingly, central banks essentially reflected the predominance of the
cognitive aspect of economy against the traditional form of normative compulsion, ie law and economy. This predominance is guaranteed not only through
the award of exclusive competences but also through guarantees of immunities,
independence and impartiality for their executive members. In this respect ordoliberalism reserves an elevated level of autonomy for the economy and symbolises
the structural coupling of politics/law (ordo-) with economy (-liberalism), that is
to say the need of normative expectations for the functioning and stability of the
cognitive status of economy. Yet, in the supranational EU, economic policy still

[32] Ch Joerges, 'Unity in Diversity as Europe's Vocation and Conflict's Law as Europe's Constitutional
Form' LSE Europe in Question Discussion paper Series, LEQS paper No 28/2010 (revised version
2013); Ch Joerges, 'The Idea of a Three-Dimensional Conflicts Law as Constitutional Form' RECON
Online Working Paper 2010/05 (2010), available at: www.reconproject.eu/projectweb/portalproject/
RECONWorkingPapers.html; Ch Joerges, 'Conflicts-Law Constitutionalism: Ambitions and Problems'
Zentra Working Paper in Transnational Studies No 10/2012 (2012), available at: https://ssrn.com/
abstract=2182092.
[33] E-U Petersmann, *International Economic Law in the 21st century* (2012) 31, 272–331.
[34] K Nicolaïdis, 'Our European Demoi-cracy: Is this Constitution a Third Way for Europe?' in
K Nicolaïdis and S Weatherill (eds), *Whose Europe? National Models and the Constitution of the
European Union* (Oxford, Oxford University Press, 2003) 137, 143–44.
[35] N Gibbs, 'Post-Sovereignty and the European Legal Space' (2017) 80 *The Modern Law Review*
812, 832.

remains within the competence of the sovereign Member States through the ordinary law-making mechanisms and, therefore, ordoliberalism prepares economic constitutionalism for a step forward in the balance of power between the cognitive and the normative. As Tuori puts it, ordoliberals sought cooperation between law and economics at a deeper-conceptual basis, thus producing reciprocal dialectics; this necessarily transformed the specifics of legal science in that lawyers ought to stand on both ends, namely law and economy; otherwise, their remaining attached to the receiving end only would bring the two ends in an undesired and unnecessary conflict.[36] Yet the management of the financial crisis, which was initially outside the EU framework and focused on the financial aspects of the crisis only, arguably alienated some of the key features upon which the Union was founded. In this respect, Mark Dawson and Floris de Witte argue that the constitutional balance safeguarding the Union's stability and legitimacy, with 'substantive', 'institutional' and 'spatial' dimensions, was altered as a result of the response to the euro crisis, such as the establishment of the ESM, the growing influence of the European Council and the creation of a stand-alone Fiscal Compact, with a lasting impact on the ability of the EU to mediate conflicting interests.[37]

The incorporation of economic narratives into the constitutional discourse means that economic principles find a place in the instrument which express par excellence the normative expectation for the future, ie the Constitution, because it is amended not by any coincidental majority but through a wider consensus. This, however, constitutes a paradox: economic activity finds a place in the Constitution as a means to achieve a higher level of protection against the legislator through norms with a macroscopic range while, at the same time, economy is a subsystem which evolves at an extremely fast pace into new, entirely unforeseeable territories. The temporal asymmetry of constitutional normativisation of economic tools is a typical example of both over- and under-inclusiveness; over-inclusiveness in that it embraces parameters that instantly become out-of-date and under-inclusiveness in that it cannot embrace evidence that lies ahead. Although this symptom is to some extent inherent to constitutional drafting due to the abstract and guiding nature of constitutional norms, the dynamics of economy essentially challenge the efficacy of enacted norms almost instantly. The paradox of macroscopic constitution and agile economy, within the same framework of economic constitutionalism, causes significant problems, mainly because law is not responsive to rapid evolution of economic tools or, conversely, because economy always finds itself one step ahead from most regulatory interventions of the State. This symptom greatly complicates the treatment of any financial crisis and caused, to some extent, the emergence of new economic constitutionalism.

---

[36] K Tuori and K Tuori, *The Eurozone Crisis. A Constitutional Analysis* (Cambridge, Cambridge University Press, 2014) xi.

[37] Teubner, *Constitutional Fragments* (2012) 35–41.

III. New Economic Constitutionalism

In new economic constitutionalism economy is upgraded to an equal status with
the politics/law subsystem and, in case of conflict, it does not concede but rather
interrelates with it and may cause a significant change of constitutional paradigm
in order to adjust to economic reality. Unlike economic constitutionalism, which
merely acknowledges the functional differentiation and dynamics of economy,
new economic constitutionalism is beset by an idea that economy is a *sine qua
non* condition precedent for the harmonious operation of the constitutional state,
superseding any other social subsystem and enjoying the same normative capacity
as politics/law. As a doctrine, new economic constitutionalism can be summa-
rised in the prophetic words of Luhmann in his Orwellian 1971 paper on world
society (*Weltgesellschaft*): he pictures this world's society as one where normative
expectations that widely supported the predominance of politics/law over any
social subsystem concede and are largely substituted by cognitive expectations
leading to a new leadership of science and technology.[38]

New economic constitutionalism in Europe entails a fresh economic constitutional identity, ie financialism, which is shared by both the sovereign Member
States and the Union itself. This new type of constitutionalism, as suggested
by Stephen Gill,[39] started developing in the 1990s through disciplinary neoliberalism, with a view to secure investor freedoms and property rights for transnational enterprises through a swinging institutional interdependence between
States and supranational entities, and was firmly established in the aftermath of
the economic crisis in early twenty-first century through new enhanced economic
governance at a supranational level.[40] Accordingly, financialism implies that the
Constitution, as properly interpreted and enforced by all state authorities, not only
tolerates and protects the economy by abstaining from offensive intrusions but
also gives priority to the economic provisions over other constitutional clauses
and, where necessary, also bends the economic provisions themselves, such as in
the case of no bail-out clauses of Articles 125/123 TFEU. This entails a process of
interpretative transformation of key constitutional notions, such as competence,
sustainability, public interest, property and access to justice.

[38] N Luhmann, 'Die Weltgesellschaft' (1971) 57 *Archiv für Rechts- und Sozialphilosophie* 1, 10–19.
[39] S Gill, 'New Constitutionalism, Democratisation and Global Political Economy' (1998) 10 *Global
Change, Peace & Security* 23.
[40] L Oberndorfer, 'A New Economic Governance through Secondary Legislation? Analysis and
Constitutional Assessment: From New Constitutionalism, via Authoritarian Constitutionalism to
Progressive Constitutionalism' in N Bruun, K Lörcher and I Schömann (eds), *The Economic and
Financial Crisis and Collective Labour Law in Europe* (Oxford, Hart Publishing, 2014) 25; L de Lucia,
'The Rationale of Economics and Law in the Aftermath of the Crisis: A Lesson from Michel Foucault'
(2016) 12 *European Constitutional Law Review* 445.

A. The Context

The shift from economic constitutionalism to new economic constitutionalism did not occur through an abrupt change of constitutional paradigm, but was rather a slow-moving process of domination of economy against all other social subsystems and its equivalent rivalry towards politics/law. This transformation process started immediately after World War II and arguably culminated in the aftermath of the 2008-onwards financial crisis. The grounds that facilitated the transition to new economic constitutionalism were, in my view: transnationalism of economic governance; transformation of the orthodox ordo-liberal perception; larger intangibility of financial assets; dismantling of politics and law; and osmosis of public and private spheres. These are outlined below.

As regards *transnationalism of economic governance*, it should be said from the outset that, from an institutional point of view, developments after the end of the war moved in parallel in the domestic and international arena. On a domestic level, the end of the war marked tremendous changes in the constitutional charters. Almost all States introduced new constitutional regimes domestically. For obvious reasons, Germany and Italy turned to parliamentary democracy with strong emphasis on dignity and the social state and the introduction of powerful constitutional courts. France, inspired by De Gaulle's personality, turned to the semi-presidential regime of the fifth republic after a short interval of parliamentary democracy. Belgium, Holland, Greece and the Scandinavian countries restored their pre-war constitutional regime. The Soviet regime dominated Eastern Europe and established Constitutions to upgrade the communist authority. Spain and Portugal were yet under the authoritarian regimes of Franco and Salazar respectively.

On an international level, immediately after the end of the war, there was a great mobility to launch new and powerful international organisations. Of course, international organisations were established as early as the beginning of the nineteenth century. The Congress of Vienna in 1814/15 was the venue that shaped the formation of allegedly the first international organisation in the world properly understood as such, ie the *Commission Centrale pour la Navigation du Rhin*.[41] The Treaty of Vienna confirmed the principle of freedom of navigation on the Rhine and authorised the Central Commission to draft a convention to that effect, eventually materialised in 31 March 1831 (the Mainz Convention). Prior to all this, in 1804, the French Empire and the Holy Roman Empire of the German Nation concluded a concession Treaty whereby it was agreed to establish a single Rhine toll in Mainz, to centralise the toll system, to use the funds to improve navigation and to settle disputes arising therefrom. Furthermore, a year earlier, in 1814, the Congress of Vienna laid down the principle of the freedom of navigation on the major international rivers of Europe. Later, in 1904,

---

[41] HWV Temperley, *The Congress of Vienna 1814–15 and the Conference of Paris 1919* (London, Historical Association, 1923).

the *Fédération Internationale de Football Association* (FIFA) was established with regard to international football regulation. Immediately after World War I, the League of Nations was founded on 10 January 1920 as a result of the Paris Peace Conference that ended the war with a principal mission to maintain world peace – obviously failing patently.

In spite of all the above, international organisations launched in the second half of the twentieth century were perceived in a different manner compared to the past. In this respect, it was widely recognised that there was a noble cause in establishing liaisons between sovereign States in order to prevent the disastrous consequences of another world conflict. The global character of the wars raised the issue of inadequacy of conventional bilateral agreements as instruments of solving disputes between the contracting States. In that regard, the States were ready to enter into wide-range multilateral agreements and, in this framework, to make significant concessions in order to demonstrate their willingness to go along with fellow States in a state of relative equality and solidarity. Furthermore, there was a common perception that due to stagnancy of the economy as a result of the wars and, especially in Europe, the decrease in work forces due to war casualties, there should be an economic boost over and above national State boundaries.

However, neither of the above grounds could provide a persuasive answer to the question as to how international organisations evolved to transnational experiments with a broadly autonomous logic and political standing, lying between domestic and international legal orders but not assimilated into either. Among the most influential transnational organisations of such hybrid quality, established between 1945 and 1960, were: the United Nations; the International Monetary Fund (IMF) founded at the Bretton Woods Conference to secure international monetary cooperation, to stabilise currency exchange rates and to expand international liquidity; the European Communities with the European Court of Justice; the European Convention of Human Rights with the Court of Strasbourg; The GATT, with its gradually developed system of judicial review (the World Trade Organisation (WTO) and the Appellate body were established in 1995); and the Inter-Governmental Maritime Consultative Organization, which later became the International Maritime Organisation (IMO).

From a societal point of view, Kjaer considers the formation of such transnational organisations as a third independent layer of social pattern reproduction unfolding within world society over and above modern statehood and feudal structures, the latter having been subsumed within modern States, albeit marginalised, through constitutional monarchies, inherited seats in the Upper House and closed networks of nobility. Accordingly, the transnational space must be understood as a conglomerate of *Eigene Structur*, reproducing an independent form of law-generating social patterns.[42] This new transnational law was, in Tuori's words, the 'true El Dorado of legal hybrids'.[43]

---

[42] PF Kjaer, *Constitutionalism in the Global Realm. A Sociological Approach* (Abingdon, Routledge, 2014) 1–2.
[43] Tuori and Tuori, *The Eurozone Crisis* (2014) 17.

As regards the *transformation of the orthodox ordoliberal perception,* in the 1970s there has been a marked shift from the ordoliberal tradition, that placed emphasis on a broadly sovereign structure and budgetary/fiscal policies concerning policies, towards a more market-oriented approach, placing emphasis on free and equal conditions of competition. This shift, set symbolically by Joerges at the publication, in 1985, of the Delors White Paper on the Completion of the Internal Market,[44] signifies a radical mutation – one might argue degradation – in the perception of the Community from a supranational state-oriented entity, which predominantly aims at integration, to a geographically prescribed area, to a market-oriented entity aiming primarily at achieving more profits and welfare. As a sequel to this evolution, the regulatory emphasis was placed not so much on the rules determining the fiscal habits of the sovereign Member States, but mostly on the rules that would guarantee the primary target of uninhibited competition between economic actors. This turn clearly upgraded private economy to a key notion in the shaping of community policies and, incidentally, in the interpretation of existing rules and principles. This eventually amounted to turning European Economic Community law from mainly constitutional to administrative and commercial in nature.

As regards the *larger intangibility of financial assets,* economic globalisation brought an extreme dominance of non-cash money (electronic money, capital transactions, securities, etc). According to the World Payments Report, globally, non-cash transaction volumes continued to grow at double-digit growth rates throughout 2015/16. Volumes grew by 10.1 per cent to reach a total of 482.6 billion, while the global e-wallet market is growing even faster, with transaction volumes estimated to a total of 41.8 billion, its main growth regions during that period emerging in Asia and Central Europe, the Middle East and Africa. In spite of the assumption that high levels of non-cash transactions can benefit society in treating corruption and payment fraud, the increased ratio of intangible transactions, as opposed to actual money transactions, has substantially changed the role and performance of private banks and other payment institutions.[45] Currently, private banks essentially administer and monitor a much greater percentage of circulation of money than state central banks, which have the monopoly on issuing money, and are, therefore, much stronger stakeholders in the economy arena and, constitute, correspondingly, a strong point of consideration for all States in determining their financial policy. This transfer of the power to create money from central to private banks has resulted in the latter acting pro-cyclically without a concern for broader economy or political/social accountability, while at the same time they are exposed as the State itself or the society. However, since private

---

[44] Ch Joerges, 'Unity in Diversity as Europe's Vocation and Conflict's Law as Europe's Constitutional Form', LSE Europe in Question Discussion paper Series, LEQS paper no 28/2010 (revised version 2013) 17–18.

[45] Capgemini and BNP Parisbas, 'World's Payment Report 2018' (2018), available at https://world-paymentsreport.com/wp-content/uploads/sites/5/2018/10/World-Payments-Report-2018.pdf.

banks can only aim at earnings and given that there can be no zero-sum growth or stability, such banks must attack the excesses of the compulsion in order to increase profits.[46] This situation leads to an arms race competition between banks over appealing banking products and an endless effort to circumvent regulatory banking restrictions in order to maximise bank benefits. This is, anyhow, the short story of Lehman Brothers and of the banking crisis of 2007–09.

As regards *politics/law dismantling*, it seems that economy has brought the two salient features of normativity into an internal conflict. The whole idea of economic constitutionalism, prior to the new era, was based on an explicit and an implicit assumption. The explicit assumption was that economy developed as a privileged subsystem having a constant place in the normative agenda of law. The implicit assumption was that economy still remained subordinate to the superseding joint subsystem of politics/law, which is the key feature of the era of constitutionalism. This unity of politics/law vis-a-vis economy was, however, seriously hampered while economy was getting all more globalised. Not only traditional sovereign States became unable to address such issues because of their increased complexity on a layer that trespassed the domain of application of domestic law, but mostly there was a crack in the cohesive alliance of law and politics. For politics seemed to concede a great portion of the authority of the political subsystem to economy.

This occurred in a variety of ways. First, economy became a goal per se for national welfare and an intrinsic part of public interest, which is by definition the pursuit of politics. Second, politicians and political parties became altogether dependent upon the subsidies by economic actors, without which it was impossible to access governance due to the exorbitant increase of electoral expenses. Third, the extremely high financial stakes of the economy resulted in corruption that greatly disintegrated the ethical values associated with the administration of public affairs. Because of all these factors the political subsystem moved from the main alliance with law to the arena of economy, which obviously had an adverse effect on the integrity of the regulation but mainly caused a certain vulnerability of politics as regards the latter's regulatory intervention in economy.

As regards the *public/private osmosis*, the current state of economy seems to produce tension to the orthodox constitutional maxim that private and public, ie State and society, are strictly differentiated. Yet, although economy becomes all the more technical and cognitive, there is a particular grey area between cognitive and normative expectations which are treated as accidental and do not produce neither normative sanctions nor cognitive learning processes and can also be covered by insurance mechanisms.[47] With reference to this distinction,

---

[46] G Teubner, 'A Constitutional Moment? The Logics of "Hitting the Bottom"' in PF Kjaer, G Teubner and A Febbrajo (eds), *The Financial Crisis in Constitutional Perspective. The Dark Side of Functional Differentiation* (Oxford, Hart Publishing, 2011) 3.

[47] N Luhmann, *Soziale Systeme: Grundriß einer allgemeinen Theorie* (Frankfurt, Suhrkamp, 1987) 442.

Renner considers that most parameters of the financial crisis as of 2007 qualify in this intermediate category which he terms 'complex expectations', since neither sanctions have been imposed nor economic structures have been substantially modified as a result of a cognitive turning point.[48] The truth is that economy has penetrated so deeply into the public sphere that the distinction from politics/law is not that clear anymore. This was made evident in the context of the sovereign debt crisis in Europe, where the endangered States were fluctuating between public and private sphere in order to secure adequate state funding. On a domestic level, sovereign debt is shifted from private debt to public debt (for instance, through rescue packages, bond purchasing or guarantees from fellow Member States or through private sector involvement schemes to reduce States' private debt); on a worldwide level, global debt is essentially transferred from advanced to emerging economies, while at the same time there is no diminution in the overall ratio of global debt to GDP.

It seems that the hyper-complexity and multicentrality of global economy has not only dislocated the territorial aspect of governance but has also, to some extent, merged the public and private operation of the States. The more the distinction between public and private becomes blurred, the more economy finds a path to penetrate strongly into the basic constitutional structures of the State.

B. The Process

Yet, a fundamental question remains unsolved in relation to the present analysis: whether there has been indeed a major transition from the era of economic consti-tutionalism that is worth qualifying as a new phase in the relationship between the Constitution and the economy, ie a new economic constitutionalism, and, if so, how this transition was effectively triggered. The financial crisis constitutes, beyond any doubt, a great constitutional moment in this respect. Both the people and the system encountered a near-catastrophe experience, as opposed to the experience of its contingency as such: in Teubner's words, the real experience of late modernity, following the triumphant victory of the autonomy of economy, is no longer what the institutional pre-conditions of their autonomy are, but rather where the limits of the expansion of the function systems are, ie the 'hitting the bottom' question.[49] From an institutional point of view, the crisis, most importantly and relevantly, brought in and consolidated a new economic constitutional iden-tity, which is in fact the key notion of the era of new economic constitutionalism.

The convergence towards a single economic constitutional identity was a parallel evolution process in national States and international entities. From the

---

[48] Renner, 'Death by Complexity' (2011) 99–100.
[49] Teubner, 'A Constitutional Moment? (2011) 10–12.

States' point of view, the focal point was historically the existence of *constitutional identity*, as a by-product of constitutionalism. The constitutional identity was shaped within the state structures because it aimed at limiting the political power of the sovereign; and sovereignty remained at state level. Although the notion of constitutional identity originated as akin to any individual State (thus many variations of constitutional identities existed), wide sharing of fundamental constitutional values (such as democracy, the rule of law and the separation of powers) led to the phenomenon of global constitutionalism on a national level.

However, in the latter part of the twentieth century there has been a colossal redistribution of the political power, in the course of which the States transferred a critical mass of their functions (relating to the economy in one way or another) to international economic entities. The latter essentially shaped their own economic model, which was then imposed on national States and merged with their long-standing constitutional identities. In that, national States exported constitutionalism and imported economic identity, thus developing an economic constitutional identity of their own.

From the point of view of the European Communities (and, by analogy, the World Trade Organisation), the starting point has historically been an *economic identity* of ordoliberalism. In spite of its domestic German origin, ordoliberalism gained wide recognition, predominantly because of economic globalisation, and was established as a model pattern for regulating the economy. Thus, it was essentially exported to the whole of Europe and became the dominant architecture of economic management. In that, it was exported to Member States not as a matter of their own sovereign choice but mostly as an imposition by the supranational entity. When the financial crisis erupted, the economic model of ordoliberalism did not only survive (since no blame was afforded to it for the ongoing predicament), but actually established itself through a strict adherence to the economic constitutional identity of financialism. Accordingly, the one-sided economic model intruded on the constitutional core of the States. On the other hand, international economic entities, due to their ever-increasing competences and their political power stemming from global economy, gradually developed a supranational quality as autonomous legal structures with constitutional specifications. In that sense, the supranational entities exported their economic identity and imported constitutionalism, thus shaping an economic constitutional identity.

In the light of the above, States and supranational entities, albeit from different angles and through different routes, converge to the economic constitutional identity of financialism, exactly because of the domination of the ordoliberal theory. This economic constitutional identity has, however, been used in a distinct manner. The States have embraced the economic constitutional identity seeking for functionality, which conventional constitutionalism failed effectively to establish in order to prevent the break-out of the economic crisis. On the other hand, the supranational entities have embraced the economic constitutional identity for legitimacy, which still remains their basic shortfall in relation to sovereign States and inhibits them from gaining a constitutional status equivalent to that of the

Member States.[50] On an EU level, the continuous effort towards European integration has continually resorted to mechanisms of nationally mediated legitimacy in order to 'borrow' legitimacy from the national level, in order to transform functional administrative legitimacy to sound democratic constitutional legitimacy.[51]

C. The Causes

The economic crisis constituted the ignition of new economic constitutionalism that changed the constitutional paradigm and brought in new economic drafting and reading as well as significant implications upon governance and politics. These consequences are discussed in detail in the following chapters. As regards the causes of the economic crisis in Europe, various explanations could be provided and have indeed been set forth by the relevant literature; the most popular explanations are non-institutional ones, ie the economic, the political, the psychological and the sociological explanation.

The *political* explanation blames neo-liberalism in Europe.[52] In this view, the economic theology which suggests that the economy should be left entirely alone from any unnecessary intervention of the State lies in a false assumption, namely that economy employs strong self-corrective mechanisms that allow it to find by itself the optimal vehicles to treat any relevant crises. In fact, due to the constant urge for accumulation of wealth, capitalism cannot operate on a self-corrective manner. Irrespective of the soundness of the argument in terms of its economic foundation, an issue that has sparked off a long-lasting and intense theoretical debate throughout the centuries, an obvious factual counter-argument would be that socialist and left-wing parties in Europe – even those that took over power in their respective countries – did not manage to articulate a credible alternative, apart from claiming for a more even distribution of wealth through a social Europe and for the release of money from richer countries to those that have suffered the most from the crisis (which is obviously a target but says nothing about the means to achieve this end). Pursuant to the prophetic saying by Poulatzas, from a Marxist point of view, there is in capitalism an 'authoritarian statism', ie a general movement of States towards authoritarianism through coercive and state surveillance to safeguard the prevailing notion of the free economy.[53]

[50] G Gerapetritis, 'Europe's New Deal: A New Version of an Expiring Deal' (2014) 38 *European Journal of Law and Economics* 91.

[51] P Lindseth, 'Reflections on the "Administrative, not Constitutional" Character of EU Law in Times of Crisis' Special Issue, Sixty Years Later: Rethinking Competing Paradigms for EU Law in Times of Crisis, (2017) 9 *Perspectives on Federalism* 1.

[52] For the same reason, this accusation may also turn against neo-conservatism in the US, although this policy is not based exclusively on the faith in economic self-growth but also argues for an interventionist administration, primarily in international affairs (when national interests seem to be at stake, eg invasion to Iraq to protect national security) but also on a domestic level (eg imposition of taxes to prevent domestic industry).

[53] N Poulatzas, *Clashes in Contemporary Capitalism* (London, New Left Books, 1975).

The *psychological* explanation blames the individual or collective market greed for more profits. Thus, the financial crisis can be put down to relevant individual attitudes that destroy any rational choices towards self-preservation. In that regard private key actors of the economy, such as bankers, entrepreneurs, funds, stock-marketers, insurance brokers and credit-ratings companies, cannot be controlled because they are not in a position to realise the macro-destruction caused to the economy or they refuse to uphold this argument, because this would go contrary to the fundamental premise of maximisation of profit-making. The sum of such individual attitudes results in collective addiction phenomena that explain the latest financial crisis, ie underlying self-destructive growth compulsions of information flows.[54]

Obviously addictions do not generally obey any rationality test: it is by definition that any addiction succumbs to irrationality, let alone collective addiction that operates in a much more subtle and persistent manner in the collective subconscious and ignores potential self-destruction effects. Thus, for instance, people at large do not see the preservation of the environment as a condition for prosperity but, mostly, as a compulsive restriction to private economic activity, which might be necessary, albeit sometimes excessive. The psychological explanation has two loopholes: first, it provides significant insight to human attitudes in the context of the crisis, yet it seems to rely exclusively on the human factor and to underestimate the significance of structures, be it institutional or economic; second, it cannot, by using exclusively the cognitive instruments of psychology, provide a certain line of distinction between greed as a pathology of excess and self-destruction on the one hand, and legitimate desire for growth which constitutes one factor of improvement and societal growth, on the other.[55]

The *sociological* explanation places emphasis on the failed process of gradual autonomy of economy as a social subsystem and its structural coupling with politics/law. Instead of effective structural coupling, economy created, based on its cognitive predominance, escape mechanisms through social practices that superseded or by-passed law. The difference lies between cognitive and normative expectations. As Luhmann set it: normative expectations (law) are counter-factually upheld in a case of crisis through institutional coercion, whereas cognitive expectations are modified in cases of crisis and accordingly result in new adaptive learning processes. The more a subsystem such as economy presents a complexity gap between internal structures and the environment the more it claims autonomy.[56]

In the case of the financial crisis, precisely because of their hyper-complex nature, economic phenomena that were shaped very rapidly after World War II established a very serious complexity gap and, accordingly, raised the issue

---

[54] Teubner (n 35) 5.
[55] ibid 7–10.
[56] Luhmann, *Soziale Systeme* (1987) 383–447.

of autonomy. It was not merely a matter of institutional struggle over power and dominance among these sub-social systems, but also politics/law was cognitively unable to understand the basics of the economy and demonstrate reflexes to rapidly evolving economic phenomena. Economic phenomena in the pre-crisis era became extremely complicated, both in terms of operation and in terms of architecture, thus creating over-complicated structures that are not easily implemented and are not easily adjustable, given the rapid evolution of the economy. This made institutions vulnerable to the unexpected turbulences of the economy. Politics/law based on a model of normative predictability, thus, failed to cooperate with the new economic facets. As Niall Ferguson puts it, in capitalism wealth mutates in a way that democracy may eliminate growth and a financial crisis may undermine democracy: 'Financial history is a roller-coaster ride of ups and downs, bubbles and busts, manias and panics, shocks and crushes ... so much about the future lies in the realm of uncertainty, as opposed to calculable risk'.[57]

There are, however, two counter-arguments to the sociological explanation. The conceptual objection is that it seems to rely considerably on a very static perception of positive law, thus ignoring the multiparty relationships developed in contemporary societies, where a great number of cumulative compulsions co-exist in a polycentric community schema with a high level of complexity, globality and uncertainty of the phenomena associated to economic activity and its interaction with law and politics. The factual objection is that there was no significant reaction on the part of the economy subsystem in the course of the post-2009 financial crisis in Europe to respond to the respective malfunctions. Theoretically, since economy by definition enjoys cognitive supremacy some reflective reaction ought to have occurred, yet this was not the case. In fact, the attempt to bridge the complexity gap only came unilaterally from the politics/law system, it is, therefore, questionable whether there was a cognitive disability on the part of the institutions to properly understand the economic deficiencies.

Finally, the *economic* explanation refers to asymmetric shocks due to lack of independent monetary policy or devaluation, to the underestimation of moral hazard that the prospects for bailouts created for the incentive of member countries to exercise budget discipline and to the imbalance caused by the dichotomy between responsibility for financial regulation that was left at the national level and for monetary policy that was conveyed to the European Central Bank (ECB). The above causes resulted in the fiscal criteria being violated repeatedly, without any significant consequences for the violating Member States, since their interest rate spreads were almost zero.[58]

---

[57] N Ferguson, *The Ascent of Money: A Financial History of the World* (New York, Penguin, 2009) 342–43.

[58] JC Shambaugh, R Reis and H Rey, 'The Euro's Three Crises' (2012) 1 *Brookings Papers on Economic Activity* 157; J Frankel 'Causes of Eurozone Crises' in R Baldwin and F Giavazzi (eds), *The Eurozone Crisis: A Consensus View of the Causes and a few Possible Solutions* (London, CEPR Press, 2015) 109.

Arguably, none of the above arguments provides a convincing explanation for the financial crisis. In fact, politics, psychology and sociology cannot, even combined, furnish rational reasons to explain how Greece could so easily destabilise the euro area, while representing in 2008 less than 1 per cent of the world's debt (today 0.32) and 4.3 per cent of Europe's debt, its nominal debt today being 322 billion euros when Italy's is 2,302, France's 2,255, Germany's 2,071 and the UK's 2,016 billion euros.[59] Only eight years after the euro was launched, sovereign debt crisis knocked on Europe's door – a situation that until then mostly occurred in developing countries. In fact, the post-2009 crisis is properly classified as international since prior crises either developed in a particular region, such as in Russia in 1998 or in Argentina in 2001, or referred to private debts, such as the East Asia crisis of 1997/98 or the Mexican crisis of 1998 (Reinhart and Rogoff, 2011). In the light of these facts, this book advances the thesis that the cause of the financial crisis, which in turn, brought in new economic constitutionalism and the upgrade of financialism, is institutional and is linked to the wide range of structural asymmetries of the European project with regard to the Union altogether and, especially, with the monetary union. These asymmetries refer to: (a) the lack of EU constitutional foundation; (b) the multiplicity of the Community project; (c) the lack of fiscal convergence of the euro area; (d) the economic divergences of euro-area Member States; and (e) the limited monitoring for financial trespasses by Member States. These are discussed in turn below.

As regards the *lack of EU legitimate constitutional foundation*, much has been said about the concessions towards democratic legitimacy and accountability, the lack of a clear vision as to where Europe is headed, even after the introduction of the single currency and the repeated devaluation of the rule of law, which has resulted in the so-called EU democratic deficit.[60] There are three reasons why this is so: first, the key actors in EU decision-making remain in the Member States themselves, operating through the intergovernmental method, with the exception of the ministers when acting in the Council in an intergovernmental manner; second, in areas where the EU has no competence to act following the Community method, there is a clear political hegemony in the form of a core of national executives from the most powerful States who take crucial decisions on major issues,

---

[59] Information drawn from Eurostat, available at https://www.statista.com/statistics/274179/national-debt-in-eu-countries.

[60] A Psygkas, *From the 'Democratic Deficit' to a 'Democratic Surplus': Constructing Administrative Democracy in Europe* (New York, Oxford University Press, 2017); Ó Fernández, *The Democratic Deficit of the European Union* (Saarbrücken, Lap Lambert Academic Publishing, 2013); K Dilek Azman, *The Problem of Democratic Deficit in the European Union: The Democratic Deficit Issue with Reference to the Acquis* (Saarbrücken, Lap Lambert Academic Publishing, 2011); WW van der Werf, *Democracy in the European Union: An Analysis of the Democratic Deficit in the European Union* (Saarbrücken, Lap Lambert Academic Publishing, 2010); D Chryssochoou, *Democracy in the European Union* (London, Tauris, 2000); SS Andersen and KA Eliassen, *The European Union: How Democratic is it?* (London, Sage, 1996); GF Mancini, *Democracy and Constitutionalism in the European Union: Collected Essays* (Oxford, Hart Publishing, 2000); G Majone, 'Europe's "Democratic Deficit": The Question of Standards' (1998) 4 *European Law Journal* 5.

such as the financial crisis or the future of Europe, in small round-tables; and, third, there is a wide involvement of non-legitimate expert fora established *ad hoc* or on a semi-permanent basis, which is addressed as the comitology issue.

The round table and comitology methods obviously fall short on the level of accountability, their procedures are to a great extent obscure and, eventually, they harm the Union's overall level of legitimacy. To this end, the Preamble of the TEU expresses the desire 'to enhance further the democratic and efficient functioning of the institutions so as to enable them better to carry out, within a single institutional framework, the tasks entrusted to them'. This deficit was once again confirmed in the course of the financial crisis. Indeed, the most striking example of lack of democratic legitimacy and adhesion to the Union's legality was the treatment of Greece's debt and deficit problem. This pathology seems to have been treated on a European level, either outside the Union or by unrepresented EU authorities.

Thus, relevant decisions have been taken by the heads of governments of the most powerful European States, mostly over dinners, as has always been the case from Maastricht onwards, and then passed on to the rest of the executives and the EU itself. This resulted in a broadly technical approach to the financial crisis, mostly at the level of Eurogroup and Euro-working group, as opposed to a highly political administration of the situation. This is to confirm Lindseth's famous quotation that the structural deficiencies of the Union combined with the strictly attributed powers stemming from the national Constitutions themselves render the European integration essentially 'administrative' rather than constitutional in nature, because the Union's complex system of governance has been unable to achieve a democratic or constitutional legitimacy in its own right.[61]

However, the question remains as to whether the European project was improperly launched from the very outset, or if it was developed in an inadequate manner. Weiler argued that the European project was in the first place messianic, whereby both the mobilising force and the principal legitimising feature were based on the nobility of the cause of peace and prosperity.[62] But, even where some democratic façade was institutionally provided at EU level, it never materialised due to a lack of political will to convert it to applied policy.[63] The effort to strengthen the EU in terms of democratic processes, stemming primarily from the Lisbon Treaty, through the empowerment of the European Parliament, the national powers in relation to the Union's subsidiarity issues as well as the forms of popular initiative, was hardly an effective remedy. This is so, particularly because of the structural deficiencies of the Union vis-a-vis the Member States and the hesitation

---

[61] PL Lindseth, *Power and Legitimacy. Reconciling Europe and the Nation-State* (Oxford, Oxford University Press, 2010) 23–32.

[62] JHH Weiler, '60 Years since the First European Community – Reflections on Political Messianism' (2011) 22 *European Journal of International Law* 303; JHH Weiler, 'The Political and Legal Culture of European Integration: An Exploratory Essay' (2011) 9 *International Journal of Constitutional Law* 678.

[63] S Bilakovics, *Democracy without Politics* (Cambridge, MA, Harvard University Press, 2012) 175–84.

towards a more substantive union, as reflected in the turmoil of the unsuccessful European Constitution. Unsurprisingly, the treatment of the 2009 financial crisis was based on administrative and logistical approaches and much less so on political and constitutional considerations.

As regards the *multiplicity of the Community project*, arguably, the Community was never a single project because of the existence of internal subsystems, national derogations and different state aspirations and/or interests. Structurally, the euro area and the Schengen area constitute self-evident indications of the various intra-Community layers, whereas the multiple derogations from those two fundamental sub-Treaties by definition stand for a variable institutional architecture. Conceptually, the main political and institutional goal of European Integration did not connote the same meaning for all stakeholders, basically the Member States. Federico Fabbrini argues that instead of a joint effort towards integration through convergence, in practice, this operates vice versa, ie with the EU Members attempting to move towards their own visions of integration, which he categorises as integration from an economic community perspective, an intergovernmental union perspective and a parliamentary union perspective.[64]

In that, the EU project produced a multi-layer and multi-speed amalgam resulting in a system of differentiated integration.[65] As Hinarejos argues, the tensions produced by such differentiated integration was substantially culminated at the time of financial crisis due to variable interests of the EU Member States and the immediate priorities of euro and non-euro countries, coupled with a need for prompt and at times politically sensitive action. It resulted in further fragmentation that jeopardises the future of the European project because of the deepening of the split and the legitimacy concerns.[66] The different understanding and practical implementation as to whether access to the euro area is compulsory for those Member States fulfilling ex post the criteria set therein (except for the States that formally opted out) is only a paradigm of this attitude.

As regards the *lack of fiscal convergence of the euro area*, there is a clear economic paradox in trying to establish a common and very inflexible centralised monetary policy, while the economic policy remains broadly decentralised within the competence of the Member States. Germany and France strongly opposed the idea of a fiscal union that would force compliance with the financial restrictions by each Member State. Instead, an allusion to a low-level 'budgetary discipline' was preferred, based on an amalgam of fiscal autonomy and the obligation of solidarity and budgetary discipline. The European Council, in its Resolution on the Stability and Growth Pact adopted in Amsterdam on 17 June 1997, stressed

---

[64] S Fabbrini, *Which European Union? Europe after the Euro Crisis* (Cambridge, Cambridge University Press, 2015) 91–184.

[65] M Avbelj, 'Differentiated Integration – Farewell to the EU-27' (2014) *German Law Journal* 191.

[66] A Hinarejos, *The Euro Area Crisis in Constitutional Perspective*, (Oxford, Oxord University Press, 2015) 103–04.

the crucial importance of securing such discipline in stage three of the Economic and Monetary Union and addressed relevant guidelines to the Member States, the Commission and the Council.

Yet, lenient economic rules essentially operated mostly as Christian morality than regular coercion. Member States were asked to cooperate in safeguarding the monetary ceilings, which indirectly set restrictions upon their liberty to exercise autonomous – mostly social – policies, while at the same time they nominally retained sovereignty in drafting such domestic policies, not only as a matter of constitutional empowerment, but also as an acceptable compromise in the allocation of competences between the EU and the euro-area Member States. Accordingly, in Europe, transnational governance presented entirely idiosyncratic characteristics.

The Union's own dynamics developed a model of institutionalised economic governance far beyond any other transnational system worldwide. In this respect, one might blame the crisis on the lack of effective regulation and monitoring institutions, or the wrongful form of institutionalisation of multiple unions instead of a single union,[67] or even the Union's lack of essential characteristics of a state-based monetary union, such as a macro-economically significant central budget and centralised banking supervision, in order to prevent banking and financial abruptness.[68] In any event, the lack of fiscal convergence rendered the monetary union project fruitless merely from an economic standpoint. In the absence of a fiscal union, austerity policy, combined with the rigidities of Europe's monetary union, has hardly been a model of social cogency and sagacity.[69]

As regards the *economic divergences of the euro-area Member States*, it appears that the contracting States not only varied significantly in their actual economic status but, on occasions, their sovereign financial interests were sharply contradictory. Such multilayer participation based on structural economic discrepancies could not stand against a procrustean monetary model which required a very strict adherence to standardised rules. This was so, because the common currency outside a fiscal union was designed mostly with a view to securing anti-inflation stability, which was a clear setback for weak economies.

As a prerequisite for participation in the euro area, the Member States were asked to waive part of their traditional sovereignty, without receiving in return any sort of warranties regarding the future of the project. Essentially, less developed States were asked to withdraw the single mechanism to respond to national economic turbulence through currency devaluation, even as a means to temporarily ease budgetary and loan pressures. In Jürgen Habermas' words, the outcasting of politics from economy through European monetarism conveyed the inability of

---

[67] Fabbrini, *Which European Union?* (2015) 1–90.

[68] P de Grauwe, *Economics of Monetary Union*, 12th edn (Oxford, Oxford University Press, 2018) 103–31.

[69] A Sen, 'The Crisis of European Democracy' *New York Times*, 22 May 2012.

national governments to stabilise the foundations of their social legitimacy and an arm's race of demolition of the social state in order to prevent default.[70]

Accordingly, although convergence constitutes by definition the goal of an international organisation aiming at unity, the EU never really took into consideration the existing inequalities of its constituent Member States, apart from strict technical economic differences. For example, in assessing Member States' actual economic capabilities and encouraging policies of convergence, the EU consistently ignored particularities concerning defence and geography, at least until the post-2015 immigration wave to Europe, which forced the Union to take proactive measures.

In all these aspects, Greece was the evident weak actor of the Union. Based on historic grounds of neighbouring conflicts in the region and as a country located at the external border of the EU, Greece had to deal with national security issues, which resulted – reasonably or not – in exorbitant defence expenditure, amounting, according to the World Bank's data, to 2.5 per cent of GDP in 2017, with a euro area average of 1.5 per cent.[71] This makes Greece one of the few alliance members to exceed NATO's goal of 2 per cent of GDP for defence spending, despite its huge financial problems, ranking second, after the US only, in proportionate defence expenses. In turn, this led to corruption that immensely augmented unrevealed defence costs to the detriment of national economy. Furthermore, illegal immigration has been, and still is, an unsolved problem because of Greece being easily accessible through continental and sea gates, notably from Asia Minor and North Africa. Today, the cost paid by the country, both financially and socially, has become explosive because of the economic crisis. Finally, the geographic disparity of Greece, given the great number of islands and mountains, has led the State to spend a huge amount of resources to maintain a satisfactory level of balanced growth. The situation has become all the more vulnerable due to the fact that the country does not support heavy industry; rather, its gross revenue mostly revolves around the provision of services, such as tourism and maritime services. Evidently, all these factors have rendered Greece a less-favoured region overall and have cultivated disparities with the rest of Europe. Despite the above, Greece became a member of the Eurozone and, as of 2001, enjoyed a seven-year prosperity period before flagrantly collapsing under a mountain of debt.[72]

Finally, it should be added that a crisis mostly affects the most vulnerable groups and cultivates internal inequalities within the endangered States; this

---

[70] J Habermas, 'The European Nation-State and the Pressures of Globalization' (1999) 44 *Blätter für Deutsche und Internationale Politik* 425.

[71] https://data.worldbank.org/indicator/MS.MIL.XPND.GD.ZS?view=chart.

[72] T Pelagidis and M Mitsopoulos, *Understanding the Crisis in Greece: From Boom to Bust*, 2nd edn (New York, Palgrave Macmillan, 2011); G Pagoulatos, 'Greece after the Bailouts: Assessment of a Qualified Failure', GreeSE Paper no 130, Hellenic Observatory, European Institute, LSE, available at www.lse.ac.uk/Hellenic-Observatory/Assets/Documents/Publications/GreeSE-Papers/GreeSE-No130.pdf (2018); J Manolopoulos, *Greece's 'Odious' Debt: The Looting of the Hellenic Republic by the Euro, the Political Elite and the Investment Community* (London, Anthem Press, 2011).

makes the financial conundrum for these States even harder, since it is the state budgets that need to respond to challenges relating to basic social needs.

On the other hand, due to the asymmetrical structure of the euro area, not only there were economic discrepancies among Member States, but also the institutional framework essentially produced, especially in the course of the post-2009 financial crisis, major conflicts of interests. First of all, the increase in the cost of government bonds in countries close to default, insofar as those retain access to markets but also in secondary markets, reduces the spreads accordingly and, correspondingly, results in a reduction in the cost of financially strong countries which, therefore, benefit – sometimes significantly – from low borrowing costs. For instance, during the period following Greece's entry into the euro area (2001–07) spreads were on average 27 basis points, relatively comparable to the German spreads; in 2008, spreads rose from 40 to about 100 basic points and overcame, in 2009, 300 basic points, in contrast with an unprecedented drop in the yields of German bonds from roughly 5.5 per cent to 2.5 per cent, attributed to the liquidity crisis which resulted in the 'flight-to-safety' investing phenomenon, ie panic leading investors to place their fortunes in the seemingly safe German bonds.[73]

Secondly, the rescue packages for Greece also strongly benefited German banks, which had obtained, until December 2009, a total portfolio of 704 billion euros-worth of bonds, including bonds from Italy and Spain, well above their own overall capital. In essence, due to the interconnection of European economies, granting financial support to a country is tantamount to granting support to all the other members of the Eurozone; this is the major difference compared to the US, where no interdependence occurs in principle, which is why Wall Street rescue after the Lehman Brothers fall was more easily manageable.[74] Altogether, by October 2009 it was German and French banks that were most exposed to the periphery of the Eurozone, with more than 40 per cent of the foreign claims on Greece, Ireland, Portugal, Italy and Spain being French and German. These collateral benefits should be added to the direct benefits of interests from the rescue packages loan repayments.[75]

Thirdly, the ECB, which participated in all Greek rescue programmes, officially declared on 10 October 2017, in response to a request by a member of the European Parliament, that it made nearly 7.8 billion euros in income interest profits from its holdings of Greek government debt acquired under its Securities and

---

[73] N Georgikopoulos and T Efthimiadis, 'The Development of the Greek-German Government Bond Spreads' *European Business Review*, 4 February 2010.

[74] Bloomberg Editorial Board, 'Hey, Germany: You got a Bail-out, too' 24 May 2012.

[75] For example, responding to a parliamentary question from the Green Party in July 2017, the German Minister of Finance confirmed that loans and bonds purchased in support of Greece over nearly a decade have resulted in profits of 1.34 billion euros for Germany. Commenting on the above, Sven-Christian Kindler, budget policy spokesperson of the German Green Party, stated: 'It might be legal for Germany to profit from the crisis in Greece, but from a moral and solidarity perspective, it is not right', https://global.handelsblatt.com/finance/germany-profits-from-greek-debt-crisis-796637.

Markets bond-buying programme in the period 2012–16, that were then redistributed to across all 19 national central banks in the euro area.[76]

Fourthly, the involvement of the IMF – a genuinely key actor in the euro area financial and stability mechanisms – in the handling of the economic crisis in euro-area Member States, in the drafting of the rescue packages agreements and in the monitoring of conditionality and of the post-programme surveillance, was not without benefit for the Fund. Irrespective of the potentially good intentions of the Fund, its financial accounts reveal that in the era of the European financial crisis there has been a tremendous increase of its profits.[77] Prior to the rescue packages, the IMF suffered serious losses, whereas out of its lending to all countries in debt crisis between 2010 and 2014 it has made a total profit of 8.4 billion euros, with Greece's contribution to this budget so far amounting to 2.5 billion euros of net profit with a full expectancy of 4.3 billion euros by 2024. Such profit comes from interest rates upon the loans at a rate of 3.6 per cent, whereas the institution is estimated to need to cover all its costs currently around 0.9 per cent according to the UK Jubilee Debt Campaign.[78] Although the profits made by the ECB and the IMF do not relate to the structural asymmetries of the EU and of the euro area, this situation clearly indicates that the decision of a Member State or of the EU or of an international organisation is in no case a zero-sum process, but it does imply serious financial consequences for all participants – consequences which are not always obvious on a first reading of an agreement.

As regards the *limited monitoring* for financial trespasses by Member States, it should be noted that in the very beginning the Union did not put in place mechanisms to respond to potential imbalances in the monetary union, therefore States exposed par excellence to external financial risks were truly vulnerable. The truth is that there were some provisions for excessive deficits in the Eurozone. Article 104 EC (now Article 126 TFEU) and Council Regulation 1467/97 of 7 July 1997 provided the legislative framework for initiating procedures against Member States violating the set deficit and debt ceilings.[79] Thus, Member States ought to avoid excessive government deficits and the Commission should monitor the development of the budgetary situation and of the sustainability of government debt, in particular compliance with budgetary discipline, with a view to identifying gross errors. If the Commission considered that an excessive deficit existed or might occur, it addressed an opinion to the Council which, in turn, acting by a qualified majority on a recommendation from the Commission decided, after an overall assessment, whether an excessive deficit existed. If so, the Council made non-public recommendations to the Member State concerned with a view to bringing that situation to an end within a given period. If no compliance

---

[76] www.ecb.europa.eu/pub/pdf/other/ecb.mepletter171010_Chountis.en.pdf?ca00752c61bdb4df6c2 27f4f3c62b98a.
[77] According to the official IMF accounts, www.imf.org/external/pubs/ft/quart/index.htm.
[78] https://jubileedebt.org.uk/news/imf-made-e2-5-billion-profit-greece-loans.
[79] OJ L 209, 02.08.1997, p 1.

occurred, recommendations might become public and the Council might decide to give notice to the Member State to take, within a specified time-limit, necessary measures to reduce the deficit and request reporting on its adjustment efforts.

If a Member State failed to comply with a decision taken, the Council could, on a recommendation from the Commission, by a majority of two-thirds of the votes of its members decide to apply or intensify one or more of a series of measures, ie:

(a)   to require the Member State to publish additional information, to be specified by the Council, before issuing bonds and securities;
(b)   to invite the European Investment Bank to reconsider its lending policy towards the Member State;
(c)   to require the Member State to make a non-interest-bearing deposit of an appropriate size with the Community until the excessive deficit had, in the view of the Council, been corrected; and
(d)   to impose fines of an appropriate size.

The Excessive Deficit Procedure could be held in abeyance if the Member State acted in compliance with the recommendations made or the notices given in the context of this very procedure. The nature of the provided sanctions obviously indicates that the Union was unprepared to deal with such a diffused financial crisis, since the imposition of a monetary penalty against a State who is already struggling with economic difficulties is obviously false disciplinary mechanics.

Yet again, the EU authorities had the opportunity to set out a controlled fiscal policy well before the crisis, in 2003, when the Excessive Deficit Procedure mechanism was initiated against Germany and France. The Council decided,[80] on a recommendation from the Commission, that an excessive deficit existed and recommended the German Government to bring that deficit to an end as rapidly as possible, by implementing various measures. It set 21 May 2003 as the deadline for taking the measures recommended. Since the measures taken by Germany were considered to be effective at that date, the Excessive Deficit Procedure was implicitly held in abeyance. The Commission considered that the measures taken were inappropriate and sent a recommendation for a decision to the Council in order for it to establish that the action taken proved to be inadequate and recommended that the Council decided to give notice to Germany to take measures to reduce its deficit by 2005 at the latest and to achieve in 2004 an annual reduction in the cyclically adjusted balance of 0.8 per cent of GDP. Almost the same procedure was followed with regard to France in the same period.[81]

In the context of the Council, on 25 November 2003 the Member States of the Eurozone voted on the Commission's recommendations; the required majority

[80] Council Decision 2003/89/EC of 21 January 2003 on the existence of an excessive deficit in Germany, OJ L 034, 11.02.2003, p 16.

[81] Council Decision 2003/487 of 3 June 2003 on the existence of an excessive deficit in France, OJ L 165, 03.07.2003, p 29.

was not, however, achieved and, thus, the Council decided not to act, at that point, and held the Excessive Deficit Procedure for both countries in abeyance. The Commission brought an action before the ECJ against the Council seeking annulment of the decisions of the Council not to adopt the formal instruments contained in the Commission's recommendations and of the Council's conclusions to hold the excessive deficit procedure in abeyance. In its judgment C-27/04 of 13 July 2004,[82] the Court, despite declaring the inadmissibility of the allegation as to the Council's failure to act, annulled the Council's conclusions on the ground that they entailed a de facto weakening of the Excessive Deficit Procedures and the recommendations thereof by relying exclusively on unilateral commitments of the Member State concerned. The Court also annulled the decision modifying the recommendations previously adopted by the Council on the ground that this would necessitate a fresh recommendation from the Commission as the institution having a right of initiative in the Excessive Deficit Procedure.[83]

Despite this bell by the Court of Justice, both disciplined and non-disciplined Member States of the euro area refused to take any appropriate measures to prevent what should have been seen as inevitable. Instead, both then President Chirac and then Chancellor Schröder asked for a loosening of the Stability Pact. Ironically, then Vice-President of the ECB Loukas Papademos, later Prime Minister of Greece, strongly opposed any curtailment of budgetary discipline by stating that allowing national governments to supervise the Stability Pact is like giving bar keys to an alcoholic. Against this background, when the financial crisis knocked on Europe's door through Greece, the Union was completely unprepared to deal with a large-scale predicament. This was particularly true for the euro area structure, considering that the EU had the Medium-Term Financial Assistance framework for Member States facing balance of payment problems and a provision for overall unforeseen circumstances (Article 122 TFEU).

It seems that Europe either undervalued the eminent dangers of forming a monetary union composed of having their own particular financial features or hypocritically refused to address the issue in order not to raise challenges with regard to a seemingly successful project. In the light of the above, the EU and the euro area had no effective mechanisms to deal with a financial crisis of the magnitude of 2009. Accordingly, the emergency measures taken were originally targeting exclusively the Greek debt crisis, aimed at dealing with the imminent threat of state insolvency and, arguably, fell outside the Community legal framework. As Drossos shrewdly put it, Greece had the institutional instruments to take the decisions deemed necessary, but no money at all, whereas the EU and the euro area had or could find the money to dump in and ideas on the

---

[82] OJ C 228, 13.07.2004, p 16.
[83] B Dutzler and A Hable, 'The European Court of Justice and the Stability and Growth Pact – Just the Beginning?', European Integration Online Papers (EIoP), vol 9, no 5 (2005), available at SSRN: https://ssrn.com/abstract=676523.

conditions for its use, but no proper institutional means at all.[84] The ad hoc mechanism turned to standing mechanisms of European economic governance in a way that, in the aftermath of the crisis, Europe is much more equipped to deal with immense lending problems of the Member States. Interestingly, the same limited monitoring occurred also in the field of the banking union with detrimental results, especially for the Irish banking system. The growth in bond funding was quite exceptional compared to the aggregate growth in bond funding in the euro area, and the focus of the Central Bank was on the strong capital adequacy ratios of the banks and not on supervisory processes to mitigate concentration risks.

Given the above structural loopholes in the architecture of the EU and the euro area, one might legitimately argue that in the absence of a solid institutional background, the eruption of the financial crisis was altogether the outcome of two factors: overreliance on monetarism and overreliance on sincere cooperation between the euro-area Member States.

Overreliance on *monetarism*, ie the economic theory basically arguing that monetary authorities must as a primarily task maintain price stability since excessive supply of money is inherently inflationary,[85] essentially stands for giving full credit to the economy that it may operate internally as a self-corrective mechanism. Exactly because of this high level of trust to economic self-reliance, adequate preventive and corrective mechanisms were launched for the case of trespasses. The monetary union project was essentially crafted for periods of normality and prosperity and not for the potentiality of things going totally wrong. Thus, the normative expectation of the law was almost totally subsumed to the cognitive and factual premises set by the noble purpose of a deeper union of the Member States. The political leadership in Europe underestimated a fundamental premise of economy, ie that it tends to become an autonomous subsystem and to trespass regulation and institutions. In 2007, the German Chancellor complimented Greece's economic growth (4.6 per cent in 2006 and 3 per cent in 2007), stating that Germany should look upon that model as a clear success story. Although money became a constitutional project of huge importance in Europe, through the clear targeting towards monetarism, traditional minimal banking regulation of assets (reserves and productive assets) versus liabilities (deposits and equity) was proved barely sufficient. The emergence of largely unregulated new market products, such as credit default swaps (CDS), investment mandates, hedge funds or derivatives and the spectacular default of the seemingly uncompromised no bail-out clause are indicative of this independent move of economy and eventually of its dominance over politics. In such fiscal dominance, structural concerns were mitigated. As Arghyrou rightly puts it, the main weaknesses of the pre-crisis European monetarism was its failure to provide credible mechanisms preventing the accumulation of unsustainable macroeconomic/financial imbalances,

---

[84] YZ Drossos, 'Yesterday' available at www.constitutionalism.gr/site/2352-yesterday (2012).
[85] M Friedman (ed), *The Optimum Quantity of Money and other Essays* (Chicago, Aldine, 1969).

to ensure market pressure towards the same outcome and to have in place a credible crisis-management infrastructure able to stabilise expectations following the crisis' eruption.[86]

Overreliance on *sincere cooperation* means that in the absence of effective and reliable monitoring and of sanctions that would operate as a credible threat, the whole institutional building relied heavily on the self-restraint that the Member States would demonstrate towards their financial obligations. Yet, this was not the only level of soft-law trust that was required for the smooth operation of the monetarist experiment. It also presupposed a high level of trust between economy and law, between economic and political actors, between the economic actors themselves, between States when pulled together in an international economic structure, between state agencies involved in the performance of the economy. This level of trust was not materialised. It seems that all institutions and stakeholders trespassed the permissible limits. Economy completely disassociated itself from politics/law and developed an own ethos outside the normative; Member States became indifferent to the rules on financial and fiscal discipline, especially after the violation of the Stability and Growth Pact by France and Germany had compromised its constraining power.[87]

The EU institutions (mostly the Commission and the Court of Justice) were extremely tolerant, Eurostat had been denied the authority to override national statistical agencies and private economic actors (such as banks) were inventively unstoppable in the pursuit of more profits; and all the above in the absence of effectively enforceable regulation. In fact, the financial crisis has revealed an interesting paradox. Prior to the financial crisis, the societal attitude was mostly leaned towards economy, which seemed appealing and trustworthy, and less so on institutions that ought to have a limited intervention to allow for economic self-correction. Once the financial crisis was in place, the institutions were blamed for not being proactive or imminently responsive to the risks associated with the crisis. This is, in fact, a very common attitude in the history of crises. In times of normality and prosperity people rely at large on flourishing subsystems, especially the economy. Yet, if a disruption occurs in the subsystem, such as in case of match-fixing in sports or financial malfunctions of a Church, people seek a normative restoration. Reliance on cognitive processes in routine times gives place to increased expectations of law and politics in times of crises. Eventually, the crisis revealed the value of institutions since cognitive processes do not suffice.

---

[86] MG Arghyrou, 'From the Euro-Crisis to a new European Economic Architecture' in DD Thomakos, P Monokrousos and K Nikolopoulos (eds), *A Financial Crisis Management: Reflexions and the Road Ahead* (Basingstoke, Palgrave Macmillan, 2015) 308.

[87] S Blavoukos and G Pagoulatos, 'The Limits of EMU Conditionality: Fiscal Adjustment in Southern Europe' (2008) 28 *Journal of Public Policy* 229.

2

Impact of New Economic Constitutionalism on Constitution-Making

New economic constitutionalism brought a significant bulk of new regulation, merely serving an economic rationality. On the level of EU law, changes occurred in secondary law, which is nonetheless considered for the purposes of the present analysis as constitutional drafting due to its supremacy over domestic Constitutions. One might reasonably include in the new economic drafting the agreements concluded between EU institutions and other organisations, mostly the IMF, on providing financial assistance to euro-area Member States encountering financial difficulties, and not only because they largely constituted the legal basis upon which domestic courts built the crisis case law. On the level of domestic Constitutions, the crisis, with a few exceptions, did not entail a wide flow of revisions in the EU Member States. With the notable exception of the insertion of the golden budgetary rule in the constitutions of some Member States, institutional adaptation to new economic Constitutions was generally made through ordinary legislation enhancing the contractual obligations of conditionality stemming from the financial assistance agreements and with a significant reversal of the pre-crisis case law. Interestingly, although the economic crisis was clearly of a constitutional magnitude, the management of the crisis did not entail extensive revision of constitutional or EU primary law, with the exception of concrete balanced budget/debt brake amendments and the provision for an emergency assistance mechanism respectively.

This chapter divides the implications of new economic constitutionalism on the economic drafting of the Constitution into three categories, ie European economic governance, economic governance in EU Member States and financial assistance to EU Member States. The aim is to present the constitutional framework within which institutional changes occurred, so as to illustrate the intrusion of economy as a key factor in regulatory drafting on the highest level as compared to the pre-crisis institutional environment.

I. European Economic Governance

A. Economic and Monetary Union

The plans for a monetary Union in the European Communities go back to the late 1960s and it was eventually the fourth attempt in 1989 by the Delors report that led to the 1992 Maastricht Treaty on European Union accord on an Economic and Monetary Union (EMU), through which Member States undertook the responsibility to coordinate their economic policies, to provide multilateral surveillance of this coordination and to respect financial and budgetary discipline. In this framework, the Treaty provided for the introduction of the euro as a single currency, of the European Central Bank (ECB) and of the European System of Central Banks (ESCB), comprising the ECB and the independent national central banks of the euro-area Member States (Article 4(a)) and set the 'convergence criteria' that the Member States ought to fulfil cumulatively to join the euro area. These were: low inflation; durability of convergence; a budget deficit of less than 3 per cent of GDP; government debt levels of less than 60 per cent of GDP with flexibility clauses for specific Member States; an independent central bank; and compliance of its statutes with the Treaties and the Statute of the ESCB and of the ECB (Article 109(j) TEC and Protocol on the convergence criteria referred to in Article 109(j)).

The prerequisite of budget deficit of less than 3 per cent must still be met after the entry of the State to EMU, whereas the other two economic conditions, although not formally a condition for remaining within the Union, after the respective entry, are de facto compulsory as their infringement has an effect on the budget deficit. Strictly speaking, all Member States meeting the convergence criteria ought to become members of the euro area, except for the United Kingdom and Denmark, which upon launching of the euro, albeit satisfying the required standards, opted out through Protocols.[1] As of 1 January 1999, the euro became the national currency in 11 out of 15 EU Member States in accounting form for transfer payments and the issuance, inter alia, of Government bonds by those States; on 1 January 2002, it was introduced as a physical currency in those 11 Member States, as well as in Greece which joined the euro area in 2001. Today, the single currency is used in 19 out of 28 EU Member States.

The definition and implementation of monetary policy within the euro area is entrusted to the ESCB (Article 127(2) TFEU).[2] Through its Governing Council,

---

[1] Although outside the euro area Andorra, Monaco, San Marino and the Vatican City have also adopted the euro as their national currency, pursuant to individual monetary agreements with the EU, since prior to introduction of the euro these 'micro-states' used the national currency of a euro-area Member State (Spain, France and Italy) as their national currency.

[2] By virtue of Article 139(2)(c) TFEU, this Article, as the majority of the provisions relating to the monetary union, only applies to the Member States whose currency is the euro, hence to the Eurosystem (a subsystem of the ESCB, consisting of the ECB and the central banks of those Member States).

the ECB regulates monetary issues in the euro area having as a primary objective to maintain price stability therein, whereby it also sets a number of key interest rates for the euro area (Article 127(1) TFEU). Economic policy of EU Member States largely remains their own responsibility, with the exception of monetary and foreign-exchange policies (Article 3(1)(c) TFEU), although they must conduct it with a view to contributing to the achievement of the objectives of the Union (Article 120(1) TFEU). Yet, coordination is pursued through a number of structures and instruments, containing rules for fiscal discipline (ie limits on government deficits and on national debt) applying to all EU Member States,[3] whereas implementation of the EU's economic governance is organised annually in a cycle, known as the European Semester.[4,5]

A cornerstone provision for fiscal discipline in the Union is that of Article 125 TFEU, introducing the 'no bail-out' clause, according to which neither the Union nor a Member State is to be liable for the commitments of another Member State or assume those commitments. This clause is to be systematically read in conjunction with Articles 122 and 136(3) TFEU, permitting ad hoc financial assistance to a Member State when seriously threatened with severe difficulties in the supply of certain products, notably in the area of energy, or caused by natural disasters or exceptional occurrences beyond its control and Article 123 TFEU prohibiting the ECB and the central banks of the Member States from granting overdraft facilities or any other type of credit facility.

B. Emergency Temporary Financial Assistance Vehicles: Stabilisation Mechanisms (EFSF, EFSM)

In the crisis era a bulk of regulation was introduced to provide for financial assistance to endangered Member States with variable legal and factual characteristics.[6] In the aftermath of the Greek sovereign debt crisis which erupted in 2009 and of the decision on the first bail-out programme for the country, and due to the continuation of the economic crisis in the euro area in general, a specific Greek Loan Facility and two temporary financial backstop assistance instruments were set in place as emergency financial assistance mechanisms, ie the European

---

[3] Below section D.

[4] Below section G.

[5] On the EMU, see P de Grauwe, *Economics of Monetary Union*, 12th edn (Oxford, Oxford University Press. 2018); M Chang, *Economic and Monetary Union* (London, Palgrave Macmillan, 2016); D Gros and N Thygesen, *European Monetary Integration: From the European Monetary System to Economic and Monetary*, 2nd edn (New York, Financial Times Prentice Hall, 1998); M Andenas, LW Gormley, Ch Hadjiemmanuil and I Harden, *European Economic and Monetary Union: The Institutional Framework* (London, Kluwer Law International, 1997); PB Kenen, *Economic and Monetary Union in Europe: Moving beyond Maastricht* (Cambridge, Cambridge University Press, 1995).

[6] For a full breadth analysis of the supranational euro area crisis measures between 2010 and 2016, see A Kyriakidis, 'EU Institutions after the Eurozone Crisis: What has Changed?' (2017) *Hellenic Review of European Law* 19.

Financial Stabilisation Mechanism (EFSM) and the European Financial Stability Facility (EFSF).

The EFSM was based on guarantees from the EU budget of up to 60 billion euros, available to all EU Member States in financial need. It enabled the European Commission to borrow from financial markets on the EU's behalf under an EU budget guarantee and, in turn, to lend the proceeds to the EU Member State in question. Repayment was fully guaranteed by the EU budget in case of default, but the beneficiary Member State ought to repay the loan principal and interests.

The EFSF was established as a *société anonyme*, outside the EU institutional framework, based on guarantees given by the euro area Member States in accordance with their share in the paid-up capital of the ECB of up to 440 billion euros available to euro-area Member States requesting financial assistance because of loss of their access to capital markets or reaching a position where they would have to pay excessively high interest rates. It was an inter-governmental body established by the Economic and Financial Affairs Council (ECOFIN) in May 2010 in the form of a Luxembourg special purpose vehicle, all euro-area Member States participating as its shareholders. The IMF decided on additional potential financial support to the euro-area countries of up to 250 billion euros. It should be noted that the participation of the IMF was deemed necessary, as it was the only international institution with experience in supervising the implementation of austerity measures on the basis of the principle of conditionality, since no such institution existed in the EU, and definitely not prior to the establishment of the European Stability Mechanism.[7]

C. Permanent Financial Assistance Vehicle: Stability Mechanism

At the meeting of the European Council of 28 and 29 October 2010, the Heads of States or Governments agreed on the need for Member States to establish a permanent crisis mechanism to safeguard the financial stability of the euro area as a whole and invited the President of the European Council to undertake consultations with the members of the Council on a limited treaty change required to that effect. The crucial statutory basis on that matter was Article 136 TFEU, according to which the Council, in order to ensure the proper functioning of economic and monetary union, might adopt measures specific to euro-area Member States to strengthen the coordination and surveillance of their budgetary discipline and to set out economic policy guidelines for them, while ensuring that they are compatible with those adopted for the whole of the Union and are kept under surveillance.

---

[7] On the EFSF, see M Stallechner and D Kolb, *The European Financial Stability Facility (EFSF) and the European Stability Mechanism (ESM)* (Munich, Grin, 2013).

For that purpose, the simplified revision procedure of Article 48(6) TEU was initiated to this effect, providing that the Government of any Member State, the European Parliament or the Commission might submit to the European Council proposals for revising all or part of the provisions only of Part Three of the TFEU, relating to the internal policies and action of the Union. The relevant decision shall in no case increase the competences conferred on the Union, and shall be adopted by the European Council by unanimity after consulting the European Parliament and the Commission, and the ECB in the case of institutional changes in the monetary area.

Indeed, upon proposal submitted by the Belgian Government and opinions rendered by the Commission, the ECB and the European Parliament, Decision 2011/199 was adopted on 25 March 2011 adding a new paragraph in Article 136 providing for the possibility of the euro-area Member States to establish a stability mechanism to be activated if indispensable to safeguard the stability of the euro area as a whole, and establishing that the granting of any required financial assistance under the mechanism would be made subject to strict conditionality.[8] According to recital (4) of the Preamble of the Decision, the stability mechanism provided the necessary tool for dealing with such cases of risk to the financial stability of the euro area as a whole as experienced in 2010, and hence helped preserve the economic and financial stability of the Union itself, without the need to have recourse to Article 122(2) TFEU, providing for Union financial assistance to a Member State threatened with severe difficulties caused by natural disasters or exceptional occurrences beyond its control. Accordingly, the final intergovernmental Treaty establishing the European Stability Mechanism (ESM Treaty) was signed in Brussels on 2 February 2012 by the then 17 euro-area Member States, entered into force on 27 September 2012 and was later signed by the countries which subsequently adopted the euro.

The European Stability Mechanism (ESM) was established as a *société anonyme*, outside the EU institutional framework, and assumed the tasks previously undertaken by the EFSF in providing financial assistance to euro-area Member States, by mobilising funding and providing stability support, to the benefit of ESM Members experiencing or threatened by severe financing problems, if that was deemed indispensable to safeguard the financial stability of the euro area as a whole and of its Member States. Assistance is provided under strict conditionality, appropriate to the financial assistance instrument chosen that may range from a macro-economic adjustment programme to continuous respect of pre-established eligibility conditions.

ESM's effective maximum lending capacity was initially fixed at 500 billion euros. It is entitled to raise funds by issuing financial instruments or by entering into financial or other agreements or arrangements with the ESM Members, credit

---

[8] OJ L 91, 6.4.2011, p 1.

institutions or other third parties. ESM is designed to be governed by a Board of Governors, a Board of Directors, a Managing Director and other dedicated staff as may be deemed necessary. The adoption of a decision by mutual agreement required, with the exception of cases of emergency, the unanimity of the members participating in the vote, whereas the Board of Governors is to take decisions by qualified majority. The liability of each ESM Member is, in all circumstances, limited to its portion of the authorised capital stock at its issue price and no ESM Member can be held liable for obligations of the ESM by reason of its membership.

According to the ESM Treaty, the procedure for granting financial stability support is initiated with an ESM Member addressing a relevant request to the Chairperson of the ESM Board of Governors, which must indicate the financial assistance instrument to be considered. Upon receipt of such a request, the Chairperson entrusts the European Commission, in liaison with the ECB, with the tasks to assess the existence of a risk to the financial stability of the euro area as a whole or of its Member States, unless the ECB had already submitted an analysis, to assess – solely or jointly with the IMF – whether public debt was sustainable and to assess the actual or potential financing needs of the ESM Member concerned. The Board of Governors decides to grant support, in which case it assigns the European Commission, in liaison with the ECB and, wherever possible, together with the IMF, with the task of negotiating, with the ESM Member concerned, a Memorandum of Understanding (MoU) detailing the conditionality attached to the financial assistance facility, that must reflect the severity of the weaknesses to be addressed and the financial assistance instrument chosen. The European Commission signs the MoU on behalf of the ESM, subject to prior compliance with the conditions set out and approval by the Board of Governors. The ESM Treaty establishes an appropriate warning system to ensure that ESM receives any repayments due by the ESM Member under the stability support in a timely manner.

The European Commission, in liaison with the ECB and, wherever possible, together with the IMF, is entrusted with monitoring compliance with the conditionality attached to the financial assistance facility. Facility instruments may include financial assistance in the form of a precautionary credit line and in the form of loans, purchase of bonds issued by an ESM Member on the primary market and operations on the secondary market in relation to bonds issued by an ESM Member. When granting stability support, the ESM aims to fully cover its financing and operating costs, including an appropriate margin. If an ESM Member fails to meet the required payment under a capital call, a revised increased capital call is made to all ESM Members with a view to ensuring that the ESM received the total amount of paid-in capital needed. The Board of Governors decides an appropriate course of action for ensuring that the ESM Member concerned settles its debt to the ESM within a reasonable period of time and is entitled to require the payment of default interest on the overdue amount.

The ESM Treaty launched significant new competencies for EU institutions, namely the Commission, the ECB and the Court of Justice. The new tasks entrusted to the *Commission* consist in assessing requests for stability support (Article 13(1) ESM Treaty), assessing their urgency (Article 4(4) ESM Treaty), negotiating an MoU detailing the conditionality attached to the financial assistance granted (Article 13(3) ESM Treaty), monitoring compliance with the conditionality attached to the financial assistance (Article 13(7) ESM Treaty) and participating in the meetings of the Board of Governors and the Board of Directors as an observer (Articles 5(3) and 6(2) ESM Treaty).

The new tasks entrusted to the *ECB* consist in assessing the urgency of requests for stability support (Article 4(4) ESM Treaty), participating in the meetings of the Board of Governors and the Board of Directors as an observer (Articles 5(3) and 6(2) ESM Treaty) and, in liaison with the Commission, assessing requests for stability support (Article 13(1) ESM Treaty), negotiating an MoU (Article 13(3) ESM Treaty) and monitoring compliance with the conditionality attached to the financial assistance (Article 13(7) ESM Treaty).

The new tasks entrusted to the *Court of Justice* consist in its new jurisdiction to rule on conflicts between ESM Members and the ESM, in connection with the latter's Board of Governors' decisions on disputes arising between an ESM Member and the ESM or between ESM Members, in connection with the interpretation and application of the ESM Treaty, including any dispute on the compatibility of the decisions adopted by the ESM, in accordance with Article 273 TFEU. The Court's judgment would be binding on the parties in the procedure (Article 37(3) ESM Treaty). Accordingly, the Court, through Articles 121 and 136 ESM Treaty may currently exercise effective judicial review on the excessive deficit procedure.[9]

On 6 December 2017, the European Commission, pursuant to the flexibility clause of Article 352 TFEU, tabled, among other instruments to complete EMU, a proposal for a Council Regulation on the establishment of the European Monetary Fund (EMF), including the EMF's Statute that would absorb the ESM as a stronger and more comprehensive crisis-management EU entity having its own legal personality.[10] Although the idea seems to have been abandoned, the Eurogroup on 3 December 2018 and subsequent European Council agreed to revise the ESM treaty in a number of significant areas, such as collective action clauses, single limb aggregation provisions and debt restructuring as precondition for ESM bailout.

---

[9] On the ESM, see M Schwarz, 'A Memorandum of Misunderstanding. The Doomed Road of the European Stability Mechanism and a Possible Way Out: Enhanced Cooperation' (2014) 51 *Common Market Law Review* 389; A Gregorio Merino, 'Legal Developments in the Economic and Monetary Union during the Debt Crisis: The Mechanisms of Financial Assistance' (2012) 49 *Common Market Law Review* 1613; S Peers, 'The Stability Treaty: Permanent Austerity or Gesture Politics?' (2012) 8 *European Constitutional Law Review* 404.

[10] ChV Gortsos, 'The Proposed Legal Famework for Etablishing a European Monetary Fund (EMF): A Systematic Presentation and a Preliminary Assessment' (2017), available at: ssrn.com/abstract=3090343.

D. Treaty on Stability, Coordination and Governance in the Economic and Monetary Union

On 2 March 2012, 25 EU Member States agreed to commit themselves to having common domestic rules of economic governance and concluded inter-governmentally the Treaty on Stability, Coordination and Governance in the Economic and Monetary Union (TSCG), which entered into force on 1 January 2013, 'desiring to promote conditions for stronger economic growth in the European Union and, to that end, to develop ever-closer coordination of economic policies within the euro area'. The Treaty introduces specific rules of economic governance, known as the Fiscal Compact (Title III of the Treaty). The Fiscal Compact came on the top of the existing EU fiscal rules, namely the 3 per cent deficit ceiling, the medium-term objective and the debt-reduction rule.

In essence, the Contracting States to the Treaty assumed the responsibility to enhance the following four aspects:

(a) *The balanced budget rule.* Structural deficits ought to be in accordance with country-specific medium-term objective and, in any case, below 0.5 per cent of GDP at market prices (Article 3(3)(b) TSCG). It is noteworthy that the structural deficit refers to deficits over the economic cycles, ie outside temporary fiscal measures and fiscal evolutions that are purely due to cyclical changes in the economy; therefore, the Contracting Parties may temporarily deviate from their respective medium-term objective or the adjustment path towards it only in exceptional strictly defined circumstances in case of 'an unusual event outside the control of the Contracting Party concerned which has a major impact on the financial position of the general government or to periods of severe economic downturn as set out in the revised Stability and Growth Pact, provided that the temporary deviation of the Contracting Party concerned does not endanger fiscal sustainability in the medium-term'.

(b) *The Government debt benchmarking.* Contracting States' government debt ought to be in principle significantly below 60 per cent of GDP at market prices and risks to long-term fiscal sustainability must be low, in which case the medium-term objective can be set as low as a structural deficit of 1 per cent of GDP at most. The difference between the government debt-to-GDP ratio and the ceiling of 60 per cent of GDP needs to be reduced at an average rate of one-twentieth per year.

(c) *Strict Excessive Deficit Procedure.* In the event of significant observed deviations from the medium-term objective or the adjustment path towards it, an automatic correction mechanism is provided, to be triggered automatically, including the obligation of the Contracting Party concerned to implement measures to correct the deviations over a defined period of time (Article 3(1) TSCG). Automatic redress related to the commitment of euro-area Member States to support proposals or recommendations from the European Commission to the ECOFIN Council if a euro-area country breaches the deficit criterion, unless this was opposed by a qualified majority of the other euro-area countries is provided to be triggered.

(d) *Reporting on planning public debt issuance.* Member States are asked to report in advance their plans to issue public debt (Article 6 TSCG).

One of the main chapters of this Treaty was the requirement imposed upon the contracting parties (in fact the 19 euro-area Member States plus Bulgaria, Denmark and Romania) to introduce the Fiscal Compact (basically the balanced budget rule and the government debt benchmarking) into their domestic legal orders, at the latest one year later, ie by 1 January 2014, 'through provisions of binding force and permanent character, preferably constitutional, or otherwise guaranteed to be fully respected and adhered to throughout the national budgetary processes'. This obligation undoubtedly constituted a very significant step towards the convergence of economic governance in Europe, a true 'fiscal stability union', through a joint action of both the EU and the EU Member States. It comprised a set of economic yardsticks that ought to be institutionally preserved by the States and the financial supervision that ought to be exercised by the EU institutions. That was indeed the added value of this Treaty vis-a-vis the original Stability and Growth Pact, not only because the substantive balanced budget rule of the Fiscal Compact replicated in large part the medium-term objective of the Pact, but mainly because a compiled framework of fiscal operation was introduced, within which discipline could be better enforced and monitored, especially against the emergence of excessive deficits.

The TSCG was drafted as an inter-governmental Treaty outside the EU legal order, after the EU Member States, in the context of the European Council, failed to agree on a new setting for economic governance to be incorporated into primary law through the TFEU. Yet, the Treaty made significant bridges with conventional EU law in the sense that, according to explicit clauses to that effect, its rules ought to be applied and interpreted in conformity with the EU Treaties and, in any case, it should be officially incorporated into EU law by 1 January 2018. On 6 December 2017, the Commission proposed a Council Directive laying down provisions for strengthening fiscal responsibility and the medium-term budgetary orientation in the Member States.[11] Yet, the scope of the proposal is limited to the euro-area Member States, with the possibility for other Member States to join on a voluntary basis.[12]

---

[11] COM(2017) 824 final.

[12] On the TSCG, see P Craig, 'The Stability, Coordination and Governance Treaty: Principle, Politics and Pragmatism' (2012) 37 *European Law Review* 231; CM Cantore and G Martinico, 'Asymmetry or Dis-integration? A Few Considerations on the New "Treaty on Stability, Coordination and Governance in the Economic and Monetary Union"' (2013) 19 *European Public Law* 463.

E. Enhanced EU Economic Governance: Six-Pack, Two-Pack, European Semester

In parallel to the ESM Treaty, three significant regulatory packages of enhanced EU economic governance were introduced setting minimum commitments for national fiscal frameworks: the Six-Pack set mostly new substantive fiscal rules, reinforcing the Stability and Growth Pact (basically Council Regulation 1466/97 on the preventive arm of the Pact and 1467/97 on the corrective arm of the Pact); the Two-Pack set mostly procedural rules of coordination, complementing the Stability and Growth Pact and transferring modules of the Fiscal Compact to the EU level; and the European Semester set the framework of sound public finances and monitoring of Member States' fiscal accounts.[13]

(a) The *Six-Pack* was adopted in November 2011 and entered into force on 13 December 2011. It consists of five Regulations of the European Parliament and of the Council (1173–1777/2011)[14] and one Directive of the Council (2011/85/EU)[15] applicable to all EU Member States, except for Regulations 1173–1174/2011 applying merely to euro-area countries. According to Regulation 1175/2011, the 'experience gained and mistakes made during the first decade of the Economic and Monetary Union show a need for improved economic governance in the Union, which should be built on stronger national ownership of commonly agreed rules and policies and on a more robust framework at the level of the Union for the surveillance of national economic policies'. Thus, the Six-Pack:

   (i) ensures stricter application of the fiscal rules by quantitatively defining what constitutes a 'significant deviation' from the Medium-Term Budgetary Objective or the adjustment path towards it in the context of the preventive arm;

   (ii) operationalises the debt criterion, so that an Excessive Deficit Procedure may also be launched on the basis of a debt ratio above 60 per cent

---

[13] Pursuant to a Franco-German proposal, a Euro Plus Pact has also been in place as of 2011 as one of the measures to stabilise the euro area through increased fiscal and economic discipline in the Member States and a more rigorous approach towards economic and financial imbalances. The nature and the limited impact of the Pact cannot, presumably, qualify it as strictly speaking an instrument EU economic governance, see H Gabrisch and K Staehr, 'The Euro Plus Pact: Competitiveness and External Capital Flows in the EU Countries' (2014) 53 *Journal of Common Market Studies* 558.

[14] Reg 1173/2011 of 16 November 2011 on the effective enforcement of budgetary surveillance in the euro area (OJ L 306, 23.11.2011 p 1); Reg 1174/2011 of 16 November 2011 on enforcement measures to correct excessive macroeconomic imbalances in the euro area (OJ L 306, 23.11.2011, p 8); Reg 1175/2011 of 16 November 2011 on the strengthening of the surveillance of budgetary positions and the surveillance and coordination of economic policies (OJ L 306, 23.11.2011, p 12); Reg 1176/2011 of 16 November 2011 on the prevention and correction of macroeconomic imbalances (OJ L 306, 23.11.2011, p 25); and Reg 1177/2011 of 8 November 2011 on speeding up and clarifying the implementation of the Excessive Deficit Procedure (OJ L 306, 23.11.2011, p. 33).

[15] Dir 2011/85/EU of 8 November 2011 on requirements for budgetary frameworks of the Member States (OJ L 306, 23.11.2011, p 41).

of GDP, which would not diminish towards the Treaty reference value at a satisfactory pace (and not only on the basis of a deficit above 3 per cent of GDP, which has been the case so far);

(iii) specifies that financial sanctions for euro-area Member States are imposed in a gradual way, from the preventive arm to the latest stages of the Excessive Deficit Procedure, and may eventually reach 0.5 per cent of GDP; and

(iv) allows more space for the imposition of sanctions for relevant violations by the euro-area Member States by introducing reverse qualified majority voting for most sanctions, ie a recommendation or a proposal of the Commission is considered adopted in the Council unless a qualified majority of Member States votes against it.

(b) The *Two-Pack* was adopted on 21 May 2013 and entered into force a week later. It consists of two Regulations of the Council and the Parliament (472–473/2013), which supplement the Six-Pack through enhanced budgetary surveillance and coordination among euro-area Member States. It integrates some of the elements of the Fiscal Compact into EU law, aiming at increased transparency of the decisions of euro-area Member States, stronger coordination in the euro area, consistency between budgetary and other economic policy processes and decisions and the recognition of the special needs of euro-area Member States under severe financial pressure. Regulation 472/2013 applies to Member States facing severe difficulties with regard to their financial stability, those receiving financial assistance and those exiting a financial assistance programme, by setting out compact rules for enhanced surveillance and setting the framework for the involvement of the Troika into EU institutional and legal operating framework;[16] Regulation 473/2013, with special rules applying to those under the Excessive Deficit Procedure, provided the Commission and Eurogroup with the authority to approve all draft budgets of the euro area Member States, and to request changes where non-compliance would be observed, before they are even considered by the national parliaments of those states.[17] The Two-Pack establishes, inter alia:

(i) an obligation of Member States to set up independent bodies monitoring compliance with national fiscal rules;

(ii) a requirement for Member States in Excessive Deficit Procedure to prepare economic partnership programmes; and

(iii) a requirement for ex ante coordination of Member States' debt issuance plans.[18]

---

[16] OJ L 140, 27.5.2013, p 1.

[17] OJ L 140, 27.5.2013, p 11.

[18] On the new economic governance in the EU through Six-Pack and Two-Pack, see A de Streel, 'EU Fiscal Governance and the Effectiveness of its Reform' in M Adams, F Fabbrini and P Larouche (eds), *Constitutionalization of European Budgetary Constraints: Comparative and Interdisciplinary Perspectives* (Oxford, Hart Publishing, 2014) 85.

(c) The *European Semester*, launched in the beginning of the financial crisis in
Europe and reshaped in 2015, is the main tool for EU regular financial control
over coordination of economic policies of EU Member States, especially of
the Fiscal Compact, until 2020. It aims at ensuring sound public finances
through prevention of excessive government debt, preventing excessive
macroeconomic imbalances in the EU at suggesting structural developments
to create more jobs and growth, and boosting investment. For that purpose,
each year the Commission:

(i) undertakes a detailed analysis of each country's plans for budget,
macroeconomic and operational reforms with a purpose to provide the
governments of EU Member States with country-specific recommendations for the next 12–18 months; and

(ii) monitors Member States' efforts towards the 'Europe 2020' targets,
ie the EU's agenda for growth and jobs for the 2010s entailing smart,
sustainable and inclusive growth as a way to overcome the structural
weaknesses in Europe's economy, improve its competitiveness and
productivity and underpin a sustainable social market economy, all in
measurable goals.

The country-specific Commission proposals, pursuant to European Semester, are endorsed and formally adopted by the Council and, eventually, it
lies with the governments of EU Member States to implement the recommendations in their respective territory, so as not to endanger their
economic position within the Union, by incorporating them into national
targets and by reporting on them as part of their annual national reform
programmes.[19]

In the light of the above modules of economic governance, a three-step budgetary cycle is introduced for euro-area Member States. The first step requires
them to publish, by 30 April every year, their medium-term fiscal plans (Stability
Programmes), together with their policy priorities for growth and employment
for the forthcoming 12 months (National Reform Programmes) in the context
of the European Semester on economic policy coordination. The second step
requires them to publish, by 15 October, their draft budgets for the following year;
those must be based on independent macroeconomic forecasts. The European

---

[19] On the European Semester, see S Bekker, 'Flexicurity in the European Semester: Still a Relevant
Policy Concept?' (2018) 25 *Journal of European Public Policy* 175; A Verdun and J Zeitlin 'Introduction: The European Semester as a New Architecture of EU Socioeconomic Governance in Theory
and Practice' (2018) 25 *Journal of European Public Policy* 137; ZM Darvas, and Á Leandro, 'The
Limitations of Policy Coordination in the Euro Area under the European Semester' (2015) 19 *Bruegel Policy Contribution* 1; M Hallerberg, B Marzinotto and GB Wolff, 'How Effective and Legitimate
is the European Semester? Increasing the Role of the European Parliament', Bruegel Working Paper
no 2011/09 (Brussels, 2011); JD Savage and D Howarth 'Enforcing the European Semester: the Politics of Asymmetric Information in the Excessive Deficit and Macroeconomic Imbalance Procedures'
(2018) 25 *Journal of European Public Policy* 212; K Efstathiou and GB Wolff, 'Is the European Semester
Effective and Useful?' (2018) 9 *Policy Contribution*, Issue 1.

Commission then reviews and gives an individual opinion on each draft budget by 30 November and, if severe non-compliance with the obligations under the Stability and Growth Pact is detected, it asks the Member State concerned to submit a revised plan and for an opinion for the euro area as a whole focusing on a comprehensive assessment of the budgetary outlook for the forthcoming year. By 31 December the euro-area Member States must adopt their budgets for the following year. To that effect, minimum requirements for national budgetary frameworks are imposed on Member States to ensure that their fiscal frameworks are in line with minimum quality standards and cover all administrative levels, whereas national fiscal planning should adopt a multi-annual perspective to attain the medium-term budgetary objectives and numerical fiscal rules should also promote compliance with the Treaty reference values for deficit and debt.

Furthermore, prevention and correction of macroeconomic and competitiveness imbalances within the euro area are envisaged through an alert system that uses a scoreboard of indicators and in-depth country studies, strict rules in the form of a new Excessive Imbalance Procedure and better enforcement in the form of financial sanctions for Member States which do not follow up on recommendations. On top of this, strict requirements for the budgetary frameworks of EU Member States are introduced in relation to accounting and statistics, forecasts, numerical fiscal rules, medium-term budgetary frameworks and transparency of general government finances and rules of comprehensive scope of budgetary frameworks.

On the basis of the produced budgetary evidence by Member States, the Commission may decide to subject to automatic enhanced surveillance in any preferable type countries receiving certain types of precautionary financial assistance. The surveillance involves the obligation of the Member States in question to adopt measures to address the sources of instability, regular review missions and the provision of more detailed or disaggregated financial sector data and quarterly reporting by the Commission to Euro Working Group. For deciding and monitoring a macro-economic adjustment programme, the Member States facing insufficient administrative capacities must seek technical assistance from the Commission and, if necessary, the Council may decide that the beneficiary Member State does not comply with the policy requirements contained in the adjustment programme. As a result, the country concerned would face financial consequences with regard to the disbursements due. The Pact also provides for minimising duplicate purveyance of Member States in a programme since, during the time of Commission monitoring, all other means of surveillance are suspended (Stability and Growth Pact monitoring, Macroeconomic Imbalance Procedure and European Semester). Most importantly, the Pact caters for the post-programme surveillance, according to which a country shall be subject to post-programme surveillance as long as it has not repaid 75 per cent of its debt, a stringent rule of post-discipline that has so far invariably applied in countries that received financial assistance.

F. ECB Asset Purchase Programmes

The ECB uses three vehicles in its approach to safeguarding an appropriate monetary policy transmission and the singleness of the monetary policy and giving an impulse to growth against deflation and economic stagnation in the euro area: the Outright Monetary Transactions (OMTs) programme aiming at countering the dysfunctions of the monetary transmission mechanism; the Quantitative Easing (QE) programme; and the asset purchase programmes (APP) aiming at fighting medium-term low inflation. They are all considered as unconventional monetary policy instruments, transcending ordinary vehicles taken in cases of economic recession (eg interest rate fluctuation, even deposit facilities).

The *OMTs programme* was announced by the Governing Council of the ECB on 2 August 2012. According to this programme, the ECB might purchase in secondary markets bonds issued by euro-area Member States. The plan was part of the set of vehicles that the ECB officially launched to support financially endangered Member States, whose bonds were not in demand or were set at an unsustainable interest rate level, thus providing a clear signal of solidarity against potential speculations of euro-area failure. The new policy required that the Member State, whose bonds would be purchased in secondary market by the ECB, ought to have come under an adjustment programme and to have received financial assistance from the ESM or the EFSM. Following approval by the Governing Council, a press release was published on 6 September 2012, entitled 'Technical features of Outright Monetary Transactions'; it announced that the Council decided on a number of technical features regarding the Eurosystem's OMTs in secondary sovereign bond markets.[20] The press release involved a series of specifications of the plan including:

(a) *conditionality*, ie strict and effective conditions attached to an appropriate EFSF/ESM programme of either macroeconomic adjustment or precautionary programme (Enhanced Conditions Credit Line), provided that they include the possibility of EFSF/ESM primary market purchases, with the possible involvement of the IMF in the design of the country-specific conditionality and the monitoring of such a programme;

(b) *duration*, ie OMTs should be warranted from a monetary policy perspective, as long as programme conditionality was fully respected and should be terminated once their objectives were achieved or when there was non-compliance with the macroeconomic adjustment or precautionary programme, with the full discretion of the ECB's Governing Council to decide on the start, continuation and suspension of OMTs;

(c) *coverage*, ie OMTs would be considered for future cases of EFSF/ESM macroeconomic adjustment programmes or precautionary programmes as well as

---

[20] www.ecb.europa.eu/press/pr/date/2012/html/pr120906_1.en.html.

for Member States then under a macroeconomic adjustment programme in the eventuality of their regaining bond market access, focusing on transactions on the shorter part of the yield curve, in particular on sovereign bonds with a maturity of between one and three years and without ex ante quantitative limits;

(d)   *creditor treatment*, ie the Eurosystem explicitly accepted the same *pari passu* treatment as private or other creditors with respect to bonds issued by euro-area countries and purchased by the Eurosystem through OMTs;

(e)   *sterilisation*, ie the liquidity created through OMTs would be fully sterilised; and

(f)   *transparency*, ie aggregate OMT holdings and their market values as well as average duration of OMT holdings and the breakdown by country would be published on a weekly and monthly basis respectively.

According to behavioural economics, such an unprecedented announcement would stimulate the market by creating 'constructive ambiguity'. In other words, the objective of the ECB was not to commit to participating as a player in the market, but rather to increase the demand for the bonds in question. The programme reflected Mario Draghi's voluntaristic statement 'I will do whatever it takes to save euro', which was essentially tantamount to *'salus euro suprema lex esto'*. Following the above-mentioned press release, in the second half of 2012, two-year government bond yields of endangered countries within the euro area, ie Italy and Spain, decreased by about two percentage points, without any significant side effects to more financially stable States, ie Germany and France, a fact that could be largely attributed to the announcement of the OMTs policy.[21] Interestingly, the policy has not been effectuated since its announcement, given that the countries leaving a MoU and regaining complete access to private lending markets did not at the time suffer from distressed interest rates, whereas Greece, six months after conclusion of the programme, did not have full access to international capital markets anyway.[22]

The *QE programme* was announced by the Governing Council of the ECB on 22 January 2015. It involved more than 2.6 trillion euros to allow the ECB to purchase 60 billion euros in combined monthly assets, including bonds issued by central governments, agencies, EU institutions and corporations each month in the secondary market against central bank money, which the issuers could use to buy other assets and extend credit to the real economy. The programme encompassed the asset-backed securities purchase programme and the covered bond purchase programme. Greek bonds, rated below investment grade, have not as yet been eligible, in spite of the country's exit from the programme.

---

[21] C Altavilla, D Giannone and M Lenza, 'The Financial and Macroeconomic Effects of OMT Announcements' (2016) 12 *International Journal of Central Banking* 29.

[22] On the OMTs programme, see ChV Gortsos, 'Legal Aspects of the European Central Bank (ECB) – The ECB within the European System of Central Banks (ESCB) and the European System of Financial Supervision (ESFS)' 2nd edn (2018), available at: ssrn.com/abstract=3162024.

Finally, in view of increased risk of a medium-term decline in prices in the context of an economic crisis entailing a risk of deflation, the ECB adopted in March 2015 a programme for the purchase of government bonds on secondary markets, namely the *PSPP programme*. Accordingly, substitute purchases were conducted if purchases of marketable debt instruments issued by the central government and agencies needed to be complemented to implement the national central banks' shares of purchases through the end of the APP in December 2018 that included all purchase programmes under which private sector securities and public sector securities were purchased. The PSPP was the largest share of the Expanded APP amounting to a volume of 1,534.8 billion euros out of 1,862.1 billion euros of the total programme.

G. Banking Union and Resolution Tools

The banking crisis in Europe demonstrated the interdependence of the domestic banking systems within the EU Monetary Union and the need for a deeper Banking Union. This union involves a higher level of transparency, more common rules and administrative standards for supervision, recovery and resolution of credit institutions. Such rules and standards would necessarily imply equal treatment of both national and cross-border banking activities, delinking of the financial health of credit institutions from the Member States in which they are located and an early warning system. For the purposes of the present analysis, a schematic description of the new framework of banking supervision and regulation, banking resolution and deposit guarantee/insurance will be presented.

It is noted in this respect that, prior to the banking crisis, with regard to rescuing credit institutions which faced insolvency issues, there were two options available, if there was no possibility to draw capital from the markets: either bankruptcy and liquidation, which was obviously a very traumatic solution for credit institutions holding a significant position in their respective market, or bail-out, suggesting that public funds should be used in one way or another to guarantee the survival of endangered credit institutions. Unlike in most of the world, in the EU bail-in, ie contribution by depositors and investors of credit institutions was not an option. EU primary law essentially prohibited bail-out of credit institutions through the prohibition, in principle, of state aid which distorted or threatened to distort competition by favouring certain undertakings or the production of certain goods (Article 107(1) TFEU), except for state aid, inter alia, remedying a serious disturbance in the economy of a Member State (Article 107(3)(b) TFEU). Furthermore, the no-bail-out clause of Article 125 TFEU indirectly included the Member States' credit institutions as well.

The unprecedented financial crisis, which in certain parts of Europe, such as in Ireland and Spain, directly affected the banking system, caused an overall revisit of the no bail-out clause and the prohibition of state aid. The interdependence of the Member States' banking systems along with the collateral effects of a possible collapse of a systemic credit institution of a Member State on the entire monetary and financial system of the Union, especially the euro area, called for new strategies and new institutional tools to be set in place. Obviously, the sovereign debt crisis and the banking crisis clearly qualified as serious disturbances in the economy, which could conceivably trigger the escape clause as regards the prohibition of state aid. The expansion of bail-out in times of financial crisis caused significant burdens to taxpayers who had, in principle, already suffered a serious decrease in their income as a result of salary/pension cuts and increased tax obligations. Consequently, a reasonable complaint against credit institutions for exploiting the moral hazard embodied into the bail-out policy and a distortion of competition against other credit institutions with balanced financial budgets was raised.

In response to this rather critical situation, the EU institutions, especially the Commission, responded with a series of instruments that aimed at launching common conditions at EU level for access to public support and the requirements for such aid to be compatible with the internal market in the light of state aid principles. These instruments – the Banking Communications, the Recapitalisation Communication, the Impaired Assets Communication and the Restructuring Communication – moved from the bail-out policy through derogations from the prohibition of state aid to a 'burden-sharing' policy in order to engage shareholders and subordinated creditors into the rescue programmes and reduce public support to credit institutions. This trend took a clear and stable form in a twofold manner in 2013/14, with:

(a) the 2013 Communication of the Commission on the application, from 1 August 2013, of state aid rules to support measures in favour of credit institutions in the context of the financial crisis (the Banking Communication on state aids to credit institutions); and

(b) Directive 2014/59/EU of the European Parliament and of the Council of 15 May 2014 establishing a framework for the recovery and resolution of credit institutions and investment firms (the Bank Recovery and Resolution Directive).

The Banking Communication on state aids to credit institutions supplemented the 2008–13 crisis rules, which remained in force, jointly determining the common EU conditions under which Member States can support credit institutions with funding guarantees, recapitalisations or asset relief and the requirements for a restructuring plan. Its characteristics include: a strictly defined bank restructuring process; criteria for restructuring and state aid; strengthened burden-sharing requirements; conditionality on restructuring and state support; and liquidation aid.

With regard to the *strictly defined bank restructuring* process, in principle, a bank needs to work out a restructuring plan, including a capital-raising plan, convincingly demonstrating how it will become profitable in the long term before receiving recapitalisation measures. If the viability of the bank cannot be restored, an orderly winding-down plan needs to be submitted instead. This process brings forward the restructuring plan, unlike the previous system, which entailed as a first triggering of the process a temporary authorisation by the Commission of recapitalisations as rescue measures pending approval of the subsequent restructuring plan. Yet, temporary approval can still be granted before the full restructuring plan is ready, provided that the competent supervisor confirms that an immediate intervention is necessary in the form of public recapitalisation to avert risks to financial stability.

With regard to the *criteria for restructuring and state aid*, financial stability remains the overarching objective and macro-economic considerations also become relevant.

With regard to *strengthened burden-sharing requirements*, credit institutions with a capital shortfall will have to obtain the contribution of shareholders and subordinated debt-holders before resorting to public recapitalisations or asset protection measures. This will level the playing field between similar credit institutions located in different Member States and it will reduce financial market fragmentation. Exceptions would be possible where financial stability is at risk or where a bank has already managed to significantly close the capital gap and the residual amount needed from the State is small compared to the size of the bank's balance sheet.

With regard to *conditionality on restructuring and state support*, failed credit institutions should apply strict executive remuneration policies up to a cap prescribed by the Communication, thus giving management the proper incentives to implement the restructuring plan and repay the aid.

Finally, with regard to *liquidation aid*, strict procedures are set in place to curtail any discretionary processes.

(a) As regards *banking supervision*, the developing EU Banking Union devised the Single Supervisory Mechanism (SSM). The SSM's main legal sources are a Council Regulation establishing a Single Supervisory Mechanism[23] and an ECB Single Supervisory Mechanism Framework Regulation.[24] It confers upon the ECB and upon national supervisory authorities (ie national central banks or other national administrative authorities) competences aiming at contributing to the safety and soundness of credit institutions and the stability of the financial system within the Union and each Member State, with full regard and duty of care for the unity and integrity of the internal market based on equal treatment of credit institutions with a view to preventing regulatory arbitrage (Article 1 of Regulation 1024/2013). SSM applies mandatorily to

---

[23] Reg 1024/2013 of the Council of 15 October 2013 conferring specific tasks on the ECB concerning policies relating to the prudential supervision of credit institutions (OJ L 287, 29.10.2013, p 63).

[24] Reg 468/2014 of the ECB of 16 April 2014 establishing the framework for cooperation within the Single Supervisory Mechanism between the ECB and national competent authorities and with national designated authorities (SSM Framework Regulation) (ECB/2014/17) (OJ L 141, 14.5.2014, p 1).

the euro-area Member States and voluntarily to the other EU countries on the basis of a 'close cooperation agreement' between the ECB and national supervisory authorities, determining the scope of close cooperation on supervisory matters (Articles 3(6) and 7 of Regulation 1024/2013).[25] Under the SSM, 'significant' euro-area credit institutions are directly supervised by the ECB; less significant credit institutions are directly supervised by their national supervisory authorities in close cooperation with the ECB.

In principle, there are objective criteria for the categorisation of credit institutions as significant and, on the basis of these criteria, the ECB can decide at any time to upgrade a euro-area bank to the status of significant and to directly supervise it, as a result of an increase of normal business activity or due to one-off events, such as mergers or acquisitions.[26] Yet, through a flexibility clause, the ECB, when necessary to ensure consistent application of high supervisory standards, may at any time, on its own initiative after consulting with national competent authorities or upon request by a national competent authority, freely decide to directly exercise all the relevant powers with regard to one or more credit institutions (Article 6(5)(b) of Regulation 1024/2013). In relation to all credit institutions established in the participating Member States, the ECB is exclusively competent for prudential supervisory purposes with a wide range of interventionist mechanisms (Article 4(1) of Regulation 1024/2013).[27]

(b)   As regards *banking regulation*, the Single Rulebook constitutes EU's post-crisis resolution framework reflecting the Basel III package and aiming at setting a single set of prudential rules for the EU financial sector to ensure

---

[25] The provisions of this Article are further specified in Decision of the ECB of 31 January 2014 on the close cooperation with the national competent authorities of participating Member States whose currency is not the euro (ECB/2014/5).

[26] The non-cumulative criteria of significance concerning credit institutions are: (a) if it is one of the three most significant credit institutions established in the respective country; (b) if the size of its total value of its assets exceeds 30 billion euros; (c) if its economic importance for the specific country or the EU economy as a whole is observed; (d) if it presents cross-border activities on the level that the total value of its assets exceeds five billion euros and the ratio of its cross-border assets/liabilities in more than one other participating Member State is above 20 per cent to its total assets/liabilities; (e) if it has received direct public financial assistance or has requested/received funding from the ESM or the EFSF. If a significant bank fails to meet all the above criteria for three consecutive years, it is downgraded to less significant and falls under the direct supervision of the national supervisor (Article 6(4) of Reg 1024/2013 and Articles 39–42 of Framework Reg 468/2014).

[27] On the SSM, see A Baglioni, *The European Banking Union: A Critical Assessment* (London, Palgrave Macmillan, 2016) 31–60; J-H Binder and ChV Gortsos, *The European Banking Union: A Compendium* (Baden-Baden, Beck – Hart – Nomos, 2016) 17–44; G Boccuzzi, *The European Banking Union: Supervision and Resolution* (London, Palgrave Macmillan, 2015) 23–47; E Wymeersch, 'The Single Supervisory Mechanism: Institutional Aspects' in D Busch and G Ferrarini (eds), *European Banking Union* (Oxford, Oxford University Press, 2015) 4.04–4.71; ChV Gortsos, 'Macro-Prudential Tasks in the Framework of the Single Supervisory Mechanism (SSM): An Analysis of Article 5 of the SSM Regulation' European Center of Economic and Financial law Working Paper Series no 2015/12 (2015); S Verhelst, 'Assessing the Single Supervisory Mechanism: Passing the Point of No Return for Europe's Banking Union' Egmont Paper no 58 (2013).

uniform application, through minimum requirements for all international credit institutions to strengthen their regulation, supervision and risk management of credit institutions and prevent systemic weaknesses. It contains: two legislative acts, ie a Regulation and a Directive of the European Parliament and of the Council;[28] non-legislative Council and (mainly) Commission delegated and implementing acts pursuant to Articles 290 and 291 TFEU; and EBA Guidelines on various aspects of the two legislative acts.

As regards, in particular, regulatory risk from government bonds held by credit institutions, which is a functional collateral of prudential regulation, Article 114(4) of the Capital Requirements Regulation (575/2013/EU) introduced the rule that exposures to Member States' central governments, and central banks, denominated and funded in the domestic currency, shall be assigned a risk weight of zero per cent. Notably, the zero per cent rule for Member States' central governments, and central banks applies as early as 1992 under Directive 89/647/EEC,[29] whereas the capital requirement to cover the credit risk to which they are exposed through their activities is calculated either through the standardised approach or through the internal ratings-based approach, the latter rendering credit risk inherent to holdings of government bonds/bills (Articles 111–141 and 142–191 of Regulation 575/2013).

The issue of the regulatory treatment of sovereign exposures is of acute importance today due to the ongoing banking and financial problems in some countries. Two reports of particular interest have been published on this matter. On 10 March 2015, the European Systemic Risk Board published a report stating that such exposures in banking and insurance sectors could be seen either as a source of fragility in the episodes of financial stress or as a factor of crisis mitigation.[30] The report argued that, from a macro-prudential point of view, the existing regulatory framework might have led to excessive investment by credit institutions in government debt, recognised the difficulty in reforming the existing framework without generating potential instability in sovereign debt markets and examined a set of possible options which might be considered. In December 2017, the Basel Committee completed its review on the regulatory treatment of sovereign risk assigned by its oversight body, by the Group of Central Bank Governors and by Heads of Supervision with very specific and radical proposals for the improvement of the current

---

[28] Capital Requirements Regulation (CRR), ie Reg 575/2013/EU of 26 June 2013 on prudential requirements for credit institutions and investment firms (OJ L 176, 27.6.2013, p 1) and Capital Requirements Directive (CRD IV), ie Directive 2013/36/EU of 26 June 2013 on access to the activity of credit institutions and the prudential supervision of credit institutions and investment firms (OJ L 176, 27.6.2013, p 338).

[29] Council Directive 89/647 of 18 December 1989 on a solvency ratio for credit institutions (OJ L 386, 30.12.1989, p 14).

[30] www.esrb.europa.eu/pub/pdf/other/esrbreportregulatorytreatmentsovereignexposures032015.en.pdf.

situation in the field.[31] Although the Committee has not reached a consensus on making any changes, such as guidance on monitoring sovereign risk, stress testing for sovereign risk and supervisory responses to the crystallisation of sovereign risk, mainly due to divergent opinions from various States and credit institutions, the Report contained a very detailed framework for understanding systemic deficiencies.[32]

In relation to banking resolution, the Single Resolution Mechanism (SRM) constitutes the second pillar of the Banking Union, its legal source being Regulation (EU) No 806/2014 of the European Parliament and of the Council of 15 July 2014 establishing uniform rules and a uniform procedure for the resolution of credit institutions and certain investment firms in the framework of an SRM and a Single Resolution Fund (SRF) and amending Regulation (EU) No 1093/2010, which entered into force on 19 August 2014.[33] It sets a system of resolution for credit institutions covered by the SSM, ie a mechanism of orderly restructuring of a credit institution by a resolution authority when that credit institution is failing or likely to fail and meets the two other criteria for resolution, as laid down in Article 18(1) SRMR, so as to prevent collateral harm to the broader economy or financial instability and to minimise costs for taxpayers, for the real economy and for the public finances of Banking Union Member States. Thus, if a credit institution fails, despite stronger supervision, the SRM allows bank resolution to be managed effectively through: a Single Resolution Board (SRB) complemented by the national resolution authorities (which are the components of the SRM – a system resembling, mutatis mutandis, the SSM); and a Single Resolution Fund (SRF) that is financed by the banking sector.

The SRB is a fully independent EU agency, acting as the central resolution authority within the Banking Union, and constituting along with the national resolution authorities of participating countries the SRM. The SRB further manages the SRF. The fund is composed of contributions from credit institutions and certain investment firms in the 19 participating Member States within the Banking Union and ensures that the economic industry, as a whole, finances the stabilisation of the system. It was intended to be gradually built up reaching the target level of at least 1 per cent of the amount of covered deposits of all credit institutions within the Banking Union by

---

[31] www.bis.org/bcbs/publ/d425.pdf.

[32] In this regard, on 24 May 2018 the European Commission set a proposal for a Regulation of the European Parliament and the Council, whose objective is to lay down a general framework for sovereign bond-backed securities (SBBSs), aiming at reducing systemic risk in the disruption in the provision of financial services due to the partial or wholly weakening of the financial system and mitigating financial fragmentation, see ChV Gortsos, 'Financial engineering coupled with regulatory incentives: Is there a strong market case for Sovereign Bond-Backed Securities (SBBSs) in the Euro-Area? A brief analysis of the European Commission's proposal for a Regulation on SBBSs' (2018), available at: ssrn.com/abstract=3244320.

[33] OJ L 225, 30.7.2014, p 1.

31 December 2023. The Fund may be used to ensure the effective application of the resolution tools, as last resort and insofar necessary in a variety
of forms (guarantees, loans, asset purchases, contributions). The Fund is not
designed to take on the losses of an institution or to recapitalise an institution. In exceptional cases, where an eligible liability or class of liabilities is
excluded or partially excluded from the write-down or conversion powers,
it might assist the institution under resolution with a total contribution that
does not exceed 5 per cent of the total liabilities, including own funds of the
institution under resolution. In order for this contribution to be activated
there must be a prior bail-in of at least 8 per cent, ie losses over and above
this threshold by shareholders and holders of relevant capital instruments
and other eligible liabilities, through write-down, conversion or otherwise.
Significantly, the December 2018 Eurogroup took a decision to backstop the
SRF by the ESM.[34,35]

The Single Rulebook in this respect features the Bank Recovery and
Resolution Directive (BRRD), which complements the SRM for the euro-area
Member States and those in a close cooperation agreement. It especially
entails:

(i)   Mandatory bail-in in case of bank failure. In such case the bank is
      put under resolution and their shareholders and subordinated credi-
      tors must participate to the rescue with their own resources, such as
      write-down of shares or conversions of subordinated debts into equity
      (Articles 43–44 BRRD).

(ii) Applicability of precautionary recapitalisation. If a solvent bank
      requires some public support in order to address capital shortfall ascer-
      tained in the framework of the national, Union or SSM stress tests,
      asset quality reviews or equivalent exercises, a capital injection can be
      provided by the State to the bank, provided that proper bail-in meas-
      ures apply to shareholders and subordinated creditors pursuant to the

---

[34] In its roadmap for deepening Europe's EMU, the Commission proposed that the future EMF could
serve as a backstop to the Banking Union: it would be activated as last-resort insurance in the event
of a bank resolution in case the resources available in the single resolution fund were insufficient, by
providing a credit line or guarantees to the fund (ec.europa.eu/commission/sites/beta-political/files/
backstop-banking-union_en.pdf, accessed 31 December 2018). Furthermore, the European Parliament
and the Council have rendered a Proposal for a regulation to amend Reg 806/2014 as regards loss-
absorbing and recapitalisation capacity for credit institutions and investment firms, COM/2016/0851
final – 2016/0361 (COD).

[35] On the SRM, see A Baglioni, *European Banking Union* (2016) 45–68; D Busch, 'Governance of the
Single Revolution Mechanism' in D Busch and G Ferrarini (eds) *European Banking Union* (Oxford,
Oxford University Press, 2015) 9.01–9.121; A Gardella, 'Bail-In and the Financing of Resolution within
the SRM Framework' in Busch and Ferrarini (ibid) 11.01–11.66; ChV Gortsos, 'The Single Resolution
Mechanism (SRM) and the Single Resolution Fund (SRF): Legal Aspects of the Second Main Pillar of
the European Banking Union', 4th edn (2018), available at: ssrn.com/abstract=2668653; GS Zavvos and
S Kaltsouni, 'The Single Resolution Mechanism in the European Banking Union: Legal Foundation,
Governance, Structure and Financing' in M Haentjens and B Wessels (eds), *Research Handbook on
Crisis Management in the Banking Sector* (Cheltenham, Edward Elgar Publishing, 2015) 117.

Banking Communication (Article 57 BRRD). Burden-sharing and bail-in tools included mostly in the Banking Communications and in the BRRD respectively essentially lead to the same result, ie imposition of the financial burden to shareholders and subordinated creditors in case of bank failure as a prerequisite for upholding state aid to the bank as a form of partly assuming capital shortfalls. Yet, neither of those two, nor any other tool within the EU, addressed the issue of property loss on the part of the bank's shareholders and subordinated creditors.[36]

(c)   Finally, as regards *deposit guarantee/insurance*, the third pillar of the EU Banking Union has been envisaged through the establishment of a European Deposit Insurance Scheme (EDIS), whose progress in terms of adopting relevant legal acts is rather slow. Accordingly, in the field of deposit guarantee, there is still only secondary legislation addressed to all EU Member States and providing for the mandatory establishment and official recognition in each Member State of at least one deposit guarantee scheme. The aim of those schemes has been to compensate bank depositors whose deposits have been considered to be 'unavailable', in order to protect depositors and to maintain stability of the banking system by preventing mass withdrawal of deposits in case of bank failure. As a result of the financial crisis, Directive 2009/14[37] required EU countries to uniformly increase their protection of deposits firstly to a minimum level of 50,000 euros and then to a minimum level of 100,000 euros by the end of 2010 in all credit institutions established in the EU and their branches within the Union.

Currently, deposit guarantee within the EU is governed by Directive 2014/49/EU of the European Parliament and of the Council 'on deposit guarantee schemes',[38] which was adopted on 16 April 2014 as part of the single rulebook (DGSD) and repealed Directive 94/19/EC of the same EU institutions as of 3 July 2015. This legislative act provides, inter alia, for the gradual reduction of the repayment period for deposit guarantees and firmly reinstates that resolving of bank failures can only take place with the use of funds

---

[36] On the Single Rulebook and the BRRD, see Boccuzzi, *The European Banking Union* (2015) 48–115; ChV Gortsos, 'A Poisonous (?) Mix: Bail-Out of Credit Institutions Combined with Bail-In of their Liabilities under the BRRD – The Use of "Government Financial Stabilisation Tools" (GFSTs)' (2016), available at: ssrn.com/abstract=2876508; G Ferrarini and F Recine, 'The Single Rulebook and the SSM: Should the ECB have More Say in Prudential Rule-Making?' in Busch and Ferrarini (2015) 5.01–5.84; M Haentjens, 'Selected Commentary on the Bank Recovery and Resolution Directive' in G Moss QC, B Wessels and M Haentjens (eds), *EU Banking and Insurance Insolvency*, 2nd edn (Oxford, Oxford University Press, 2017), 177–318; V de Serière, 'Recovery and Resolution Plans of Banks in the Context of the BRRD and the SRM: Some Fundamental Issues in Busch and Ferrarini (n 35) 10.01–10.86.

[37] Directive 2009/14/EC of the European Parliament and of the Council of 11 March 2009 on deposit-guarantee schemes as regards the coverage level and the payout delay (OJ L 68, 13.3.2009, p 3). This Directive replaced Directive 94/19 of the European Parliament and of the Council of 30 May 1994 on deposit-guarantee schemes (OJ L 135, 31.5.1994, p 5), merely requiring a minimum level of harmonisation between national deposit guarantee schemes.

[38] OJ L 173, 12.6.2014, p 149.

provided by the credit institutions participating in the deposit guarantee schemes and not by resorting to taxpayers.[39]

Although Directive 2014/49/EU set a very solid basis in an attempt to improve consumer confidence in financial stability across the internal market and to preserve financial stability, deposit guarantee schemes still remain national; this is inconsistent with the other pillars of the bank safety net in the course towards the establishment of a genuine European Banking Union. In addition, national deposit guarantee schemes are still designed merely for small credit institutions due to the low target level for their funding set in the Directive.[40]

II. Economic Governance in EU Member States

A. State Economic Model

In relation to the provisions referring to the state economic model, there are three categories of national Constitutions: the economically open-ended Constitutions, the free-market/competition-oriented Constitutions and the mixed social/free-market economy Constitutions.

The *open-ended Constitutions*, although containing certain aspects of financial activity within the national territory, contain no specific definition of the national prevailing economic model, thus allowing a wide margin to the Government in each particular era to apply a variable economic programme. This is the case, for example, in Greece, where there is no constitutional prescription institutionally protecting the free market economy and the possibility of significant state intervention is secured (Article 106(1)). Yet, even in such cases, one might reasonably argue that accession to the EU, which has a definite model based on free market economy, in conjunction with the principle of supremacy of EU law, has essentially casted new light upon the pre-existing constitutional clauses. Irrespective of this sort of transformation of the original reading of the Constitution, the truth is that EU Member States, while remaining within the Union, have no discretion to opt for any other economic model than that of the free market. Obviously, the transfer of sovereign national powers to the EU, especially in the field of free movement and the Monetary Union, for those countries which are part of the euro area,

---

[39] On the EU framework governing deposit guarantee schemes see, N Kleftouri, *Deposit Protection and Bank Resolution* (Oxford, Oxford University Press, 2015); Baglioni (n 27) 111–24; Boccuzzi (n 27) 130–53; ChV Gortsos, 'Deposit Guarantee Schemes: General Aspects and Recent Institutional and Regulatory Developments at International and EU Level' (2016), available at: ssrn.com/abstract=2758635; O Shy, R Stenbacka and V Yankov, 'Limited Deposit Insurance Coverage and Bank Competition', FEDS Working Paper no 2014-53 (2014), available at: ssrn.com/abstract=2477933.

[40] Article 10(2), see ChV Gortsos, *The New EU Directive (2014/49/EU) on Deposit Guarantee Schemes: An Element of the European Banking Union* (Athens, Nomiki Bibliothiki, 2014).

signifies that economically neutral domestic Constitutions have lost their elasticity and have been sized in an EU procrustean model of market economy. Accordingly, the all-embracing purpose of the Constitutions has been significantly shrunk in the economic reality of the EU.

The *free-market/competition-oriented Constitutions* have adopted, explicitly or implicitly, the EU economic pattern. This is the case in a significant number of Constitutions of the EU Member States, especially those which emerged in the aftermath of the dissolution of former socialist States of Eastern Europe. Certain Constitutions explicitly use the language of preservation of competition or safeguard from anti-monopoly practices or equivalent: of Austria, specifying that public servants must safeguard competition and implement economic inspection (Article 20(2)); of Bulgaria, declaring that the State shall establish and guarantee equal legal conditions for economic activity to all citizens and legal entities by preventing any abuse of a monopoly status and unfair competition (Article 19(2)); of Slovenia, entailing that unfair competition practices and practices which restrict competition in a manner contrary to the law are prohibited (Article 74(4)); and, of Ireland, according to which the State shall direct its policy towards securing, inter alia, that the operation of free competition shall not be allowed to develop in a way that results in the concentration of the ownership or control of essential commodities in the hands of a few individuals to the common detriment (Article 45(2)(iii)).

On some occasions, national Constitutions employ a joint wording involving both free market and competition principles. This is the case, for example, of the Constitutions: of Romania, indicating that the national economy is a free market economy, based on free enterprise and competition and that the State is expected to ensure free trade, protection of loyal competition, the creation of a favourable framework for the use of all production factors and the protection of national interests in economic, financial, and currency transactions (Article 135); of Hungary, providing that the economy shall be based on work which creates value and freedom of enterprise and that the State shall ensure the conditions for fair economic competition against any abuse of a dominant position (Article M(1)); of Croatia, specifying that entrepreneurial and market freedom shall be the basis of the economic system and that the State shall ensure all entrepreneurs an equal legal status on the market explicitly prohibiting abuse of monopoly position (Article 49(1)); and of Lithuania, entailing that the economy shall be based on the right of private ownership, freedom of individual economic activity and initiative, alongside the prohibition of monopolisation of production and of the market and protection of freedom of fair competition (Article 46(1) and (4)).

Outside the EU, the most striking example of pompous free market/competition wording is provided by the Russian Constitution, to the effect that in the country the integrity of economic space, free flow of goods, services and financial resources, support of competition, and the freedom of economic activity shall be guaranteed (Article 8).

The *mixed social free-market economies Constitutions form* an amalgam of free market and social economy stipulations. The difference between an open-ended and a mixed economy Constitution is that in the latter case there is much less discretion left on governments to apply an economic policy of their choice, since the pattern is constitutionally defined and must respect the mainstays of social free-market economy, even though by definition this is a pattern that could reasonably embrace a great number of variables. Thus, even the neutral model subsumes organisation of economic functions (medium- and long-term basis with a view to macro-prosperity), but only the mixed model enhances the planning of the economy (ie policy directions and limitations of private economy). In mixed models, the State normally holds a significant part of economic planning, the control and monopoly of the coin and credit and the competence to intervene in sectoral/geographical sections.

In one way or another, most of the European Constitutions reserve the general economic policy for the State with further variables of social restrictions upon individual economic activity. Under the Constitution of Spain, free enterprise is recognised within the framework of a market economy, yet the State is empowered to plan general economic activity by an act in order to meet collective needs, to balance and harmonise regional and sectorial development and to stimulate the growth of income and wealth and a more equitable distribution thereof (Section 38). Thus, the Government shall draft planning projects in accordance with forecasts supplied by self-governing Communities and with the advice and cooperation of unions and other professional, employers' and financial organisations (Section 131). Furthermore, the Constitution stipulates that in the framework of the consumer protection rationale, the law shall regulate domestic trade and the commercial product licensing system (Section 51). Finally, the State guarantees and protects the exercise of free enterprise aiming at productivity in accordance with the demands of the general economy and, as the case may be, of 'economic planning' (Section 38).

According to the Constitution of Italy, the legislator has the mandate to introduce appropriate programmes and controls so that public and private-sector economic activity may be oriented and coordinated for social purposes (Article 41(3)). More explicitly in terms of its combined character, the Constitution of Poland provides that the domestic economic system is a social market economy, based on the freedom of economic activity, private ownership, and solidarity, dialogue and cooperation between social partners (Article 20). The Constitution of Slovakia similarly provides that the state economy is based on the principles of a socially and ecologically oriented market economy, whereas at the same time it protects and encourages competition (Article 55). In the same vein, under the heading 'directive principles of social policy', the Constitution of Ireland provides that the State shall favour and, where necessary, supplement private initiative in industry and commerce (45(3)(i)), since the constitutional reservation for regulatory intervention of the State, when read in conjunction with other social restrictions of the Constitution, irrespective of the safety constitutional net of the subsidiarity clause through 'necessary' supplement, intimates a mixed economic model. Interestingly, the Constitution provides that the State shall, in particular, direct its policy towards securing that the ownership and control of the material resources of the community may be distributed among private individuals and the various classes in a way that best serves the common good (Article 45(2)(ii)).

Yet, the most detailed framework of national economic mixed model is provided under the Portuguese Constitution, which is in any case the most extensive domestic constitution in Europe. According to this Constitution, the country is based on fundamental constitutional principles with a view to achieving, inter alia, 'economic democracy' (Article 2). This means that the financial system 'shall be structured by law in such a way as to guarantee the accumulation, deposit and security of savings, as well as the application of the financial resources needed for economic and social development' (Article 101), whereas the fiscal system shall aim to satisfy the financial needs of the State and of other public bodies and to ensure a fair distribution of income and wealth (Article 103(1)).

Furthermore, in the economic field the State shall be under a primary duty to ensure the efficient operation of the markets, in such a way as to guarantee a balanced competition between businesses, counter monopolistic forms of organisation and repress abuses of dominant positions and other practices that are harmful to the general interest (Article 81); the economy shall be organised on the basis of the principle that the public, private and cooperative social sectors shall coexist in the ownership of the means of production and the coexistence of three sectors of ownership of the means of production shall be guaranteed (Article 80 and 82(1)); economic development shall be democratically planned (Article 80); and, finally, the State's commercial policy shall aim, inter alia, at healthy competition between commercial agents, the rationalisation of distribution circuits, combatting speculative activities and restrictive commercial practices and the development and diversification of external economic relations (Article 99).

Overall, the Portuguese mixed economic model is defined by the guiding constitutional clause providing that 'private economic enterprise shall be undertaken freely within the overall frameworks laid down by this Constitution and the law and with regard for the general interest' (Article 61(1)), 'within the overall framework of a mixed economy' (Article 80(b)).

The currency and its circulation are invariably determined either by the State itself or by an independent central bank pursuant to the ordoliberal model. In some instances, moreover, the proper Constitution determines the official national currency, such as the forint in Hungary (Article K) and the Leu/Ban in Romania. (Article 137(2)). In the latter case it is specifically stated that, following Romania's accession to the EU, the replacement of the national currency by the EU currency and its circulation shall be regulated by organic law. A relevant clause also exists in the Greek Constitution according to which the sovereign power to mint or issue currency does not impede the participation of Greece in the process for European economic and monetary unification, in the wider context of European integration (Interpretative Clause under Article 80(2)). Also, the regulation and/or monopoly of credit obviously exercise significant influence upon the market. Constitutional clauses for the regulatory monopoly of coordination and control of credit can be found in the Constitutions of Italy (Article 47(1)) and Ireland, the latter aiming constantly and predominantly at the welfare of the people as a whole (Article 45(2)).

A number of Constitutions provide for sectoral/geographical intervention in economy. Thus, national Constitutions may favour and promote certain aspects and forms of private economic activities, either by setting relevant initiatives or merely as declaratory economic paternalism. Although this is a guiding principle for the legislator to take up particular preferential sectoral measures, it does not per se turn a free market constitutional model to a mixed economy model, in that it lies with the ordinary legislator to launch such measures and normally citizens have no justiciable claim against the State regarding a request for initialisation of such policies. For example, the Constitution of Italy provides that the State encourages and safeguards savings in all forms (Article 47(1)) and promotes house and farm ownership and direct and indirect shareholding in the main national enterprises through the use of private savings (Article 47(2)). The Constitution of Greece provides that the State takes all measures necessary to promote, especially, the economy of mountainous, insular and frontier areas (Article 106(1)). Finally, the Constitution of Lithuania, in a more general wording, mandates the State to support economic efforts and initiative that are useful to society (Article 46(2)).

B. Economic Liberty

Apart from the institutional acknowledgment of an economic model through a specific constitutional clause, domestic Constitutions further guarantee the freedom to exercise an economic activity, which to some extent determines the scope of the economic model of the State. Thus, the provision for uninhibited pursuance of an economic activity naturally inclines towards a more market-oriented model. By way of contrast, the existence of various conditions in the exercise of this right might well stand for a more social-oriented economy that reserves a more interventionist role for the State. In that, it is equally important to identify the constitutional scope of acknowledgment of the right as well as the constitutional restriction upon their exercise.

The right to pursue an economic activity is constitutionally secured in a variety of forms:

(a) guarantee of free economic enterprise/initiative through free access, engaging in and exercise of economic or entrepreneurial activity, such as in the Constitutions of Italy (Article 41(1)), Denmark (Article 74), Portugal (Articles 61(1) and 80(c)), Estonia (Article 31), Slovenia (Article 74), Bulgaria (Article 19(2)), Romania (Article 45) and Hungary (Article 12(1));

(b) state encouragement of private economic enterprise or stimulation of economic progress, such as in the Constitutions of Ireland (Article 45), Croatia (Article 49(3)) and Malta (Article 18);

(c) freedom of commerce and industry, such as in the Constitution of Luxembourg (Article 11(6));

(d) freedom to choose and/or exercise private profession, such as in the Constitutions of Luxembourg (Article 11(6)), Finland (Article 18(1)) and Hungary (Article XII(1));

(e) establishment of equal legal conditions for economic activity to all citizens and legal entities or guarantee of equal legal status on the market to all entrepreneurs, such as in the Constitutions of Denmark (Article 74), Bulgaria (Article 19(2)) and Croatia (Article 49(2));

(f) general protection of the investments or prohibition from diminution of the rights acquired through the investment of capital, such as in the Constitutions of Croatia (Article 49(4)) and Bulgaria (Article 19(3));

(g) guarantees to set up cooperatives and other forms of association of citizens and legal entities in the pursuit of economic gain, such as in the Constitutions of Estonia (Article 31) and Bulgaria (Article 19(4));

(h) freedom to participate in the economic life of the country, such as in the Constitution of Greece (Article 5(1)).

Notably, some Constitutions, such as the Greek Constitution, provide that provisions on freedom of economic activity belong to the hard core of the Constitution and cannot be amended through the process of amendment, thus enjoying a perpetual status within the institutional structure of the State (Article 110).

In addition to the above, a number of domestic EU Member States' Constitutions safeguard the position of consumers within the economic activity, a human right and a state policy at the same time, which indirectly creates a space for the economic model of free market and for uninhibited participation in the economy of the country. This might involve a general protection clause, such as in the case of the Constitutions of Lithuania (Article 46) and Bulgaria (19(2)). It might, however, also include a more detailed guidance to the State as to the aims to be pursued by the legislator or the means of the corresponding protection. This is the case, for example, of the Constitutions of Spain, Portugal and Poland.

The Spanish Constitution provides that:

(a) the public authorities shall guarantee the protection of consumers and users and, by means of effective measures, safeguard their safety, health and legitimate economic interests; and

(b) the public authorities shall promote the information and education of consumers and users, foster their organisations, and hear them on those matters affecting their members (Section 51(1) and (2) respectively).

The Polish Constitution provides that the public authorities shall protect consumers, customers, hirers or lessees against activities threatening their health, privacy and safety, as well as against dishonest market practices (Article 76).

Finally, the Portuguese Constitution not only provides that the State shall be under a primary duty to guarantee consumer rights and interests (Article 81(i)), and that one of the objectives of commercial policy must be consumer protection (Article 99(e)), but further specifies, in rather unusual detail for a constitutional charter, the scope of permitted advertising, ie that it is regulated by law and that all forms of concealed, indirect or fraudulent advertising shall be prohibited (Article 60(2)), and the rights of consumer associations, ie freedom of establishment, rights to receive support from the State, the right to be heard in relation to consumer protection issues and a presumption of locus standi in defence of their members or of any collective or general interests (Article 60(3)).

An interesting aspect of the right to economic activity relates to the nationality of those exercising it and the origin of the investment. With regard to non-nationals, the respective right can, in most Constitutions, be exercised by them also. Yet, on occasions, reservations apply. Thus, under the Estonian Constitution, ordinary legislation may differentiate the status of aliens and stateless persons as regards the right to engage in enterprise and to form commercial undertakings and unions (Article 31). In the same vein, the Portuguese Constitution stipulates that regulation of economic activity and investment by foreign private individuals and corporate bodies should aim to ensure that they contribute to the country's development and to the defence of national independence and the interests of workers (Article 87). Naturally, there is no constitutional room to provide restrictions on EU citizens and legal entities in the relevant matters, to the extent that EU law guarantees free movement and establishment.

With regard to foreign investments, some Constitutions provide for a preferential treatment of capitals brought in from abroad and invested in the domestic economy as an additional incentive for investments. This occurs in two ways. First, in the form of the ability to withdraw the capital and/or the profits produced therefrom, which again could not be in principle deprived of, due to EU law commitments, such as the Constitution of Croatia, providing that 'foreign investors shall be guaranteed free transfer and repatriation of profits and the capital invested' (Article 49(5)). Secondly, in the form of guarantee of a steady entrepreneurial environment at a higher constitutional level to prohibit the ordinary legislation from amending such privileges, especially concerning tax obligations upon the economic activity concerned, such as the Greek Constitution with regard to foreign capitals invested in the country and the maritime operations upgrading relevant statutes to a constitutional level (Article 107).

Almost all Constitutions that guarantee freedom to pursuit an economic activity impose, in a variety of forms, some restrictions on the bearers of this right, stemming from the need to reconcile it with the right of others and with the community welfare. Broadly speaking there are two types of qualifications, the social and the liberal ones. In the category of social qualifications, national

Constitutions prohibit the exercise of the right to economic activity when this might harm or is incompatible with:

(a) the national and/or public interest or general good, such as in the Constitutions of Denmark (Article 74), Croatia (Article 50(2)), Poland (Article 22), Romania (Article 135(2)(b)) and Slovenia (Article 74);
(b) the general welfare, such as in the Constitution of Lithuania (Article 46(3));
(c) the State/general economy, such as in the Constitutions of Spain (Section 38) and Greece (Article 106(1));
(d) the prevailing morals/good usages, such as in the Constitution of Greece (Article 5(1));
(e) the safety or State security, such as in the Constitutions of Italy (Article 41(2)) and Croatia (Article 50(2));
(f) the environment, such as in the Constitution of Croatia (Article 50(2));
(g) social peace, such as in the Constitution of Greece (Article 106(1)); and
(h) public health, such as in the Constitution of Croatia (Article 50(2)).

In this category, one might also include the prohibitions in the exercise of sectoral economic activities in the pursuance of a legitimate public purpose, including: the constitutional prohibition of non-concentration of ownership of the media, such as that included in the Constitutions of Portugal (Article 39(1)) and Greece (Article 14(9)); and the prohibition of an owner, partner, main shareholder or management executive, as well as their relatives and spouses, of an information media enterprise to take on personally or through a legal entity a public procurement, such as in the Greek Constitution (Article 14(9)).

Again, the most detailed social restriction of the right to economic activity is to be found in the Constitution of Portugal, which provides that the State should encourage business activity, particularly that of small and medium-sized enterprises, and to monitor compliance with the respective legal obligations, especially by businesses that engage in activities that are of general interest to the economy, to intervene in the management of private businesses only on a transitional basis, in cases expressly provided for by law and, as a general rule, subject to prior judicial ruling, while the legislator is authorised to indicate basic sectors in which participation is forbidden for private businesses and other bodies of a similar nature (Article 86). In the category of liberal qualifications, private economic activity should not contravene human dignity and liberty or the rights of others, such as in the Constitutions of Italy (Article 41) and Greece (Article 5(1)).

The particular constitutional paradigms of Sweden and Portugal are worth noting in the course of the present analysis. The Swedish Constitution provides a counter-safety valve on restrictions upon economic activity by setting the rule that limitations affecting the right to trade or practice a profession may be introduced only in order to protect an overriding public interest and never solely in order to further the economic interests of a particular person or enterprise (Chapter 2, Article 17(1)). The Portuguese Constitution introduces a clause of a rather symbolic significance, providing that society and the economy shall be organised on the basis of the principle, inter alia, that the economic power shall be subordinated to democratic political power (Article 80(a)).[41]

C. State Ownership

Most Constitutions include provisions to secure exclusive State property in some particular assets and the process of nationalisation of private enterprises when so required by a compelling public interest. The provisions for public owned property refer to:

(a) the enactment of a statute establishing certain property as the exclusive ownership of the State for the purposes of safeguarding the needs of the society, the interests of the general public, the public welfare and the advancement of the national economy, such as in the Constitutions of the Czech Republic (Article 11(2) of the Charter of Fundamental Rights and Basic Freedoms) and Slovakia (Article 20(2));
(b) the possibility of the State to introduce a monopoly in any economic field, such as in the Constitution of Poland (Article 216(3));
(c) the possibility of the State to introduce a monopoly in particular fields of public interest, including those of railway transport, the national postal and telecommunications networks, the use of nuclear energy, the manufacturing of radioactive products, armaments and explosive and powerful toxic substances, such as in the Constitution of Bulgaria (Article 18(4));
(d) the *ipso jure* State property upon all natural resources, including all possible forms of energy, such as in the Constitution of Ireland (Article 10(1));
(e) the *ipso jure* property of society or property and enterprises that have or that may acquire the character of a public service or *de facto* monopoly, such as the constitutional order in France (Preamble to the Constitution of 27 October 1946);
(f) the *ipso jure* State possession of vital services for the people, including construction, maintenance and operation of the tracks of federal railways, sovereign functions in the area of posts and telecommunications, waterways and state functions relating to inland shipping, motorways and highways used by long-distance traffic on state commission, post services for a certain period of time, such as the German Constitution (Articles 87e(3) and (5), 87f, 89, 90 and 143b).

[41] On economic rights enshrined into domestic Constitutions, see A Eide, C Krause and A Rosas (eds), *Economic, Social and Cultural Rights: A Textbook*, 2nd edn (Leiden, Brill, 2001); T Daintith, 'The Constitutional Protection of Economic Rights' (2004) 2 *International Journal of Constitutional Law* 56.

The nationalisation process is provided through:

(a) the compulsory participation of the State as shareholder or its effective control in any company, such as in the Constitution of Finland (Article 92(1));

(b) public ownership, when so required by the public interest, of natural resources and of the means of production, such as in the Constitution of Portugal (Article 80);

(c) the compulsory purchase of an enterprise operating as a monopoly or being of vital significance to the State or of outstanding importance for the national economy, for example some energy sources or other natural resources, such as in the Constitutions of Italy (Article 43), Hungary (Article 38(1)), Cyprus (Article 25(3)) and Greece (Article 106(3)); and

(d) the possibility that land, natural resources and the means of production may, for the purpose of socialisation, be transferred to public ownership or other forms of public enterprise, such as in the Constitution of Germany (Article 15).

D. State Economic Institutions

Many European Constitutions provide that certain public authorities are established with specific competences of an economic nature. This mostly involves the establishment of central banks, supervisory authorities and economic committees.

The establishment of state central banks reflects an ordoliberal principle requiring a strong independent institution, normally accountable to the Parliament, which generally issues binding legal regulations within the scope of its power, comprising monetary competences of note-issuing and currency; this is case of the Constitutions of Finland (Article 91(1)), Portugal (Article 92), Hungary (Article 41), Slovakia (Article 56), Croatia (Article 53), the Czech Republic (Article 98(1)), Estonia (Article 111) and Slovenia (Article 152).

It was Germany which provided the prototype of EU ordoliberal constitutionalism through a state central bank (Article 88) and adherence to price stability policy, which were the result of World War II and the consequent fear of inflation. This model, as reflected in the Basic Law, enhances first and foremost a strong and independent central bank with decisive competences in the determination and implementation of monetary policy. The Constitution provides that the State shall establish a note-issuing and currency bank as the Federal Bank, whose responsibilities and powers may, within the framework of the EU, is transferred to the ECB, which is independent and committed to the overriding goal of assuring price stability (Article 88).

This constitutional clause is of a rather unusual nature, in the sense that it provides for transfer of competences to an EU institution, ie the ECB, to which the proper Constitution assigns certain characteristics regarding its independence and financial purposes. Presumably, this provision lies clearly outside the domain of the constitutional charter, since it involves the architecture of another legal system, and is therefore interpreted mostly as a condition precedent for the transfer of competences from the national to the international banking authority: insofar as the ECB remains independent and is committed to the overriding goal of assuring price stability, the competences of the German Central Bank may constitutionally be transferred to the former. Interestingly, although a number of European Constitutions provide for the establishment of a central bank, some of them explicitly conferring the status of an independent authority, few Constitutions expressly refer to the orientation of such credit institutions; for example, the Czech Constitution explicitly provides that National Bank's primary purpose shall be to maintain price stability (Article 98(1)).

The constitutional establishment of supervisory authorities is provided either in the form of an independent authority or in the form of a court. The most elaborate constitutional paradigms of an independent supervisory authority are the German Stability Council (Article 109a), the Austrian Public Audit Office (Articles 121–128) and the Slovak Supreme Audit Office (Articles 60–63).

The German Stability Council is a joint Federation and *Länder* body, which was established in 2010 and is composed of the Federal Minister of Finance, the *Länder* finance ministers and the Federal Minister for Economic Affairs and Energy. The Federal Minister of Finance and the chair of the *Länder* Finance Minister Conference co-chair the Stability Council. It exercises continuing supervision of budgetary management upon both levels of the State to avoid a budgetary emergency, on the basis of statutory conditions and procedures for ascertaining the threat of budgetary emergency and corresponding principles for the establishment and administration of programmes for taking care of budgetary emergencies. The Law on the domestic implementation of the Fiscal Compact of 15 July 2013 added the competence of the Stability Council to monitor the budgets of the Federation, *Länder*, local authorities and social insurance funds to ensure that these, taken together, comply with the upper limit for the general government structural deficit of 0.5 per cent of GDP set by the Fiscal Compact and to make proposals in case of a breach of the upper limit of the structural budgetary deficit.

The Austrian Public Audit Office acts as agent for the Lower House, ie the National Council, *and* is independent from the Federal Government and the Land Governments. Its competences include, inter alia, the examination of the spending of public funds by the Federation, the *Länder*, the municipal associations, the municipalities and other legal entities, the drawing up of the final federal budget accounts before submission to the Lower House, the countersignature (by its President) of all vouchers about financial debts of the state legality on grounds of the legality of the borrowing and the correct registration in the ledger of the national debt, the periodical report on undertakings and agencies average incomes, the assessment of the management of the Federation, of endowments, funds and institutions administered by Federal authorities, of enterprises where the State holds majority shares or de facto control by other financial, other economic, or organisational measures, of corporations under public law using federal funds, and the investigations on alleged misuse of public revenue or breaches of the law.

Constitutional paradigms of a court of law operating as a supervisory authority are the courts of audit in Germany and Greece. The German Court of Audit
audits the accounts and determines whether public finances have been properly
and efficiently administered by the Federation, conducts surveys of authorities
outside the federal administration and the *Länder* and submits an annual report
to both Houses of Parliament and the Federal Government (Article 114(2)). The
Greek Court of Audit controls the expenditures of public authorities, the public
procurement contracts of high value and the accounts of public officials entrusted
with financial competences and, thereby, accountable (Article 98(1)). The Slovak
Supreme Audit Office is an independent body carrying out audit of the management
of budgetary resources of the State, of all sorts of revenues, liabilities, guarantees
of all public authorities (State, municipalities, state-controlled institutions), of
individual/entities within the framework of foreign development programmes
and of legal entities carrying out activities in the public interest (Article 60).
The Office submits reports on the results of its auditing activity to the National
Council of the Slovak Republic at least once a year and whenever requested to do
so by the Parliament, ie the National Council.

The establishment of committees is provided in a variety of ways. The first type
of committee involves independent advisory bodies to the Government and/or
the Parliament, such as the Economic and Social Council provided for by the
Constitution of Portugal (Article 92), the Economic and Social Council provided
for by the Constitution of Romania (Article 141); the Economic and Social
Council provided for by the Constitution of France (Articles 69–71). The French
Economic, Social and Environmental Council, which is a rather voluminous institution comprising 233 members appointed for a five-year term, renewable once
on a consecutive duty, represents the civil society and reflects upon economic,
social and environmental matters, promotes cooperation between different groups
and takes part in the resolution of relevant matters. Upon request by the Government, the Council gives its opinion on any regulatory initiative and may also be
consulted by the Government or Parliament on any affair of its respective field
of interest. Finally, the Italian Constitution provides for the National Council for
Economics and Labour, composed of experts and representatives of the economic
stakeholders and serving as a consultative body for Parliament and the Government; this council also has the competence to initiate legislation and to contribute
to drafting economic and social legislation (Article 99).

The second type of committees refers to parliamentary committees with various competences. One of the most powerful committees of such nature provided
for by the Swedish Constitution is the Committee on Finance, which prepares
general guidelines for economic policy and the determination of the national
budget, the activities of the Central Bank of Sweden, monetary, credit, currency
and central government debt policy, the credit and finance markets, the commercial insurance market, the National Audit Office, insofar as it does not rest with
the Committee on the Constitution to prepare these matters; local government
finance, the State as employer, national statistics, accounting, audits and administrative efficiency, State property and public procurement in general, other

questions of administrative finance, not solely concerned with a particular subject area, budgetary questions of a technical nature, estimates of State revenue and coordination of the national budget, matters concerning appropriations falling within expenditure areas, economy and financial administration, general grants to local government, interest on central government debt, the contribution to the EU (Chapter 3 Article 5 and Supplementary provision 4.6.2).

E. Rules of Economic Governance

Not many Constitutions of EU Member States included rules of economic governance prior to the conclusion and entry into force of the TSCG, the most notable exception being the German fiscal prototype, composed of eight extensive constitutional articles of 1,558 words exclusively devoted to budgetary rules (Articles 109–115). The Constitutions of Poland and France also had similar rules of economic governance, the former having a debt brake as of 1997 and the latter providing for a requirement for balancing State accounts as of 2008. However, the Fiscal Compact commitment of the contracting parties gave an impulse to introduce such rules.

In a 2017 Report on the implementation of the Fiscal Compact commitments,[42] the European Commission concluded that all Contracting Parties significantly adapted their national fiscal frameworks as a result of the relevant requirements. Such convergence was made possible in two ways: first, by putting in place in various forms core requirements ('the substance of the Fiscal Compact'), ie binding and permanent balanced budget rules and correction mechanisms triggered automatically in the event of significant deviations were observed; second, by setting independent national fiscal institutions with an adequate monitoring mandate in their domestic legal orders, either through constitutional amendment or statutory incentives or alternative forms of binding frameworks.

In this respect, apart from differences stemming from the diversity of the constitutional and legal frameworks of the Contracting Parties, the Commission further noted:

(a) 'distinct approaches to flexibility within the correction mechanisms as well as in varying ambitions, beyond the minimum requirements, in the setting and mandate of national independent monitoring institutions';

(b) a difference of approach concerning the scope given to specific national rules and procedures, with some States developing their own provisions while others placing increased emphasis on consistency with the Stability and Growth Pact, thus relying on decisions from EU institutions, eg on the triggering of the correction mechanism and the setting of the required correction.

---

[42] Report from the Commission presented under Art 8 of the Treaty on Stability, Coordination and Governance in the Economic and Monetary Union of 22 February 2017, C(2017) 1201 final; and, Communication from the Commission. The Fiscal Compact: Taking Stock of 22 February 2017 C(2017) 1200 final.

Eventually, the report found that, albeit in various formats and with diverse substantive regulations, all Contracting States were in principle compliant with the requirements set in Article 3(2) TSCG and with the common principles in light of the formal commitment provided by the national authorities to apply the comply-or-explain principle in line with the common principles with some per country reservations referring to various mostly procedural issues.

On many occasions, for diverse reasons concerning either a political choice, such as in the case of Bulgaria, Greece and Cyprus, or failure to satisfy the procedural requirements for a constitutional amendment, such as in the case of France, or a judicial hindrance set upon the process, such as in the case of Belgium, the obligations stemming from the Fiscal Compact were transposed by statute. In some instances, intermediate regulatory vehicles were selected for that purpose, such as an organic law in France,[43] an upgraded law in Italy,[44] or a cooperation agreement between the federal State and the federated entities and/or municipalities in Belgium and Austria.

The foregoing analysis is basically limited to presenting examples of domestic Constitutions relating to the Fiscal Compact mandate, since the argument lies with the premise that there has been a change in the constitutional drafting and reading. Such constitutional amendments have, to some extent, been introduced in Austria, Belgium, Estonia, Spain, Finland, Italy, Lithuania, Latvia, Portugal and Slovenia. The presentation will not be exhaustive; it merely aims at identifying key constitutional elements (not, in principle, statutory or of any other type), which are rarely prior and more often subsequent to the deadline for domestic incorporation of the Fiscal Compact; this indicates a significant change of paradigm in the economic governance of the respective States. This is why the issue in question is not presented by country but rather in a material typology of three categories, ie general discipline and stability clauses, balanced budget rule and government debt benchmarking and state borrowing.

III. General Discipline and Stability Clauses

The German Basic Law expressly sets the framework of monetary policy with an explicit reference that all state authorities ought to pursue such financial goals and that the State ought to comply with the commitments assumed in the context of EU law. In particular, the Basic Law provides that both the Federation and the

---

[43] The Organic Law on the Programming and Governance of Public Finances voted by both Houses (Assemblée Nationale on 19 November 2012, Senate on 22 November 2012).

[44] Law 243/2012. Upgraded law can be repealed, modified or waived only expressly by a subsequent law passed by the same special majority and approved by the two plenary sessions of the parliamentary Chambers, whereas no statutory delegation applies on those matters for the Government to regulate such fields.

Länder shall jointly discharge the obligations of the State resulting from legal acts of the European Community for the maintenance of budgetary discipline pursuant to former Article 104 TEC and shall, within this framework, give due regard to the requirements of an overall economic equilibrium/macroeconomic balance (Article 109(2)). Furthermore, there is a constitutional clause to the effect that a federal law may establish principles applicable to both the Federation and the *Länder* governing budgetary law with a view to cyclically appropriate budgetary management and long-term financial planning (Article 109(4)).

In the same logic, the Constitution of Spain includes three relevant clauses. The policy clause provides that public authorities shall promote favourable conditions for social and economic progress and for a more equitable distribution of regional and personal income 'within the framework of an economic stability policy' (Section 40(1)). The budgetary clause provides that all public administrations must conform to the principle of budgetary stability (Section 135(1)). The decentralisation clause provides that the self-governing communities shall take the appropriate measures for effective implementation of the principle of stability in their rules and budgetary decisions (Section 135(6)). Furthermore, the Constitution authorises the enactment of an Organic Law to address the distribution of the limits of deficit and debt among the different public administrations, the exceptional circumstances under which such limits may be disregarded and the manner and time in which deviations are corrected (Section 135(5a)).

The Constitution of Hungary includes in the 'Foundations' section a relevant principle according to which the country shall observe the principle of balanced, transparent and sustainable budget management. In this respect, the National Assembly and the Government shall have primary responsibility for the observance of this principle, whereas the Constitutional Court, the courts, the local governments and other state organs are also obliged to respect it in performing their duties (Article N). The most interesting parameter of this constitutional stipulation is that the Constitutional Court of the country is also included among the state organs that ought to cater for the implementation of sound budget management, only insofar as the state debt exceeds half of the country's GDP (as a result of the conflict of state braches that resulted in the constitutional revision).

Finally, the Italian Constitution provides that all levels of government in the State must contribute to ensuring compliance with the economic and financial constraints imposed under EU law (Article 119(1)).

IV. Balanced Budget Rule

The requirement for a balanced budget is well-articulated in the Basic Law and contains the following characteristics:

(a) the budget shall be balanced with respect to revenues and expenditures on all state level budget, ie Federation and the *Länder;* in the case of federal enterprises and special trusts, only payments to or remittances from them need to be included;

(b)   budgets must be balanced without revenue from credits whatsoever for the *Länder* and must not exceed 0.35 per cent in relation to the nominal gross domestic product for the Federation; and

(c)   exceptional circumstances ought to be taken into account, thus the Federation and the *Länder* may introduce rules with a view to taking into consideration, symmetrically in times of upswing and downswing, the effects of market developments that deviate from normal conditions, as well as exceptions for natural disasters or unusual emergency situations that are beyond governmental control and substantially harmful to the State's financial capacity, in which case a corresponding repayment plan *(Tilgungsregelung)* must be adopted (Articles 109(3) and 110(1)).

It is noteworthy that the balanced budget rule of the Basic Law does not employ the totality of the Fiscal Compact mandate, since it merely applies to the Federation and the *Länder*, but not to the municipalities and the social security institutions. The additional obligations stemming from the Fiscal Compact did not result in a constitutional amendment but were incorporated through ordinary federal legislation concerning budgetary principles, ie Law on the domestic implementation of the Fiscal Compact of 15 July 2013.

Other Constitutions establish a substantive budgetary rule with direct reference to the EU ceilings, as applicable. Thus, the Constitution of Spain provides that the State and the self-governing communities may not incur a structural deficit that exceeds the limits established by the EU for its Member States. It further provides that an organic law shall determine the maximum structural deficit the State and the self-governing Communities may have in relation to GDP and explicitly states that local authorities must submit a balanced budget (Section 135(2)). The Constitution also provides an escape clause, according to which the limits of the structural deficit may be exceeded only in cases of natural disasters, economic recession or extraordinary emergency situations that are beyond the control of the State and significantly impair either the financial situation or the economic or social sustainability of the State (Section 135(4)). Finally, the Constitution provides the enactment of an organic law to set the methodology and procedure for calculating the structural deficit (Section 135(5)(b)).

Reference to EU law is also made by the Constitution of Italy in a much more holistic manner, indicating that:

(a)   the State shall balance revenue and expenditure in its budget, taking into account the adverse and favourable phases of the economic cycle (Article 81(1));

(b)   general government entities shall ensure balanced budgets in accordance with EU law (Article 97(1)); and,

(c)   that the revenue and expenditure autonomy of municipalities, provinces, metropolitan cities and regions is subject to the obligation to balance their budgets (Article 119(1)).

Maximum deviations from the budgetary equilibrium were provided by statute (Law 243/2012).

The Constitution of Austria generally provides that authorities of all state levels must aim at securing an overall balance and sustainable balanced budgets in the conduct of their economic affairs and have, therefore, to coordinate their budgeting with regard to these goals (Article 13(2)). Furthermore, on a federal level a federal law provides that there is a ceiling of structural deficit of 0.35 per cent of GDP with qualifications for extraordinary economic cycles and natural catastrophes. The law was not passed with the required majority of two-thirds of the total number of deputies in order to acquire constitutional ranking and, therefore, applies as an ordinary statute.

The Constitution of Slovenia provides in this respect that revenues and expenditures of the budgets of the State must be balanced in the medium term without borrowing or that revenues must exceed expenditures. The mandate allows for temporary deviations of the balanced budget rule when exceptional circumstances affect the State (Article 148(2)). Yet again, the ordinary legislator is authorised to set the manner and time frame for the implementation of the principle referred to in the preceding paragraph, the criteria for determining exceptional circumstances, and the course of action when those arise, with a requirement, however, of a qualified majority vote of two-thirds of all deputies (Article 148(3)).

V. Government Debt Benchmarking and State Borrowing

In relation to government debt benchmarking (ie a debt brake and state borrowing) there are two types of domestic constitutional provisions. The procedural rule entails that the borrowing of funds and the assumption of securities obligations, guarantees or other commitments that may lead to expenditures in future fiscal years shall require authorisation by a federal law specifying or permitting computation of the amounts involved, such as the relevant provision in the German Basic Law (Article 115(1)). The substantive rule contains specific ceilings concerning state borrowing.

The Basic Law provides in this respect that revenue obtained by the borrowing of funds should not regularly exceed 0.35 per cent in relation to the GDP, taking into account that symmetrically potential effects on the budget in periods of upswing and downswing must be taken into account. Deviations of actual borrowing from the credit ceiling of 0.35 per cent are to be recorded on a control account, whereas debits exceeding the threshold of 1.5 per cent in relation to the nominal gross domestic product are to be reduced in accordance with the economic cycle.

The Constitution contains an escape clause in cases of natural catastrophes or unusual emergency situations beyond governmental control and substantially harmful to the State's financial capacity, in which case the credit limits may be exceeded on the basis of a decision taken by the Lower house, accompanied with a repayment plan within an appropriate period of time (Article 115(2)).

Interestingly, pre-existing borrowing ceilings are not entirely identical to those contained in the Fiscal Compact. The entry into force of the borrowing rules of the German Constitution was set for the budgetary year 2011, but the *Länder* could deviate from it until 31 December 2019 (Article 143 d(1), the relevant clause for the federation was until 31 December 2015 and has already elapsed).

A direct bridge to EU law is made by the Italian Constitution, which provides that the sustainability of public debt pursuant to EU law shall be ensured by general government entities (Article 97(1)) and, in particular, that no recourse shall be made to borrowing except for the purpose of taking account of the effects of the economic cycle or, subject to authorisation by the two Houses approved by an absolute majority vote of their Members, in exceptional circumstances (Article 81(2)).

The Constitution of Spain seems to be the most elaborate in this respect (Section 135(3)). On the one hand, it lays down the procedural rule that in order to issue public debt bonds or to contract loans the State and the self-governing communities must be expressly authorised by an Act of Parliament. On the other hand, it explicitly refers to the TFEU as a ceiling for the total volume of public debt of all public authorities in relation to the State's GDP. It further provides that loans taken out to repay the interest and capital of the State's Public Debt shall always be deemed to be included in budget expenditure and their payment shall have absolute priority and shall not be subject to amendment, provided that they conform to the terms of issue. The same escape clause applying to the deficit also applies to the public debt allowing a margin. The limits of the structural deficit and public debt volume may be exceeded only in case of natural disasters or serious economic upsets (Section 135(4)).

The Constitution of Hungary lays down the principle of sustainable debt. Accordingly, the Parliament is prohibited from adopting an Act on the central budget where this would result in state debt exceeding half of the country's GDP (Article 36(4)). As a result, no borrowing may be contracted and no financial commitment may be undertaken in the course of the implementation of the central budget if such borrowing or commitment would lead to the state debt exceeding half of the GDP (Article 37(2)). The Constitution provides for a derogation from the constitutional ceiling when there is a declared special legal order and to the extent necessary to mitigate the consequences of the circumstances triggering this status, or, in case of an enduring and significant national economic recession, to the extent necessary to restore the balance of the national economy (Article 36(6)). According to the Constitution, a special legal order occurs in cases of a state of national crisis, of a state of emergency, in a state of preventive defence due to a danger of external armed attack or in order to fulfil an obligation arising from an alliance, in a terrorist threat-situation, in case of an unexpected invasion by external armed groups and in case of natural disasters or industrial accidents endangering life and property (Articles 48–53).

The Constitution provides a series of preventive measures if state debt exceeds half of the country's GDP. First, the Parliament may only adopt an Act on the central budget that provides for state debt reduction in proportion to the GDP (Article 36(5)). Second, no borrowing may be contracted and no such financial commitment may be undertaken in the course of the implementation of the central budget if this would result in an increase, compared to the previous year, of the ratio of state debt in relation to the GDP (Article 37(3)). Third, and most importantly, the Constitutional Court may review the Acts on the central budget, the implementation of the central budget, central taxes, duties and contributions, customs duties and the central conditions for local taxes in terms of conformity with the Constitution exclusively in connection with the rights to life and human dignity, the protection of personal data, freedom of thought, conscience and religion, or the rights related to citizenship. It may annul these Acts on these grounds, either because they have been adopted in infringement of these rights or because there has been a breach of the procedural requirements laid down in the Constitution for the adoption and the promulgation of such Acts (Article 37(4)).

The Constitution also caters for two further relevant issues, namely that the restrictive legislation taken because of surpass of the ceiling continues to apply, even in case the country falls below the threshold (Article 37(5)), and that ordinary legislation lays down the method for calculating state debt and the GDP as well as the rules relating to the implementation of budgetary rules (Article 37(6)).

Interestingly, compared to the Hungarian Constitution, the Constitution of Poland sets a different threshold when it comes to public debt. In particular, it provides that it is not permissible to contract loans or to provide guarantees and financial securities which would generate a national public debt exceeding three-fifths of the value of the annual GDP; the method for calculating the value of this figure and the national public debt is specified by statute (Article 216(5)). Furthermore, there is an additional procedural clause, according to which state borrowings, guarantees and financial sureties by the State are only permitted on the basis of a statute, such as the relevant provision of the Constitution of Slovenia (Article 149), or in accordance with principles and in the framework of procedures specified by statute, such as in the Constitution of Poland (Article 216(4)). Finally, the German Basic Law contains a rule which is peculiar to the federal system of governance and applies in cases of sanctions imposed for breaches of budgetary discipline imposed by EU rules. Accordingly, EU sanctions shall be borne by the Federation and the *Länder* at a ratio of 65 to 35 per cent. In solidarity, the *Länder* as a whole shall bear 35 per cent of the charges imposed on them according to the number of their inhabitants; 65 per cent of the charges imposed on the *Länder* shall be borne by them according to their degree of causation (Article 109(5)). The Spanish Constitution, on the other hand, delegates an organic law to lay down

the principles of responsibility of each public authority in case of breach of the
budgetary stability objectives (Section 135(5c)).

VI. Financial Assistance to EU Member States

A. Prior to Emergency Mechanisms

Prior to the establishment of emergency financial assistance mechanisms, the EU
had treated such difficulties of EU countries, especially through EU Balance of
Payments (BoP) assistance facility based on Council Regulation (EC) 332/2002
and Article 143 TFEU, enabling multilateral agreements with the European States,
the IMF and, less so, with the World Bank. That was the case of Hungary, Latvia
and Romania in 2008 and 2009.

In the case of Hungary, suffering from serious market turbulences and difficulties in refinancing government and external debt, the IMF, the European
Commission staff and the Hungarian authorities agreed, in October 2008, that
the country would receive 20 billion euros overall in multilateral financial assistance, ie 6.5 billion euros from the EU, 12.5 billion euros from the IMF and
one billion euros from the World Bank. A series of policy conditions, such as
fiscal consolidation, fiscal governance, financial sector regulation and supervision
and other structural reforms were attached to the financial assistance. Eventually, Hungary received 14.2 billion euros, with no financial assistance drawn from
the World Bank. The balance of payments programme for Hungary expired on
3 November 2010 and the country was then subject to post-programme surveillance until January 2015, when it repaid 70 per cent of its EU loan.[45]

In the case of Latvia, where the economic situation was deteriorating
rapidly and concerns had been voiced with regard to the viability of the banking sector, the IMF, the European Commission staff and the Latvian authorities
agreed, in December 2008, that the country would receive an overall amount
of 7.5 billion euros in multilateral financial assistance, ie 3.1 billion euros from
the EU, 1.7 billion euros from the IMF, 0.4 billion euros from the World Bank,
0.4 billion euros from the European Bank for Reconstruction and Development,
the Czech Republic and Poland and 1.9 billion euros from Sweden, Denmark,
Finland, Norway and Estonia. A series of policy conditions were attached to the
financial assistance, aiming at facilitating external and internal adjustments, stabilising the economy and restoring economic policy credibility. These conditions
included fiscal consolidation, fiscal governance, financial sector regulation and

---

[45] European Commission, 'Financial assistance to Hungary', available at ec.europa.eu/info/
business-economy-euro/economic-and-fiscal-policy-coordination/eu-financial-assistance/
which-eu-countries-have-received-assistance/financial-assistance-hungary_en.

supervision and other structural reforms. The programme expired on 19 January 2012 and the country was subject to a three-year post-programme surveillance.[46]

In the case of Romania, the country suffered from large internal and external imbalances in the form of a 5.7 per cent of GDP budget deficit and an 11.6 per cent of GDP current account deficit that resulted in capital inflows and depreciation by more than 30 per cent of the national currency in 18 months. Thus, the IMF, the European Commission staff and the Romanian authorities agreed, in May 2009, that for the period of 2009–11 the country would receive an overall amount of 20 billion euros in multilateral financial assistance, ie five billion euros from the EU, 13 billion euros from the IMF, one billion euros from the World Bank and one billion euros from the European Investment Bank and the European Bank for Reconstruction and Development. A series of policy conditions, such as fiscal consolidation, fiscal governance, financial sector regulation and supervision and other structural reforms, were attached to the financial assistance. After the conclusion of the programme Romania was under post-programme surveillance, which ended in April 2018 as the country repaid more than 70 per cent of its EU loan. During that period Romania received three precautionary Balance of Payments Assistance programmes due to difficulties regarding its balance of payments.[47]

B. Greece

Greece was the first euro-area Member State to receive financial assistance through the emergency mechanisms (and, therefore, the first euro-area country to receive financial assistance from the IMF) in order to deal with the sovereign debt crisis. Overall, Greece was settled to receive three bail-out packages, totaling 309 billion euros (73, 150 and 86 billion euros in 2011, 2012 and 2015 respectively).

Greece had not qualified to join the euro area in 1999, but joined in 2001, despite having a budget deficit well in excess of three per cent of GDP and government debt in excess of 100 per cent of GDP.[48] Greece's membership to the euro area created an unprecedented rally of private-sector purchases of government bonds

---

[46] European Commission, 'Financial assistance to Latvia', available at: ec.europa.eu/info/business-economy-euro/economic-and-fiscal-policy-coordination/eu-financial-assistance/which-eu-countries-have-received-assistance/financial-assistance-latvia_en; European Commission, Directorate-General for Economic and Financial Affairs, 'EU Balance-of-Payments assistance for Latvia: Foundations of success', Occasional Papers 120 | November 2012: ec.europa.eu/economy_finance/publications/occasional_paper/2012/pdf/ocp120_en.pdf.

[47] European Commission, 'Financial assistance to Romania', available at: ec.europa.eu/info/business-economy-euro/economic-and-fiscal-policy-coordination/eu-financial-assistance/which-eu-countries-have-received-assistance/financial-assistance-romania_en.

[48] In order to achieve such statistics, the then Greek Government concluded a restructuring scheme of a Goldman Sachs off-market swap in order to avoid registry of 2.8 billion euros in the debt. The swap was eventually included in the heat of the crisis into the 2010 budget with the value of 5.2 billion euros and is estimated to cost eventually 16 billion euros until its expiration in 2037.

resulting in interest rates going significantly down; this motivated a significant growth in the economy. Yet, in the 2000s, budget deficit and overall government debt levels increased significantly, while at the same time, due to the participation in the monetary union, national governments were unable to reduce interest rates or devalue the currency to stimulate economic growth. Greece was, in short, unable to implement its own monetary policy to meet its fiscal and political needs. As of the Lehman Brothers fall, lenders and investors rapidly abandoned the country and interest rates deviated significantly from the equivalent of other euro-area States in a very short period of time.

On 27 April 2009, the Council adopted a decision confirming the existence of an Excessive Deficit Procedure in Greece. Unlike in Ireland, Greek banks were not affected by the banking crisis, since they did not have Lehman Brothers toxic bonds, but merely maintained Greek government bonds. On 2 and 21 October 2009, the newly elected Greek Government transmitted to Eurostat data on the government deficit and debt for the period of 2005–08, and a forecast for 2009, substantially revising all relevant figures upwards and blurring the national financial situation even further.[49] On its 10 November 2009 conclusion, the ECOFIN invited the Commission to prepare a report on the renewed problems in the Greek fiscal statistics. Approximately at the same time, the Council also invited the Commission to recommend appropriate measures to be taken in this situation.

On 8 January 2010, the Commission, responding to those calls, issued the Report on Greek Government Deficit and Debt Statistics[50] accusing the Greek authorities, in a rather unusual manner for the standards of technical courtesy normally employed by the Commission, for incapacity and hypocrisy, in spite of the fact that all statistical data had been confirmed by the relevant services of the Commission at the time of their timely submission. In this report, the Commission essentially instigated the forthcoming financial developments concerning Greece. It first noted that data revisions of that magnitude are rather akin to Greece and illustrated the lack of quality of the national fiscal statistics and of macroeconomic statistics in general and showed that the progress in the compilation of fiscal statistics in the country and the intense scrutiny of the Greek fiscal data by Eurostat since 2004 had not sufficed.

In general terms, the Commission found two fundamental problems with the domestic statistics. The first set of problems concerned methodological weaknesses and unsatisfactory technical procedures of the national statistical authority and of other national services that provide data and information to this authority,

---

[49] The 2008 deficit was revised to 7.7 per cent of GDP (from 5 per cent reported by Greece and validated by Eurostat in April 2009), whereas the estimate for the 2009 budget was revised to 12.5 per cent of GDP (from 3.7 per cent reported by Greece in spring), reflecting on, inter alia, the impact of the economic crisis, budgetary discrepancies in an electoral year and accounting decisions. The latter eventually closed at 15.2 per cent of GDP.

[50] COM(2010) 1 final, dated 08.01.2010.

such as the General Accounting Office and the Ministry of Finance. The second set of problems resulted from

> inappropriate governance, with poor cooperation and lack of clear responsibilities between several Greek institutions and services ..., diffuse personal responsibilities, ambiguous empowerment of officials, absence of written instruction and documentation, which leave the quality of fiscal statistics subject to political pressures and electoral cycles.

In the Commission's view, those findings indicated that, on top of the serious problems observed in the functioning of other areas involved in the management of Greek public revenues and expenditures, the institutional set-up did not guarantee the independence, integrity and accountability of the national statistical authorities.

In response to the imminent threat of Greek insolvency, on 2 May 2010 the euro-area Member States, together with the IMF, set up an ad hoc mechanism to provide 110 billion euros of financial assistance to Greece in the form of bilateral loans over three years, including a voluntary contribution from the private sector, the extension of maturities and lowering of lending rates. As a condition for receiving the loans, the Greek Government declared its commitment to launch a series of strict austerity measures, including significant reductions in salaries and pensions, redundancies in the public sector, curtailment of social benefits, privatisation of publicly owned enterprises and a great number of structural reforms. Furthermore, the adherence to the austerity programme was agreed to be constantly supervised by a troika composed of representatives of the European Commission, the IMF and the ECB, and a European task force was settled in Greece to provide technical assistance on the proposed changes.

On 15 March 2010, Law 3833/2010, entitled 'Protection of the national economy – Urgent measures to respond to the financial crisis' was published in the Official Gazette. This Law retrospectively reduced the salaries of public servants by 12 to 30 per cent and set a new pay ceiling. On 3 May 2010 the Minister of Finance and the Governor of the Bank of Greece, representing the Hellenic Republic, and the EU Commissioner for Economic and Monetary Affairs, signed an MoU setting out in detail the measures comprising a three-year programme drawn up by the Greek authorities after consultation with the European Commission, the ECB and the IMF providing significant salary and pension cuts and tax adjustments. Three days later, Law 3845/2010 essentially ratified the conditionality set out by the MoU and reduced public sector salaries by a further eight per cent.

The second EU-IMF bail-out programme for Greece, totaling 130 billion euros, included a bail-in programme of 53.5 per cent debt write-down for private Greek bondholders, in exchange for Greece committing itself to reduce its debt-to-GDP ratio from 160 per cent to 120.5 per cent by 2020. On 27 November 2012, the euro-area finance ministers and the IMF agreed to a revised rescue package for Greece, including lower interest rates on Greek bail-out loans and a debt-buyback programme, with a relative revision of debt-to-GDP ratio to 124 per cent by 2020 substantially below 110 per cent by 2022.

On 5 July 2015, in a national referendum in Greece, voters overwhelmingly rejected austerity package submitted by the institutions. Nonetheless, the Government, which had strongly supported the 'no' vote over the referendum, under the imminent threat of Grexit, reversed course and accepted a third bail-out programme worth up to 86 billion euros, which was voted with by the Greek Parliament on 16 July 2015. The Greek Government accepted, among other measures, to implement tax reforms, cut public spending, privatise state assets and reform labour laws. The IMF did not participate in the third bail-out programme, claiming unsustainability of the Greek debt, which ran contrary to the statutes of this international organisation.

At the time of the economic crisis and in spite of the three financial assistance programmes and the substantial write-down of public debt in 2012, Greece's GDP shrunk by more than 25 per cent. Greece exited the last programme in August 2018, yet severe post-programme surveillance is in place.[51]

C. Ireland

Ireland, albeit the first country to be hit by the financial crisis, was the second euro-area Member State to receive financial assistance through the emergency mechanisms in December 2010 to deal with the crisis erupted predominantly in the banking sector and the property market. It amounted to 67.5 billion euros, ie 22.5 billion euros from the IMF, 22.5 billion euros from the EFSM and 17.7 billion euros from the EFSF, along with bilateral loans from the UK (3.8 billion euros), Sweden (0.6 billion euros) and Denmark (0.4 billion euros). Financial assistance was accompanied by Ireland's own contribution to the package of 17.5 billion euros through the treasury cash buffer and investments of the national pension reserve funds and by an economic adjustment programme for the period 2010–13.

Prior to the crisis, in the decade before 2007, the largest Irish banks developed immensely in relation to their international bond borrowings, overcoming half the country's GDP as a result of a rather offensive banking policy towards the property market. As in other parts of the developed world, primarily in the US,

---

[51] C de Waal, *Beyond the Bail-Outs: The Anthropology and History of the Greek Crisis* (London, Tauris, 2018); A Marketou, 'Greece: Constitutional Deconstruction and the Loss of National Sovereignty' in T Beukers, B de Witte and C Kilpatrick (eds), *Constitutional Change through Euro-Crisis Law* (Cambridge, Cambridge University Press, 2017) 179; MG Arghyrou and J Tsoukalas, 'The Greek Debt Crisis: Likely Causes, Mechanics and Outcomes' (2011) 34 *The World Economy* 173; G Pagoulatos, 'State-Driven in Boom and in Bust: Structural Limitations of Financial Power in Greece' (2014) 49 *Government and Opposition* 452; J Milios and D Sotiropoulos, 'Crisis of Greece or Crisis of the Euro? A View from the "Periphery"' (2010) 12 *Journal of Balkan and Near Eastern Studies* 223.

the property market was in full bloom with very extensive sales and purchases, resulting in a bubble in property pricing and a tremendous total stock of mortgage loans in Ireland, even higher than the level of international bond borrowings.

The economic and financial crisis faced by Ireland in 2008 had serious effects on the financial stability of both the Irish banks and the country in general. This was so because of the relative size of the banking sector compared to the size of the national economy. With the eruption of the crisis and the consequent withdrawal of the international lending markets, the Irish banks suffered a significant liquidity problem to deal with withdrawal requests and faced an imminent risk of insolvency since their assets went very low, due to the decline of the worth of their property against their liabilities.

On 2 October 2008, the Irish Parliament enacted the Credit Institutions (Financial Support) Act 2008, which provided a 440 billion euro state guarantee to six Irish banks for two years for all uncovered retail and corporate deposits, interbank deposits, senior unsecured debt, asset-covered securities and dated subordinated debt, as a temporary support mechanism prior to recapitalisation so as to continue to transfer money to the Irish real economy and prevent possible collapse. It further provided for a very discretionary framework for the involvement of the State in endangered banks, according to which the Minister could provide financial support in respect of the borrowings, liabilities and obligations of any credit institution or subsidiary which the Minister might specify by order having regard to the extent and nature of the obligations undertaken (including the degree of control over possible abuse of the financial support) or which might be undertaken in the future and the relevant resources available to him/her.

Financial support could be provided by individual agreement, a scheme made by the Minister or otherwise, in a form and manner determined by the Minister and on such commercial or other terms and conditions as the Minister might think fit, including conditions regulating the commercial conduct of the credit institution to which the support was provided, and in particular conditions to regulate their competitive behaviour. The Minister might also require the credit institution to fulfil the requirements imposed by the Central Bank or equivalent authority and might subscribe for, take an allotment of or purchase shares and any other securities in a credit institution to which financial support is provided. The Minister might moreover withdraw or revoke financial support provided to a credit institution in accordance with the terms or conditions of the financial support.

Finally, under the Act the Minister was fully entitled to create and issue securities:

(a) bearing interest at any appropriate rate or no interest;
(b) for any cash or non-cash deferred consideration; and
(c) subject to such terms and conditions as to repayment, repurchase, cancellation and redemption or any other matter.

The Government negotiated a deal with the Central Bank of Ireland (CBI), which set out the conditions under which the latter would provide endangered banks with the necessary Emergency Lending Assistance (ELA), provided that permission by the ECB was granted. Finally, Ireland's two largest banks (Bank of Ireland and Allied Irish Bank) were recapitalised with an injection of 3.5 billion euros each. Furthermore, the Minister for Finance issued promissory notes to the value of 31 billion euros to two credit institutions, namely the Irish Bank Resolution Corporation and the Educational Building Society, with a repayment liability of three billion euros per year from the State's budgetary expenditure.

Notwithstanding the measures taken by Ireland to support the banking sector, the markets continued to lose faith in the Irish banks and the financial situation of Ireland continued to deteriorate. In those circumstances, the Irish authorities produced an economic and financial adjustment programme, based on which, on 21 November 2010, they applied for financial assistance to the EFSF and to the IMF. The economic adjustment programme attached to the financial assistance provided for immediate strengthening and comprehensive overhaul of the banking sector, fiscal adjustment to restore fiscal sustainability and to correct excessive deficit by 2015 and growth-enhancing reforms, in particular of the labour market, to facilitate the return to a robust and sustainable growth.

Responding to the above commitments, the Credit Institutions (Stabilisation) Act 2010 was enacted by the Irish Parliament on 21 December 2010 to address the serious, continuing disruption to the economy and the financial systems, the continuing serious threat to the stability of certain credit institutions in the State and the financial system in general, and to implement the reorganisation of credit institutions to achieve the financial stabilisation of those credit institutions and their restructuring in the context of the National Recovery Plan 2011–14 and the EU/IMF Programme of Financial Support for Ireland. The Act provided, inter alia, that the Minister, having consulted with the Governor of the ECB, might issue orders proposing that a credit institution should be directed within a specified period to take or refrain from taking any action, for which the Minister shall apply ex post to the High Court for a 'direction order' (Section 7). The Act explicitly provided that a direction order might include a provision to the effect that any power exercisable by the members of the credit institution concerned in general meeting might be exercised instead by the Minister (Section 47).

Indeed, by Implementing Decision 2011/77, the Council approved the Irish programme and made financial assistance available under the EFSM. On 16 December 2010, Ireland and the Commission entered into a MoU whereby Ireland assumed the responsibility to ensure the reorganisation and recapitalisation of its national banks, on the basis of the results of a Prudential Capital Assessment Review and a Prudential Liquidity Assessment Review published by the Central Bank of Ireland.

Ireland successfully exited its three-year programme in December 2013, after having met the vast majority of policy conditions under the programme and having restored investor confidence in the State and credit institutions. Nonetheless, it remains subject to post-programme surveillance until at least 75 per cent of the financial assistance received has been repaid and, at least, until 2031.[52]

D. Portugal

Portugal was the third country to receive financial assistance through the emergency mechanisms, amounting to 78 billion euros, ie 26 billion euros from the EFSM, 26 billion euros from the EFSF and 26 billion euros from the IMF. The official request for financial assistance was submitted on 7 April 2011. In response to this request an economic adjustment programme was agreed on 17 May 2011 at the Eurogroup/ECOFIN meeting in Brussels, for the period 2011 to mid-2014. Thereafter, in June 2011, three memoranda were signed, and the European Council confirmed the economic and financial adjustment programme for Portugal in its Implementing Decision 2011/344 of 17 May 2011, aiming at recovering the Portuguese economy, restoring confidence in the State and in the banking sector and supporting growth and employment. It provided for deep structural reforms, including fiscal devaluation, reforms of the labour market, the judicial system, network industries, and the housing and services sectors, and for fiscal consolidation strategy, including freezing wages, limiting job promotions, reducing high-paid state pensions, increasing sales tax on certain items, privatising public companies and limiting the duration of unemployment benefits.

In the course of implementation of the programme, the Government introduced, inter alia, the following Bills:

(a) Budget Laws for the years 2011 and onwards, introducing significant salary and pension cuts along with other austerity measures significantly affecting the status of employees, especially those engaged in the public sector;
(b) a number of amendments to the Labour Code and other employment statutes (eg Law No 75/2014); and
(c) Bill 177/XXII on the process of 'requalification of public sector' employees, facilitating redundancies, as a substitute to the original mobility scheme that was frustrated, allowing surplus public employees to be included in a list for placement for a maximum of 12 months, at the end of which they could choose to remain, without remuneration, on the waiting list for a possible placement or select termination of employment and, potentially, unemployment benefits.

---

[52] International Monetary Fund, *Ireland: Lessons from its Recovery from the Bank-Sovereign Loop* (Washington, IMF, 2016); S Coutts, 'Ireland: Traditional Procedures adapted for Economic Emergency' in T Beukers, B de Witte and C Kilpatrick (eds), *Constitutional Change through Euro-Crisis Law* (Cambridge, Cambridge University Press, 2017) 230; KPV O'Sullivan and T Kennedy, 'What Caused the Irish Banking Crisis? (2010) 18 *Journal of Financial Regulation and Compliance* 224; K Cardiff, *Recap: Inside Ireland's Financial Crisis* (Dublin, The Liffey Press, 2016).

Furthermore, it provided for the change of legal status of certain public servants appointed to established posts in the public sector and guaranteed the holding of their posts to employees working on an employment contract with fewer guarantees of permanency.

In June 2014, Portugal successfully exited its three-year economic adjustment programme and was put under post-programme surveillance until at least 75 per cent of the financial assistance received has been repaid, which is expected to last until 2035.[53]

E. Cyprus

Cyprus was the fourth country to receive financial assistance through the emergency mechanisms in 2012–13 to deal with the imminent crisis erupted predominantly in the banking sector. It amounted to 10 billion euros, among which nine billion were covered by the ESM and one billion by the IMF. Financial assistance was accompanied by an economic adjustment programme for the period 2013–16.

Prior to the financial crisis, the banking sector in Cyprus experienced a tremendous boom with a very high percentage of deposits. During the first few months of 2012, certain banks established in Cyprus, including Laïki *[Popular]* Bank and Bank of Cyprus, encountered financial difficulties. On 25 June 2012, Cyprus requested before the Eurogroup financial assistance from the EFSF or the ESM to recapitalise endangered banks. In a statement dated 27 June 2012, the Eurogroup indicated that the financial assistance requested would be provided by the EFSF or the ESM in the framework of a macro-economic adjustment programme to be negotiated between the Cypriot Government and the Commission, the ECB and the IMF. An agreement was reached in March 2013, including the essentials of the economic adjustment programme attached to the financial assistance, and was welcomed by a Eurogroup statement on 16 March 2013.

Two days later, Cyprus declared bank holidays on 19 and 20 March 2013; this was eventually extended until 28 March 2013. During the suspension of the functioning of the banks and following a rejection by the Cypriot Parliament of a bill relating to the introduction of a levy on all bank deposits in Cyprus, the Law of 22 March 2013 was enacted, whereby the Central Bank of Cyprus was entrusted, together with the Ministry of Finance, with the resolution of the institutions covered by that law. The law also gave authorisation to the Central Bank, by decree, to mandate restructuring of the debts and obligations of an institution under resolution, including by means of the reduction, modification, rescheduling or renewal of the principal or outstanding amount of any type of claim, existing or future, against that institution, or by means of a conversion of debt instruments

[53] J Rodrigues and J Reis, 'The Asymmetries of European Integration and the Crisis of Capitalism in Portugal' (2012) 16 *Competition and Change* 188; O Blanchard, 'Adjustment within the Euro: The Difficult case of Portugal' (2007) *Portuguese Economic Journal* 1.

or obligations into equity. In addition, this law provided that deposits of up to 100,000 euros were insured, and were thus excluded from the above measures.

By Decrees No 103 and No 104 of 29 March 2013, the Bank of Cyprus and Laïki Bank were officially put into resolution. On 24 April 2013, the ESM's Board of Governors decided to grant stability support to Cyprus in the form of a financial assistance facility and approved the negotiated draft MoU. On 26 April 2013, the MoU was signed by the Commission, specifically mandated for that purpose by the ESM, the Minister for Finance of Cyprus and the Governor of the Central Bank of Cyprus. On 8 May 2013, the ESM's Board of Directors approved the agreement relating to the financial assistance facility.

The economic adjustment programme involved a series of financial, fiscal and structural reforms in the country with a view:

(a) to restructure credit institutions, strengthen supervision and address expected capital shortfalls;
(b) to correct the excessive government deficit through measures to reduce current primary expenditure and maintain fiscal consolidation through increase of the efficiency of public spending, enhancement of revenue collection and improvement of the functioning of the public sector; and
(c) to support competitiveness and sustainable and balanced growth through a wage indexation system and the removal of obstacles to the functioning of services markets.

In essence, the impugned scheme essentially involved taking over, by Bank of Cyprus, of Laïki Bank's insured deposits, for the conversion of 37.5 per cent of Bank of Cyprus's uninsured deposits into shares with full voting and dividend rights, and for the temporary freezing of another part of those uninsured deposits, with a provisional buy-back of shares.

In March 2016, Cyprus successfully exited its three-year economic adjustment programme by restoring financial stability, improving public finances and reinstating sustainable economic growth. Cyprus is subject to post-programme surveillance until at least 75 per cent of the financial assistance received has been repaid and in any case until 2029.[54]

F. Spain

Spain was the fifth country to receive financial assistance through the emergency mechanisms for the period 2012–13 to deal with the crisis erupted predominantly in the housing market. It amounted to 41.33 billion euros covered by the ESM.

[54] P Demetriades, *Diary of the Euro Crisis in Cyprus: Lessons for Bank Recovery and Resolution* (Cham, Springer, 2017); J Theodore and J Theodore, *Cyprus and the Financial Crisis: The Controversial Bail-Out and what it Means for the Eurozone* (London, Palgrave Macmillan, 2015); A Michaelides and A Orphanides (eds), *The Cyprus Bail-In: Policy Lessons from the Cyprus Economic Crisis* (London, Imperial College Press, 2016); SA Zenios, 'Fairness and Reflexivity in the Cyprus Bail-In' (2016) 43 *Empirica* 579; A. Michaelides, 'Cyprus: From Boom to Bail-In' (2014) 29 *Economic Policy* 639.

Prior to the crisis, in 2011, as was also the case in other countries in a similar situation, the country enjoyed a tremendous property boom, great growth rates, excessive credit expansion by banks, very low unemployment rates and a strong domestic construction industry. With the emergence of the crisis, property prices dropped significantly, while mortgages remained unpaid to a large extent; this resulted in credit institutions suffering exorbitant losses, with an increase in the government deficit as a collateral effect.

Because of the unstable banking system market, money became rather expensive and the Spanish authorities requested financial assistance for the recapitalisation of the banking sector on 25 June 2012. On 20 July 2012, the Eurogroup approved assistance for up to 100 billion euros and conditionality regarding the reform in the Spanish banking sector. This assistance programme had some particular characteristics in relation to other bail-out programmes in Europe: the amount was smaller in relation to the size of the domestic economy; the money aimed to assist only the restructuring of the country's banks through the government's intervention; the only creditor was the ESM; and the programme only lasted 18 months.

Spain successfully exited its programme in December 2013, after having restructured the savings banks sector, not only through recapitalisation but also through regulation that aimed to increase the level of accountability in the administration of savings banks, so as to refocus their business models on retail and small and medium enterprise lending. In the same period, state access to private funding markets became easier, bank deposits were rising and the country regained international competitiveness. Yet, the ESM will monitor Spain through post-programme surveillance, without any new conditionality, until the loan has been fully repaid in 2027.[55]

---

[55] L Sanchez, 'Spain: Dealing with the Economic Emergency through Constitutional Reform and Limited Parliamentary Intervention' in T Beukers, B de Witte and C Kilpatrick (eds), *Constitutional Change through Euro-Crisis Law* (Cambridge, Cambridge University Press, 2017) 199; F Carballo-Cruz, 'Causes and Consequences of the Spanish Economic Crisis: Why the Recovery is [sic] Taken so Long?' (2011) 3 *Panoeconomicus* 309; S Royo, 'Lessons from the Economic Cfrisis in Spain' (New York, Palgrave Macmillan, 2013).

3

Impact of New Economic Constitutionalism on Constitutional Interpretation

The most spectacular change in the era of new economic constitutionalism has been the change in constitutional interpretation due to the omnipresence of financialism. From the perspective of EU law, this phenomenon has been as transformations in the basic rules of EU economic constitution, reflecting the acceptance of financial assistance to euro-area Member States and the replacement of market discipline of domestic economies by bureaucratic discipline.[1] From the point of view of domestic constitutional orders, this phenomenon reflects a significant concession of the domestic sovereignty and the rule of law so as to safeguard the overriding effect of stability. This chapter presents the case law produced in the context of the financial crisis (see section I below) and an analysis of the shift in case law regarding the human rights' doctrine, in particular the case of property (section II).

I. The Financial Crisis Case Law

The financial crisis case law is presented on the basis of two criteria. The first criterion is geographic and reflects the judicial attitudes in particular legal orders. The second concerns the specific material issues that dominated the case law in each particular geographic territory, such as institutional building (in the EU), social state decrease as a collateral to financial assistance prior to the establishment of EU mechanisms (in Hungary, Latvia and Romania), salary and pension cuts as a result of bail-out and the relevant conditionality (in Greece and Portugal), government bonds and bank deposit cuts as a result of bail-in schemes (in Greece and Cyprus) and shareholders' rights as a result of bank recapitalisation schemes (in Ireland). The distinctive classification of the relevant case law is necessary for a better understanding of the analysis regarding the change of constitutional

---

[1] M Ioannidis, 'Europe's New Transformations: How the EU Economic Constitution has Changed during the Eurozone Crisis' (2013) 53 *Common Market Law Review* 1237.

paradigm that follows. Obviously other legal systems have also been affected by the financial crisis, yet the above-mentioned countries seem to present the strongest characteristics of a reversal of the case law.[2] The presentation of the relevant case law is made on three levels, ie domestic case law, EU case law and the ECtHR case law.

A. EU and Euro-area Institution Building

i. Domestic Courts

National courts of the euro-area Member States were called upon to respond to various challenges against new financial assistance mechanisms and their implications on EU and/or the Member States. A first category of grounds were national law-related: whether domestic constitutional processes and division of competences were respected in the financial assistance decisions taken mostly inter-governmentally; whether the requirement that the Fiscal Compact be transposed to domestic law, preferably through constitutional amendment, amounted to a bypass of the constitutional revision processes; and whether conditionality clauses (mostly austerity measures and resolution of credit institutions) amounted to constitutional human rights violations.

A second category of grounds were EU-related: whether the EU and the EU institutions enjoyed the competence to introduce relevant financial tools; whether an amendment to launch rescue mechanisms through simplified procedures amounted to a Treaty procedural violation; whether financial assistance tools were compatible with the EU Treaties prohibiting specific activities, mostly the Member States' bail-out or state aid; whether resolution of credit institutions violated EU law on the administration of companies; and whether measures stemming from national measures, usually via conditionality clauses, amounted to human rights violations under EU law. A third category of grounds were ECHR-related.

a. Germany

The most active domestic court in the crisis era has been the German Federal Constitutional Court (*Bundesverfassungsgericht – BVerfG*), which issued three sets of two decisions each: two judgments relating to the procedural rights of the German Lower House (*Bundestag*) on European affairs; two relating to the substantive competence of the Parliament concerning financial assistance to

---

[2] Eg, for Spain, see A Ruiz Robledo, 'The Spanish Constitution in the Turmoil of the Global Financial Crisis' in X Contiades, (ed), *Constitutions in the Global Financial Crisis: A Comparative Analysis* (Farnham, Ashgate, 2013) 141.

Greece and ratification of the new crisis treaties; and three on EU competence claim concerning the compatibility of the OMT and PSPP programmes to EU primary law.[3]

In relation to the first set of judgments, the Court held in Judgment of 28 February 2012 (the ESM Treaty case),[4] on domestic constitutional process ground, that the transfer of the competence to review European state aids to a nine-member parliamentary sub-committee, as opposed to the plenary, was unconstitutional on the ground of the principle of representative democracy (Article 38.1 of the Basic Law). The Court drew from this fundamental constitutional principle a guarantee that every MP individually enjoyed both freedom in the exercise of their mandate and equal status against each other as a representative of the entire people, unless differentiations were justified by a compelling constitutional clause. In the light of the above, the Court declared that the German *Bundestag* exercised its function, especially to matters pertaining to the budget and its overall budgetary responsibility, as a body of representation in its entirety and through the participation of all its Members in debates and decision-making, not through individual Members, a group of Members or the parliamentary majority. Accordingly, transfer of decisive competencies to a parliamentary committee could only be tolerated if, cumulatively, it served a public interest of constitutional rank and the principle of proportionality was strictly observed, which was not the case on the merits of the impugned Act on the Assumption of Guarantees in Connection with ESM (Article 3(3) ESM Treaty).

In Judgment of 19 June 2012 (the ESM and Euro Plus Pact case),[5] again on domestic constitutional process claims, the Court emphatically ensured the right of the national Parliament to be effectively informed on EU matters pursuant to the constitutional clauses that:

(a)   the Bundestag and, through the Bundesrat, the Länder shall participate in matters concerning the EU (Article 23(2) first sentence);
(b)   the Federal Government shall notify the Bundestag of such matters comprehensively and at the earliest possible date (Article 23(2) second sentence); and
(c)   before participating in EU legislative acts, the Federal Government shall provide ex ante the Bundestag with an opportunity to state its position and ex post take it into account throughout the negotiations (Article 23(3)).

First, in relation to the *nature* of the impugned act, ie the issue of whether the ESM constituted an EU matter triggering the above participation right of the *Bundestag*, the Court estimated that EU matters included not only EU legislation, but also agreements under international law if they supplemented or stood

---

[3] PM Huber, 'The Rescue of the Euro and its Constitutionality' in W-G Ringe and PM Huber (eds), *Legal Challenges in the Global Financial Crisis: Bail-outs, the Euro and Regulation*, (Oxford, Hart Publishing, 2015) 9; P Eleftheriadis, 'The Euro and the German Courts' (2012) 128 *Law Quarterly Review* 216.

[4] 2 BvE 8/11.

[5] 2 BvE 4/11.

in another particular proximity to EU law on account of their contents: the more complex a matter was, the more deeply it intervened in the sphere of competences of the legislature and the more it resembled a formal resolution or agreement, thus giving rise to requirements as to the quality, quantity and timeliness of the information that ought to be furnished to the legislature.

Second, in relation to the *quality and quantity* of the evidence that ought to be provided, the Court ruled that objective information of the Parliament was intended to enable it to exercise effectively its constitutional right of participation.

Third, in relation to the *time* of submission of relevant information, the Court held that the *Bundestag* must receive the information from the Federal Government at the latest at a time which it enabled it to consider the matter in depth and to prepare an opinion before the executive makes binding declarations on legislative acts of the EU and intergovernmental agreements.

Fourth, in relation to the *restrictions* of the parliamentary right of participation, the Court accepted that limits to the obligation to inform the House might derive from the principle of the separation of powers, especially the confidentiality of the Government's core executive responsibility, including initiative, consultation and action which was generally confidential; therefore, there was no right of information at the stage prior to conclusion of the executive deliberation of the matter in question, but once the policy was concluded.

In the light of the above, the Court held that the Federal Government violated the rights of the German Bundestag by failing to:

(a) inform it directly before and after the meeting of the European Council of 4 February 2011 timely and comprehensively about the structuring of the ESM and, in particular, by failing to send the draft of the ESM Treaty prior to the publication of the Council Decision of 25 March 2011 at the latest;

(b) inform the *Bundestag* before the above meeting of the European Council of the initiative of the Federal Chancellor for a closer economic policy coordination of the euro-area Member States; and

(c) inform the *Bundestag* timely and comprehensively that the Heads of Governments and States decided to launch the Euro Plus Pact (ie an interim intergovernmental tool to increase fiscal and economic discipline in the Member States and stabilise the euro area).

In relation to the second set of cases, Judgment of 7 September 2011 (the EFSF and First Adjustment Programme for Greece case)[6] was rendered responding to three constitutional complaints against a statute to implement the EFSF and to allow the payment of an emergency loan for the financial assistance to Greece, claiming violation of the right of the Bundestag to make decisions about the budget and, therefore, an interference with the right to democracy. The Court dismissed the appeal but affirmed that any large amount of financial assistance

---

[6] Joined Cases 2 BvR 987/10, 2 BvR 1485/10, 2 BvR 1099/10.

had to be approved by Parliament as the forum of democratic legitimacy, thus requiring an interpretation of the relevant legislation as imposing prior involvement of the Parliament on every decision by the Federal Government to accord financial guarantees under the EFSF.

Once again, the focal point for the Court was representative democracy, and for the first time in such explicit terms, the citizens' constitutional right to elect the Bundestag (Article 38(1)). In the Court's view, this fundamental right would suffer from a loss of substance of the citizens' power to rule, if competences belonging to the domestic present or future Parliament were transferred to supranational institutions, thus rendering *de jure* or *de facto* impossible the materialisation of the political will of the citizens through representation. The Court placed special emphasis on the assertion that decisions on public revenue and public expenditure, including a system of intergovernmental administration, constituted a key function of popular will in order for the representatives to remain accountable to citizens and for adequate information to be diffused to allow for an informed electorate. In that regard, the Court declared that the *Bundestag* might not transfer its budgetary responsibility to any mechanisms which might decide in favour of exorbitant burdens without prior explicit legislative consent. Thus, any large-scale financial assistance of the Federal Government taken in a spirit of solidarity and involving public expenditure on an international or EU level must be specifically approved by the Parliament, while at the same time sufficient parliamentary influence on the manner in which the funds made available are dealt with must be secured, otherwise the budgetary autonomy of the Parliament would be curtailed.

In the light of the above, the Court upheld the financial assistance to Greece, as not exceeding the boundaries of budgetary autonomy of the Parliament, but explicitly required the German Government to accompany its ratification of the ESM Treaty with two declarations under international law clarifying that nothing in the Treaty could be interpreted as increasing the share of Germany to the ESM capital without the approval of the *Bundestag* or as depriving the *Bundestag* of the right to obtain all information about the internal functioning of the ESM.

In Judgment of 12 September 2012 (the ESM and Fiscal treaty case),[7] applications were lodged by a history record of plaintiffs (76 MPs, left-wing political party *Die Linke*, professors of Economics and 41,000 citizens) requesting an interim injunction essentially to prohibit the Federal President from signing the statutes passed by the two Houses of Parliament on 29 June 2012, thus preventing the ratification of the ESM Treaty and the TSCG, until a decision is rendered in the principal proceedings. The Court dismissed the remedy but gave very strict guidance to the effect that the *Bundestag*:

(a) must retain control of fundamental budgetary decisions even in a system of intergovernmental governance;

[7] 2 BvR 1390/12.

(b)   should not agree to European financial mechanisms which may result in incalculable burdens with budget significance without prior mandatory consent;

(c)   ought to make its decisions on budget revenue and expenditure free of other-directedness by the EU institutions or the authorities of other Member States so as to remain permanently the master of its decisions;

(d)   must individually, rather than *in globo*, approve large-scale federal aid measures on the international or EU level, made in solidarity and resulting in expenditure; and

(e)   ought to be able to have access to the information needed to exercise its budgetary competence.

Finally, the last set of decisions (EU institutions' competences) related to the validity of decisions of the ECB's Governing Council on OMTs and PSPP plans. In Order of 14 January 2014,[8] the Court, for the first time in its 65-year history, made a reference for a preliminary ruling to the Court of Justice, conveying significant concerns on the mechanism in question as to whether it fell within the ambit of the competences of the ECB as explicitly specified in the Treaties. The judicial proceedings were initiated through various constitutional actions brought by several groups of individuals, including a group supported by more than 11.000 signatories, and the left political party *Die Linke*, in respect of an alleged failure of the Federal Government and the Lower House to act with regard to those decisions, and an application, in dispute resolution proceedings between constitutional bodies.

The applicants submitted that:

(a)   the OMT decisions constituted, overall, an ultra vires act in as much as they were not covered by the mandate of the ECB and infringed Article 123 TFEU on the prohibition to furnish overdraft facilities or any other type of credit facility; and

(b)   those decisions breached the principle of democracy entrenched in the Constitution and thereby impair German constitutional identity.

The Court expressed strong concerns as to the validity of the impugned acts and noted that the mandate assigned to the ECB must be strictly limited in order to meet the democratic requirements. With regard to the extent of judicial review, the Court declared that compliance with the limits concerned must be subject to comprehensive judicial review pursuant to the principle of conferral of powers and that in accordance with the Court of Justice's case law the independence of the ECB did not preclude such review, since that independence related only to the powers that the Treaties confer on the ECB, but not to the definition of the extent and scope of its mandate. The Court confirmed the standing of the applicants

---

[8] 2 BvR 2728/13.

by stating that even if the impugned decisions were to be regarded as merely declaratory, ie an announcement of the adoption of future acts, that would not in itself render the application inadmissible, since preventive legal protection might be necessary in order to avoid irreparable consequences.

The relevant reference for a preliminary ruling involved an extremely elaborate set of questions which essentially amounted to the question of validity of the ECB's Governing Council's OMTs policy embodied into the press release of 6 September 2012 as:

(a) violating Articles 119, 127(1) and (2) TFEU and Articles 17 to 24 of the Protocol on the ESCB and the ECB, by exceeding the monetary policy mandate of the ECB and encroaching upon the competence of the Member States, in particular, as linked to economic assistance programmes of the EFSF or of the ESM (conditionality), as provided for the purchase of government bonds of selected Member States only (selectivity), as provided for the purchase of government bonds of programme countries in addition to assistance programmes of the EFSF or of the ESM (parallelism) and as undermining the limits and conditions laid down by assistance programmes of the EFSF or of the ESM (circumvention); and

(b) violating Article 123 TFEU, ie the prohibition of monetary financing of Member States, given that it did not provide for quantitative limits for government bond purchases (volume), it did not provide for a time gap between the issue of government bonds on the primary market and their purchase by the ESCB on the secondary market (market pricing), it allowed all purchased government bonds to be held to maturity (interference with market logic), it did not contain any specific requirements for the credit standing of the government bonds to be purchased (default risk) and it provided for the same treatment of the ESCB as private or other holders of government bonds (debt cut).

The Court also submitted 10 additional questions of interpretation in the event that the Court of Justice did not consider the impugned decision to be admissible for a preliminary ruling. Overall, the Court expressed the view that Article 123 TFEU explicitly prohibited the ECB from acquiring government bonds directly, which would essentially be tantamount to monetary financing and found that the policy was ultra vires on EU law grounds by resulting in the ECB designing economic (as opposed to strictly monetary) policy due to its direct link to the ESM and the EFSM and its lack of generality due to selective application to countries receiving financial assistance.[9]

After the decision of the Court of Justice affirming the validity of the ECB policy in C-62/14 *Gauweiler and others*, the case went back to the German Constitutional

[9] M Wendel 'Exceeding Judicial Competence in the Name of Democracy: The German Federal Constitutional Court's OMT reference' (2014) 10 *European Constitutional Law Review* 263; J Bast,

Court for final judgment. That Court upheld the ruling of the Court of Justice in Judgment of 21 June 2016.[10] Accordingly, it allowed the German Central Bank (*Bundesbank*) to participate in a future implementation of the OMT programme, insofar as the prerequisites set out by the Court of Justice in *Gauweiler* were met, ie if (cumulatively):

(a) purchases were not announced;
(b) the volume of the purchases was limited from the outset;
(c) there was a minimum period between the issuing of the government bonds and their purchase by the ESCB that is defined from the outset and prevents the issuing conditions from being distorted;
(d) only government bonds of Member States are purchased that have bond market access enabling the funding of such bonds;
(e) purchased bonds were held until maturity only in exceptional cases; and
(f) purchases were restricted or ceased and purchased bonds are remarketed should the continuing intervention become unnecessary.

Obviously, the domestic Court withdrew its particularly strict line of argumentation in the first referring judgment, but insisted on the conditions that ought to be met for the policy to be compatible with the national Constitution in order to secure the integrity of its decision-making, thus considering that a fair judicial compromise was made in order to safeguard its prestige and the integrity of its case law.

Finally, stakeholders brought constitutional actions before the Constitutional Court following on the ground that the decision on the PSPP for the purchase of government bonds on secondary markets introduced by the ECB and subsequent extensions went beyond the powers of the EU institutions. The applicants submitted that the German Federal Central Bank ought not to participate in the asset purchase programme and that the Federal Government and the Central Bank were obliged to take suitable measures against the challenged programme. In Order of 18 July 2017,[11] the Court identified violation of the prohibition of monetary financing and excess of the monetary policy mandate of the ECB over Member States sovereign powers, ie violation of the principle of conferred powers and of the prohibition of monetary financing and referred a number of questions to the Court of Justice on the compatibility of the programme with the EU law, further requesting an expedited procedure pursuant to Article 105 of the Rules of Procedure of the Court of Justice as the nature of the case arguably required that it be dealt with within a short time.

'Don't Act Beyond your Powers: The Perils and Pitfalls of the German Constitutional Court's Ultra Vires Review' (2014) 15 *German Law Journal* 167; FC Mayer, 'Rebels without a Cause? A Critical Analysis of the German Constitutional Court's OMT Reference' (2014) 15 *German Law Journal* 111.
[10] 2 BvR 2728/13.
[11] 2 BvR 859/15, 2 BvR 980/16, 2 BvR 2006/15, 2 BvR 1651/15.

b. Poland

In 2010, the Constitutional Tribunal of Poland rendered its judgment on the constitutionality of the Treaty of Lisbon on an application by a group of Members of the Lower House (*Sejm*) and the Upper House (Senate), as violating fundamental aspects of the Constitution, such as the relationship between the State and international organisations in conjunction with the democratic principle, sovereignty and constitutional supremacy (Articles 90, 2, 4 and Article 8 and Preamble to the Constitution), in the absence of national statutory regulations stipulating the participation of the domestic Houses in the process of determining the national stance in every case of possible adoption of legal acts by the EU institutions.[12] Although the case is not directly related to the crisis case law, it is one of the most elaborate judgments rendered by national courts in relation to key issues raised in the context of the economic crisis concerning national sovereignty, especially through domestic parliaments' involvement in key decisions rendered by the EU institutions and affecting national policies; it constituted the basis for the subsequent judgment concerning the ratification of the stability mechanism.

As regards the preservation of state sovereignty vis-a-vis the Union, the Court held that since the transfer of competences to the EU institutions was not irrevocable, the relations between exclusive and shared competences had a dynamic character and the Member States merely assumed the obligation to jointly conduct state duties in areas of cooperation, while, since they retained *Kompetenz-Kompetenz*, they remained sovereign subjects in the light of international law.

The Tribunal held that the domestic Constitution merely allowed for such transfer upon express consent by the Polish Parliament or by way of national referendum, on certain matters, which meant a prohibition to confer all the competences of a domestic institution, to confer competences in relation to all matters of a sector and to confer core competences of a state organ. Accordingly, if such transfer of powers required a constitutional amendment, the national Parliament should make a decision to that effect or amend EU regulations, or ultimately withdraw from the Union altogether, since, in the context of EU membership, national sovereignty meant the absolute power of the Polish nation to determine its own fate; the normative manifestation of this is the constitutional identity of the State, enshrined in the inalienable competences of its organs. Core issues pertaining to the constitutional identity of the State were, therefore, excluded from the power to confer competences.

With regard to accession to the EU, a relevant limitation of national sovereignty was compensated, in the Court's view, by the right of the Member State to take part in the EU decision-making. Especially in relation to the Treaty of Lisbon providing for amendment of the Treaties outside the ordinary revision procedure, last resort unanimity operated as a guarantee of respect for the sovereignty of the

---

[12] Polish Constitutional Tribunal Judgment of 24 November 2010, K 32/09.

Members States, to some extent manifested in the early-warning process reserved for the domestic Parliaments. Accordingly, the Parliament reserved a critical mass of intervention in the formation of EU law: primary law amendments ought to be approved by all Member States; national Parliaments (both Houses, if this is the case, such as in Poland) must be notified about the proposals for applying the ordinary revision procedure of the Treaties; under the ordinary revision procedure, representatives of the national Parliaments take part in the Convention composed by the European Council to adopt recommendations and every House has a guaranteed right to vote in the event of a decision not to convene a Convention; and, finally, secondary law is created with the participation of the representatives of governments of the Member States in the Council and in the European Parliament, with the express requirement of the Protocol on the role of national parliaments that they ought to express their views on draft legislative acts of the Union.

It is, therefore, for the Polish Parliament to:

(a)   decide to what extent and for the implementation of which European policies, as well as with what intensity, and what consequences, it will make use of the possibilities provided for in the Treaty of Lisbon; and

(b)   devise appropriate solutions and requirements concerning the fulfillment of constitutional requirements akin to the protection of the State's sovereignty in the process of European integration so as to prevent conflicts between the Government and the Parliament.

The Tribunal placed particular emphasis on the Polish Cooperation Act on cooperation of the Council of Ministers with the Houses of Parliament in matters related to the membership of the country to the EU (posterior to the application lodged to the Tribunal), providing that the Council ought to submit the draft acts to the *Sejm* and the Senate before the position is adopted and there is a duty of consultation with the appropriate authority in the two Houses. With this rationale, the Tribunal eventually found that the provisions of the Treaty of Lisbon were compatible with the Polish Constitution, yet acknowledging that parliamentary competences associated with national sovereignty could not be curtailed in the EU context.[13]

A most relevant case for the purpose of the present analysis is, for obvious reasons, the Judgment of the Constitutional Tribunal in 2012 concerning the procedure for the ratification of Council Decision 2011/199.[14] The application was filed by a group of *Sejm* Deputies alleging violation of the process for conceding competences to international organisations in conjunction with the internal

---

[13] K Budziło (ed), *Selected Rulings of the Polish Constitutional Tribunal Concerning the Law of the European Union – 2003–2014*, Studia i Materiały Trybunału Konstytucyjnego (Warsaw, Biuro Trybunału Konstytucyjnego, 2014) 192, available at http://trybunal.gov.pl/uploads/media/SiM_LI_EN_calosc.pdf.

[14] Polish Constitutional Tribunal Judgment of 26 June 2013, K 33/12.

parliamentary proceedings of the Lower House, the process for promulgation of domestic laws, the competences of the Council of Ministers and the process for adopting state budget (Articles 88, 90, 120, 146 and 219 of the Constitution). The basic premise of the Tribunal, largely relying on the Treaty of Lisbon ruling, was that the constitutional clause allowing for transfer of powers to international organisations could not include core competences that would prevent Poland from functioning as a sovereign and democratic State. The Tribunal held that the dynamic system of the EU was reflected in the simplified revision procedure provided by the impugned act, only in the cases where this does not lead to an increase of Union competences, which would require ratification of a new international agreement by the Polish Parliament.

As regards the EU competence issue, the Tribunal, adhering to the then recent Court of Justice Judgment on *Pringle*,[15] held that it merely confirmed the competence of the Member States to establish a stability mechanism, whereas the Union itself was granted no new competences. The Tribunal refrained from rendering a ruling on the compatibility of the ESM Treaty with the Constitution, since, at that moment, Poland was neither a signatory to the Treaty nor had it commenced the ratification process. Yet, it made an obiter statement to the effect that a decision to join the euro area and to adopt the ESM Treaty might require a constitutional amendment with regard to the position of the National Bank and the Tribunal of State (the Court examining liability of high state officials) and, in any case, the ratification of such Treaty would require prior consent granted by statute on the ground of special constitutional proceedings reserved for international agreements entailing, inter alia, membership to an international organisation or considerable financial responsibilities imposed on the State (Article 89(1) ESM Treaty).[16]

c. France

In France, the Constitutional Council held, in a rather laconic judgment of 9 August 2012,[17] that the Fiscal Compact, especially the budgetary constraints thereof, did not require a constitutional change, hence validating accession of France to the TSCG. The Constitutional Council was seised by the President of the Republic on 13 July 2012, in accordance with Article 54 of the Constitution, in order to answer the question as to whether the authorisation to ratify the TSCG required a constitutional amendment to that effect.

As to the substance of the Treaty, the Council held, first of all, that the State had already been bound by rules of budgetary discipline under the TFEU and Protocol No 12, thus the introduction of new thresholds concerning balanced budgets and debt ceilings did not affect the essential conditions for the exercise of national

---

[15] Below section B ii.
[16] Budziło, *Selected Rulings* (2014) 295.
[17] 2012-653 DC.

sovereignty. As to the requirement that the Fiscal Compact clauses be transposed into domestic law through binding and permanent provisions, preferably constitutional, the Council made references to Article 55 of the French Constitution, providing that Treaties or agreements duly ratified or approved shall, upon publication, prevail over Acts of Parliament, and, therefore, once France has ratified the TSCG and it has entered into force, its substantive rules were directly applicable and prevailed over any contrary statutory provision, thus the legislator ought to respect those stipulations when adopting budget and social security laws.

Yet, the Council noticed that if the State opted for implementing such rules through binding and permanent provisions, a constitutional revision would be required, since prerogatives of the Government and the Parliament concerning fiscal and budget laws would be affected. The Council made particular reference to the nature of organic laws in the context of French constitutional law, setting the framework for programming laws relating to multi-year public finance guidelines, finance and social security laws. Moreover, it instructed the legislature to include – in order to comply with the requirements of the Fiscal Compact the medium-term objective and the adjustment path of the general government fiscal position – the correctional mechanism of the general government and the independent institutions operating throughout the budget process concerning compliance with the balanced budget rules and, where appropriate, the automatic correction mechanism.

Interestingly, in an obiter dictum, the Council stressed the point that in the future it would take into account the opinions rendered by the independent financial authorities when controlling the conformity of relevant legislation with the Constitution, in particular to assess whether the principle of sincerity (*principe de sincérité*) of budget laws is respected. Furthermore, the Council made the point that Article 8 of the TSCG, establishing the jurisdiction of the Court of Justice to exercise a controlling function on the fulfillment of the requirements of the Fiscal Compact, did not undermine the essential conditions for the exercise of national sovereignty. Thus, it concluded that an organic law would suffice to transpose the substantive commitments assumed by the Compact and no constitutional amendment was necessary to authorise ratification of the TSCG.[18]

d. Belgium

In Judgment 62/2016 of 28 April 2016, the Constitutional Court of Belgium ruled on a case brought by citizens and non-profit organisations against various acts of the federal and the Flemish Parliament, which approved the TSCG. Given the particularities of the Belgian federal system, the main problem was to ensure that

---

[18] S Pierré-Caps, 'Le Conseil Constitutionnel et la Stabilité Economico-Financière' (2013) 30 *Civitas Europa* 145; X Magnon, 'Décision n° 2012-653 DC du 9 août 2012, Traité sur la Stabilité, la Coordination et la Gouvernance au sein de l'Union Economique et Monétaire' (2012) 92 *Revue française de droit constitutionnel* 860.

all state layers would abide by the balanced budget rule, given that the overall budget of Belgium in the European Semester is composed separately for the federal State and for its regions and communities, with political coordination but without any formal legal mechanism to resolve disputes. The option advanced was to introduce a cooperation agreement between state actors that would rank above ordinary law and would ensure compliance with budgetary rules by local governments.

The most relevant ground of annulment was that the adopted Fiscal Compact deprived domestic institutions of exercising their competence to safeguard fundamental social rights according to the Belgian Constitution. In essence, the Court, although having declared that under no circumstances can the national identity inherent to the fundamental, political and constitutional structures or to the fundamental rights be undermined, found no violation of the principles of representative democracy. The reasoning of the Court was that although admittedly the Fiscal Compact set out detailed budgetary restrictions and monitoring process by the EU institutions and proposed, without strictly requiring it, constitutional embodiment of the balanced budget rule (Article 3(2)), the domestic House of Representatives remained the sole competent body to draft and implement every year at its full discretion the budget, in which all State accounts and expenditure must be included, whereas the national Constitution explicitly provides that the exercise of specific powers can be assigned by treaty or by law to institutions of public international law (Articles 174 and 34 of the Constitution respectively). Eventually, the Court held the application inadmissible because there was no direct causal link between the parliamentary acts and the damage suffered by the applicants, because of the possibility of future imposition of burdens as a result of the Fiscal Compact.[19]

e. Estonia

Perhaps the most elaborate judgment on most of the issues relating to the new architecture of economic governance in Europe was provided by the Supreme Court of Estonia in its Judgment of 12 July 2012.[20] In that decision the Court found no violation of the constitutional principle of parliamentary democracy in the provisions of the ESM Treaty which in effect diluted the national voting share by introducing, by way of derogation to the ordinary unanimity-based decision-making, the possibility to resort to an emergency voting procedure (requiring a qualified majority of 85 per cent of the votes cast by the Board of Directors of the ESM), when failure to urgently adopt a decision to grant or implement financial

---

[19] P Gérard and W Verrijdt, 'Belgian Constitutional Court Adopts National Identity Discourse: Belgian Constitutional Court No 62/2016, 28 April 2016' (2017) 13 *European Constitutional Law Review* 182.

[20] No 3-4-1-6-12.

assistance would threaten the economic and financial sustainability of the euro area (Article 4(4) ESM).

Interestingly, the Court was convened on a request by the Chancellor of Justice, pursuant to the competence attributed by the Constitution of Estonia to challenge international agreements in order to guarantee that Estonia would not enter into international agreements which would be in conflict with the Constitution. The submissions of the Chancellor of Justice broadly referred to the constitutional division of powers and the EU competence and hierarchy of norms. The constitutional claim was that the Treaty interfered with the principles of parliamentary democracy, especially with the exclusive budgetary powers of the Parliament. The Chancellor had recourse to the essence of parliamentary democracy as embodying the chain of legitimacy and political responsibility, where the executive power ought to be liable to the Parliament and the Parliament, in turn, to the people, in whom the supreme authority is vested.

In advancing this argument, the Chancellor additionally made the following factual statements with regard to the impugned Treaty:

(a) Estonia would be required to irrevocably and unconditionally subscribe the authorised capital stock to a level up to 8.5 per cent of GDP (as opposed eg to Estonia's contribution to the IMF amounting to 0.7 per cent of GDP), which would not only be added to the sovereign debt but would also clearly diminish the economic options of the Parliament;

(b) the requirements under which the ESM could grant financial assistance to an endangered State, as well as the conditionality imposed thereon, were very vaguely drafted in a manner that the domestic Parliament was essentially deprived of any say in such a decision, especially in the light of the volume of proprietary obligations which might prompt the ESM to approve financial assistance and of the fact that Estonia maintained no veto right since the required qualified majority would require the consent of merely the six major countries;

(c) there was a linguistic discrepancy that significantly loosened the terms under the emergency procedure, whereby the volume of financial assistance was limited only to the general lending volume of the ESM, ie whether a failure to urgently adopt a decision would threaten the economic and financial sustainability of the euro area to a significant extent.

The Chancellor challenged the overall suitability of the legitimate aim concerning the monetary stability of the euro area, in that the process could not be very prompt and expedient since, on some occasions (reference was made to Germany), approval by domestic parliaments was a condition precedent, thus the speed and efficiency of decision-making was not guaranteed in cases where one country whose contribution is more than 15 per cent (Germany, France or Italy) opposed the decision, while the rest of the countries, as well as the European Commission and the ECB, considered it necessary.

In a quite sound response, the Court placed emphasis on the significance of the budget for the polity and the necessary State discretion on the matter.

The Court admitted that there was indeed interference by the Treaty, in that the Parliament would be deprived of its full scope of competence in determining the State's budgeting policy. It then proceeded to assess such interference against the legitimate interests and objectives of the Treaties, ie to guarantee the efficiency of the decision-making mechanism to eliminate a threat to the economic and financial sustainability of the euro area in case of emergency, which was closely related to Estonia's stability itself. In order to draw the balance between conflicting values, the Court made use of the principle of proportionality and concluded that the ESM Treaty constituted an appropriate, necessary and reasonable vehicle for the achievement of the relevant objective and not a very strict one in itself.

Interestingly, the Constitutional Court took the opportunity to address two further issues albeit not strictly necessary for deciding the case. The first related to domestic parliamentary processes, where the Court decided that, in principle, the Constitution wouldn't be violated in case a parliamentary committee was empowered to review the activities of the Government and render binding opinions upon the executive or if that committee adopted an opinion on behalf of the Parliament in connection with certain issues. In the latter case. however, the Parliament should not be deprived of its competence to decide on the relevant matter, because the legislature could not be restricted merely to receiving information. Accordingly, the budgetary powers of the Parliament would be curtailed if a binding opinion only by the EU Affairs Committee sufficed to authorise financial assistance under the ESM Treaty, given that an amendment to the state budget might be necessary after taking the decision on granting financial assistance and, therefore, the Parliament might urge the Government to take steps in order to assume financial responsibilities.

The Court also dealt with the broader issue of Estonia's membership to the EU on the assumption that the ESM Treaty might in the future supersede EU law. Under this hypothesis, it was argued that the ESM process could go beyond the mandate given by the Estonian people through the referendum concerning accession to EU. In that case, as in any other case of a new EU founding treaty or amendments to such treaty that would lead to a deeper integration process and give rise to a more extensive delegation of competences by Estonia to the EU, it might be vital to amend the Constitution through the appropriate parliamentary deliberation. Yet, under the current circumstances there was no reason to declare the unconstitutionality of a Treaty technically lying outside the EU framework.

On this sovereignty issue, strong dissent was expressed by eight out of 19 judges of the plenary of the Court. According to various dissenting opinions the challenge by the Chancellor ought to have been upheld, basically on ground of curtailment of parliamentary sovereignty in Estonia. Justice Jüri Ilvest argued that the Constitution of Estonia did not give the Parliament the right to ratify the ESM Treaty without holding a referendum, for the people remain the only sovereign:

> Sovereignty is not an object of trade which one composition of the Riigikogu can (though maybe in the interests of Estonia) waive 'a bit', hoping that the next composition will bargain something back. A reading of Article 4(4) of the Treaty *introducing qualified majority instead of unanimity* clearly shows that what is gone is gone.

Yet the most striking dissenting view was that of Justice Luik:

> (R)egardless of how hard I try, I cannot understand how emergency assistance/assistance increasing the burden of debt of a state/bank allows in the long run to guarantee the economic and financial sustainability thereof and of the entire euro area .... So I find that the beliefs of the Supreme Court *en banc* in the mystical efficiency of the ESM in safeguarding the prosperity of the euro area Member States, including Estonia, ... do not fit in the boundaries of intelligent probability. Capital is a phenomenon guided by the principle of absolute greed. It means that capital always moves there where the biggest gain can be expected, being completely indifferent to ethics and other spiritual values. Therefore also being indifferent to the preservation of the Estonian nation, language and culture ... A financial crisis is a phenomenon of a global value crisis ... A value crisis is chaos in thinking, characterised by aimlessness, shallowness and vagueness, lack of fundamental values as fulcrums, the center of multiplicity of values is occupied by material gain. In lack of an ethical discipline the reigning political authority deems also the people/person as an instrument. Time will tell whether/when/how the value system of Estonia will change.[21]

f. Ireland

In the context of a bank recapitalisation scheme, Mr Pringle, a member of the Irish Parliament, opposed the participation of Ireland in the ESM Treaty. On 13 April 2012, Mr Pringle brought before the High Court (Ireland) an action against the defendants in the main proceedings in support of which he put forward both constitutional and EU claims. The constitutional claim was based on the ground that the ESM Treaty would transfer sovereign monetary powers and powers of monetary policy of the State to the new international institution and that any ratification would be unlawful and unconstitutional in the absence of approval by the people of Ireland in a referendum.

The EU claims suggested incompatibility of both Decision 2011/199 and the ESM treaty vis-a-vis the TEU and TFEU. As regards the former, the claim was that it was unlawfully adopted pursuant to the simplified revision because it entailed a prohibited alteration of the competences of the EU and that it was inconsistent with provisions of the EU Treaties concerning the economic and monetary union and with general principles of EU law, including the principle of legal certainty. As regards the ESM Treaty, he claimed that:

(a) it was essentially creating an autonomous and permanent international institution for euro-area Member States with the objective of circumventing the prohibitions and restrictions laid down by the provisions of the TFEU in relation to economic and monetary policy;

(b) it conferred new competences and duties on the EU institutions, which were incompatible with their functions as defined in the EU Treaties; and

---

[21] C Ginter, 'Constitutionality of the European Stability Mechanism in Estonia: Applying Proportionality to Sovereignty' (2013) 9 *European Constitutional Law Review* 335.

(c)   it was incompatible with the general principle of effective judicial protection and with the principle of legal certainty.

By a judgment of 17 July 2012 the High Court dismissed Mr Pringle's action in its entirety.[22] Mr Pringle brought an appeal against that judgment before the Supreme Court of Ireland, which delivered on 31 July 2012 its Judgment,[23] to stay proceedings and make a reference to the Court of Justice with a significant number of preliminary questions concerning both the validity of Decision 2011/199 and, indirectly, the compatibility of the ESM Treaty with a number of provisions of the TEU, the TFEU and the EU Charter of Fundamental Rights. On the issue of constitutionality, the Court held that the ESM did not involve concession of national sovereignty to such an extent that it amounted to a breach of the Constitution but merely pursued a defined policy of the government rather than an inappropriate transfer of executive powers. It finally dismissed the application for an injunction, on ground that this could result in significant and irreversible damage for Ireland's economy and for the euro area as a whole.

g. Slovenia

In the course of the economic crisis, the Bank of Slovenia, following state aid clearance by the European Commission, proceeded to the recapitalisation of two banks, the rescue of a third one, and the winding up of two more banks with capital shortfalls that did not allow them to have sufficient assets to satisfy their creditors and to cover the value of deposits. The measures included writing off equity and hybrid capital and subordinated debt. In the event of insolvency or winding up of the issuing entity, the holders of subordinated rights (financial instruments which share certain characteristics with debt products and certain characteristics with shares in equity capital), were to be paid after the holders of ordinary debentures, but before shareholders. In exchange for the financial risk thus assumed by their holders, those financial instruments offered a higher rate of return.

A number of applications for review of constitutionality were brought before the Constitutional Court of Slovenia by individuals, the National Council and the Ombudsman. Those applications related to whether provisions of the domestic law on the banking sector of 23 November 2006 as applicable to the main proceedings (Uradni list RS, No 99/10), on the basis of which the contested measures were adopted, providing for exceptional measures designed to ensure the recovery of the banking system, were compatible with the Slovenian Constitution, and in particular with the principles of non-retroactivity and of legitimate expectations and proportionality and the right to property and with European law protecting the rights of the shareholders and the right to property.

---

[22] *Pringle v The Government of Ireland and others* [2012] IEHC 296.
[23] *Pringle v Government of Ireland and others* [2012] IESC 47.

In its Judgment of 6 November 2014, the Court interpreted the plan as interfering with the Banking Communication but stayed the proceedings considering that it did not have jurisdiction to rule on a question of interpretation or validity of EU law representing the legal basis for the provision of national law whose constitutionality was challenged. Accordingly, it decided to refer seven questions to the Court of Justice essentially requesting guidance on the compatibility of the Banking Communication with:

(a)   the property right as enshrined in Article 17 of the Charter of Fundamental Rights of the European Union;

(b)   Directive 2012/30 of the European Parliament and of the Council of 25 October 2012 on coordination of safeguards which, for the protection of the interests of members and others, are required by Member States of companies within the meaning of the second paragraph of Article 54 of the Treaty on the Functioning of the European Union, in respect of the formation of public limited liability companies and the maintenance and alteration of their capital, with a view to making such safeguards equivalent;[24] and

(c)   Directive 2001/24 of the European Parliament and of the Council of 4 April 2001 on the reorganisation and winding up of credit institutions.[25]

ii. EU Courts

Four judgments of the Court of Justice are the most influential in setting the case law for the post-crisis EU architecture: the *Pringle* case refers to the legality of the establishment of the ESM; the *Gauweiler* and the *Weiss* cases refer to the legality of the ECB's policy of buying state bonds in the secondary market; and the *Kotnik* case refers to the legality of the EU bail-in tools to subordinated creditors.

In Judgment of 27 November 2012 in Case C-370/12, *Pringle*, 12 governments, the Commission, the Parliament and the Council intervened in the case, which the Court heard through the accelerated procedure before a full court composed of all 27 judges. The Court upheld the compatibility of Decision 2011/199 and of the ESM Treaty with EU law. Somewhat arbitrarily, the responses of the Court to the questions set by the order for reference can be classified in three categories: the ultra vires arguments; the new competences arguments; and the no-bail-out clause.

With regard to the EU ultra vires allegations of the plaintiff, the Court essentially made six syllogisms on the interpretation of the Treaties:

(1)   The amendment of Article 136 TFEU by Decision 199/2011 was purely declaratory and confirmed a power that the Member States already had; it created no legal basis for the Union to be able to undertake any action which was not

---

[24] OJ L 315, 14.11.2012, p 74. The Directive is no longer in force as of 19 July 2017.
[25] OJ L 125, 5.5.2001, p 15.

possible before the entry into force of the amendment, especially given that the granting of any financial assistance under that mechanism would be made subject to strict conditionality.

(2) Although the challenged stability mechanism established by the ESM Treaty was developed outside the framework of EU law, it directly contributed to the financial stability of the euro area so as to strengthen the economic governance of the EU; consequently, it could not possibly affect the exclusive competence held by the Union in the area of monetary policy for the euro-area Member States (Article 3(1)(c) TFEU).

(3) The stability mechanism did not fall within the monetary policy and, accordingly, under the Union's exclusive competence: the purpose of the ESM was not to maintain price stability (by setting key interest rates for the euro area or by issuing euro currency), but rather to meet the financing requirements of euro-area Member States experiencing or threatened by severe financing problems, if indispensable to safeguard the EU and/or national financial stability, funded from paid-in capital or by the issue of financial instruments. Accordingly, the recapitalisation by ESM of financial institutions and the necessary borrowing for that purpose (irrespective of any collateral consequence concerning increase on the amount of euro currency in circulation and possibly on inflation), constituted a breach of the exclusive competence of the Union on monetary policy or, particularly, the ECB's competence to regulate money supply in the euro area.

(4) The ESM Treaty was an international agreement, the operation of which did not affect the common rules on economic and monetary policy of the Union and, therefore, did not jeopardise in any way exclusive competences of the Union in the defence of the common interest. In that view, the conditionality prescribed by the ESM Treaty did not constitute an instrument of harmonisation of Member States' economic policies that is incompatible with primary law, but was intended to ensure the relevant coordinating measures adopted by the Union, especially Council's recommendations to Member States with excessive deficits (Article 126(7) and (8) TFEU), since conditionality must explicitly be consistent with such recommendations (Article 13(3) and (4)).

(5) The list of specific exceptional circumstances under which the Union grants ad hoc financial assistance to a Member State when it is seriously threatened with severe difficulties beyond its control (Article 122 TFEU) was not exclusive and did not preclude other stability mechanisms, such as the ESM.

(6) The prohibition on ECB to provide credit facilities or purchase debt instruments (Article 123 TFEU), did not apply to any other EU institution which might legitimately do so if not precluded by other EU law provisions.

On top of the above statements, the Court held that Decision 2011/199 satisfied the condition that a revision of the TFEU by means of the simplified revision procedure may concern only provisions embodying EU policies and internal actions.

With regard to the allegations concerning *new competences* established for EU institutions,[26] the Court held that there was an issue with Article 13 TEU on conferred powers, since neither the TEU nor the TFEU confers on the Union a specific competence to establish a permanent stability mechanism such as the ESM.[27] In relation to the new competencies conferred on the *Commission*, the Court found that they fell within the rubric of powers which the euro-area Member States were entitled to entrust to institutions outside the EU framework on two conditions: that the duties belong to areas which do not belong to the exclusive competence of the Union; and that the duties do not alter the essential character of the powers conferred on those institutions by the TEU and the TFEU.

On the first condition, the Court held, in a very laconic statement, that the activities of the ESM fall under economic policy, in which EU does not have exclusive competence. On the second condition, the Court stated that the new duties assigned to the Commission, 'important as they are',[28] do not entail any power to make decisions of its own and solely bind the ESM. Furthermore, the new duties did not alter the Commission's essential character as an authority that 'shall promote the general interest of the Union' and 'shall oversee the application of Union law' (Article 17(1) TEU), in the sense that by its involvement in the ESM Treaty, it promotes the general interest of the Union and seeks to ensure that the MoUs concluded by the ESM are consistent with EU law.

In relation to the new *ECB* competencies, the Court found that the above two criteria for allocation of powers to institutions outside the EU framework were met, in that statutorily the ECB supports the general economic policies in the Union (Article 282(2) TFEU) and is entitled to participate in international monetary institutions (Articles 6(2) and 23 of the Statute of the ESCB).[29]

Finally, in relation to the *Court of Justice's* new competences, the Court held that the new fields of jurisdiction fell within the ambit of Article 273 TFEU entailing that the Court shall have jurisdiction in any dispute between Member States which relates to the subject matter of the Treaties, if the dispute is submitted to it under a special agreement between the parties. Accordingly, the relevant Article 37(3) of the ESM Treaty qualified as 'special agreement', since there was nothing to preclude such agreements given in advance with reference to a whole class of pre-defined disputes, whereas at the same time the class of disputes to be submitted to the jurisdiction of the Court was related to the subject-matter of the Treaties. Furthermore, rather as an obiter dictum, the Court noted that a dispute linked to the interpretation or application of the ESM Treaty was also likely

---

[26] Above ch 2 section I C.

[27] Thus, the Court rejected the argument set forth by the applicant that the euro-area Member States should have established enhanced cooperation between them in order to be entitled to make use of the EU institutions within the ESM instead of conferring duties to EU authorities through the ESM Treaty on the ground that enhanced cooperation according to Art 20(1) TEU could be established only where the Union itself was competent to act in the area concerned by that cooperation.

[28] Para 161.

[29] OJ 2010 C 83, p 230.

to bear upon the interpretation or application of EU law, since, according to the ESM Treaty, the MoUs with Member States receiving financial assistance must be fully consistent with EU law and, in particular, with the measures taken by the Union in the area of coordination of the economic policies of the Member States.

With regard to the allegation of the plaintiff that there was a violation of the *no-bail-out clause* of Article 125 TFEU, the Court arguably set the most important ruling in *Pringle*. The Court widely used methodological tools of literal interpretation suggesting that if the Treaty wished to launch an exhaustive list of instruments for financial assistance it would have used the language of derogation from Article 125 TFEU in the event of grant based on Article 122. In that regard, the limited wording of Article 123 on exceptional ad hoc financial assistance suggested *a contario* that *some* financial assistance to a Member State could be deemed permissible.

Having established that financial assistance is not altogether prohibited, the Court went on to assess which forms of financial assistance were compatible with Article 125 TFEU. Accordingly, it had recourse to the objective pursued by this Article as reflected in the preparatory work relating to the Treaty of Maastricht, namely to ensure that the Member States follow a sound budgetary policy and remain subject to the logic of the market when they enter into debt by maintaining budgetary discipline and, eventually, the financial stability of the monetary union. Applying a teleological standard of interpretation, the Court delineated that such measures could only be permissible if cumulatively satisfying two criteria, ie to be indispensable for the safeguarding of the financial stability of the euro area as a whole while being subject to strict conditions and to not frustrate the incentive of the recipient Member State to conduct a sound budgetary policy (the moral hazard issue).

The Court found that both criteria applied in all forms of financial assistance established by the Treaty since the ESM did not act as guarantor of the debts of the recipient Member State, the latter remaining liable to its creditors for its financial commitments. Furthermore, the granting of financial assistance in the form of a credit line, loans or government bonds purchased by the ESM on the primary or secondary market, did not imply that it assumed the debts of the recipient Member State but essentially amounted to the creation of a new debt, including an appropriate margin, owed to the ESM. Finally, the Court, in justifying the legality of the impugned EU acts, placed emphasis on the provision that financial assistance could only be triggered as a last resort mechanism in case it appeared indispensable to safeguard the financial stability of the euro area as a whole and of its Member States and on the statutory requirement of 'strict conditionality' to ensure that the assisted Member States kept on pursuing a sound budgetary policy.[30]

---

[30] P Craig, 'Pringle and Use of EU Institutions Outside the EU Legal Framework: Foundation, Procedure and Substance' (2013) 9 *European Constitutional Law Review* 263; P Craig, 'Pringle: Legal Reasoning, Text, Purpose and Teleology' (2013) *Maastricht Journal of European and Comparative Law* 14; Ch Koedooder, 'The Pringle Judgment: Economic and/or Monetary Union?' (2013) 37 *Fordham*

The second major judgment of the Court of Justice in this field is C-62/14 *Gauweiler and others* of 16 June 2015. With regard to the *admissibility* of the request for a preliminary ruling, the Court overruled three objections relating to the nature of the impugned act:

(a)   that it lacked legal effects vis-a-vis third parties;
(b)   that the request for a preliminary ruling was vague and conditional because of the referring court's reservation to go contrary to the Court of Justice's ruling; and
(c)   that the structure proceedings before the referring Court by-passed the conditions for individual challenging of EU acts as set out in article 263 TFEU.

In that respect the Court of Justice, adhering to the principal judgment *Melloni*,[31] held that questions concerning EU law enjoyed a presumption of relevance and it was in principle bound to give a ruling, since it could only refuse to give one where it was quite obvious that the interpretation or the determination of validity of a rule of EU law had no relation to the actual facts of the main action or its purpose, where the problem was hypothetical, or where the Court did not have necessary factual or legal material. Nor did the fact that the OMT programme had not been implemented and required further legal action render the reference inadmissible, since under German law preventive legal protection might be granted in such a situation if certain conditions were met.

With regard to the *merits* of the case, broadly three general grounds were examined by the Court: ultra vires; violation of the prohibition of direct financing; and breach of procedural requirements. Regarding *competence*, the Court found that it was within the competence of the ECB to develop the impugned programme as part of the monetary policy of the Union, which is exclusive when it comes to the euro-area Member States (Article 3(1)(c) TFEU).

Since the ECB could admittedly adopt measures which were necessary to carry out its tasks in accordance with the rules on monetary policy, the critical question was what constitutes monetary policy since the TFEU contained no precise definition. In assessing whether the OMTs policy fell within the ambit of the monetary policy, the Court employed a teleological methodology by trying to identify the objectives of the programme. The impugned press release used the language of safeguarding both an appropriate monetary policy transmission and the singleness of the monetary policy. The Court emphasised on the latter, based on the letter of 119(2) TFEU and its effect to preserve and to contribute to the primary objective of price stability, irrespective of whether a programme such as OMTs might also be capable of contributing incidentally to the stability of the euro area, which is a matter of economic policy.

International Law Journal 110; C Herrmann, 'Pringle v Ireland. Case C-370/12' (2013) 107 *American Journal of International Law* 410; P-A van Malleghem, 'Pringle: A Paradigm Shift in the European Union's Monetary Constitution' (2013) 14 *German Law Journal* 141.

[31] CJEU Judgment of 26 February 2013 in Case C-399/11, *Melloni*, para 29.

The Court held that there might be a possible indirect effect of the OMT programme in furthering the economic policy objectives of adjustment programmes, thus treated as equivalent to an economic policy measure. Yet, the ESCB is anyhow set to support the general economic policies in the Union and, as the Court noted, its ability to influence price developments by means of its monetary policy decisions in fact depended, to a great extent, on the transmission of the 'impulses' which the ESCB sent out across the money market to the various sectors of the economy. Accordingly, measures that were intended to preserve the transmission mechanism may be regarded as pertaining to the primary objective of price stability. In any case, the Court noted that in order to achieve the objectives of the ESCB and to carry out its tasks, as provided for in primary law, the ECB and the national central banks might, in principle, operate in the financial markets by buying and selling outright marketable instruments in euro (Article 18(1) of the Protocol on the ESCB and the ECB). A fortiori, the Court thought that the conditionality of the OMTs programme was in a position to ensure that the monetary policy measures adopted would not work against the effectiveness of the economic policies followed by the Member States and operate as counter incentives for sound budgetary policy.

Regarding the alleged violation of *prohibition of direct financing* of Member States (Article 123(1) TFEU), the Court placed emphasis on the specific conditions, namely that:

(a) the Member States could not, in determining their budgetary policy, rely on the certainty that the ESCB would at a future point purchase their government bonds on secondary markets; and
(b) the programme in question could not be implemented in a way which would bring about a harmonisation of the interest rates applied to the government bonds of the euro-area Member States, regardless of the differences arising from their macroeconomic or budgetary situation.

Regarding breach of *procedural requirements,* the Court found no manifest error of assessment on the merits of the case on the ground of the duty to give reasons (and of the more substantive allegation for violation of proportionality). It ruled that it stemmed from the challenged press release and from the explanations provided by the ECB in the course of the judicial proceedings that the programme was based on an analysis of the economic situation of the euro area, according to which, at the date of the programme's announcement, interest rates on the government bonds of various euro-area Member States were characterised by high volatility and extreme spreads, caused, in part, by the demand for excessive risk premia for the bonds issued by certain Member States. Consequently, the Court of Justice altogether upheld the validity of the OMTs programme.[32]

---

[32] T Tridimas and N Xanthoulis, 'A Legal Analysis of the Gauweiler Case' (2016) 23 *Maastricht Journal of European and Comparative Law* 1; P Craig and M Markakis, 'Gauweiler and the Legality of Outright Monetary Transactions' (2016) 41 *European Law Review* 1; A Hinarejos, 'Gauweiler and the

In Judgment of 11 December 2018 in Case C-493/17 *Weiss and others*, the Grand Chamber of the Court of Justice, widely relying on *Gauweiler*, found that the PSPP programme did not exceed the ECB's mandate and did not infringe the prohibition of monetary financing. On the competence issue, the Court held that the programme fell within EU's exclusive competence in the area of monetary policy for the euro area Member States and adhered by the principle of proportionality by considering all potential adverse effects arising on implementation of the programme. In particular, it was held that the purpose of the PSPP programme to encourage a return of inflation rates to levels below, but close to, two per cent over the medium term was legitimate and the measure taken did not constitute a manifest error of assessment.

The Court found that the measure was falling into the rubric of monetary measures and was not equivalent to an economic policy measure, since in order to exert an influence on inflation rates, measures might lawfully produce certain effects on the real economy. In that respect, the Court noted that if the ESCB were precluded altogether from adopting such measures also incurring economic effects, that would in represent an insurmountable obstacle to its accomplishing the task assigned to it by EU primary law.

On the substantive issue of alleged monetary financing, the Court ruled that the implementation of the programme was not equivalent to a purchase of bonds on the primary markets and did not amounted to an increased level of moral hazard. This was so, according to the Court, because a private operator could not be certain when purchasing bonds that they would actually be bought by the ESCB in the foreseeable future and any Member States could not possibly determine its budgetary policy without taking account of the fact that continuity in the implementation of the PSPP was in no way guaranteed and, therefore, it could not rely on it in the medium term. In so deciding, the Court took into account the restriction of the total monthly volume of public sector asset purchases, the subsidiary nature of the PSPP programme, the distribution of purchases between the national central banks in accordance with the key for subscription of the ECB's capital, the purchase limits per issue and issuer and the stringent eligibility criteria based on a credit quality assessment.

In Judgment of 19 July 2016 in Case C-526/14, *Kotnik and others v Državni zbor Republike Slovenije*, the Court of Justice upheld the 2013 Banking Communication

---

Outright Monetary Transactions Programme: The Mandate of the European Central Bank and the Changing Nature of Economic and Monetary Union' (2015) 11 *European Constitutional Law Review* 563; F Fabbrini, 'After the OMT Case: The Supremacy of EU Law as the Guarantee of the Equality of the Member States' (2015) 16 *German Law Journal* 1003; S Simon, 'Direct Cooperation has Begun: Some Remarks on the Judgment of the ECJ on the OMT Decision of the ECB in Response to the German Federal Constitutional Court's First Request for a Preliminary Ruling' (2015) 16 *German Law Journal* 1025; H Sauer, 'Doubtful it Stood ...: Competence and Power in European Monetary and Constitutional Law in the Aftermath of the CJEU's OMT Judgment' (2015) 16 *German Law Journal* 971.

on state aids to banks, which established the burden-sharing principle by imposing financial burden to subordinated creditors prior to state aid in case of bank failure. The Court essentially assessed three grounds of review. First, the Court assessed the state aid prohibition vis-a-vis the burden-sharing principle enshrined in the Banking Communication. It held that burden-sharing was not binding on the Member States, in the sense that it could not impose independent obligations upon them, but that it merely established conditions designed to ensure that state aid granted to the banks in the context of the financial crisis might qualify as a serious disturbance in the economy of a Member State as identified by the Commission on a wide discretionary assessment. In this sense, the burden-sharing principle was found compatible with Articles 107–109 TFEU, on the prohibition of state aid, as being specifically designed to prevent recourse to state aid merely by obtaining a contribution from subordinated creditors prior to capital injection by the State.

Second, regarding the prohibition of increase or reduction in the capital of a public limited liability company without a decision by the company's general meeting (Articles 29, 34, 35 and 40 to 42 of Directive 2012/30), the Court held that general provisions were not applicable in that case, since the applicable Banking Communication had a different and specific scope in serious disturbance of the economy, falling within the concept of 'reorganisation measures', insofar as these measures were adopted by an administrative or judicial authority and were not decided upon and implemented by the shareholders or the subordinated creditors, without the interference of any state action (Article 2 of Directive 2001/24).

Third, regarding the right to property, the Court made a differentiation between shareholders and subordinated creditors of the distressed banks. For shareholders, the Court held that they must fully bear the risk of their investments and, since they are liable for the debts of the bank up to the amount of its share capital: the scale of their losses would, in any event, be identical, regardless of whether those losses are caused by a court insolvency order because no state aid is granted or by a procedure for the granting of state aid which is subject to the prerequisite of burden-sharing. For subordinated creditors, the Court held that their rights are hybrid and, therefore, there is a fair balance requiring their contribution if a bank becomes distressed, since those creditors are to contribute only after losses are first absorbed by equity and if there are no other possibilities available to overcome any capital shortfall or where the bank no longer meets the minimum regulatory capital requirements. And all this without prejudice to the 'no creditor worse off principle', enshrined also in the impugned Banking Communication: subordinated creditors should not receive less, in economic terms, than what their instrument would have been worth if no state aid was to be granted.[33]

---

[33] V Babis, 'State Helps Those who Help Themselves: State aid and Burden-sharing' University of Cambridge Faculty of Law Research Paper no 62/2016 (2016), available at: ssrn.com/abstract=2858360;

B. Hungary, Latvia and Romania: Social State Decrease and Right to Property

i. Domestic Courts

Courts in Central and Eastern Europe issued a very large number of judgments concerning austerity measures and their impact on human rights. Some of the impugned measures were introduced by the respective States before 2010 and were challenged afterwards, whereas others came after the eruption of the crisis. Judgments from Hungary, Latvia and Romania are, indicatively, cited below. The criterion for the selection of the countries and of the judgments has been the quantity of the relevant case law and their impact in the general level of protection of human rights, with a view to assessing whether this case law has brought in a change in the traditional paradigm of the rule of law.

The Constitutional Court of Hungary has probably been the judicial forum with the highest ratio of rulings on unconstitutionality of the relevant legislation. Thus, the Court found a violation of the Constitution in: Judgment 33/2012 (legal status and remuneration of judges); Judgments 8/2011 and 29/2011 (dismissal of civil servants); Judgment 37/2011 (imposition of a special tax); Judgment 184/2010 (retroactive taxation); Judgment 8/2010 (parameters of wealth tax); and Judgment 127/2009 (quasi taxation of family allowances). On the other hand, the Administrative and Labour Court of Hungary in its Judgment of 20 June 2013 found that the reductions in disability allowance were constitutional.

Yet, there is a strong particularity in the case of Hungary. In the wake of the annulment of the tax legislation of the Government by the Constitutional Court, there was a fierce constitutional crisis after 2010, which resulted in a revision of the Constitution in 2013, seriously affecting the structure of the judiciary and the scope of judicial review on budgetary and tax issues:

(a)   the powers of the Constitutional Court were limited, as the Court was prevented from referring to its pre-2012 case law and its power to review substantive constitutional amendments was removed;
(b)   the retirement age for judges was lowered to allow for new appointees; and
(c)   the President of the National Judicial Office (a government appointee) was constitutionally permitted to transfer cases from one court to another at his/her own discretion.

Indeed, Hungary is the only country where there was a strong conflict between the Government and the judiciary as a result of the case law produced by the latter. In many respects the political context resembled the 1932–1937 clashes

S Lucchini, J Moscianese, I de Angelis and F di Benedetto, 'State Aid and the Banking System in the Financial Crisis: From Bail-out to Bail-in' (2016) *Journal of European Competition Law and Practice* 1.

between the US Supreme Court and President Roosevelt, especially his court-packing scheme that never found a path in the Congress. Interestingly, the highly controversial constitutional revision that significantly curtailed judicial powers was adopted along party lines within the Parliament.[34]

The Latvian Constitutional Court has been particularly active as regards case law concerning the reduction of social entitlements. Indicatively: Judgment in Case 2009-08-01 (cancellation of pension indexation – constitutional); 2009-43-01 (pension cuts – unconstitutional); 2009-44-01 (reduction to benefit for working parents – constitutional); 2009-76-01 (cuts to pensions of the public servants of the Ministry of the Interior – unconstitutional); 2009-88-01 (cuts to early pensions of military personnel – unconstitutional); 2009-11-01 (cuts in salaries of judges – unconstitutional); and 2010-21-01 (cuts to funding of occupational pensions – constitutional). The Latvian Constitutional Court has widely used a balancing process between the restrictions upon human rights and the benefit of the community and concluded in most cases that the latter ought to prevail. It is perhaps the Court that used in the strictest manner the legal tool of proportionality in assessing the impugned measures.[35]

The Constitutional Court of Romania has also delivered a great number of judgments concerning allowances: Judgment 414/2009 (public-sector employment conditions – unconstitutional); Judgments 872–874/2010 (pension and salary cuts of public servants – partly unconstitutional); Judgment 1655/2010 (time extension of salary cuts – constitutional); Judgment 1658/2010 (ceiling for public servants' bonuses – constitutional); Judgment 765/2011 (cut in maternity leave and child-raising allowance – constitutional); Judgments 74/2011 and 575/2011 (curtailment of labour union rights – constitutional); and Judgment 383/2011 (liberalisation of working conditions – constitutional).

In the above cases the Court was based on two key premises. First, the financial crisis amounted to a constitutional emergency that fell par excellence within the ambit of economic security, justifying measures interfering with social rights, without prejudice to the application of the principle of proportionality. Second, salaries did not enjoy the same level of constitutional protection as pensions, in that the former were subject to the public interest qualification for the economic sustainability of the State, whereas the latter were essentially based on contributions that had already been paid by the pensioners at the time of their work. Accordingly, within the scope of the necessity test, salary cuts could be constitutionally

---

[34] M Bogaards, 'De-democratization in Hungary: Diffusely Defective Democracy' (2018) 25 *Democratization* 1481; Z Szente, 'Breaking and Making Constitutional Rules: The Constitutional Effects of the Financial Crisis in Hungary' in X Contiades (ed), *Constitutions in the Global Financial Crisis. A Comparative Analysis* (Farnham, Ashgate, 2013) 245; N Chronowski and G-O Fruzsina, 'The Hungarian Constitutional Court and the Financial Crisis' (2017) 58 *Hungarian Journal of Legal Studies* 139.

[35] R Balodis and J Pleps, 'Financial Crisis and the Constitution in Latvia' in X Contiades (ed), *Constitutions in the Global Financial Crisis. A Comparative Analysis* (Farnham, Ashgate, 2013) 115; C Kilpatrick, 'Constitutions, Social Rights and Sovereign Debt States in Europe: A Challenging New Area of Constitutional Inquiry' in T Beukers, B de Witte and C Kilpatrick (eds), *Constitutional Change through Euro-crisis Law* (Cambridge, Cambridge University Press, 2017) 279.

tolerated as temporary measures, because of the expediency to produce immediate beneficial results for the national economics, whereas pension cuts much less so.[36]

ii. EU Courts

Interestingly, it was not the Constitutional Court of Romania but mostly regional Romanian courts (courts of first instance of Dambovita and Alba and the Court of Appeal of Brasov) that made references for a preliminary ruling to the Court of Justice concerning salary cuts in the public sector on the ground of property violations of the ECHR and infringement of the right to property and the principles of equal treatment and non-discrimination of the EU Charter of Fundamental Rights. The Court of Justice, in 2011, used the jurisdictional mechanism of lack of jurisdiction and issued orders to that effect.[37] The orders were founded on Article 53(2) of the Rules of Procedure of the Court, providing that where it is clear that the Court has no jurisdiction to hear and determine a case or where a request or an application is manifestly inadmissible, the Court may, after hearing the Advocate General, at any time give a decision by reasoned order without taking further steps in the proceedings (Article 93(a) of the Rules of Procedure).

Interestingly, the case law of inadmissibility of such cases changed altogether with Judgment of 27 June 2017 in Case C-258/14 *Florescu and others v Casa Judeţeană de Pensii Sibiu.* The case was brought to the Court by reference from the Court of Appeal of Alba Iulia, Romania, for a preliminary ruling. Pursuant to a MoU concluded between the European Community and Romania in 2009, the disbursement of every installment of the financial assistance granted to the latter by the EU was to be carried out subject to the satisfactory implementation of the economic programme, including, among others, reduction of the public sector wages, revision of the pension system to help improve the long-term sustainability of public finances and structural reforms of the public administration (concerning decision-making structures, division of responsibilities among institutions, internal organisation of key ministries, oversight and accountability for implementation and adequacy of staffing levels and human resource management).

Pursuant to the MoU provisions, Law 329/2009 restricted some aspects of preexisting pension rights, especially relating to the rules on combining a pension with employment income. Individuals, at the same time part of the judiciary and the academia, claimed that such restrictions, although their pension accrued in

---

[36] Kilpatrick, 'Constitutions' (2017); B Selejan-Gutan, 'Social and Economic Rghts in the Context of the Economic Crisis' (2013) 4 *Romanian Journal of Comparative Law* 139.

[37] CJEU Order of 14 December 2011 in Case C-462/11, *Cozman v Teatrul Municipal Târgovişte*, request for a preliminary ruling from the Court of Dambovita (Tribunalul Dâmboviţa); CJEU Order of 14 December 2011 in Case C-434/11, *Corpul Naţional al Poliţiştilor v Ministerul Administraţiei şi Internelor (MAI) and others*, request for a preliminary ruling from the Court of Alba (Tribunalul Alba); and, CJEU Order of 15 November 2012 in Case C-369/12, *Corpul Naţional al Poliţiştilor - Biroul Executiv Central*, request for a preliminary ruling from the Court of Appeal of Brasov (*Curtea de Apel, Braşov*).

respect of over 30 years of contributions, were contrary to EU law on various grounds (Articles 6 TEU, 110 and 267 TFEU, Articles 17, 20, 21 and 47 ChFR, the principles of legal certainty, effectiveness and equivalence, Article 2(2)(b) of Council Directive 2000/78/EC of 27 November 2000 establishing a general framework for equal treatment in employment and occupation),[38] notwithstanding the fact that law was adopted in order to comply with the MoU.

The domestic Court made a reference to the Court of Justice with two sets of questions: the principal question was whether the MoU might be regarded as an act, decision or communication having legal force and interpreted by the Court; the substantive question was whether curtailment of individual rights to secure sound national finances was compatible with EU law. The answer in the principal question was in the affirmative: the MoU gave concrete form to an agreement between the EU, represented by the Commission, and a Member State on an economic programme negotiated by the parties, whereby the latter undertook to comply with predefined economic objectives in order to be able, subject to fulfilling that agreement, to benefit from financial assistance from the latter. Accordingly, the MoU fell in the heading of validity and interpretation of acts of the institutions, bodies, offices or agencies of the Union that triggered the jurisdiction of the Court (Article 267(b) TFEU). The answers in the substantive questions were that:

(a)   the MoU, although mandatory, contained no specific provision requiring the adoption of a national law which barred retired officials of the public institutions from receiving a salary in addition to the pension;
(b)   the EU Charter of Fundamental Rights did not preclude national legislation prohibiting the combining of a net public-sector retirement pension with income from activities carried out in public institutions if the amount of the pension exceeded a certain threshold; and
(c)   there was no indirect discrimination in the meaning of Article 2(2)(b) of Council Directive 2000/78/EC for different categories of public servants receiving a pension and a salary.

Albeit rejecting on the merits, most importantly, *Florescu* constitutes a milestone judgment in that the Court of Justice accepted the financial assistance MoUs signed between the Union institutions and the Member States as legal instruments of EU relevance, thus assuming the role of protector of the EU social law especially through the EU Charter of Fundamental Rights.[39]

[38] OJ 2000 L 303, p 16.
[39] M Markakis and P Dermine, 'Bailouts, the Legal Status of Memoranda of Understanding, and the Scope of Application of the EU Charter: Florescu' (2018) 55 *Common Market Law Review* 643; K Lenaerts and J Gutiérrez-Fons, 'The European Court of Justice as the Guardian of the Rule of EU Social Law' in F Vandenbroucke, C Barnardm and G de Baere (eds.), *A European Social Union after the Crisis* (Cambridge, Cambridge University Press, 2017) 407.

iii. European Court of Human Rights

In case *Fábián v Hungary* of 15 December 2015,[40] a public sector pensioner complained before the Court of Strasbourg that, following an amendment to the Pension Act, his old-age pension was suspended because he had taken up post-retirement employment as a civil servant, while those working in the private sector and some public officials (such as government ministers and mayors) were not affected by this restriction. The complaint was based on three grounds:

(a) violation of the right to property because of deprivation of part of his pension;
(b) violation of the prohibition of discrimination because of the difference in treatment against pensioners working in the private sector; and
(c) unjustified difference in treatment between pensioners employed in different categories within the public sector.

Although the Chamber of the Court admitted the Government's submission that the suspension of the pension had the legitimate aim of reducing public expenditure, it unanimously held that there had been a violation of the prohibition of discrimination under Article 14 in conjunction with Article 1 of Protocol No 1 on grounds of (b) and (c) since there was no reasonable and objective justification in the difference in treatment between public servants' salaries and private sector pensions also burdening the state budget.

The Grand Chamber reversed the unanimous decision of the Chamber decision in its Judgment of 5 September 2017. The Court dismissed the application on the merits as regards the first two grounds and as inadmissible as regards the third ground, due to the fact that it had been introduced outside the six-month time-limit (Article 35(1) and (4) ECHR). On the property claim, in spite of the overall curtailment of the pension allowance, the Court relied on its prior case law, according to which the modification or discontinuance of supplementary retirement benefits or the reduction of a pension by way of forfeiture constituted neither an expropriation nor a measure to control the use of property, but merely amounted to interference with the peaceful enjoyment of property.

In so deciding, the Court placed emphasis on the following:

(a) the coherence of state policy, ie that the suspension of pension payments at issue was part of a package of measures aimed at assuring the long-term sustainability of the Hungarian pension system and reducing public debt;
(b) the extent of the loss of benefits, ie that it did not refer to either permanent, complete loss of the applicant's pension entitlements or the reduction thereof, but rather the suspension of a temporary nature of monthly pension payments and would be resumed when the applicant left State employment;
(c) the aspect of personal choice left to the applicant, ie not to re-enter state employment; and

---

[40] ECtHR Judgment of 15 December 2015, *Fábián v Hungary*, Application no 78117/13.

(d) the effect of the measure on the applicant's means of subsistence, ie that the suspension by no means took him below the subsistence threshold.

The Court felt obliged to say a word justifying the one-sided assessment of the facts vis-a-vis its settled case law as regards the need to draw a fair balance between the demands of the general interest of the community and the requirements of the protection of the applicant's fundamental rights which prohibits the imposition of any excessive individual burden. It accordingly held that this test could not be based solely on the amount or percentage of the loss suffered, but must be examined in the light of all the relevant factors; a reasonable thought, since on the record of the case there was no reduction but a suspension altogether. As regards the non-discrimination argument between public servants and private sector employees, the Grand Chamber considered this to be a policy choice merely subject to manifest lack of a reasonable basis, which was not the case on the merits of the file.[41]

In pilot cases *Markovics v Hungary*,[42] *Béres v Hungary*[43] and *Augusztin v Hungary*,[44] the Court dealt with the complaints of over 13,500 persons in 1,260 applications concerning the restructuring of retired servicemen's pensions in Hungary, resulting in pensions being subject, for the first time, to general personal income tax rate, which meant eventual cuts of an average of 15 per cent (460 euros for the applicant with the lower pension), and unanimously declared the applications inadmissible. The applicants complained that this conversion constituted an unjustified and discriminatory interference with their property rights. The Court found that the reduction in the applicants' benefits had been reasonable and commensurate since under the new scheme:

(a) they continued to receive a service allowance reasonably related to the value of their previous service pension;
(b) the rationalisation of the pension system was indeed an aim justifying difference in treatment and a commensurate reduction of benefits and reflecting a reasonable relation of proportionality; and
(c) the applicants had not been altogether deprived of their only means of subsistence and were therefore not placed at risk of having insufficient means to live on.

Another important case, currently pending before the Court of Strasbourg, is *Albert and others v Hungary*.[45] This case is about the devaluation of shareholders' rights as a result of a very extensive banking sector restructuring programme in Hungary, especially as regards saving and cooperative banks. The applicants complained that the cumulative effect of the restructuring rules amounted to an

---

[41] Below section II C a.
[42] ECtHR Judgment of 24 June 2014, *Markovics v Hungary*, Application no 77575/11.
[43] ECtHR Judgment of 24 June 2014, *Béres v Hungary*, Application no 19828/13.
[44] ECtHR Judgment of 24 June 2014, *Augusztin v Hungary*, Application no 19829/13.
[45] ECtHR Judgment of 4 April 2017, *Albert and others v Hungary*, Application no 5294/14.

unjustified interference with their property rights, which was further discriminatory given the arbitrary inclusion/exclusion of various financial institutions within the scope of the new legislation.[46] In particular, the applicants asserted, inter alia, breach of their property rights due to changes in ownership ratios, in shareholder rights and in the management over a savings bank which resulted in the nationalisation of the bank and in the deprivation of their ownership rights to establish or amend the banks' Articles of Association. In its Decision of 27 April 2017, the Fourth Section of the Court reiterated its consolidated case law that a company share with an economic value can be considered a possession and declared the case admissible, without prejudging the merits of the case, which is currently pending.

C. The Greek Bail-out Scheme: Salary/Pension Cuts in the Public Sector

i. Domestic Courts

A great number of judgments relevant to the implementation of the Greek bailout programmes, especially concerning the austerity measures introduced thereunder, have been rendered by the national courts. The most significant judgments were rendered by the supreme administrative court of the country, ie the Council of State:

- 668/2012 (first financial assistance MoU regarding salary/pensions cuts applying to public sector and other relevant issues – constitutional);
- 1972/2012 (surtax on properties with electricity connection – constitutional);
- 1685/2013 (surtax upon personal income tax for 2010 – constitutional);
- 3354/2013 (temporary pre-pension set aside applying to public servants – unconstitutional);
- 1902/2014 (transfer of public real estate assets to a privately operating fund – constitutional);
- 1906/2014 (privatisation of the Athens water supply company – unconstitutional);
- 2192/2014 (salary cuts applying to military and public security servants – unconstitutional);
- 3169/2014 (temporary pre-pension set aside applying to vocational trainers – constitutional);
- 3404–3405/2014 (salary cuts applying to special scientific staff of independent authorities – constitutional);

---

[46] Act no CXXXV of 2013 on the Integration of Cooperative Credit Institutions and the Amendment of Certain Laws Regarding Economic Matters.

- 4741/2014 (salary cuts applying to academics – unconstitutional);
- 532/2015 (real estate tax – constitutional);
- 2287–2290/2015 (further pensions cuts applying to the public sector – unconstitutional);
- 2653/2015 (solidarity surtax applying to professionals – constitutional).

Among the voluminous remaining case law of the Hellenic Council of State, a number of key judgments (with wide effects, involving case law reversal or presenting variations in the level of protection among different categories of employees) are cited hereinafter, classified according to their subject-matter.

Concerning, the *MoU* enhancing conditionality and the *salary cuts* in the public sector, the main trend of the case law was that such cuts were in principle constitutional given the legitimate aim of rescuing the country from financial default. In milestone Judgment 668/2012, the plenary of the Council rejected the applications lodged by trade unions, professional chambers, other legal entities and individuals challenging Law 3833/2010, enshrining the conditionality of the first MoU. In a very elaborate judgment, comprising 129 pages, the Council rejected all grounds on their merits. Following a very extensive historical assessment of the domestic economy, going back to its first steps in 1830, it concluded that:

(a) the financial assistance MoU was not an international treaty because the contracting parties had not undertaken any mutual commitments and, in any case, it contained no enforcement mechanisms or legal sanctions for non-compliance;
(b) the impugned measures would indeed have significant financial impact on the state budget (salary/pension cuts of 0.5 and 0.2 per cent of GDP for 2010 and 2011 respectively; holiday bonus cuts of 0.6 and 0.2 per cent of GDP for 2010 and 2011 respectively); and
(c) the aim of preventing financial default of the State justified taking the impugned measures, which were temporary, consistent and sustainable.

In Judgments 3404–3405/2014, the Council of State added that a salary of a certain amount was not guaranteed, as the system of remuneration depends on the various and specific financial, social and political circumstances and, as an obiter dictum rather, that the impugned measures were justified in the light of the constitutional clause stipulating that the State is entitled to claim of all citizens to fulfil the duty of social solidarity (Article 25). By way of exception, the Council of State considered that salary cuts of judges, academics and military/public security servants were unconstitutional. This case was rather predictable for the judiciary given that, according to settled case law, judges' salaries ought to be equivalent to those of other high officials of the Government and the Parliament, pursuant to the constitutional clause establishing that their remuneration shall reflect their high office. However, no equivalent constitutional stipulation exists for academics and military servants. This is why the Council, in order to strike down the respective

salary cuts, after significant cuts that had already been imposed on those professional categories, tried to establish differences in the nature and scope of their
professional conditions and duties.[47]

Overall, it seems that in assessing the constitutionality of salary cuts, the
Council of State entered into a policy of identity choices. This judicial policy may
find some support in the letter of particular constitutional provisions, but is always
vulnerable to the allegation that the courts essentially draft salary policies based
on subjective criteria of how important or distinct the provision of services by
specific public servants is.

As regards *pension cuts*, in the first phase of the economic crisis (2010–15), the
Council of State consistently upheld the constitutionality of such statutory provisions, broadly maintaining the same rationale it employed with regard to salary
cuts.[48] Judgments 2287–2290/2015 marked an outstanding reversal in the relevant
case law, which arose as a challenge to a further cut on main and supplementary
pensions. In the meantime, there had been a series of direct or indirect reductions,
ie cuts on holiday allowances, imposition of a solidarity contribution on main and
supplementary pensions, further reductions for pensioners fewer than 55 years
old, etc.

In its turning point for case law, the Council of State stressed three preliminary
points. First, social insurance – as opposed to private insurance – was not based on
pure remuneration between contributions and benefits but should also cater for a
satisfactory standard of living close to the level achieved while working. Second,
the State had a positive obligation to take care of the proper functioning of the
social security organisations and the sustainability of their funds for the sake of
future generations. Third, reduction of social security could be implemented insofar as two prerequisites cumulatively apply: a procedural requirement of a prior
detailed study on the fairness and effects of the pension cuts; and a substantive
requirement to observe proportionality and human dignity. In spite of the identified unconstitutionality, the Council of State held that its ruling should only apply
ex post and, therefore, pensioners could not claim damages for past reductions.

As regards the *employment status* of public servants, the Greek Constitution
contains a rather unique provision, namely that they cannot be removed from
public service provided that their organic post (established by law) still exists
(Article 103(4)). This high level of protection for public servants, due to a long
history of illegitimate appointments and dismissals in the public sector on grounds
of political beliefs, has made it rather difficult for the State to introduce schemes
aiming at the reorganisation and rationalisation of the public sector. In this context,
the Council of State ruled on the constitutionality of the dispensability scheme

---

[47] Judgment 4741/2014 for academics and Judgment 2192/2014 for military and public security
servants.

[48] For instance, Judgments of the Hellenic Council of State 668/2012, 1285/2012, 2287/2015,
2288/2015.

transferring redundant public employees to a list for placement (decided as a collateral to the overall restructuring of the public sector), which after a prescribed period of time might lead to mandatory dismissal.

In Judgment 3354/2013, the Council held that this process was unconstitutional: although admittedly budgetary reasons might lead to reorganisation, rationalisation and limitation of the over-expanded public sector, such measures should observe the constitutional guarantee with regard to the status of public servants and the principle of equality, prohibiting the use of criteria not causally linked to the operational needs of the public service, such as the age of the employee, and merely allowing criteria associated to the constitutional principle of meritocracy, such as qualifications, competence, and performance of the employees. By way of contrast, in later Judgment 3169/2014, the Council found that temporary pre-pension set aside for teachers in the field of vocational training was constitutional because it was based on operational and organisational needs of the administration and that suffices for the State to exercise the margin of appreciation it possesses when it comes to the state architecture.

As regards the *privatisation schemes*, which included a number of public companies in the field of networks and provision of services, the most notable judgment is 1906/2014 of the Council of State with regard to the project of sell-out of the shares belonging to the state-owned Athens water supply company. The Council found the project to be unconstitutional on the grounds that it breached the constitutional right to health, which is formulated in Greece both as an individual right and as a public policy principle (Articles 5(5) and 21(3) respectively), mandating the State to ensure that the supply of potable water would remain continuous, adequate and affordable to meet the hygiene requirements. Therefore, the Council found that the full privatisation of the public company, for the sake of servicing the public debt, contravenes the Constitution to the extent that it entails the alienation of the State from the majority of the share capital of the company in question and thus the governmental supervision.

On the other hand, in Judgment 1902/2014 the Council held that it was constitutional to transfer a real estate property within the broader city of Athens (*Elliniko* region, the area of the former Athens airport, currently the largest non-built metropolitan space) to the Hellenic Republic Asset Development Fund, a *société anonyme* established and owned by the Greek Government to administer public assets, with the prospect of being commercially exploited through a public auction. The Council of State, taking into account the rebuilt of the area in question because of its size and significance, rejected the allegations of the applicants, namely two neighbouring municipalities, on the grounds that the project did not in principle entail social and environmental consequences contrary to the Constitution and EU law and that it did not usurp competences of the municipalities, since there was no constitutional mandate for the transfer of state property to them.

As regards the imposition of *extraordinary and multiple taxation*, due to urgent financial needs, the Council of State found all relevant burdens compatible with the constitutional principle of proportionate and universal taxation (Article 4(5)),

the partial prohibition of retroactive taxation (Article 78(2)), the general principle of equality (Article 4(1)) and the principle of proportionality (Article 25(1)).
Accordingly, it held that:

(a)   the diminution of the enormous budget deficit and of the excessive public
      debt was a compelling public interest that justified taking onerous tax meas-
      ures at wide discretion;[49]

(b)   a fair balance between burdens upon individuals/entities and the urgent need
      to raise public income was struck;[50]

(c)   a different tax treatment between individuals and legal entities, with impo-
      sition of a surtax upon the former only and exclusion of the latter, did not
      exceed the limits of the legislature's discretion to reform the tax system in
      accordance with general and objective criteria;[51]

(d)   the imposition of an extraordinary surtax upon personal income tax with
      reference to the income of previous years did not violate the non-retroactivity
      of taxation, in that this criterion does not appear to be inappropriate since
      it is merely used as the most recent and safe indicator of the tax capacity in
      order to identify the richer citizens and impose the relevant taxes on them;[52]

(e)   the imposition of a real estate tax, irrespective of whether these assets
      produce any income or not, did not violate the constitutional guarantee for
      proportionate taxation and the right to property;[53]

(f)   the imposition of professional and solidarity taxes for self-employed individ-
      uals, based on criteria linked to the time of exercise of a profession, the place
      and the relevant population, as well as the creation of layers of taxpayers with
      different percentages of financial burdens, fell within the State discretion to
      draw a variable taxation system;[54] and

(g)   the imposition of more than one type of taxes upon the same tax indicator for
      specific categories of taxpayers, such as the income (eg cumulatively private
      income taxation and professional and solidarity tax) did not, in principle,
      violate the protection of property and the proportionality test, since the
      principle *ne bis in idem* was not applicable in the field of imposition of tax
      burdens.[55]

A slight reversal, not yet consolidated, seems to apply in the field of tax case law
as of 2017, with some judgments curtailing the powers of the tax authorities in
imposing taxation and controlling adherence to tax obligations. In that regard,
the Council of State found a violation of the principle of equality in the statutory determination of a different tax indicator for listed as opposed to non-listed

---

[49] 2563/2015.
[50] 1972/2012, 532/2015, 2563/2015.
[51] 1685/2013, 2809/2017.
[52] 1685/2013.
[53] 532/2015.
[54] 2563/2015.
[55] 2563/2015, 1222/2017.

companies, since the mere fact that the former follow the international accounting standards and publish financial statements is not adequate to justify differential treatment.[56] Most importantly, the Council of State restricted the competence of the relevant tax authority to exercise controls upon individuals and legal entities for non-conformity with tax regulations.

The case arose in the context of recurrent statutory extensions of the general deadline provided by the Code of Income Taxation, which allowed tax controls and, in turn, set out an obligation to maintain all evidence concerning tax obligations, for a period of five years (Article 84(1)). Prior to 2017 the Council of State had ruled that such an extension did not amount to a constitutional violation, on the ground that it aimed at securing an even allocation of tax burdens and a tax conscience along with the need for state revenue. Yet, in Judgment 1738/2017 this statutory practice was deemed unconstitutional as violating the principles of legal certainty and legitimate expectations, stemming from the general constitutional clause for the protection of the rule of law, in conjunction with the prohibition of tax retroactivity and the requirement that no tax should be levied without a statute enacted by Parliament, specifying the subject of taxation and the income, the type of property, the expenses and the transactions or categories thereof to which such tax pertains (a reflection of the no taxation without representation dogma).

In particular, the Council held that:

(a) the rule of law, thus interpreted, required, due to the serious economic repercussions of tax rules for individuals and entities, clarity and predictability of such rules, that have to apply rigorously;

(b) both tax obligations and penalties imposed for their violation should not threaten taxpayers indefinitely but there must be a clear and predictable deadline, the starting and ending point of which should be concretely specified by law and should not depend on actions of a public authority (eg from the date of issuance or notification of a control order or from the amount of tax obligation that the tax authority ought to determine);

(c) the limitation period must, overall, be reasonable and compatible with the principle of proportionality so as to secure a series of compelling public interests:

   (i) effective tax control without the risk on the part of the tax authority to determine the exact amount of the obligation and to eventually collect it after the personal and/or legal status of individuals and entities are modified;

   (ii) the mobilisation of the tax authority to act promptly and not merely close to the deadline date;

---

[56] 753/2018. The decision is not final, given that the Section of the Council referred the case to a broader composition of the Section composed of seven members, as opposed to the ordinary five-member composition.

(iii)   the rationalisation of national policies in the sense that the State must be able to roughly determine its revenue in a timely manner so that it can allocate its expenditure;

(iv)   the substantive protection of taxpayers from legal uncertainty (which is present anyway because of the mutability of tax legislation) in the exercise of their right to pursue economic activities, with significant collateral benefits for the economic growth of the country;

(v)   the procedural protection of taxpayers by minimising the risk that they would no longer be in a position to adduce adequate evidence exercising their right to defence, after a long period of time from the event giving rise to the financial obligation.[57]

In spite of some minor judicial corrections in the taxation system in Greece in the aftermath of the sovereign debt crisis, there is one thing that is clearly missing from the case law of the Council of State when dealing with tax burdens imposed on individuals and entities. This is the cumulative effect of multiple tax burdens and the cumulative effect of tax burdens in conjunction with other State-imposed burdens, predominantly social security contributions, although proportionality does require a holistic assessment of the personal status of each person. Only in marginal cases, where the courts inclined towards striking down the relevant legislation, eg salary cuts of academics and military servants, was such cumulative effect taken into account. In fact, Greece features on the top of the Organisation for Economic Cooperation and Development's (OECD) 34 Member States with regard to taxes and social security burdens on individuals and entities, on the top of the EU index of unemployment, among the countries with the highest property taxation, on the top of tax hikes per GDP between 2007 and 2016 with an amazing increase of 7.4 percentage points (with half of the States reducing their tax rates in the same period and just four, ie Argentina, Mexico, Slovakia and Estonia, with an increase of over three percentage points).[58]

ii. EU Courts

In Judgment of 3 May 2017 before the General Court in Case T-531/14, *Sotiropoulou and others v Council*, the applicants brought an action before the EU General Court, on the basis of Article 268 TFEU, seeking compensation on the basis of non-contractual liability for the reduction of their main pensions as a result of the adoption of a series of allegedly unlawful decisions of the Council addressed

---

[57] X Contiades and IA Tassopoulos, 'The Impact of the Financial Crisis on the Greek Constitution' in X Contiades (ed), *Constitutions in the Global Financial Crisis. A Comparative Analysis* (Farnham, Ashgate, 2013) 195; A Marketou, 'Greece: Constitutional Deconstruction and the Loss of National Sovereignty' in T Beukers, B.de Witte and C Kilpatrick (eds), *Constitutional Change through Euro-crisis Law* (Cambridge, Cambridge University Press, 2017) 179.

[58] OECD, *Tax Policy Reforms 2018: OECD and Selected Partner Economies* (Paris, OECD Publishing, 2018).

to Greece in activation of the collective mechanism provided for in Article 126 TFEU. The Court dismissed the action, which relied on two pleas in law:

(a)   a competence plea alleging infringement of the principles of conferral of powers and subsidiarity; and
(b)   a human rights plea concerning infringement of fundamental rights.

As regards the competence plea, the applicants submitted that, in adopting the contested decisions, including detailed measures, policies and interventions in the social security and pension system, the Council exceeded the powers accorded to it by the Treaty and trespassed Greece's exclusive competence to determine its economic policy. Although the Court rejected the plea as inadmissible, it also made a substantive evaluation of the lawfulness of the impugned acts by indicating that they were compatible with EU law, to the extent that they were adopted in order to strengthen and deepen the necessary budgetary surveillance on a situation of excessive deficit.

As regards the human rights plea, the applicants submitted rapid deterioration in the standard of living in direct infringement of the EU Charter of Fundamental Rights with regard to the applicants' right to human dignity (Article 1 ChFR), their right as elderly persons to lead a life of dignity and independence (Article 25 ChFR) and their right to social security benefits and social services providing protection in cases such as old age (Article 34(1) ChFR). On the facts of the case, the Court identified that the contested decisions were adopted after it was found that the deterioration in the public finances of Greece threatened the financial stability of the euro area in general, the budgetary measures were thoroughly discussed with the Greek Government and agreed jointly by the Commission, the ECB and the IMF and, therefore, they fall within the Council's wide discretionary power. On this plea again, the Court made an auxiliary comment, to the effect that, irrespective of the non-manifest unlawfulness of the impugned acts, there was no causality in the damages incurred by the applicants, since the rights of access to social services and the social security benefits were not absolute prerogatives but could legitimately be restricted, where necessary to serve a compelling interest. Such an interest was found in the case, in view of the imminent threat of Greece's default, in ensuring fiscal consolidation, reducing public expenditure and supporting the national pension system, conjunctively amounting to the Union interest to ensure the budgetary discipline of the euro-area Member States and to safeguard the euro area's financial stability.

iii. European Court of Human Rights

In Judgment of 7 May 2013 *Koufaki and ADEDY*,[59] salary cuts in Greece were challenged before the European Court on Human Rights as violating Article 1 of Protocol No 1 to the Convention. The first applicant, Ms Ioanna Koufaki,

---

[59] ECtHR Judgment of 7 May 2013, *Koufaki and ADEDY v Greece*, Application no 57665/12.

was a Greek national working as a member of the scientific staff of the Greek Ombudsman's Office, a public law entity, whereas ADEDY (Supreme Administration of Public Servants Union) was the public sector employees' national union in Greece, representing several unions of public-sector workers employed on a permanent basis or under private law by the State, corporations governed by public law and the local and regional authorities, with an aim to defend the economic, social and professional interests of public-sector workers, including with regard to pension issues.

In their argumentation, the applicants submitted that the right of all public-sector employees to payment of their salary formed part of their possessions and fell within the sphere of protection of their right to property; therefore, infringement of this right amounted to a deprivation of possessions. They claimed that the public interest of adducing public income, eliminating the budget deficit and securing the stability of public finances was not sufficient, but the State ought to have drawn up a detailed economic study examining in advance all alternative solutions and measures with a less drastic impact. The applicant further argued that the legislature ought to have examined whether the impact of these measures would be permanent or temporary, whether the scope and duration of the restrictions imposed were compatible with the aim pursued and whether they were accompanied by compensatory measures (for instance, a reduction in direct or indirect taxation and in the price of basic essentials, a reduction in working hours, a permission to have another occupation, a lowering of interest rates or a reduction in loan repayments). The Labour Union also complained that the impugned legislation introduced horizontal cuts, irrespective of the level of salary, thus affecting high and low earners alike.

The Court identified that interferences served a legitimate public interest to remedy the acute budgetary crisis and to consolidate state finances. It reiterated that there was no individual right to a pension of a particular amount and found no evidence that Ms Koufaki's situation had worsened to the extent that she risked falling below the subsistence threshold – a settled pre-crisis case law.[60] Eventually, the Court, making extensive use of both the explanatory report accompanying Law 3833/2010[61] and of Judgment 668/2012 of the Hellenic Council of State, held that a fair and proportionate balance was struck between the legitimate public interest involved and the relative curtailment of the applicants' property rights.

---

[60] ECtHR Judgment of 1 June 1999, *Skorkiewicz v Poland*, Application no 39860/98; ECtHR Judgment of 10 April 2001, *Kuna v Germany*, Application no 52449/99; ECtHR Judgment of 18 June 2002, *Blanco Callejas v Spain*, Application no 64100/00; ECtHR Judgment of 31 May 2011, *Maggio and others v Italy*, Application nos 46286/09, 52851/08, 53727/08, 54486/08 and 56001/08, para 55.

[61] 'The worst crisis in the public finances for decades', which '[had] undermined the country's credibility, thwarted efforts to meet the country's lending needs and pose[d] a serious threat to the national economy'. The report stated that finding a way out of the crisis represented 'a historic responsibility and a national duty' and that Greece had undertaken to 'achieve fiscal consolidation on the basis of precise targets and a precise timetable'.

D. The Portuguese Bail-out Scheme: Salary/Pension Cuts in the Public Sector

i. Domestic Courts

A great number of judgments relevant to the implementation of the Portuguese programme were rendered by the Constitutional Court:

- 399/2010 (surtax upon personal income tax for 2010 – constitutional);
- 396/2011 (salary cuts stemming from Budget Law for 2011 – constitutional);
- 353/2012 (suspension of thirteenth and fourteenth salary in the public sector stemming from Budget Law 2012 – unconstitutional);
- 187/2013 (suspension of holiday payments in the public sector and imposition of burdens on unemployment benefits stemming from Budget Law 2013 – unconstitutional);
- 474/2013 (dismissals through requalification stemming from statute – unconstitutional);
- 602/2013 (diminution of labour protection in private sector stemming from the Labour Code – unconstitutional);
- 160/2013 (statutory increase of working hours in the public sector – constitutional);
- 862/2013 (statutory cuts on public sector pensions to achieve relative convergence – unconstitutional);
- 413/2014 (salary cuts in the public sector, taxation upon social benefits and suspension of public sector pension supplements stemming from Budget Law for 2014 – unconstitutional);
- 572/2014 (imposition of the special solidarity contribution stemming from Budget Law for 2014 – constitutional);
- 574/2014 (statutory salary cuts for the public sector for the years 2014–2018 – unconstitutional);
- 575/2014 (statutory special sustainability contribution on pensions – unconstitutional);
- 745/2014 (increase of public servants' contributions for national health care – constitutional). Some of the above-mentioned judgments are cited below.

The selection is based on the significance of the judgments, mostly those striking down legislation relating to the austerity measures or referring questions to the Court of Justice.

Challenges of the three Budget Laws for the years of the programme were arguably the most significant case law contribution of the Constitutional Court. The first decision to hold the Budget Law unconstitutional was Judgment 353/2012, concerning the constitutionality of the 2012 Budget, in particular its provisions suspending holiday and Christmas allowances for public servants and pensioners where the amount received exceeded 600 euros for the three years of the international assistance programme, ie 2012–14. The Court found a breach of the principle of equality and proportionality, on the grounds that only servants and pensioners of the public sector suffered cuts and that the Government failed to seek other more equitable alternative solutions to reduce state expenses.

In spite of the fact that the annulment referred to the budget of 2012, the Court postponed its effect, so that restoration of salaries and pensions would occur as of 2013, since at the time of issuance of the judgment a large part of the year had already elapsed. The dissenting opinion justified the salary cuts with reference to the domestic constitutional mandate towards European integration, requiring respect for the principle of loyal cooperation and entailing that Portugal should do its utmost to reinforce the European identity and to strengthen the European States' actions in favour of democracy, peace, economic progress and justice in the relations between the people (Article 7(5)) and to the commitments stemming from membership to the euro area that came with the financial assistance.

By Judgment 187/2013, the Budget Law for 2013 was declared unconstitutional by the Constitutional Court, again on the grounds of violation of the equality clause, in its parts concerning:

(a)   the suspension of the payment of holiday allowances or equivalent to the public officials;
(b)   the suspension of the payment of holiday allowances or equivalent to the retired individuals and pensioners; and,
(c)   the mandatory contribution on sickness and unemployment benefits (six and five per cent respectively).

Other aspects of the Budget Law were considered by the Court as compatible with the Constitution, namely the reduction of salaries of public officials obtaining a gross monthly salary exceeding 1,500 euros, the reduction in the payment of overtime work to public officials, the extraordinary solidarity contribution on pensions with a monthly value exceeding 1,350 euros, the reduction of supports and the extraordinary surcharge on personal income tax. The dissenting opinion again upheld the constitutionality of the austerity measures on the grounds of adherence to the European integration project. Finally, in Judgment 413/2014, the Constitutional Court examined the Budget Law for 2014 imposing a further cut on public salaries. The Court, as expected, found unconstitutionality on the grounds of equality, using the already established case law by that time. In this judgment, nevertheless, the Court did not suspend the effects of its ruling but implemented it for the remainder of 2014 (as of the date of the ruling – 30 May 2014).

Outside the salary and pensions cut, the most important ruling came in Judgment 474/2013 of 29 August 2013 concerning the constitutionality of governmental Bill 177/XXII on the dispensability scheme of public sector employees. This 'requalification programme' came as a substitute to the original mobility scheme that was withheld. It provided for the change of the legal status of certain public servants appointed to organic placements in the public sector and guaranteed the holding of their posts to employees on a contract labour relationship with less guarantees of permanency. The case was referred to the Court by Portugal's President, Aníbal Cavaco Silva for a preventive ruling concerning the constitutionality of certain provisions of the Bill on job security (Article 53) in conjunction with the constitutional principles of proportionality and legitimate expectations (Article 18).

The Court discarded some parts of the Bill on the grounds that:

(a) the criteria set by the statute to decide on redunduncies were vague and inconcrete and, therefore, did not secure adequate guarantees to prevent dismissals without just cause;

(b) it violated the principles of proportionality and legitimate expectations in relation to the restriction of the right to employment security;

(c) it amounted to an unconstitutional deterioration of the labour relationship through the change of the legal status of the employees; and,

(d) it instigated a different treatment for public servants as opposed to employees in the private sector who can only be dismissed on adequately proved market, structural or technological grounds but not on cost reduction grounds.

On a number of cases the ordinary Portuguese Courts took the path of a reference to the Court of Justice for a preliminary ruling concerning salary cuts of members of the judiciary and of the rest of public sector employees. As regards the remuneration cuts of the judiciary, in its decision of 7 January 2016, the Supreme Administrative Court dealt with the constitutionality and the compatibility of Law 75/2014 with EU law which temporarily reduced, as of October 2014, the remuneration of a series of office-holders and employees performing duties in the public sector, including the remuneration of the judges of the Court of Auditors (*Tribunal de Contas*) through a 'salary management' scheme.

The Trade Union of Portuguese Judges, *Associação Sindical dos Juízes Portugueses*, acting on behalf of the members of the Court of Auditors, brought a special administrative action before the Court seeking the annulment of the scheme, the repayment of the lost portion of salaries plus default interest at the statutory rate, and a declaration that the persons concerned were entitled to receive their salaries in full. The Court acknowledged that the cuts were based on mandatory requirements for reducing the Portuguese State's excessive budget deficit during the year 2011 in the framework of EU law by the decisions granting financial assistance to that Member State. It then emphasised on the constitutional and Union law principle of judicial independence and impartiality (Articles 203 of the Portuguese Constitution, 19(1) TEU and 47 of the Charter of Fundamental Rights of the EU), applicable both to Courts of the European Union and national courts. Given that, in the Court's view the independence of judicial bodies depended on the guarantees attached to their members' status, including remuneration. In the light of the above, it referred a question to the Court of Justice as to whether the relevant provisions of the TEU and the Charter should be interpreted as precluding the reduction of remuneration applied to the judiciary in Portugal, where imposed unilaterally and on an ongoing basis by other constitutional authorities and bodies.

As regards the salary cuts of the general public sector, the Portuguese trade unions challenged before the Employment Court of Porto the austerity measures included in the State Budget Law for 2011, especially concerning cuts to public sector wages and suspension of payment and bonuses in state-owned BPN – *Banco Português de Negócios*. The bank was nationalised in 2008 and its employees became public servants. Despite a collective agreement reached by the State and the unions in 2011, the bank decided to lower the wages of its employees and to set aside parts of the collective agreement, relying on the State Budget Law, which enabled instant and unilateral implementation of horizontal and sectoral labour measures. Applicants mostly relied on alleged violations of labour rights guaranteed by primary EU law, especially by reference to Article 31(1) ChFR on fair and just working conditions, entailing that every worker has the right to working conditions that respect his/her health, safety and dignity.

In Judgment of 6 January 2012, the Court suspended the process and made a reference to the Court of Justice for a preliminary ruling, setting a number of questions that could be classified as follows:

(a) whether the principle of equal treatment was applicable to the public sector or to public undertaking employees and, if so, whether salary cuts only to those employees violated that principle on the ground of the public nature of the employment relationship (the non-discrimination question);

(b) whether a unilateral modification by the State, without the employee's consent, of the contract to introduce salary cuts violated labour dignity (the unilateral State interference question);

(c) whether unforeseeable and unexpected salary cuts violated labour dignity of the employees (the legitimate expectations question);

(d) whether employees were entitled to fair remuneration which ensured that they and their families could enjoy a satisfactory standard of living pursuant to the labour dignity clause (the minimum wage question); and

(e) whether the State had to look beforehand for existing alternative measures to consolidate public finances in a case of serious economic and financial crisis (the *ultimum refugium* question).

The same Court made another reference to the Court of Justice for a preliminary ruling with its judgment of 22 May 2012. This reference questioned the compatibility with EU law of Article 21 of the Budget Law for 2012, which abolished in full the payment of holiday allowance for workers whose monthly pay was equal to or greater than 1,100 euros and abolished in part the payment of that allowance for workers who received pay of 600 to 1,100 euros per month, although those allowances were explicitly provided in the respective collective agreement. By the same token, the Employment Court of Lisbon, under practically identical factual and legal premises, with judgment of 28 October 2013 referred to the Court of Justice a question also concerning the suspension of payment of holiday and Christmas bonuses or similar benefits stemming from Budget Law for 2012. The questions of the referring Court were somewhat simpler, merely emphasising the non-discrimination argument.[62]

ii. EU Courts

On three occasions of references for a preliminary ruling by Portuguese employment tribunals, the Court of Justice ruled that it clearly lacked jurisdiction with regard to the request. Pursuant to Article 267 TFEU, the Court can only interpret EU law within the limits of the powers conferred on the EU, while the EU Charter of Fundamental Rights is addressed to the Member States only where they implemented EU law (Article 51(1) of the ChFR) and does not create any new powers or alter the powers of the Union (Article 6(1) TEU). Under those circumstances, with the Order of the Sixth Chamber of the Court of Justice of 7 March 2013 in Case C-128/12, *Sindicato dos Bancários do Norte and others*, the Court found that the reference for a preliminary ruling by the Employment Tribunal of Porto contained no concrete evidence to suggest that Budget Act for 2011 implemented EU law, despite relevant doubts expressed by the national court. Since the Court of Justice could not establish its own jurisdiction, it dismissed the case.

Interestingly, the Tribunal made another reference without waiting for the Court to give a ruling on the first one. The Court of Justice in its Orders of 26 June 2014 in Case C-264/12 *Sindicato Nacional dos Profissionais de Seguros e Afins* of the same Tribunal and of 21 October 2014 in Case C-665/13, *Sindicato Nacional dos Profissionais de Seguros e Afins*, responding to a reference by the Employment Tribunal of Lisbon for a preliminary ruling concerning broadly the same questions, found that it lacked jurisdiction and dismissed the relevant cases in roughly the same manner.

Lastly, the Court of Justice upheld the admissibility and gave a preliminary ruling on the merits in Judgment of 27 February 2018 in Case C-64/16, *Associação Sindical dos Juízes Portugueses and others*, concerning remuneration cuts of the members of the Court of Auditors of Portugal. Predictably the European Commission, which was present in the case to defend the compatibility of the Portuguese reduction scheme with EU law, relied on the then recent case law of the Court denying admissibility of references by the Portuguese Employment Courts. Yet, the Court of Justice held that in the case in question, the order for reference contained sufficient information to enable the Court to understand the reasons why the referring court sought interpretation of the relevant primary law provisions of Article 19(1) TEU and 47 ChFR for the needs of the main proceedings.

---

[62] JEM Machado, 'The Sovereign Debt Crisis and the Constitution's Negative Outlook: A Portuguese Preliminary Assessment' in X Contiades (ed), *Constitutions in the Global Financial Crisis. A Comparative Analysis* (Farnham, Ashgate, 2013) 219; Kilpatrick (n 35).

In deciding the actual question, the Court relied on six premises:

(1) To challenge before the national courts the legality of any decision or other national measure relating to the application of an EU act to them. This judicial architecture finds its expression to the value of the rule of law stated in Article 2 TEU, according to which the EU is founded on values, such as the rule of law, common to the Member States in a society in which justice prevails; thus, mutual trust between national courts and tribunals is based on the fundamental premise that Member States share a set of common values on which the EU is founded.

(2) As regards the *requirements of the rule of law*, these are guaranteed by a full and effective judicial system through courts and tribunals. Since national courts and tribunals, in collaboration with the Court of Justice, jointly fulfil an EU duty, the Member States are obliged, by reason, inter alia, of the principle of sincere cooperation (Article 4(3) TEU), to provide remedies that are sufficient to ensure effective judicial protection for individual parties in the fields covered by EU law, through a system of effective legal remedies and procedures before courts or tribunals.

(3) As to the *requirements for a body to be qualified as a court*, for the purposes of EU law, the relevant criteria were whether it was permanent, its jurisdiction was compulsory, its procedure *inter partes*, it applied rules of law and it was independent. Indeed, the Portuguese Court of Auditors qualified as a court, since it applied EU law (on actions relating to the EU's own resources and the use of financial resources from the EU) and decided on questions concerning the prior review of the validity of the measures, contracts or other instruments giving rise to public expenditure or debts, inter alia, in the context of public procurement procedures.

(4) As to the *specifics of judicial independence*, provided by Article 47 ChFR, referring to access to an 'independent' tribunal as one of the requirements linked to the fundamental right to an effective remedy, such independence was deemed essential to the proper working of the judicial cooperation system embodied by the preliminary ruling mechanism. In the Court's view, independence presupposed that the body concerned exercised its judicial functions in full autonomy, without being subject to any hierarchical constraint or subordinated to any other body and without taking orders or instructions from any source whatsoever liable to impair the independent judgment of its members and to influence their decisions. Like the protection against removal from office of its members, remuneration commensurate with the importance of the members' functions constituted a guarantee that was essential to judicial independence.

(5) As to the *impact of salary cuts on judicial independence*, the Court of Justice found that the reason to eliminate excessive budget deficit and to adhere to the conditionality attached to financial assistance was legitimate and that remuneration reductions were relatively limited and temporary in nature.

(6)   The measures were not discriminatory since they applied not only to the members of the Court of Auditors, but, more widely, to various public office-holders and employees performing duties in the public sector, including the representatives of the legislature, the executive and the judiciary, thus they were properly included in the general policy measures seeking a contribution from all members of the national public administration to the compelling austerity effort.

Accordingly, the Court responded to the referring court that the EU law principle of judicial independence did not preclude general salary-reduction measures upon judges, linked to requirements to eliminate an excessive budget deficit and to an EU financial assistance programme.[63]

E.   The Greek Bail-in Scheme: Haircut on Government Bonds

During the first years of the financial crisis (2010–11) the institutional investors, ie banks and other credit organisations, negotiated a reduction ('haircut') in the nominal value of their shares on bonds and an adjusted mode of reimbursement of the remainder. At the time, there was an official list of 81 Greek securities maturing up to 2020, which were eligible for exchange, including government bonds, international bonds and Greek organisation bonds, with a total face value of 199.5 billion euros, 134.5 billion of which were held by private-sector creditors, thus being eligible for participation in the Private Sector Involvement agreement (PSI). This project, aiming at restructuring the Greek public debt and rendering it more sustainable, was a combined action of the Greek Government, the euro-area Member States, the ECB, the IMF and private investors.

On 8 May 2010, following an adverse normal evaluation by the financial markets of bonds issued by the Greek Government and the consequent upset of financial stability of the euro area, the ECB adopted Decision 2010/268[64] on temporary measures relating to the eligibility of marketable debt instruments issued or guaranteed by the Greek Government. The decision introduced a temporary suspension of the Eurosystem's minimum requirements for credit quality thresholds, as specified in the Eurosystem credit assessment framework rules for marketable assets (Section 6.3.2 of the General Documentation, Article 1(1)), to the effect that credit quality threshold should not apply to marketable debt instruments issued by the Greek Government and by entities established in Greece and fully guaranteed by the Greek Government. Such assets could constitute eligible collateral for the purposes of Eurosystem monetary policy operations, irrespective of their external credit rating (Articles 2 and 3 of ECB Decision 2010/268 respectively).

---

[63] L Pech and S Platon, 'Judicial Independence under Threat: The Court of Justice to the Rescue in the *ASJP* Case' (2018) 55 *Common Market Law Review* 1827.
[64] ECB/2010/3 (OJ 2010 L 117, p 102).

According to said Decision, this exceptional measure would apply temporarily until the ECB's Governing Council considered that the stability of the financial system allowed for the normal application of the Eurosystem framework for monetary policy operations (Recital 5 of Decision 2010/268). The day after, the ECB's Governing Council decided and publicly announced that, in view of the exceptional circumstances in financial markets at the time, characterised by severe tensions in certain market segments hampering the monetary policy transmission mechanism and the effective conduct of monetary policy towards medium-term price stability, a temporary securities markets programme should be initiated. Indeed, on 14 May 2010, the ECB adopted Decision 2010/281,[65] establishing a securities markets programme, according to which the ECB and the euro-area national central banks, pro rata to their percentage shares in the key for subscription of the ECB's capital, and in direct contact with counterparties, might conduct outright interventions in the euro-area public and private debt securities markets. The programme formed part of the Eurosystem's single monetary policy and was designed to apply temporarily with the objective to address the malfunctioning of securities markets and to restore an appropriate monetary policy transmission mechanism. Pursuant to this programme, Eurosystem central banks might purchase on the secondary market eligible euro marketable debt instruments issued by the central governments or public entities of the euro-area Member States (Articles 1 and 2).

On 1 July 2011, the Institute of International Finance (IIF), the most acknowledged collective global association of financial institutions,[66] officially declared its commitment to working with its membership and other financial sectors, the public sector and the Greek authorities to deliver substantial cash-flow to Greece, as well as to lay the basis for a more sustainable debt position through a voluntary, cooperative, transparent and broad-based effort to support the State. On 21 July 2011, the Heads of States/governments of the euro area and the EU institutions made a joint statement to welcome both the institutional measures to assist in the Greek crisis, as well as the private sector contribution scheme. On 17 November 2011, the Greek Ministry of Finance announced the commencement of consultations with holders of Greek bonds in preparation for a voluntary exchange of those bonds with a notional haircut of 50 per cent of the nominal value of Greek debt held by private investors.

[65] ECB 2010/5 (OJ 2010 L 124, p 8). The Decision was taken on the basis of the first indent of Art 127(2) TFEU and, in particular, Art 18(1) of the Statute.

[66] The IIF is the global association of the financial industry, with close to 450 members from 70 countries. Its mission is to support the financial industry in the prudent management of risks; to develop sound industry practices; and to advocate for regulatory, financial and economic policies that are in the broad interests of its members and foster global financial stability and sustainable economic growth. IIF members include commercial and investment banks, asset managers, insurance companies, sovereign wealth funds, hedge funds, central banks and development banks, see www.iif.com/about.

On 17 February 2012, the ECB delivered a positive opinion on a relevant draft Greek parliamentary bill suggesting collective action clauses. On 23 February 2012, Greek Law 4050/2012 was enacted providing for activating collective action clauses in order to require anyone not wishing to take part in the operation to participate, provided that at least two-thirds of the individual bondholders acceded to the agreement voting collectively without distinction by series.[67] On 27 February 2012, the ECB adopted Decision 2012/133,[68] which had the effect of suspending the eligibility of Greek debt instruments as collateral for the purposes of Eurosystem monetary policy operations, on the ground that the adequacy of such collateral had been further negatively affected by the Government's decision to launch a debt exchange offer in the context of private sector involvement to holders of state marketable debt instruments.

On 1 March 2012, the European Commission, acting on behalf of the Member States of the euro area, and the Hellenic Republic reached a draft agreement to the effect that:

(a)   the latter would launch an exchange offer for outstanding eligible bonds with a view to reducing the nominal value by 53.5 per cent;
(b)   bondholders would be offered to exchange existing bonds for new bonds of the Hellenic Republic with a new nominal value of 31.5 per cent of the original nominal value;
(c)   in addition, 15 per cent of the original nominal value would be provided to bondholders in the form of notes; and
(d)   an amount of up to 35 billion euros would be used to facilitate the maintenance of eligibility, as collateral for Eurosystem monetary policy operations, of marketable debt instruments issued or guaranteed by the Greek Government, by putting in place a buy-back scheme for as long as a default or selective default rating is assigned to the Hellenic Republic or its bonds as a result of the debt exchange offer.

Consequently, the Governor of the Bank of Greece, who had been appointed to manage the procedure, declared that the bondholders had agreed to the proposed amendments and that 91.05 per cent of the outstanding receivables had been covered by the procedure. The Cabinet ratified the result, which, therefore, covered all the capital constituted by the selected bonds, including those held by the applicants. The old bonds were exchanged for new ones worth 53.5 per cent less in terms of nominal value. The exchange applied to bonds held by all individuals and legal persons, merely through the consent of a qualified majority of bondholders, through the inclusion of collective action clauses in the bonds.

[67] Prior to Law 4050/2012, Art 8(2) of Law 2198/1994 provided that if the State fails to comply with its obligations at the time of maturity of the governmental bonds, each investor might demand its claim against the State.
[68] ECB/2012/2 (OJ 2012 L 59, p 36).

i. Domestic Courts

On 23 April 2012 individual investors that had not consented to the PSI, in spite of the State's invitation to take part in the exchange procedure, and having suffered curtailment in the value of their bonds, applied to the Council of State for judicial review. The applicants turned against acts implementing Article 1 of Law 4050/2012 on the grounds of deprivation of their right to property and freedom to conclude contracts stemming from the right to one's personality, in conjunction with the principle of proportionality (Articles 17, 5(1) and 25(1) of the Greek Constitution respectively), principles of EU Law and Article 1 of Protocol No 1 to the ECHR, by unilaterally introducing collective action amounting to a 53.5 per cent reduction in the nominal value of their bonds.

In Judgments 1116–1117/2014, the plenary of the Council rejected all grounds on their merits. As a matter of principle, the majority opinion considered that buying government bonds was not a riskless investment. Regarding the actual inability of the Greek State to pay, the Council took for granted that since 2010 the sustainability of Greek public debt, the highest percentage of which was due over the next few years following the hearing of the case, had become impossible to be served either through public revenue, due to the prolonged recession of the national economy, or through borrowing from the market, which was at the time essentially prohibited due to the total loss of the State's creditworthiness. Besides that, until recovery of the national economy, the Greek Government could only draw limited funds through the IMF and loan facility financing agreements with the euro-area Member States. Therefore, the pursuit of a renegotiation for a part of public debt, concerning the private sector creditors, was legitimate and expected to have a positive outcome.

Arguably, the most interesting part of the judgments was the one regarding the legality of the process pursued, where the Council identified that the Greek Government had broadly observed international good practices, such as those in the UK and the US, especially relating to collective action clauses. Thus, all bondholders ought to have been lawfully invited to participate in their assembly with votes corresponding to the nominal value of their securities, whereas the result of the voting was binding upon all investors, even those not participating. The Council of State placed emphasis on the procedure that had been followed, namely the rules processed by the EFS sub-Committee on EU Sovereign Debt Markets, after consultation with the ECB, the IMF and other investment institutions and approval by the Economic and Financial Committee as Model Collective Action Clause for the EU Member States, who were contracting States in the Treaty establishing the ESM. Finally, regarding the constitutionality of interference with property rights, the Council held that, given the urgency and extremity of the economic crisis, the PSI scheme did not appear as a disproportionate interference with the right to property and the 53.5 per cent reduction of nominal bond value was indeed 'particularly serious' but 'not inappropriate, unnecessary or excessive'.[69]

---

[69] Contiades and Tassopoulos, 'The Impact' (2013); Marketou, 'Greece' (2017).

ii. EU Courts

In Judgment of 7 October 2015 in Case T-79/13, *Accorinti and others v ECB*, the applicants (Greek Government bond shareholders) filed a claim for damages following the adoption by the ECB of Decision 2012/153 and the Greek PSI. In the applicants' submission, the ECB acted unlawfully, causing the EU to incur liability, on a number of occasions, namely by:

(i) concluding the exchange agreement of 15 February 2012 with the Hellenic Republic, which the applicants asked the Court to order the ECB to disclose;
(ii) refusing to participate in the restructuring of the Greek public debt, as a result of which the Hellenic Republic was forced to obtain new financial assistance; and
(iii) adopting Decision 2012/153, which made the eligibility of the Greek bonds as collateral subject to a buy-back scheme made available only to the national central banks, although those bonds did not satisfy the credit quality conditions.

The applicant sought damages based on:

(a) non-contractual liability of the ECB in respect of an unlawful act, pursuant to Articles 268 and 340 TFEU, on the grounds of breach of legitimate expectations and proportionality, ultra vires because of the prohibition of any type of credit facility in favour of Member States and of purchase of debt instruments by the ECB directly from them (Article 123 TFEU and Article 21 of Protocol No 4 on the Statute of the ESCB and of the ECB) and of the strict definition of objectives and tasks of the ESCB (Article 127 TFEU), and excess of discretion on the part of the ECB, and discrimination/misuse of powers because the exchange agreement provided for a 'preferential creditor status' of the Eurosystem central banks in order to escape the haircut albeit being in a situation in which there was a conflict of interests, on account of its position within the Eurogroup 'troika' and, at the same time, its role, contrary to Article 5 TEU, as creditor of the Hellenic Republic and the guardian of its monetary policy; and
(b) non-contractual liability of the ECB in respect of a lawful legislative measure.

On claim (a) with respect to damage caused by an *unlawful* act, the Court assessed the cumulative criteria for non-contractual liability, namely the unlawfulness of the alleged conduct of the EU institution, the fact of damage and the existence of a causal link between the alleged conduct and the damage complained of, eventually dismissing all alleged grounds of illegality. The misuse of powers plea was dismissed on the ground that preferential treatment of the ECB was specifically intended to preserve the central bank's margin for maneuver and to ensure the continuity of the smooth functioning of the Eurosystem as well as to provide the national central banks with enhanced credit so that they may continue to accept Greek bonds as appropriate collateral for the purposes of Eurosystem credit operations.

The Court found that the plea was particularly vague, succinct, overlapping and 'intrinsically contradictory',[70] in that, admittedly, the ECB's conduct to which they take exception, in particular the conclusion of the exchange agreement, was intended to avoid the involvement of the Eurosystem central banks in the restructuring of the Greek public debt that would mean sacrificing part of the value of the Greek bonds held in their respective portfolios; however, such unconditional involvement would have been specifically in danger of being classified as intervention having an effect equivalent to that of the prohibited direct purchase of State bonds by those central banks.

On the alternative claim (b) with respect to damage caused by a *lawful* act coming within the legislative sphere of the EU, the Court rejected the argument, in principle, by excluding that such liability may occur, also by reference to the Member States' legal orders. It then assessed whether the individual damage in question could qualify as unusual and special. With regard to the 'unusual' nature of the damage, ie exceeding the limits of the economic risks inherent to activities in the economic sector in question, which might be capable of substantiating such liability, such operations were carried out on particularly volatile markets, often subject to hazards and uncontrollable risks as regards the increase or decrease in the value of such bonds, which might invite speculation in order to obtain high returns in the very short term. Therefore, even on the assumption that all the applicants were not involved in speculative operations, they had to be aware of those hazards and risks of a considerable loss in the value of the bonds they purchased. That applied *a fortiori* because, even before the beginning of its economic crisis, the issuing Greek State had already been faced with high indebtedness and a high deficit.

Accordingly, the damage sustained on account of the PSI could not be classified as 'unusual' or 'special' since it did not affect the particular circle of economic operators in a disproportionate manner by comparison with others.[71] In fact, the applicants, like all other private investors, admittedly with the exception of the Eurosystem central banks, were subject to the PSI and, given the large number of investors concerned, identified in a general and objective manner by reference, in particular, to the serial numbers of the bonds in question, the applicants could not be considered to belong to a special category of economic operators who were affected in a disproportionate manner by comparison with others.

iii. European Court of Human Rights

In Judgment of 21 July 2016, *Mamatas and others v Greece*,[72] the forcible participation by the applicants, who were individuals holding Greek State bonds, was

---

[70] Para 114.
[71] Para 120.
[72] ECtHR Judgment of 21 July 2016, *Mamatas and others v Greece*, Application nos 63066/14, 64297/14 and 66106/14.

challenged before the Court of Strasbourg, which found no violation of the Convention. The applicants were 6,320 Greek nationals who held Greek State bonds of amounts ranging from 10,000 to 1,510,000 euros and had refused the proposed exchange. They claimed deprivation of or, alternatively, illegal interference with their right to property, in conjunction with violation of the non-discrimination clause, when compared with other creditors, particularly the major creditors and the ECB as referential creditor.

In the first place, the Court once again reiterated its self-restraint when it comes to States' social and economic policies. It then declared that the forcible haircut of government bonds did not qualify as deprivation but merely as interference with the peaceful enjoyment of possessions. In assessing whether the interference pursued a public-interest aim, it considered that during that critical period of severe crisis, when the country was facing an enormous deficit and was incapable of paying its debts, the authorities should have endeavoured to find solutions and could have legitimately taken action to maintain economic stability and restructure the debt in the general interest of the community.

With regard to the proportionality of the impugned measure, the Court concluded that the applicants had not suffered any 'special' or 'excessive' burden, in view, particularly, of the States' wide margin of appreciation in that sphere and of the reduction of the commercial value of the bonds, which had already been affected by the reduced solvency of Greece. In the Court's view, the level of participation in the process of various private bondholders made no difference in legal terms given that they all had the possibility, acting prudently, to sell their bonds in the secondary bond market prior to the conclusion of the exchange scheme. The fact that, unlike other bondholders, the applicants had not consented to the exchange operation, which had, therefore, been imposed on them under the new collective action clauses, did not, as such, affect the assessment of the proportionality of the interference aiming at saving the State from default.

The judicial approach lies in an underlying assumption that investing in bonds is never risk-free; the Court relied significantly upon this assumption, in the sense that bondholders should have been aware of the vagaries of the financial market and the risk of a possible drop in the value of their bonds, considering the Greek deficit and the country's large debt, even before the crisis. According to the Court, there is a considerable lapse of time between the time of issue of such a security and the date of its maturity; during this time unforeseeable events occur, which can substantially affect the issuer's solvency, even if the issuer is a State, and thus cause the bondholder to incur subsequent financial losses. Moreover, the Court found no violation of the principle of equality in the bond exchange procedure among various investors, because of the inherent difficulty to apply variable standards to each category and because of the absolute need to act promptly so as not to jeopardise the effectiveness of the project. In subsequent Judgment of 16 January 2018, *Kyrkos and 33 other applications v Greece*, the Court reaffirmed its position that the exchange programme introduced by the Greek government did not violate Articles 1 of Protocol No 1 and 14 to the Convention.[73]

F. The Cyprus Bail-in Scheme: Bank Deposit Cuts

i. Domestic Courts

On 6 June 2013, the Supreme Court of Cyprus dismissed several hundreds of actions for annulment against the Central Bank of Cyprus with regard to national measures (Decrees 103/2013 and 104/2013) providing for the bail-in.[74] The Supreme Court of Cyprus held that the depositors who were affected by the bail-in measures had no direct interest in bringing an action for annulment against the Decrees in question. In this view, the contested Decrees were addressed solely to the Cypriot banks and were not directly concerned with the relationship between the State and individuals. Furthermore, the Cypriot court found that the question of lawfulness of the contested acts was an issue pertaining to private rather than public law, therefore, it lacked competence, and the applicants alleging having suffered damage from the sale ought to have applied to the ordinary courts on the ground of violation of contractual commitments by the Laïki Bank.

In this view, the impugned decrees both *ratione materiae* and *ratione personae* referred directly to the Laïki Bank: the restructuring scheme affected merely the banking operations and, therefore, only involved the Bank; neither the Bank's shareholders, nor the applicant depositors were involved in the scheme and, since the latter were merely creditors of the bank, 'the nature of their interest in the case is different'. The Court went on to make an analysis of the relationship between the depositor and the bank and the level of (contractual) faith developed in this respect.

As regards the nature of the relationship, the Court identified that the depositor delivered money to the bank, which was then melted in the Bank's entire assets and were considered as the Bank's own assets. As of the moment of deposit of the money, the Bank merely owed the money to the depositor, according to the terms of the deposit agreement; the depositor, therefore, no longer had any proprietary right but merely a contractual claim upon the deposited money.

The Court drew three analogies to substantiate its conclusion *a majore ad minus*:

(a) in the case of use of a bank deposit box, depositors remained holders and proprietors of anything inserted in the deposit boxes and in case of loss or damage they might request the return or restoration *in natura*;

---

[73] ECtHR Judgment of 16 January 2018, *Kyrkosand v Greece*, Application no 64058/14.

[74] Supreme Court of Cyprus Judgment of 7 June 2013, Case No 553/2013, *Christodoulou and others v Kentriki Trapeza Kyprou and others*; Supreme Court of Cyprus Judgment of 9 October 2014, Case no 1034/2013, *Dimitriou and others v Kentrikis Trapezas Kyprou and others*.

(b) in the case of bank shareholders, they were proprietors of the respective shares of the Bank's property, however they might be affected insofar and to the extent that the actual shares were influenced; and

(c) in the case of land-owners whose properties were confiscated, they were directly affected, whereas, by way of contrast, creditors of the land-owners would have no standing to challenge the expropriation act even if they were adversely affected.

On the jurisdiction issue, the Attorney-General suggested in his opinion that the impugned normative decrees subsumed as many individual administrative acts as the number affected by the scheme depositors of the Laïki Bank and, therefore, there was public law jurisdiction on the matter.

On an auxiliary basis, the Supreme Court rendered two significant obiter dicta. The first dictum concerned the argument of discrimination between Cypriot and Greek/English depositors because the latter were not affected by the bail-in burden because of the takeover of some transactions of branches of Laïki Bank established abroad. The Court held that, indeed, there was a different treatment which set the depositors in Greece and in England in a 'preferential position' that, in turn, made the overall burden to be carried by Cypriot depositors more onerous. Given, however, that the sale of certain operations of Laïki Bank in Greece and in England brought in significant income, the Court raised the question of whether the benefit was equivalent to the level of contribution that would have been asked by the respective depositors if they had been part of the bail-in project on an equal footing with the Cypriot depositors. Anyhow, the Court abstained from making a conclusive ruling since the complaints failed to meet the admissibility conditions.

The second dictum concerned the relevant considerations in assessing the damage allegedly suffered by the applicants. Interestingly, the Court called the civil courts, if such claims were to be raised before them, pursuant to the law and 'consolidated legal principles concerning the cause of damage and the proof and assessment of its extent', to take into account all evidence to be produced by the State in a calculus as to whether the position of the depositors would have been better if, instead of the bail-in scheme, a liquidation process had commenced.[75]

ii. EU Courts

In Joined Cases C-8/15 P to C-10/15 P of 20 September 2016, *Ledra Advertising Ltd and others v European Commission and ECB*, the applicants, depositors at Bank of Cyprus and Laïki Bank, appealed before the Court of Justice against Orders of the General Court of 10 November 2014,[76] concerning the validity of the MoU

[75] J Giotaki, 'The Cypriot "bail-in litigation": A First Assessment of the Ruling of the Supreme Court of Cyprus' (2013) 28 *Journal of International Banking and Financial Law* 485.

[76] GCEU Judgment of 20 September 2016 in Case T-289/13, *Ledra Advertising v Commission and ECB*; GCEU Judgment of 10 November 2014 in Case T-290/13, *CMBG v Commission and ECB*; GCEU

on Specific Economic Policy Conditionality concluded between the Republic of Cyprus and the ESM on 26 April 2013 and for compensation for damage allegedly suffered by the applicants as a result of the bail-in clauses inserted into the Memorandum and of the infringement of the Commission's and the ECB's supervisory duty. The grounds of the claim were breach of the right to property pursuant to Article 17 ChFR and Article 1 of Protocol No 1 to the ECHR.

At first instance, the General Court had declared the application in part inadmissible and in part unfounded, on the ground that the adoption of the Memorandum did not originate with the Commission and the ECB and, therefore, there was no EU law link, in spite of negotiations with the Cypriot authorities on a macro-economic adjustment programme pursuant to a statement by the Eurogroup of 27 June 2012 and of provision of technical expertise, advice and guidance. The appeal was held admissible by the Court of Justice and the orders under appeal were set aside on the ground that, although the participation of the EU institutions, admittedly, did not entail any power to make decisions of their own, the Commission ought to promote the general interest of the Union and oversee the application of Union law. Eventually, the Court of Justice proceeded to give final judgment in the matter and dismissed the application on its merits as lacking any foundation in law.

The Court merely elaborated on the alleged violation of the right to property over deposits, shares or bonds in the above-mentioned banks on three particular aspects of the restructuring scheme: first, the takeover by Bank of Cyprus of the insured deposits in Laïki and the maintenance of uninsured deposits in Laïki pending its liquidation; secondly, the conversion of 37.5 per cent of uninsured deposits in Bank of Cyprus into shares with full voting and dividend rights; and, third, the temporary freezing of another part of the uninsured deposits. Given that the Court concluded that the first condition for non-contractual liability, ie unlawfulness attributed to an EU institution, was not fulfilled, it found the claim unsustainable and did not proceed to the question of the causal link with the damage incurred.

In the light of the unlawfulness test, the Court reiterated that a sufficiently serious breach of a rule of law intended to confer rights on individuals must be established. Initially, the Court admitted that, whilst the Member States did not implement EU law in the context of the ESM Treaty, so that the EU Charter of Fundamental Rights was not addressed to them in that context, on the other hand the Charter was binding on the EU institutions even when acting outside the EU legal framework. Moreover, in the context of the adoption of a memorandum, the Commission was deemed bound under both the general task of overseeing the application of EU law (Article 17(1) TEU) and its duty to ensure that the MoUs concluded by the ESM were generally consistent with EU law. The Court then

---

Judgment of 10 November 2014 in Case T-291/13, *Eleftheriou and Papachristofi v Commission and ECB*; GCEU Judgment of 10 November 2014 in Case T-293/13, *Theophilou v Commission and ECB*.

proceeded to examine on the merits the allegation for a flagrant violation of the property right, as enshrined in the Charter. In this context, the Court ruled that the right to property was not absolute and that its exercise might be subject to restrictions justified by objectives of general interest pursued by the EU that did not constitute, in relation to the aim pursued, a disproportionate and intolerable interference, impairing the very substance of the right guaranteed.

In this vein of argument, the Court identified in the context of the this case:

(a)   that the objective of ensuring the stability of the banking system of the euro area as a whole was de jure legitimate;

(b)   that financial services – banks and credit institutions – played a central role in the EU as an essential source of funding for businesses that were active in the various markets;

(c)   that banks were often interconnected and certain of their number operated internationally with the result that failure of one or more banks was liable to spread rapidly to other domestic or foreign banks which, in turn, might produce negative spill-over effects in other sectors of the economy.

In view of the legitimate objective to ensure the stability of the banking system in the euro area, and having regard to the imminent risk of financial losses to which depositors with the two banks concerned would have been exposed if the latter had failed, the Court held that the bail-in programme did not constitute a disproportionate and intolerable interference impairing the very substance of the appellants' right to property and could not, therefore, be regarded as unjustified restrictions on that right. Thus, no unlawfulness on the part of the Commission was found. In this case, the Opinion of Advocate General Nils Wahl of 21 April 2016, although conceding that, even when acting outside the Union framework, EU institutions must scrupulously observe EU law and deploy their best endeavours to prevent an imminent conflict, this obligation could not generate liability for damage allegedly suffered because of the Commission's action or inaction as 'Guardian of the Treaties'.

As regards the scope of Commission's supervision, the Advocate General argued that its duty to observe the EU rules, especially the Charter, when acting outside the EU legal framework, does not mean that it is required to *impose* the Charter's standards on acts which are adopted by other entities or bodies acting outside the EU framework. The Commission's and the ECB's conduct when negotiating and/or signing the particular MoUs ought, in principle, to be attributed to the international organisation on behalf of which they carried out those tasks (the ESM), and not to the international organisation of origin (the EU). In fact, by invoking an alleged failure to act by the Commission, the appellants intended to circumvent the fact that the ESM, and the ESM alone, was responsible for the acts which it adopts pursuant to the ESM Treaty.

In Judgment of 20 September 2016 in joined cases C-105/15 P to C-109/15 P, *Mallis and others v European Commission and ECB*, the applicants appealed before the Court of Justice against Orders of the General Court of 16 October 2014, by which it dismissed their actions for annulment of the Eurogroup statement of 25 March 2013 concerning the restructuring of the banking sector in Cyprus. The statement indicated that the Eurogroup had reached an agreement with the Cypriot authorities on the key elements of a future macro-economic adjustment programme, which was supported by all the euro-area Member States, as well as by the Commission, the ECB and the IMF, and welcomed the plans for the restructuring of the financial sector that were mentioned in the annex to that state-ment. The applicants requested annulment of the Eurogroup statement, which took its final form through domestic Decree 104 of the Governor of the Central Bank of Cyprus as the representative and/or agent of the ESCB, which in essence constituted a joint decision of the ECB and the Commission, upholding the sale of certain operations of Laïki Bank.

The General Court had rendered the application inadmissible on the ground that the Eurogroup was merely classified as 'forum for discussion' at ministerial level, between representatives of the euro-area Member States, and not a decision-making body. Although the Court admitted that provision was made in Article 1 of the Protocol No 14 annexed to the TFEU for the Commission and the ECB to take part in its meetings, the Eurogroup remained, nevertheless, an informal forum of the ministers of the Member States concerned. Furthermore, it had found that there was nothing to support a finding that the Eurogroup was under the control of the Commission or the ECB or that it acted as an agent of those institutions and, therefore, the impugned statement could not have been imputed to those EU institutions by virtue of the control allegedly exerted by them over the ESM. Accordingly, the Eurogroup's statement could not be regarded as a meas-ure intended to produce legal effects with respect to third parties, but aimed to inform the general public of the existence of a political agreement between the Eurogroup and the Cypriot authorities reflecting a common intention to pursue the negotiations in accordance with the statement's terms.

The Court of Justice found the appeals admissible but dismissed them as unfounded. It broadly upheld the reasoning of the General Court and added some additional dicta. First, concerning the nature of the Eurogroup, it focused on the term 'informally' used for it in the wording of Protocol No 14 and that the Euro-group was not among the different configurations of the Council of the European Union enumerated in Annex I to its Rules of Procedure adopted by Council Deci-sion 2009/937 of 1 December 2009.[77] Accordingly, the Eurogroup could not be equated with a configuration of the Council or be classified as a body, office or agency of the Union within the meaning of Article 263 TFEU. Second, the Court broadly reiterated the findings in *Pringle*, that an action for annulment is avail-able against all measures adopted by the EU institutions, whatever their nature or form, which were intended to have binding legal effects capable of affecting the interests of the applicant by bringing about a distinct change in the applicant's legal position.

---

[77] OJ 2009 L 325, p 35, the list of which is referred to in Art 16(6) TEU.

Examining those competences in the light of that case, the Court found that the Commission and the ECB were lawfully entrusted, by the Board of Governors of the ECB, with the task of negotiating with the Cypriot authorities a macro-economic adjustment programme. Whilst the ESM Treaty entrusted the Commission and the ECB with certain new tasks relating to the attainment of the objectives of that Treaty, first, those duties did not entail the exercise of any power to make decisions of their own and, secondly, the activities pursued by those two institutions within the ESM Treaty committed the ESM alone. Accordingly, the Court held that the fact that the Commission and the ECB participate in the meetings of the Euro-group does not alter the nature of the latter's statements and could not result in the statement at issue being considered to be the expression of a decision-making power of those two EU institutions. Nor was there anything in the impugned statement reflecting a decision of the Commission and the ECB to create a legal obligation on the Member State concerned to implement the measures which it contains. Thus, the adoption by the Republic of Cyprus of the law that created the legal framework necessary for the restructuring of the banks concerned and empowered the Central Bank of Cyprus to adopt implementing decrees could not be regarded as having been imposed by a presumed joint decision of the Commission and the ECB.[78]

The General Court had once again the opportunity to deal with the lawfulness of the restructuring scheme in Cyprus in Judgments of 13 July 2018 in Case T-680/13 *Chrysostomides and Co and others v Council and others* and in Case T-786/14 *Bourdouvali and others v Council and others*. The case for non-contractual liability as a result of those measures was brought by individuals and companies who were at the time depositors, shareholders or bondholders at Laïki and Bank of Cyprus. As regards the alleged violation of the right to property, the General Court referred to its judgment in *Ledra*. Furthermore, the Court had, for the first time, the opportunity to deal with the lawfulness of the conversion of bonds of Bank of Cyprus into shares and the reduction of the nominal value of its ordinary shares. Again, the Court concluded that those measures did not constitute a disproportionate and intolerable interference with the right to property, since the measure intended to restore the equity capital of Bank of Cyprus and, thus, to ensure the stability of the Cypriot financial system and the euro area in its entirety.

According to the Court, this measure was proportionate to the objective pursued, since less restrictive alternatives would not have been feasible or would not have allowed the expected results to be achieved. Furthermore, on the ground of alleged discrimination, the Court measured the sale of the Greek branches against the right to property and found that the sale took place in an open, transparent and non-discriminatory procedure and served the compelling interest to avoid any contagion between the Cypriot and Greek banking and financial systems

---

[78] On *Ledra* and *Mallis*, see N Xanthoulis, 'ESM, Union Institutions and EU Treaties: A Symbiotic Relationship' (2017) 1 *International Journal for Financial Services* 23.

so as to maintain financial stability. The Court also discarded in their entirety arguments of alleged breach of non-discrimination and legitimate expectations and, given that an unlawful conduct alleged against an EU institution could not be identified, abstained from the assessment of the other two premises for establishing the non-contractual liability of the European Union and dismissed the case as unfounded.

G. The Irish Bank Recapitalisation Scheme: Shareholders' Rights

i. Domestic Courts

In *Collins v Minister for Finance and others*,[79] the Irish Supreme Court dealt with the constitutionality of Section 6 of Credit Institutions (Financial Support) Act 2008, establishing a state financial assistance mechanism for credit institutions, which was the legal basis for the restructuring of Irish Bank Resolution Corporation and the Educational Building Society. The plaintiff Joan Collins TD, Councilor at the Dublin City Council, brought proceedings before the Divisional High Court claiming that: the Minister acted ultra vires in issuing the promissory notes; and Section 6 amounted to an unconstitutional delegation to the Minister of the parliamentary power to approve expenditure. The High Court rejected the claims and Collins appealed to the Supreme Court, which dismissed the appeal.

Concerning the ultra vires claim, the Court held, in a rather laconic manner, that the technical requirements of the Act had been met. On the unconstitutionality claim, the Court found no trespass concerning delegation of power in financial matters since the Act provided sufficient limitations on the Minister's power to grant financial assistance. In so concluding, the Court elaborated both on the state expenditure process established by the Constitution of Ireland (Article 17.2) and on the mechanism to provide financial assistance to endangered banks; it found that in both cases a wisely crafted system of checks and balances existed. With regard to the authorisation for state expenditure, it held that neither the Government, nor the Lower House or the legislature could validly authorise the expenditure of public money without the approval of the other branch: the Lower House *(Dáil)* was not permitted to require expenditure by vote or resolution; the legislature *(Oireachtas*, ie the two Houses and the President of the Republic) was not permitted to enact a law providing for public expenditure except on the formal recommendation of the Government and upon signature by the Prime Minister; the Government was not entitled to expend money where not specifically authorised by law, both as to the purpose and manner of expenditure.

---

[79] [2016] IESC 73, delivery date 16 December 2016.

With regard to the state financial assistance to banks an elaborate multi-stage process was in place: the relevant decision was formed by the Minister, after consultation with the Governor and the Regulatory Authority, and had to be endorsed by the legislature, involving a threefold assessment of the seriousness of the situation:

(1)   that there was a serious threat to the stability of credit institutions in the State in general or that there would be such a threat if the functions under the Act were not performed;
(2)   that the performance of those statutory functions was necessary for maintaining the stability of the financial system in the State; and
(3)   that the performance of those functions was necessary to remedy a serious disturbance in the economy of the State.

After establishing that the system did not amount to a usurpation of constitutional powers, the Court acknowledged the exceptional circumstances and the wide discretion of the legitimate political power in such a case. Concerning the pleading that the 2008 Act did not provide for a ceiling in the financial support to be decided by the Minister, the Court responded that the Constitution did not expressly or by implication require such a limit, even if the exposure could indeed, as in the case in question, be 'enormous';[80] and that, by way of analogy, the state budget legislation imposed no limit on the amount of national debt that the State can accrue 'even though such borrowings may burden present and future generations, and constrain present and future decisions in relation to the economy'.[81]

Furthermore, the Irish High Court by a decision of 2 December 2014, *Dowling v Minister for Finance*,[82] rejected the applications lodged by members and shareholders of mother company ILPGH for the setting aside of the Direction Order, approved by the Court itself in a rather administrative capacity, to the effect of recapitalisation, essentially amounting to nationalisation, and delisting of ILP. The applicants claimed breach of Articles 8, 25 and 29 of the Second Directive 2012/30 because of lack of approval by the general meeting of all relevant decisions. The Minister and both mother and affiliate companies rejected that argument, relying on EU primary and secondary law,[83] which arguably mandated Ireland to take measures necessary to defend the integrity of its own financial system, notwithstanding the provisions of the Second Directive, in order to secure the safety of an institution of systemic importance for Ireland and the EU.

---

[80] Paragraph 83.
[81] Paragraph 85, referring to s 54 of the Finance Act 1970.
[82] [2014] IEHC 418.
[83] Directive 2001/24, Reg No 407/2010, Implementing Decision 2011/77, Arts 49, 65, 107, 119, 120 and 126 TFEU and on the provisions in Title VIII of Part III of the FEU Treaty.

The Court extensively assessed the factual premises of the case and decided to make a reference for a preliminary ruling to the Court of Justice asking two questions:

(a)   Does the Second Directive preclude in all circumstances the making of a Direction Order on foot of the opinion of the Minister that it was necessary, where such an order had the effect of increasing a company's capital and lowering the nominal value of the company's shares without the consent of the general meeting and of allotting new shares without offering them on a pre-emptive basis to existing shareholders?

(b)   Is the Direction Order in breach of EU Law?

Piotr Skocczylas and Scotchstone Capital (third and fourth named applicants in the Dowling case) were refused leave to appeal to the Supreme Court in a determination handed down by the Supreme Court on 15 May 2018.[84]

ii. EU Courts

The Court of Justice took over and examined the request for a preliminary ruling of the Irish High Court in Judgment of 8 November 2016 in Case C-41/15, *Dowling and others*. In its legal reasoning, the Court identified that the aim of the Second Directive was to achieve minimum equivalent protection for both shareholders and creditors of public limited liability companies. It was conceded that in that case the Direction Order was not a measure taken by a governing body of a public limited liability company as 'part of its normal operation', but was an exceptional measure taken by the national authorities intended to prevent, by means of an increase in share capital, the failure of such a company that would threaten the financial stability of the EU. The protection conferred by the Second Directive on the shareholders and creditors of a public limited liability company, with respect to its share capital, did not, in the Court's view, extend to a national measure of that kind, such as the Direction Order, taken by the national authorities (be that judicial or administrative), that might be adopted in a situation where there was a serious disturbance of the economy and financial system of a Member State and that was designed to overcome a systemic threat to the financial stability of the Union, due to a capital shortfall in the company concerned.

Although there was, admittedly, a clear public interest in ensuring, throughout the EU, a strong and consistent protection of shareholders and creditors, that interest could not be held to prevail in all circumstances over the public interest in ensuring the stability of the financial system established by those amendments. Given the self-evident state of serious disturbance of the economy and the

---

[84] [2018] IE Supreme Court Determination 72. See, D Gwynn Morgan, 'The Constitution and the Financial Crisis in Ireland' in X Contiades (ed), *Constitutions in the Global Financial Crisis: A Comparative Analysis* (Farnham, Ashgate, 2013) 63.

financial system of Ireland, the impugned measures did not, thus, contravene the provisions of the Second Directive.

II. Human Rights Case Law Revisited: The Case of Property

Based on the above case law presentation, the following section identifies the judicial shift in the area of protection of human rights in the crisis era. Although a number of rights have been affected and effectively challenged before the courts of law (mostly social rights such as the rights to health and education as well as labour rights), the emphasis of this chapter is placed on the right to property as a basic case study. This is so not only because in the pre-crisis era this right has been the cornerstone of the liberal state and has presented an uncompromising tendency towards more recognition and protection, but also because it is exactly in the right to property that case law seems to have taken a striking shift both in domestic and international legal orders in Europe. Yet, to the extent that the forthcoming analysis touches upon structural features and horizontal techniques of judicial review, the rationale applies *mutatis mutandis* to the assessment by the courts of all human rights, at least those which are fully enforceable according to the respective case law. In any case, all constitutional mechanisms and concepts presented have emerged as a result of the new relationship between economy and the Constitution and the predominance of financialism.

The right to private property is recognised by all Constitutions, alongside public ownership. In the field of the protection of individual property, perhaps more than any other fundamental human right, there has been a significant convergence in the standards of guarantee of the rule of law within the European Communities, later the European Union, after World War II. Especially as of the early 1990s, with the development of case law widening the scope of property so as to embrace contractual and other non-tangible rights, the Court of Justice, the European Court of Human Rights and the domestic constitutional and supreme courts have come closer together, so that one can reasonably claim that the protection of property constitutes today a pan-European guarantee. The fundamental inspiration was drawn, on an international level, from the Universal Declaration of Human Rights, proclaimed by the United Nations General Assembly in Paris on 10 December 1948, providing that 'everyone has the right to own property alone as well as in with others' and that 'no one shall be arbitrarily deprived of his property'. With some reservations, there is a basic common core of protection of individual property in domestic Constitutions, which generally comprises a general guarantee, ie that individual property is protected by the State, and strict conditionality on expropriation, ie that compulsory purchase of property can only occur on the basis of law, for the advancement of public interest, without any discriminatory character and with full compensation determined by a court of law.

The crisis case law has brought a significant shift in the perception of the right to property on a European level in three respects:

(i) the scope of protection has become narrower by eliminating non-tangible property claims;
(ii) the intensity of review has been softened based on the political/techni-cal or exceptional character of the nature of the cases brought before the court in the course of implementation of measures pertaining to financial stability; and
(iii) the instruments of review, ie non-discrimination, legitimate interest, propor-tionality and legitimate expectations, have mutated so as to strongly enhance economic considerations in judicial review.

Obviously, to the extent that the scope of the right is narrower, the judicial review is shallower and the vehicles of review less interventionist, very reasonably the right to property is altogether revisited and at the end of the day devalued.

A. The Scope of Protection

Prior to the crisis, a rather consolidated set of principles applied to domestic and international European law. This set of principles has been shaped gradually through milestone decisions of domestic constitutional courts, the EU Courts and the European Court on Human Rights. The most salient feature of this develop-ment has been, especially after the 1990s, the equation of the level of protection of all assets that could have a financial value or even a legitimate expectation of such value, irrespective of whether this could be a tangible or intangible asset, such as rights stemming from contracts, intellectual property rights, rights deriv-ing from participations in companies and state debt holdings. The enlargement of the scope of property had been most outstanding not only because it appeared to be universal, but mostly because it reflected an informal case law adaptation to contemporary needs, without any amendment to Constitutions or international covenants. It was merely the evolutionary interpretation of the respective courts that produced this development without the need to proceed to an explicit consti-tutional recognition of the upgraded status of the intangible rights. This can be attributed predominantly to the general understanding that the broadening in the scope of the property rights was both conceptually and pragmatically a natural and uncontestable legal adjustment.

The evolution of the idea of property as a common good and as a private acqui-sition is better understood in John Locke's doctrine enshrined in Chapter V of his Second Treatise on Government,[85] where the great philosopher provided a

---

[85] J Locke, *Second Treatise of Civil Government* (originally published 1690, Indianapolis, Hackett 1980).

dogmatic bridge between property as a means of survival and wealth of people, on the one hand, and privately owned property, on the other. His premises were as follows:

(1) Each individual possessed his or her body.
(2) Each individual possessed property, without the need to have recourse to the consent of the community, on the ground of his or her added physical labour.
(3) Each individual possessed property to the extent that it could reasonably and without excess be actually used to their advantage.
(4) In order to treat excess of property of the individual beyond the state of nature they must use money as a means of exchange and trade in view of the continuity of property based on physical labour.[86]

In the course of the time, the three first premises of Lock's doctrine, were totally absorbed by the last premise, and monetarism became tantamount to the common good. The full extent of trade in any possible product and the mostly ideological dominance of the predominance of money as a single way to achieve progress and wealth, essentially casted away the subsistence premise, which arguably set a threshold on how much property one might reasonably claim. Thus, economy, which is the basic tool of money, became an autonomous subsystem disassociated from any conceptual preconditions that could reasonably operate as restrictions upon it.

Since trade was not supposed to be subject to any community restrictions, the number of products based on money became endless. The main conception of property as tangible goods, land and products of the land, was based on an unsophisticated model of exchange of goods that was no longer in a position to satisfy the need for further wealth, because of the finite character of physical assets. Thus, the new products were intangible, exactly because of their infinite nature and, consequently, of their potential to produce unlimited wealth. Reasonably, the property focus was transferred to intangible property, which disassociated property from the requirement of physical labour and the subsistence ceiling. In turn, this conceptual evolution could not but exercise great influence upon the case law concerning property.

The classical perception of tangible property, upon which most of the national Constitutions and the international legal instruments had been built, needed a comprehensive re-evalutaion. This was necessary because the traditional legal tools of protection of tangible property, ie the procedural and substantive requirements of expropriation, were clearly inadequate to serve the target of safeguarding intangible property at the same level of effectiveness. Therefore, gradually, there was an outstanding case law adjustment in order to involve those assets to the

---

[86] MH Kramer, *John Locke and the Origins of Private Property: Philosophical Explorations of Individuals, Community, and Equality* (Cambridge, Cambridge University Press, 1997); WH Hamilton, 'Property – According to Locke' (1932) 41 *Yale Law Journal* 864.

general rubric of protection of property. Interestingly, this task was entrusted to the domestic and international courts rather than the natural institutional guards of sovereignty, ie the constitutional legislatures on a domestic level and the international fora on a transnational level.

This, presumably unprecedented, enterprise of constitutional change, was rather disparate, uneven and differentiated. Although historically there has been, as of the great constitutional texts of the seventeenth century in England and the revolutions at the end of the eighteenth century, a remarkable convergence in the constitutional wording concerning the protection of property, the process of reshaping to embrace intangible assets was not an easy process. Indeed, the common constitutional values of the western world safeguarded private tangible property as a cornerstone of the community operation and as a salient feature of human liberty, but were rather indifferent, if not suspicious, when it came to the challenges of protecting the new forms of property. The tremendous transfer of economic competences to international organisations in the post-war era, most significantly to the European Communities, created a fertile ground to develop this radical transformation of the right to property.

Yet, the single market was not built upon the idea of a new form of private property. Rather, the idea was to create a new vision concerning institutional, as opposed to personal, guarantees (ie freedom of competition, public procurements) and economic, as opposed to classical proprietary liberties. Only indirectly could there be an upgrade of the level of protection and the scope of private property as a result of the acknowledgment of institutional guarantees and economic liberties. This might furnish some explanation as to why, although the basic principles operated as of the beginning of the Communities in the 1950s, the formal acknowledgment of the broader right to property came only half a century later with the incorporation of the EU Charter of Fundamental Rights, while the new scope of property had already been established through other judicial fora.

On the level of the ECHR, the Council of Europe, drawing inspiration from the Universal Declaration of Human Rights, embraced the right to property in Article 1 of Protocol No 1 to the Convention. According to settled case law of the Court of Strasbourg, this Article comprises three distinct rules:

(1) The first rule, set out in the first sentence of the first paragraph, is of a general nature and enunciates the principle of the peaceful enjoyment of property ('every natural or legal person is entitled to the peaceful enjoyment of his possessions').

(2) The second rule, contained in the second sentence of the first paragraph, covers deprivation of possessions and subjects it to certain conditions ('no one shall be deprived of his possessions except in the public interest and subject to the conditions provided for by law and by the general principles of international law').

(3) The third rule, laid down in the second paragraph, recognises that the Contracting States are entitled, inter alia, to control the use of property in

accordance with the general interest (the State has the right 'to enforce such laws as it deems necessary to control the use of property in accordance with the general interest or to secure the payment of taxes or other contributions or penalties').

The three rules are not, however, distinct in the sense of being unconnected. The second and third rules are concerned with particular instances of interference with the right to peaceful enjoyment of property and should, therefore, be construed in the light of the general principle enunciated in the first rule. Interference by a public authority with the peaceful enjoyment of possessions can be justified if three principles are cumulatively met:

(a) *Lawfulness*: a deprivation of possessions is authorised only subject to the conditions provided for by law; the States have the right to control the use of property by enforcing laws, and any interference ought to be compatible with the rule of law, which presupposes, among other things, that domestic law must be accompanied by procedural guarantees affording to the individual or entity concerned a reasonable opportunity of presenting their case to the responsible authorities for the purpose of effectively challenging arbitrary interferences with property.

(b) *Legitimate aim in the public interest*: an interference with the enjoyment of property must pursue a legitimate aim in the public interest, whereas in cases involving a positive duty, there must be a legitimate justification for the State's inaction, in either case justified only under very exceptional circumstances.

(c) *Fair balance*: any adverse effect on property must strike a fair balance between the demands of the general interest of the community and the requirements of the protection of property. In particular, there must be a reasonable relationship of proportionality between the means employed and the aim sought so that the person concerned does not have to bear a disproportionate and excessive burden to inhibit the practical and effective enjoyment of property.[87]

In the light of the above and with relevance to the main topic of the present analysis, four sets of judgments of the pre-crisis case law of the Court of Strasbourg will be presented below, reflecting the wide scope of protection of intangible assets: the Greek landmark case *Stran* (1994), which upgraded contractual claims to the level of tangible property rights; the Polish cases on credit redress for land abandoned after World War II, which established the principle that state emergencies of any intensity and significance could not per se justify disproportionate state interference with property rights (2004–2007); cases concerning revocation of licences

---

[87] D Popovic, *Protecting Property in European Human Rights Law* (Utrecht, Eleven International, 2009); AR Coban, *Protection of Property Rights within the European Convention on Human Rights* (Aldershot, Ashgate, 2004); L Sermet, *The European Convention on Human Rights and Property Rights*, Human rights files No 11 rev (Strasbourg, Council of Europe, 1998).

granted by the State, most relevantly stemming from bank restructuring and insolvency, which established the rule that financial and banking crises do not relieve the State from the obligation to respect the possession of interested parties (2005); and, the Russian cases on premium and commodity bonds, which explicitly established the positive obligation of the State to redeem bondholders (2010–2013).

As regards the broadening of the scope of the right to property, the principal Judgment *Stran Greek Refineries and Stratis Andreadis v Greece*,[88] found a violation of the right to property in an application against Greek Law 1701/1987 abolishing a contractual arbitration clause and, in effect, the award of the arbitration tribunal thereof that had awarded damages to the applicants, while at the moment of the enactment of that statute the ordinary Greek courts had both at first instance and on appeal held that there was no ground for such annulment. The applicants claimed a violation of their rights to fair trial and property. As regards the former ground, the Court concluded that the State (being at the same time the regulator and a party in the litigation) had infringed the applicants' rights by intervening in a manner that was decisive to ensure a favourable outcome of the proceedings.

As regards the latter ground, the Court shaped for the first time in such clarity the case law protecting contractual claims as property by responding to two questions: what constituted 'possession' and what amounted to 'deprivation'. Concerning the meaning of possession according to Article 1 of Protocol No 1, the criterion set by the Court was whether the claim was 'sufficiently established to be enforceable'.[89] This statement came as a response to the principal thrust of the Government's argument that neither the domestic judgment, insofar as it had not become final, nor the arbitration award, that was based on a terminated arbitration clause producing an invalid procedure, were sufficient to establish the existence of a claim against the State. The Court unequivocally held that the arbitration award clearly recognised the State's liability and, according to its wording, it was final and binding, since it did not require any further implementation measures but was automatically enforceable. In fact, at the moment when that Law was passed, the ordinary Greek courts had by then already held twice – at first instance and on appeal – that there was no ground for such annulment and, therefore, there was room to consider that the arbitration award was not a claim sufficiently established to be enforceable. Therefore, the debt arising from a final and binding arbitration award qualified as a possession in the meaning of the Convention.

As regards the nature of deprivation of property, the Court held that there was no need to have physical transfer of the asset in question, but it sufficed that there was an issue of effective deprivation of property. On the merits of the case,

---

[88] ECtHR Judgment of 9 December 1994, *Stran Greek Refineries and Stratis Andreadis v Greece*, Application no 13427/87.
[89] Paragraph 59.

the Court considered that Law 1701/1987 was tantamount to an interference with the applicant's possession, in the sense that it made it impossible for the applicants to ensure the enforcement of the favourable arbitration award. The State, by choosing to intervene at that stage of the proceedings by a law which invoked the termination of the contract in question in order to declare the arbitration clause void and to annul the arbitration award, 'upset, to the detriment of the applicants, the balance that must be struck between the protection of the right of property and the requirements of public interest'.[90]

With *Stran*, the Court of Strasbourg essentially got in line not only with the economic reality but also with International Arbitration Tribunals which had dealt with similar cases where the States, acting as *imperium*, substantially curtailed the rights of private entities stemming from an agreement with the States as *fiscus*.[91] The cases, which mostly arose in the context of nationalisation of companies, which were state concessionaires for the exploitation of local sources of wealth, as a result of a coup or state concession, had resulted in the determination of two basic principles concerning the extent of the property right of the private contracting parties in such circumstances: first, the State may unilaterally amend or terminate a contract with individuals or entities provided that it pays compensation; and, second, the State may not terminate essential clauses of the contract, such as the arbitration clause which would allow bypass of all other contractual commitments of the contracting party. The *Stran* case law exerted a diffused influence upon domestic case law in Europe, which, some instantly and solidly and some more sporadically, harmonised the constitutional status of property with the new broader spectrum, and broadly remained intact until the cases arising after the financial crisis.

The second set of cases concerned claims brought by a great number of people against Poland for compensatory land in respect of property abandoned as a result of boundary changes following World War II. At that time, the Polish State undertook to compensate persons who had been 'repatriated' from the so-called 'territories beyond the Bug River', which no longer formed part of Poland, in respect of property which they had been forced to abandon. Such persons were entitled to have the value of such property deducted either from the price of immovable property purchased from the State or from the fee for 'perpetual use' of State property. Between 1990 and 2005, several laws were passed which made it practically

---

[90] Paragraph 74.

[91] Shufeldt Arbitration Tribunal, *Shufeldt Claim (Guatemala v USA)*, Award of 24 July 1930, 2 RIAA (Reports of International Arbitral Awards) 1080; Permanent Court of International Justice decision of 14 December 1936, *The Losinger & Co Case (Discontinuance), Switzerland v Yugoslavia*, Order, Series A/B No 69; Arbitral awards in *Lena Goldfields Company Ltd v Soviet Government*, Annual Digest and Reports of Public International Law Cases, vol 5 (1929–1930) (case no 258); Arbitration Tribunal *Texaco Overseas Petroleum Company and California Asiatic Oil Company v Government of the Arab Republic of Libya*, preliminary decision of 27 November 1975, YCA 1979, at 177, International Law Reports, vol 53, 1979, 389, Clunet 1977, at 350.

impossible to satisfy individual claims for the remainder of the compensation due to a new law setting the ceiling for compensation at 20 per cent of its original value.

In fact, in 2002, the Polish Constitutional Court declared unconstitutional various statutory provisions restricting the possibility of satisfying entitlement to compensation for abandoned property. In the relevant Judgment of 22 June 2004, *Broniowski v Poland*,[92] the Grand Chamber of the Court of Strasbourg delivered its principal judgment in the case finding that there had been a violation of Article 1 of Protocol No 1 originating in a systemic problem connected with the malfunctioning of the Polish legislation and called Poland to ensure, through appropriate legal measures and administrative practices, the implementation of the property right in question in respect of the remaining Bug River claimants. Furthermore, in assessing the fair balance between the pursuit of the public interest and the protection of property, the Court held that an overall examination of the various interests at issue ought to take place 'behind appearances and investigate the realities of the situation complained of', such as the relevant compensation terms in case of deprivation and the conduct of the parties, including the means employed by the State and their implementation.

The Court held that the Polish State, by imposing successive limitations on the exercise of 'the applicant's right to credit', and by applying the practices that made it unenforceable and unusable in practice, rendered that right illusory and destroyed its very essence. The state of uncertainty in which the applicant found himself as a result of the repeated delays and obstruction continuing over a period of many years, for which the national authorities were responsible, was in itself incompatible with the right of peaceful enjoyment of possessions, notably with the duty to act in good time and in an appropriate and consistent manner where an issue of general interest was at stake. In such a case what the Convention required was that the amount of compensation was 'reasonably related' to its value with reference to the particularities of each case. In the case before the Court, in view of the fact that the applicant had received a mere two per cent of the compensation due under the domestic legislation, there was no cogent reason for the Court to conclude that a fair balance was struck.[93]

The third set of cases are licence revocation cases. In fact, Judgment of 24 November 2005, *Capital Bank Ad v Bulgaria*,[94] comes closer to the issue of banking crisis and to the contemporary discussion concerning the diminution of the property rights as a result of the post-2007 banking crisis. In that case, the Court dealt with the serious financial crisis unfolded in Bulgaria in 1996–97,

---

[92] ECtHR Judgment of 22 June 2004, *Broniowski v Poland*, Application no 31443/96.

[93] On 4 December 2007 in its decisions in ECtHR Judgment of 4 December 2007, *Wolkenberg and others v Poland*, Application no 50003/99 and ECtHR Judgment of 4 December 2007, *Witkowska-Tobola v Poland*, Application no 11208/02 the Court held that the new Bug River compensation scheme launched by the Polish State met the requirement set out in its pilot case, *Broniowski*, a great number of cases followed to the same effect on 12 December 2007 which ended the pilot-judgment procedure dealing with systemic problems.

[94] ECtHR Judgment of 24 November 2005, *Capital Bank Ad v Bulgaria*, Application no 49429/99.

leading to economic instability, considerable inflation and the failure of a number of state-owned and private banks. As a response to that and after negotiations with the IMF, the country adopted a currency board, whereby its national currency became pegged to the German mark, and also established a completely new strict legislative framework regulating the activity of banks. On the basis of the new regulatory framework, the Bulgarian National Bank consecutively declared the applicant Capital Bank insolvent, appointed a special administrator to supervise the activities, revoked its licence and put it into compulsory liquidation.

The findings were that the overall amount of the applicant bank's outstanding major loans was more than 20 times greater than the amount of its capital (including paid-up capital and reserves), when the regulatory maximum was eight times. Considering that the situation put at risk the bank's ability to operate and posed certain other problems with its financial standing, it decided to restrict the bank's operations. In particular, it prohibited it from taking deposits, granting loans or other credit facilities, purchasing bills of exchange or promissory notes, entering into foreign-currency or precious-metals transactions, entering into deposit transactions, acting as a surety or guarantor or providing security to third parties, effecting non-cash operations, clearing current accounts of third parties and conducting factoring transactions. In this context, the Court held that in such a sensitive economic area as the stability of the banking system the Contracting States enjoy a wide margin of appreciation and that in certain situations there might be a paramount need to act expeditiously and without advance notice in order to avoid irreparable harm to the bank, its depositors and other creditors, or the banking and financial system as a whole.

Yet, the Court concluded that in spite of the fact that the revocation of the applicant bank's licence took place during a banking crisis, it did not appear that 'it was a matter of such urgency that any delay occasioned by some sort of formal procedure would have been unduly prejudicial'.[95] Furthermore, applying the necessity test to identify whether milder means existed to avoid total revocation of the bank's licence swiftly and seamlessly, which was by definition the most drastic solution, the Court held that a number of alternative options existed to attain the desired results of safeguarding the interests of the applicant bank's depositors and other creditors and protecting the stability of the banking system: revocation procedures could have been confidential and not open to the public; more expedited processes so as to avoid the damaging consequences of any undue delay; a provisional, instead of a total, suspension of the bank's licence pending the examination of the bank's objections and representations; and a process of an internal administrative appeal.

Since there was no evidence that the above or other alternatives had been considered, the Court came to the conclusion that the interference with the applicant bank's possessions was not surrounded by sufficient guarantees against

[95] Paragraph 136.

arbitrariness and, thus, it violated the right to property, without further assessing the quality of the public interest invoked by the Bulgarian Government or the existence of a fair balance between protection of property and such interest.

In broadly the same period, the Court of Strasbourg rendered a number of other judgments concerning revocations of licences in broadly equivalent circumstances. In Judgment of 10 July 2007, *Bimer SA v Moldova*,[96] the applicant company had signed a contract for an unlimited period with the Leuşeni Customs Office, at the border between Moldova and Romania, providing for the opening of duty free shops on the territory of the customs zone and obtained two lawful (at that time) licences for the operation of duty-free shops at land, water and air-border crossings. While the company operated the licensed business for three years, subsequent legislation restricted duty-free sales merely to international airports and on-board aircraft flying international routes, which resulted in the closure of the applicant's businesses. The Court of Strasbourg held that the applicant company's licences to run a business constituted a possession and their termination was unlawful and, thus, amounted to an interference with the right to the peaceful enjoyment of possessions.

Furthermore, in Judgment of 28 July 2005, *Rosenzweig and Bonded Warehouses LTD v Poland*,[97] the applicants had been granted by both the Polish and the German authorities a licence to run a bonded warehouse in Słubice, which was later expanded for exporting merchandise via the border crossing. The expansion was revoked five months later on the ground that it was not in conformity with an interstate agreement with Germany regarding the border crossings and trans-border movements of goods and persons. The Court placed emphasis on the criticism exercised by the domestic Supreme Court, on occasions, concerning the lawfulness of the impugned withdrawal and, especially, on the proportionality of the measure and was not convinced that the only alternative to a total revocation of licence would be a total lack of control, which altogether amounted to a violation of the right to property. All the above judgments were founded upon a premise, applying in all economic sectors, that the economic interests connected with the running of business were 'possessions' and that the maintenance of the licence was significant asset.[98]

Finally, the fourth set of cases concerned the legal effects of state succession from former USSR to Russian Federation in two types of state debts issued by the former sovereign: premium bonds and commodity bonds.

State *premium bonds* were issued in 1982 by the USSR Government in order to finance certain State projects with a redemption date by 2004 at the latest. In

---

[96] ECtHR Judgment of 10 July 2007 *Bimer SA v Moldova*, Application no 15084/03.
[97] ECtHR Judgment of 28 July 2005 *Rosenzweig and Bonded Warehouses LTD v Polan*, Application no 51728/99.
[98] Also see ECtHR Judgment of 7 July 1989, *Tre Ttraktörer v Sweden*, Application no 10873/84, para 53.

between, the Russian Federation acknowledged their succession in respect of the USSR's obligations and gave the options of either conversion to bondholders or redemption under, at the time, unspecified terms. Some bondholders took up the option of conversion to new 1992 Russian bonds, whereas others retained their original premium bonds anticipating the redemption terms and conditions. Although regulations on the conversion were adopted in 2000, the actual conversion did not start and application of the regulations was repeatedly postponed.

Soviet State *commodity bonds* gave their bearers the right to purchase consumer goods, such as refrigerators, washing machines, tape recorders, passenger cars and, the most popular among agricultural workers and companies, Urozhay-90 bonds ('Harvest-90') allowing priority purchasing of goods in high demand. In 2009, the federal Buyout Act, relevant to the Urozhay-90, provided for the procedure for the buyout of bonds with an amount equivalent to the nominal value of the bonds divided by 1,000, without the commodity exchange option any more. A number of bondholders filed an application before the Court of Strasbourg alleging breach of their property rights in conjunction with their legitimate expectation that the State would repay the nominal value of the bonds. The Court found that the Russian Government had not given any satisfactory justification for their continuous failure over many years to implement an entitlement conferred on the applicants by domestic legislation.[99]

The Court developed four syllogisms.

(1) On the issue of the *scope* of protection, the securities in question were considered possessions, given that under the ECHR this term has had an autonomous meaning, not limited to the ownership of material goods and independently from the formal classification in domestic law.

(2) On the issue of the extent of the *positive obligation* of the State to give effect to the right to property, the Court held that whether a case was analysed in terms of a positive duty of the State or in terms of interference by a public authority which needs to be justified, the criteria to be applied did not differ in substance and relate to the fair balance which needs to be determined between the competing interests of the individual and of the community as a whole.

(3) On the issue of the *legitimate aim* in the invoked public interest to justify interference with the property right, economic reconstruction as a response to State succession and financial turbulence do fall within this category, irrespective of subsequent relative prosperity and wealth in recent years.

---

[99] ECtHR Judgment of 11 February 2010, *Malysh and others v Russia*, Application no 30280/03; ECtHR Judgment of 18 March 2010, *Tronin v Russia*, Application no 24461/02; ECtHR Judgment of 2 December 2010, *Yuriy Lobanov v Russia*, Application no 15578/03; ECtHR Judgment of 10 April 2012, *Andreyeva v Russia*, Application no 73659/10; ECtHR Judgment of 26 February 2013, *Fomin and others v Russia*, Application no 34703/04.

(4) Most importantly, on the issue of the *fair balance*, it was held that it was for the State to adduce adequate evidence that a proper balance was sought, irrespective of the relevant gravity of the public interest involved.

On the merits of the Russian bond cases, the fact that an opportunity had been given for conversion of the 1982 State premium bonds into 1992 Russian bonds did not relieve the State of its obligation to ensure a fair balance between public and private interests in respect of the bonds retained by bondholders. It was, therefore, required that the Russian State fulfilled, timely and in an appropriate and consistent manner, the legislative promises it had made in respect of claims arising out of the 1982 bonds. In that, the State had failed to legislate on the conditions for implementation of the bondholders's entitlement and was mandated by the Court to launch a scheme to satisfy the relevant claims. In spite of State interventions to comply with these judgments, the Court in Judgment of 3 July 2018, *Volokitin and others v Russia*,[100] once again found a violation of Article 1 of Protocol No 1, in that Russia had not put into effect a mechanism for effective implementation.

On the level of EU law on property, the Charter of Fundamental Rights, applicable in the area of competence of the Union, provides in Article 17(1) that:

(a) everyone has the right to own, use, dispose of and bequeath his or her lawfully acquired possessions;

(b) no one may be deprived of his or her possessions, except in the public interest and in the cases and under the conditions provided for by law, subject to fair compensation being paid in good time for their loss; and

(c) the use of property may be regulated by law in so far as is necessary for the general interest.

Yet, even before the enactment of the Charter, the Court of Justice had held that fundamental rights formed an integral part of the general principles of law, stemming from the Union legal order, the common constitutional traditions of the Member States and the relevant international treaties. According to the Court's case law, fundamental rights were not absolute, but must be considered in relation to their social function and, consequently, restrictions might be imposed on the exercise of those rights, in particular in the context of a common organisation of a market, provided that they reflect a general interest of the Union and did not constitute a disproportionate or intolerable interference impairing the very substance of those rights.[101]

Especially with respect to property rights, three judicial authorities are cited hereinafter: *Hauer* (1976) and *Eridania* (1979), both of a more general nature, established the criterion of proportionality in the restrictions of property rights

---

[100] Application no 74087/10.
[101] CJEU Judgment of 14 May 1974 in Case 4/73, *Nold v Commission*; CJEU Judgment of 13 July 1989 in Case 5/88, *Wachauf v Germany* (1989), paras 17–18.

concerning planting restrictions and quotas; and, most importantly, *Pacifis* (1994), which assessed the compatibility of State interference with the shareholders' rights in cases of restructuring and insolvency of banks with the protection of property.

In the field of property rights, in the emblematic Judgment of 13 December 1973, *Hauer v Land Rheinland-Pfalz*, on a reference for a preliminary ruling by the Administrative Court (*Verwaltungsgericht*) of Neustadt, one of the issues at stake before the Court of Justice was the compatibility of Article 2 of Council Regulation 1162/76,[102] imposing a general prohibition for a period of three years, on new planting of vines on land not previously used for growing vines intended, according to the Preamble to the Regulation, to put an end to the considerable imbalance in the table wine market and to put a brake on production. The Court found no violation of the right to property since the impugned measure was required by the superior general interest in order to avoid a situation of severe crisis within the common agricultural market, therefore justified by the objectives of general interest pursued by the Community.

In so deciding, the Court placed emphasis on the social aspect of property and assessed the restriction in view of the proportionality test. Accordingly:

(a) the public interest involved was justified, given that considerable table wine surpluses emerged in the last few years before the enactment of the Regulation, leading to a fall in prices and serious disturbances on the market, threatening the objectives of the agricultural policy, ie the stabilisation of markets and the guaranteed existence and income for producers, the free movement of goods and the political and social harmony within the Community;

(b) the pursuit of the public interest involved was made by the Community authorities in a systematic and comprehensive manner, since a whole system of coordinated measures was enacted in order to treat the existing problem, including not only direct restrictions on production (prohibition on planting and reconversion premiums) but also measures pertaining to the organisation of the market (preventive distillation, extension of private storage of grape) and measures to improve quality;

(c) the prohibition, though radical, was essential for the attainment of those objectives, in that it could not have been tackled by methods less coercive upon the individual;

(d) the restriction was applicable for a limited period;

(e) the restriction was also taken in the interest of the commercial operators themselves;

(f) the restriction did not adversely affect the substance of the right to property, since it did not restrict the owner's power to make use of his land except in one of the numerous imaginable ways; and

---

[102] Council Regulation 1162/76 of 17 May 1976 (OJ L 135, 24.5.1976, p 32).

(g) the prohibition fell within the legislature's freedom of action in order to over= come a serious crisis by adopting temporary ad hoc solutions so as to gain time in order to work out long-term structural solutions.

The Court has also applied the standard criteria on interferences with prop= erty rights in other fields of imposition of restrictive measures in the free commerce.[103] In Case 230/78, *Eridania – Zuccherifici SpA v Minister of Agriculture and Forestry*, of 27 September 1979, in a reference by the Regional Administra= tive Court (*Tribunale Amministrativo Regionale*) of Latium, the referring Court requested, inter alia, if it could be considered that the exercise of a discretion= ary power of substantial scope, both as regards its preconditions and its effect on the basic quotas inherent in the economic activity of individuals, illegitimately interfered with the fundamental rights protected by the Community. The case referred to the establishment of a possibility for a reduction of five per cent in the basic sugar quotas prescribed for the undertakings of all the Member States, pursuant to which Italian decree of 28 February 1976 allocated to the sugar under-takings operating in Italy basic quotas for sugar.[104]

The Court held that basic quotas, ie quantities of sugar in respect of which the undertakings enjoyed the guarantees as to price and marketing provided for producers in the context of the common organisation of the market, did not restrict the economic activity of the undertakings in question but merely fixed the quantities of production which might be marketed in accordance with the special arrangements established by the common organisation of the market in sugar to protect and assist the production of basic products in the Community. Accordingly, it ruled that an undertaking could not claim a vested right to the maintenance of an advantage obtained from the establishment of the common organisation of the market and enjoyed at a given time. In those circumstances, the Court reiterated the *Hauer* test, entailing measurement of the quality and value of the purpose of an act against the adverse effects produced for the property rights of the individuals and entities and held that a reduction in such an advantage could be considered as constituting an infringement of the right to property.

---

[103] See CJEU Judgment of 17 October 1989 in Case 85/87, *Dow Benelux NV v Commission*; CJEU Judgment of 17 October 1989 in Cases 97–99/87, *Dow Chemical Ibérica SA v Commission*; CJEU Judg= ment of 18 October 1989 in Case 374/87, *Orkem v Commission*; CJEU Judgment of 13 December 1991 in Case C-18/88, *RTT v SA GB-Immo-BM*; CJEU Judgment of 18 October 1989 in Case 27/88, *Solvay et Cie v Commission*. See also the prohibition of Sunday trading cases where the Court held that such interference with the right to economic activity and property served an object which was justified under Community law and reflected choices relating to particular socio-cultural characteristics, thus being a justifiable measure, CJEU Judgment of 23 November 1989 in Case 145/88, *Torfaen Borough Council v B&Q plc*; CJEU Judgment of 28 February 1991 in Case 312/89, *Union départementale des syndicats CGT de l'Aisne v SIDEF Conforama, Société Arts et Meubles and Société Jima*; CJEU Judgment of 28 February 1991 in Case 332/89, *Ministère Public v Merchandise*; CJEU Judgment of 16 December 1992 in Case C-169/91, *Council of the City of Stoke-on-Trent and Norwich City Council v B & Q plc*.

[104] Pursuant to Article 24 of Council Regulation (EEC) No 3330/74 of 19 December 1974 (OJ L 359, 31.12.1974, p 1) and Article 2(1) of Council Regulation 3331/74 of 19 December 1974 (OJ L 359, 31.12.1974, p 18).

Undoubtedly, the most relevant Court of Justice case law from the point of view of the subject matter of the present analysis is Judgment of 12 March 1996 in Case C-441/93, *Pafitis and Trapeza Kentrikis Ellados AE and others*, where the Court defended the right to property of the shareholders of a Bank, on the ground of the Second Council Directive, which was the key EU regulatory instrument in that respect.[105] The Directive mainly protected shareholders rights to participate in the decision-making process of the company as a collective company body or, reversely, provided that no major decision affecting their status could be taken without their participation. In particular, any increase in capital ought to be decided upon by the general meeting and be published along with the increase in the subscribed capital (Article 25). Strict provisions also applied for the body, the ceiling and the time period of a potential authorisation to increase share capital, as well as the separate decisions that ought to be taken where there were several classes of shares. Furthermore, it was provided that whenever the capital was increased by consideration in cash, the shares ought to be offered on a pre-emptive basis to shareholders in proportion to the capital represented by their shares (Article 29).

The Court of Justice had, from the early stages of the implementation of the Second Directive, interpreted the relevant provisions so as to prevent any bypasses of the shareholders rights.[106] A special Greek law[107] provided that where the capital of a bank was eroded as a result of losses or where the Monetary Commission considered that, for any other reason, a bank's capital was not commensurate with its needs, the Commission would call on the bank to reinstate the capital lost or to increase the capital within a period of not less than 60 days set by it and where a bank was unable, or refused to increase its capital, or obstructed supervision, or infringed any rule, the Monetary Commission might either withdraw the bank's licence to trade, thereby putting it into liquidation, or appoint an administrator.

On 13 September 1984 the Governor of the Bank of Greece placed Bank of Central Greece (*Trapeza Kentrikis Ellados*) under the supervision of a temporary administrator, called on the bank to increase its capital in order to stabilise the conduct of its business and mandated the temporary administrator, acting in the capacity of the general meeting, to unilaterally amend the statutes of the Bank. In order to give effect to that increase, the temporary administrator invited the

---

[105] Second Council Directive 77/91 of 13 December 1976 (OJ L 26, 31.1.1977, p 1). The Second Directive was codified in 2000 through Directive 2000/12. As of 3 December 2012, it is no longer in force pursuant to Directive 2012/30 of the European Parliament and of the Council of 25 October 2012 (OJ L 315, 14.11.2012, p 74), which was, in turn repealed as of 19 July 2017 by Directive 2017/1132 of the European Parliament and of the Council of 14 June 2017 (OJ L 169, 30.6.2017, p 46).

[106] CJEU Judgments of 30 May 1991 in Joined Cases C-19/90 and C-20/90, *Karella and Karellas*, paras 25–26 and 31; CJEU Judgment of 24 March 1992 in Case C-381/89, *Syndesmos Melon tis Eleftheras Evangelikis Ekklisias and Others*, paras 32–33; and CJEU Judgment of 12 November 1992 in Joined Cases C-134/91 and C-135/91, *Kerafina-Keramische und Finanz-Holding and Vioktimatik*, para 18.

[107] Special Law 1665/1951.

shareholders, by notice published in the political and financial press, to exercise their pre-emptive rights in relation to the increase within a period of 30 days and invited any interested third parties to participate in the increase upon expiry of that period. Since the plaintiffs had not exercised their pre-emptive rights by the end of that period, the new shares were ultimately allotted to third parties. Subsequently, the capital was increased on three further occasions in 1987, 1989 and 1990 by the general meeting of the Bank, with corresponding amendments being made to its statutes. The result was a huge dilution of the old shareholders' company rights. Both decisions, ie temporary administration and share capital increase, were subsequently ratified by law.

The old shareholders brought an action against the Bank and its new shareholders on the grounds that:

(a)   the decisions taken by the temporary administrator without the general meeting of shareholders having been convened were contrary to the Second Directive;

(b)   the three subsequent increases of capital and the corresponding amendments to the statutes were null and void, and therefore the new shareholders had acquired neither the status of shareholders nor the right to participate in the general meeting; and

(c)   the mandate of the temporary administrator had anyway lapsed automatically upon the expiry of a reasonable period.

The Athens Civil Court of First Instance referred to the Court of Justice three preliminary questions concerning the interpretation of Articles 25 and 29 of the Second Directive. The Court of Justice upheld the arguments of the applicants in the main proceedings and provided very strong support to the requirements set out by the Second Directive, thus consolidating its significance within the Community structure, in line with its general case law. The main axis of the rationale of the Court, responding to the Government's argument that exceptional circumstances justified the impugned measure, which essentially codified prior case law, was that the objective of the Second Directive to ensure a minimum level of protection for shareholders in all Member States entails its application in any instance and without concessions when it comes to unusual or exceptional circumstances.

The conceptual shift of the right to property in the crisis case law is expressed essentially through two modules in the case law of the European courts. The first module is a return to the social aspect of property. This aspect seems to have become again the most salient feature in the protection of property. Most importantly, social burdens, especially taxation and social security contributions, seem to become a privileged field where not only the State does claim the share of every individual or entity for the operation of the State and the services provided thereof, but they also become the main tool to escape the imminent economic crisis in European States through an understanding of social solidarity. This is why a court shall not have recourse to the cumulative effect of burdens and shall accept extremely wide latitude of discretion of the state authorities when imposing such burdens. In that regard, judicial review becomes illusionary: active in theory, powerless in practice.

The second module is a de-scoping of property so as to devaluate the level of protection awarded to intangible property rights, ie the exact opposite to the one that had been consistently followed in the twentieth century, more evidently in its last quarter in Europe. This is not to intimate that physical property is regaining exclusivity in the characterisation as property. Intangible assets can still qualify as property, yet in a rather weak position from the point of view of its relevant protection. The mitigation of the protection of intangible assets essentially destroys what constitutes their very essence, namely the credit. Intangible property, exactly because of the lack of any physical reference of value, needs a core understanding among the actors of this arena that the worth embodied in the asset carries value commonly respected both as a matter of regular obedience to law and as a necessary requirement for economy stability and social cohesion. Without this level of protection of credit, intangible assets become volatile altogether and broadly determined by unpredictable, if not random, factors.

The post-crisis legislation and case law clearly underestimates credit and overvalues the risk associated with intangible assets. This is why the Court of Strasbourg, in assessing the Greek PSI in *Mamatas*, accepted very easily, almost as a self-evident conclusion, that haircuts do not constitute 'deprivation' of, but merely 'interference' with, the right to property. Yet, the substantiation of the statement is very poor and results in a wide paradox. In the Court's reasoning, if someone is forcibly obliged to withdraw one euro there is a case of deprivation, whereas if someone is forcibly obliged to withdraw one million euros of guaranteed securities there is merely a case of interference with peaceful enjoyment of property. Interestingly, the Court itself admitted that the State intervention amounted to a 'drastic fall of debt owed to the applicants', ie qualitatively particularly burdensome. Yet, this was not adequate to consider the haircut as constituting deprivation of the right to property on the ground that the individuals, by assuming the government bonds, made an investment whose value 'could have fluctuated according to the trends of the markets and the economic situation of the issuing State'.[108] The case law upgrade of the role of risk in any sort of intangible property is particularly true for banking products, ie bank deposits, state bonds and shareholdings.

Bank deposits, at least according to the pre-crisis institutional framework, constituted property. Such assets were essentially equivalent to tangible assets, in the sense that they were considered as a risk-free security whereby the bank assumed the responsibility to hold the deposit and be ready at any time to return it with the contractually provided interest applying at any given time. Although the banks were entitled to use the deposits for further loans or investments, the basic

---

[108] Paragraph 94.

task of deposit banks, as opposed to investment banks, was to be ready at any time to satisfy a claim for withdrawal of the deposit on the part of the depositor.

Government bonds were also widely protected under property clauses in the pre-crisis era both from a commercial and from a legal point of view. From a commercial viewpoint, when holding a Government bond or bill, which is usually a bond of a limited period of up to a year, its investor is exposed mainly to four risks:

(a)   credit risk, ie the probability that the Government will not be able to repay its debt, which is the main factor determining the level of the coupon of the bond/bill at the time of the issuance/pricing;
(b)   market risk, applying to sell-outs prior to its maturity, ie the probability that the market value of the bond/bill will decrease throughout its duration, for example due to an increase in interest rates by the central bank;
(c)   liquidity risk, applying to secondary market sell-outs, ie the probability that there is no demand when the investor wishes to sell;
(d)   foreign-exchange risk, ie the risk that the value of the investment will decrease if the currency in which the bond/bill is denominated depreciates vis-à-vis the currency of reference for the investor, a risk that was seriously depreciated in the euro area with the relevant convergence in the context of the euro as an international reserve.

At any rate, exposures to central governments or central banks denominated and funded in the national currency of the borrower were assigned a zero per cent risk weight. This attitude reflected the idea that States were by definition reliable and trustworthy and that products enjoying state guarantee could not fail or be put at risk. Yet, the ongoing fiscal crisis in the euro area, particularly the Greek Government bond exchange programme under the PSI, demonstrated that this provision is one of the most prominent examples of regulatory failure, in that it provided a false incentive for investment in government bonds denominated in euro without a substantial credit risk assessment and with a zero capital charge.[109]

Thus, from a regulatory point of view, government bonds could only be characterised as risk-free economic activity that created a rather high level of expectation that was tantamount to a very low risk investment, practically a deposit. This was further enhanced by the domestic legislation. In Greece, prior to the financial crisis, Article 8(2) of Law 2198/1994 provided that if the State fails to comply with its obligations at the time of the maturity of governmental bonds, each investor might demand its claim against the State; nonetheless, Law 4050/2012 on the PSI made the haircut on such bonds mandatory even to those in disagreement, thus depriving their right to raise the claim against the State.

---

[109] ChV Gortsos, 'The Proposed Legal Framework for Establishing a European Monetary Fund (EMF): A Systematic Presentation and a Preliminary Assessment (2017)', available at: ssrn.com/abstract=3090343.

From a legal point of view, government bonds also constituted 'possessions' falling under the protection of the right to property, especially in the meaning of Article 1 of Protocol No 1 to the ECHR. Applying the *Stran* criteria one could easily conclude that, as in all cases of regular bonds issued by sovereign States, in that case there was a claim sufficiently established to be enforceable. This is so because sovereign bonds include the essential characteristics that make the claim definitive and predictable in its implementation, ie the maturity time, the amount due on the maturity time and general terms and conditions applicable to the bonds.

This was also the case with the Russian commodity bonds. Given that Soviet securities had been recognised as Russian Federation Government debt, through the 1995 Commodity Bonds Act, and that such recognition entailed compensation or redemption, those securities were considered possessions in the meaning of Article 1 of Protocol No 1 and the applicants admittedly had a 'proprietary interest':[110] the concept of possession has an autonomous meaning not limited to the ownership of material goods and is independent from the formal classification in domestic law. The Court denies the status of possession only when a minimum specific property content is absent from intangible assets, such as in the case of a domestic rule that is laconic, without defining the actual scope of the State's obligations and the manner of their discharge, thus merely expressing a hope and not a credible commitment.

By way of analogy, the Greek Government bonds left no margins in their implementation; this is why bonds in general do not require any secondary legislation to be implemented, but are directly enforceable under their specific terms and conditions once they are issued. In that context, bond purchase constitutes a firm and legitimate contractual commitment assumed by the State and producing full expectation of satisfaction at the maturity date.

As regards the scope of protection of government bonds under property, a very extensive analysis was made in Judgments 1116-1117/2014 of the Hellenic Council of State concerning the bail-in scheme resulting in the haircut of Greek bonds. The majority of the Council considered that investing in bonds and other securities issued or guaranteed by States, as a legal relationship of financial loyalty, involved the risk of property loss. In this view, this risk existed even if the law governing the securities did not provide the possibility of renegotiating their terms, such as their nominal value, the coupon or their maturing time, before their time of expiration. The rationale for the existence of risk was that between the issuing date of the bond and its maturing, there was a sufficient time period during which unforeseen events were likely to occur; events that could substantially restrict the financial capabilities of the issuer of the securities, ie the State.

---

[110] ECtHR Judgment of 11 February 2010, *Malysh and others v Russia*, Application no 30280/03, paras 65, 68, 80; ECtHR Judgment of 18 March 2010, *Tronin v Russia*, Application no 24461/02; ECtHR Judgment of 2 December 2010, *Yuriy Lobanov v Russia*, Application no 15578/03; ECtHR Judgment of 10 April 2012, *Andreyeva v Russia*, Application no 73659/10; and ECtHR Judgment of 26 February 2013, *Fomin and others v Russia*, Application no 34703/04, para 25.

When such events occur, the State may lawfully renegotiate under the clause *rebus sic stantibus*, which defines the general principle *pacta sunt servanda*. In fact, the Council made a categorical preliminary statement that bonds and other tangible or intangible securities did not have asset value in transactions, in which case a stronger property violation would have been potentially upheld, but merely a contractual value embodied into a foreseeable claim for payment when the bond would mature. In that sense, in the Council's view, the serious curtailment of the nominal value of the state bonds could not be tantamount to a (partial) expropriation entailing full compensation within the meaning of the relevant constitutional clause (Article 17(2)), which merely applies when there is a deprivation of tangible assets with an asset value in itself. Accordingly, the reduction of the bonds' nominal value merely triggered the protection of a legitimate expectation for future income, secured through the constitutional clause guaranteeing the implementation of contractual commitments assumed by individuals or entities free of external interventions by State action, be it executive or legislative.

The majority opinion held that, given the urgency and extremity of the erupted crisis, the PSI scheme did not appear as disproportionate interference with the right to property: the 53.5 per cent reduction of nominal bond value (estimated up to 78.5 per cent if the additional measure of delay in their maturity time was added) was 'particularly serious' but 'not inappropriate, unnecessary or excessive'. There were two major dissenting opinions in the Judgment: one relying on property; and one relying on economic freedom. The first dissenting view found a property violation in the seemingly unjustified inclusion in the scheme of the bondholders who had not consented to the haircut, which was basically negotiated and agreed upon between professional investors / funds and the Greek Government Furthermore, this view identified a failure to draw a fair balance between the legitimate interest to prevent the country's default and the right to property, in that the applicants suffered actual losses and there was no proportionality between the damage and the justified public interest of fixing the sustainability of the Greek public debt. At this point, the dissenting opinion found that there was no convincing argument or report to substantiate the inclusion in the scheme of non-participating and non-consenting bondholders, thus the Court could not identify whether such inclusion was necessary for the accomplishment of the intended public purpose. In fact, according to this view, less restrictive alternatives could have applied to serve equally well the relevant public aim, such as the suspension of public debt payment, the extension of the maturity date and the limitation of the amount of interest due. The justices of this group also placed emphasis on the fact that during the parliamentary debates on the impugned statute there were serious concerns by the deputies of all political parties of the opposition.

The second dissenting view considered the State intervention tantamount to a unilateral, mandatory and detrimental change of status of the bondholders amounting to breach of Article 5(1) of the Constitution, which guarantees, in principle, the freedom to participate in the economic life (including the right to conclude and implement contracts) and of Article 106(1), which provides that the State shall plan and coordinate economic activity in the country, aiming at safeguarding the economic development of all sectors of the national economy in order to consolidate social peace and protect the general interest. In that view, the essential content of holding a bond was tantamount:

(a) to the obligation of the issuer, and correspondingly to the right of the bearer, for payment of the nominal value of the security upon its maturity time; and

(b) to the possibility of trading and participating in the economic life of the country, due to its transferability in the secondary financial market until its maturity time.

Accordingly, the rights deriving from bond holding fell within the meaning not only of property but also of the constitutionally protected freedom of contract. Thus, statutory interference with an established contractual relationship constituted an exceptional measure that could only be taken on the basis of general and appropriate criteria, within a reasonable time after the contract was concluded and only for reasons of public interest, such as national economy.

In response to the argument that collective action clauses were envisaged by international security practice and by Article 12(3) of the ESM Treaty (to be incorporated to all new securities of euro-area Member States issued after 1 January 2013), the minority view insisted on the dominant perception of freedom to enter into a binding agreement that could not be altered through external statutory mechanisms and on the scope of the ESM treaty arguably falling outside the present case *ratione temporis*, given that the bonds in question had been issued well before its entry into effect. Accordingly, the bearers of a property right could not be deprived of the value of their respective assets without their consent and without compensation, even when a majority of those in the same legal situation do consent to have their property rights collectively diminished; a third-party agreement could not substitute the autonomy of will of a bondholder, who was not party to that contract, even if his or her right was generic in nature (*res inter alios acta*).

Shareholders' rights under the Second Directive and the case law of the European Court of Human Rights also qualified as property, protected accordingly. The *Pafitis* and the Russian commodity bonds case law indeed leave very small room to support that the post-crisis case law was indeed compatible with the prior case law principles. In *Pafitis*, the Court of Justice held that the majority of Directives protecting shareholders sought to uphold and extend the right of establishment and the freedom to provide services in the banking sector, by means of specific provisions applicable to banks irrespective of the factual surroundings of each case. Moreover, the numerous provisions concerning supervision, which confer on the competent authorities, in certain circumstances, the power to require a credit institution to remedy, within a specified period of time, an insufficiency of assets, do not affect the powers of the organs of the credit institution in question to make their own arrangements to rectify matters.

With this rationale, the Court drew a clear line of distinction between company directives protecting shareholders' rights and banking directives which establish the requirements, especially that of money deposits, which are applicable to the financial institutions. The Court emphatically declared that national rules concerning the need to protect the interests of savers and, more generally, the equilibrium of the savings system, ought to apply strict supervisory rules in order to ensure the continuing stability of the banking system, without depriving the organs of a credit institution of the powers vested in them: the interests at issue could be given equal and appropriate protection by other means, such as

> the creation of a generalised system to guarantee deposits, which seek to achieve the same result but do not impede attainment of the objective pursued by the Second Directive of providing a minimum level of protection for shareholders in all the Member States.[111]

Thus, the Court set an unequivocal red line of protection for the shareholders that the domestic legislator could not cross through emergency clauses. The unequivocal wording of the Court that the Second Directive applies equally at times of financial calmness as well as at times of banking turbulence was replaced by the distinction based on the surrounding circumstances, introduced in the crisis case *Kotnik*. Thus, the shareholders' rights were subject to a variable level of protection. Most importantly, there was a clear shift in the principal perception of the legislation on the matter. From the predominance of the shareholders rights as a fundamental right, the Court of Justice turned to the priority of the systemic operation of the banking sector, as a safety net for the smooth operation of the market, where financing is by definition a key issue for the welfare of banks.

B. The Intensity of Review

In the crisis case law two major grounds have been widely exploited to mitigate the intensity of judicial review: the political/technical nature of the relevant policies; and the exceptional circumstances surrounding the financial crisis cases. In the post-crisis era, the courts seem to uphold as a matter of principle that State choices, aiming at restoring financial balance and consolidation, present a highly political/technical element.

i. Political/Technical Acts

With regard to judicial self-restraint in cases of a political/technical nature of the relevant policies, the underlying principle is the democratic legitimacy of the political branches of governance, as opposed to that of the judiciary, and the

---

[111] Paragraph 51.

expertise on particular issues that call for a more elaborate and in-depth look into the specifics of a case. Although in the pre-crisis era wider discretion was recognised to the state authorities to implement their policies when the decision was of such nature and there was admittedly a compelling public interest, this discretion could not go as far as to curtail the core of the rights interfered with.

With regard to cases with a strong political element, the Court of Strasbourg, in the Polish Bug River cases, held that in situations involving succession of State territories, which entail an exceptionally difficult exercise of balancing the rights at stake, as well as the gains and losses of the different persons affected by the process of transforming the State's economy and legal system, the choice of measures may necessarily involve decisions restricting compensation for the taking or restitution of property to a level below its market value and, thus, Article 1 of Protocol No 1 does not guarantee a right to full compensation under all circumstances. Yet, 'that margin, however considerable, is not unlimited, and the exercise of the State's discretion, even in the context of the most complex reform of the State', such as fundamental changes of a country's system in the form of transition from a totalitarian regime to a democratic form of government and the reform of the State's political, legal and economic structure, phenomena which inevitably involve the enactment of large-scale economic and social legislation, 'cannot entail consequences at variance with Convention standards'.[112]

With regard to the cases where the impugned decision involved a highly technical judgement, the European Court of Human Rights also moderates the intensity of judicial review. This is, for example, the case in the field of town planning, which results in significant interferences with the right to property. In Judgment *Elia slr v Italy*, where the complaint referred to measures aiming at protecting the natural or cultural heritage, the Court acknowledged that the State interference with the right to property met the requirements of the general interest on the ground that 'in an area as complex and difficult as that of spatial development, the Contracting States should enjoy a wide margin of appreciation in order to implement their town-planning policy'.[113] In the same vain, in *Sporrong and Lönnroth v Sweden* the Court held that although admittedly the States in this technical field enjoyed a wide margin of appreciation, it could not 'fail to exercise its power of review and must determine whether the requisite balance was maintained in a manner consonant with the applicants' right to the peaceful enjoyment of their possessions' and, accordingly, the ordinary intensity of judicial review applied, involving a balancing review process.[114]

In the post-crisis era the judicial attitude changes significantly. On the level of EU case law, the EU courts insisted that it is not for the judiciary to substitute

---

[112] ECtHR Judgment of 22 June 2004, *Broniowski v Poland* Application no 31443/96, paras 181–82.

[113] ECtHR Judgment of 2 August 2001, *Elia slr v Italy* Application no 37710/97.

[114] ECtHR Judgment of 23 September 1982, *Sporrong and Lönnroth v Sweden*, Application nos 7151, 7152/1975), para 69. Also see ECtHR Judgment of 2 December 2010, *Anonymos Touristiki Etairia Xenodocheia Kritis v Greece*, Application no 35332/05, para 45.

their opinion for that of the legitimate institutions. Thus, in both *Pringle* and *Gauweiler*, it explicitly acknowledged a wide margin of appreciation to the EU institutions on policy and technical decisions. Most indicatively, in *Sotiropoulou*, the General Court emphasised that only a manifest and serious breach on the part of an EU institution could trigger the non-contractual liability of the Union, so as to allow the institutions to take on complicated decisions of economic policy without the imminent fear of liability. In this assessment the relevant criteria were the complexity of the situations to be regulated, the difficulties in applying or interpreting the provisions and, in particular, the margin of discretion enjoyed by the issuing authority. Accordingly, the Court concluded that, in general, the impugned budgetary measures taken in Greece were thoroughly discussed with the domestic Government and agreed jointly by the Commission, the ECB and the IMF and, therefore, they did not appear to be manifestly unjustified or exceeding the limits of the Council's wide discretionary power to provide for various cost-saving measures, including with regard to pensions.

At ECHR level, the Court of Strasbourg, in *Koufaki*, conceded that the Contracting Members enjoy quite a wide margin of appreciation in regulating their social policy, since budgetary decisions commonly involve considerations of political, economic and social issues. In the Court's view, this margin becomes even wider when the issues further involve an assessment of the priorities as to the allocation of limited state resources, essentially the implementation of social policies and state structures: 'when general policy issues, on which sharp differentiations might reasonably exist in a democratic state, there is a need to pay particular attention to the role of the national decision-maker'.[115] In all such cases, the courts must, therefore, apply a low-intensity judicial control and should not require a thorough justification for the decision affecting human rights or a very detailed prior evaluation of less restrictive alternatives. Reasonably the Court significantly downgraded the threshold of annulment of the impugned measures, in the sense that a decision taken in support of the compelling financial interests of the State might be quashed on substantive grounds only if there is a manifest error or unreasonableness.

Furthermore, in *Fábián*, the Court held that in the field of social security and pensions the State enjoyed a wide margin of appreciation to draw different layers of employees (within public administration, or public/private employees) and, provided that the legislature chose a method that could be regarded as reasonable and suited to achieving the legitimate aim being pursued, there could be no assessment as to whether the legislation represented the best solution for dealing with the problem or whether the legislative discretion should have been exercised in another way: 'Decisions involving such distinctions were policy judgments which were in principle reserved for the national authorities, which had direct democratic legitimation and were better placed than an international court to evaluate

---

[115] Paragraph 39.

local needs and conditions'.[116] The doctrine of 'policy judgment' in determining labour categories essentially upgraded the state discretion to immunity in relation to the establishment of labour conditions upon any category of public servants.

On the level of domestic courts, the Irish Supreme Court's judgment in *Collins v Minister for Finance and others* set the principle in an unequivocal manner that although financial policy choices could significantly constrain the freedom of action of future parliaments and such competences ought to be performed 'conscientiously and carefully', the Court had no function in considering the wisdom of decisions taken by the other branches of government. In this view, the Court had only limited capacity to ensure, through judicial review, that the constitutional body responsible to make such decisions, whether they were 'wise or foolish, trivial or far reaching', were indeed allowed to do so within the limits imposed by the Constitution.[117]

In the same line of argumentation, in Judgment 668/2012, the Hellenic Council of State held that the legislature's discretion to deal with the critical financial situation was subject merely to marginal judicial review for their effectiveness, and on the merits of the case it sufficed that the impugned measures did indeed have a significant financial impact for the state budget in order to serve the legitimate aim of economic rescue of the country. Thus, the evidence that salary/pension cuts of the first programme would save 0.5 and 0.2 per cent of GDP for 2010 and 2011 respectively and holiday bonus cuts would save 0.6 and 0.2 per cent of GDP for 2010 and 2011 respectively sufficed for the Council to uphold the constitutionality of the measures, considering they were suitable and necessary.[118]

In the same line, the Council held in Judgments 1972/2012 and 532/2015 that the legislature had wide discretion to formulate the tax system, including determination of the appropriate method and timing of taxation, on the condition that the measures were taken on the basis of general and objective criteria, taking into account contemporary socio-economic circumstances.

Finally, with regard to the establishment of a social security system, the Latvian Constitutional Court, albeit applying in the main a balancing review process in the light of the constitutional clause that everyone has the right to social security in old age, for work disability, for unemployment and in other cases as provided by law (Article 109), acknowledged a significant margin of appreciation on the part of the Government to reallocate public benefits so as to achieve an effective, sustainable and fair system, within the constitutionally enshrined fundamental rights but without being limited by the social acquis of certain categories of workers and pensioners.[119]

---

[116] Paragraph 124.
[117] Paragraph 86.
[118] Similarly, Judgments 3404-3405/2014 of the Council of State.
[119] Judgment in Case 2010-17-01, para 7. Also see Judgment in Case 2009-08-01 and in Case 2009-44-01.

Although the constitutional courts of the lender States were indeed less inclined to defer on financial rescue packages through the European mechanisms, on some occasions they exercised some judicial self-restraint. Thus the German Federal Constitutional Court, although probing deeply into matters of parliamentary participation in such schemes, ruled in the case of the EFSF and First Adjustment Programme for Greece that, given the wide latitude of political discretion in the field, there was no constitutional violation neither in the provisions of the EU Treaties against parliamentary budgetary autonomy, both presupposing and requiring direct national democratic legitimacy, nor with regard to the probability of having to pay out on future guarantees or future soundness of the federal budget stemming from financial assistance to Greece. The same line was followed by the Estonian Constitutional Court in its judgment of 12 July 2012, regarding State discretion to draft the budget, where the Court considered that the budget was not only an instrumental manual for the revenues and expenditures but also the means to guarantee the fundamental rights and freedoms in the country, in the sense that the Parliament, on a proposal by the Government, decided in a widely discretionary manner whether to authorise government borrowing or other financial obligations related to the budgetary powers.

As regards the intensity of judicial review with political choices of the Government, there is an interesting antithesis with the stance of the UK Supreme Court in *R (on the application of Miller and another) v Secretary of State for Exiting the European Union*,[120] concerning the competence to initiate the process for the UK exiting the EU, pursuant to the 2016 British referendum. In spite of the obviously political nature of the question and the highly controversial matter in the domestic politics, the Court did not hesitate to decide on the merits of the case against the privilege that would allow the Government to initiate the process alone and to demand an Act of Parliament thus providing. The Lords felt obliged to declare at the outset of the case that the issue was not one relating to the wisdom of the decision to withdraw from the EU, the terms of withdrawal, the timetable or arrangements for withdrawal, or the details of any future relationship with the Union, or the merits of the decision to exit the EU, that are not issues 'which are appropriate for resolution by judges, whose duty is to decide issues of law which are brought before them by individuals and entities exercising their rights of access to the courts in a democratic society', but merely a matter of allocation of constitutional competences so as to proactively address allegations for interfering with political value judgments.[121]

The post-crisis case law in Europe, which upgraded the criterion of the political/technical nature of the case in determining the intensity of judicial review, is questionable both in terms of its doctrinal soundness and in terms of the results that it may produce. As Everson and Joerges notice, the discrepancy between the

---

[120] [2017] UKSC 5.
[121] Paragraph 3.

German Federal Constitutional Court's exclusive commitment to the interests of its country and the Court of Justice's commitment to the integration project has caused a risk of a new kind, namely the primacy of discretionary politics in the management of the crisis and the failure to develop any criteria against which the legitimacy of these practices might be assessed.[122] Obviously, the lower level of direct legitimacy of the judiciary does not by any means decrease the scope of the constitutional competences assigned to it. Indeed, respect by the judiciary for the separation of powers and for the constitutional status of each branch of governance traditionally takes the form of minimal control when the case reflects political choices, thus qualifying as act of government *(act de gouvernement)*.

However, treating *all* cases arising in the context of financial crisis as entailing complex technical judgments or political choices per se for the sake of degrading the intensity of judicial review is doctrinally unsustainable and practically leaves ample space to the political branches of government for uncontrollable authoritarian decisions, especially in cases which strongly involve interferences with human rights. In this way, the classical approach to judicial review, according to which judicial review becomes more intense when human rights, especially those characterised by each legal system as fundamental, are at stake, is curtailed, if not totally subverted. Indeed, from the early case law of the Court of Justice, prior to the wide recognition in the Community legal order of the obligation to respect human rights as a matter of Community general principle and, later as part of primary EU law, there was strong evidence that the Court proceeded to a more thorough judicial review, mostly involving the proportionality test, only insofar the impugned measure affected the rights of individuals, following good practices of domestic supreme courts.[123]

ii. Exceptional Circumstances

The reference to exceptional circumstances, either explicitly or implicitly, to justify taking measures that serious hamper human rights has been one of the most oft-repeated references of the post-crisis case law, both on domestic and international

---

[122] M Everson and Ch Joerges, 'Who is the Guardian for Constitutionalism in Europe after the Financial Crisis? LSE 'Europe in Question' Discussion Paper Series no 63/2013, 22–23.

[123] See, for instance, the Opinion of 18 September 1980 of Advocate General Reischl in Case 138/79, *Roquette Frères v Council*. In the US legal order, 'strict scrutiny' is the peak in terms of intensity of judicial control, over the 'intermediate scrutiny' and 'rational basis test' consisting only of the investigation of whether the contested measure has been unreasonable. Strict scrutiny leads the judicial reasoning to a level of substantive evaluation and, respectively, results in such a high burden of proof that the chances for annulment of the impugned measure rapidly increase. The selection of the type of control essentially predisposes the final result of the judgment: strict scrutiny is 'strict in theory, fatal in fact', according to the often-repeated saying, first used by in G Gunther, 'The Supreme Court, 1971 Term', (1972) 86 *Harvard Law Review* 8. In this judicial context, the Supreme Court takes on the strict scrutiny test in categories cases where there is a serious interference with right valued highly by the US constitutional order, such as cases of racial discrimination constituting suspect classifications, see, eg, *Yick Wo v Hopkins* 118 US 356 (1886).

level. This marks a significant turn from pre-crisis case law, where the principle was that constitutional rights apply in full also at hard times. The most obvious such case law, with clear relevance to the present analysis, came from the Court of Justice in *Pafitis*. With reference to the Second Directive seeking to ensure a minimum level of protection for shareholders in all the Member States, the Court declared that such safeguards would be seriously frustrated if the Member States were entitled to derogate from the provisions of the Directive by maintaining in force rules, 'even rules categorized as special or exceptional' under which it is possible to decide by administrative measure, separately from any decision by the general meeting of shareholders, to effect an increase in the company's capital.[124] The Court, accordingly, explicitly discarded the argument that supervisory rules stemming from banking legislation were provisions dictated by the public interest and, therefore, ought to prevail in case of a banking crisis.

Irrespective of its undeniable significance for the well-being of the States, the Second Directive applied to credit institutions under the same conditions as to any other undertaking, in the absence of any express exception. With *Pafitis*, the Court awarded a distinctive value to the shareholders' rights, the stability of the system and the effective safeguard of the right to property without any hierarchy in the applicability of legal norms depending on the surrounding circumstances. By the same token, on ECHR level, eg in the Russian commodity bond cases, it was ruled that exceptional circumstances, even if reflected in the most radical form of state succession, which by definition connote a wide margin of discretion for the State to take reconstruction measures, do not relieve the State from the obligation to seek and achieve a proper balance and, accordingly, the public interest cannot altogether outweigh the property right involved.[125]

The case law scenery changed immensely in the post-crisis era on all European layers, albeit in different manners. On EU level, the financial crisis case law essentially differentiated regulation applying under ordinary conditions and regulation applying under exceptional conditions. The most illustrative such cases are those concerning the protection of bank shareholders against recapitalisation schemes set in place without their consent, mostly in *Kotnik* and *Dowling*. The Court of Justice held, accordingly, without any detailed reasoning, that the Second Directive generally protecting shareholders' rights from external interventions only applied under normal conditions, whereas exceptional circumstances involving serious economic disturbances allowed for regulatory space outside the Second

---

[124] Paragraphs 38–39.

[125] Also see, on the succession from the former Czechoslovakia, inter alia, ECtHR Judgment of 28 September 2004, *Kopecký v Slovakia*, Application no 44912/98, para 35; ECtHR Judgment of 12 February 2003, *Zvolský and Zvolskáv v Czech Republic*, Application no 46129/99. For the enactment of laws in the context of German reunification see ECtHR Judgment of 2 March 2005, *Von Maltzan and others v Germany*, Application nos 71916/01, 71917/01 and 10260/02. In the latter set of cases, the Court held that, in certain circumstances, the retrospective application of legislation whose effect is to deprive someone of a pre-existing possession may constitute interference that is liable to upset the fair balance.

Directive. In this way the Court opened the gate to, and eventually upheld, the exceptional circumstances that could go contrary to the express letter of EU law and drew a clear line of distinction between ordinary circumstances, where the shareholders' rights in the banking sector are fully fledged (the principle) and circumstances caused because of lack of adequate funds and danger of insolvency where emergency tools apply that set aside the requirement that the shareholders necessarily participate in the decision-making process (the exception). Therefore, at the time of normality the right to property fully applies, whereas at times of financial abnormality the right somewhat concedes. This ruling fully reversed, without any convincing argumentation, the *Pafitis* case law of that same Court.

At ECHR level, there has been a repeated use of exceptional circumstances surrounding the austerity measures. In *Mamatas*, for example, the Court of Strasbourg strongly reiterated that in situations involving serious and controversial regulation, with significant economic impact throughout the country, national authorities should enjoy wide discretion not only to choose the measures to guarantee the respect of the economic rights or to regulate the reports of ownership in the country, but also to take the necessary time to implement them.[126] Yet, in more general terms, in the context of a change of political and economic regime, a rather conclusive argument *a majore ad minus* applies: if under such radical and exceptional circumstances the State still carries, in principle, an obligation to respect the right to property, even in conditions of wide discretion on the part of state authorities, it follows that in a sectorial crisis, such as a banking or financial crisis, irrespective of its intensity, the self-evident legitimate interest of state reconstruction cannot altogether outweigh the right to property.

On a domestic level, judicial retreat on grounds of exceptional circumstances occurred, in a more subtle manner. The Irish Supreme Court held, in *Collins v Minister for Finance and others*, that the statutory provisions authorising the Minister to initiate the process of State financial assistance to endangered banks would, under normal conditions, probably be held unconstitutional: 'It was a permissible constitutional response to an exceptional situation. It cannot therefore be considered to be a template for broader Ministerial power on other occasions'.[127] Furthermore, in Judgment 1116/2014 of the Hellenic Council of State on the PSI, the Council held that especially in 'exceptional circumstances which call for general economic and social measures', in view of the economic collapse of the country, the public authorities had had wide discretion to assess the most appropriate measures to safeguard a fair balance between the general public interest and the property right involved; in such cases, any court of law can only exercise a 'marginal review of constitutionality' of the impugned statutes.[128] Interestingly, the Council used the rationale of exceptional circumstances to also

---

[126] Paragraph 89.
[127] Paragraph 84.
[128] Paragraphs 32, 39.

outcast the discrimination argument against various distinctive categories of investors.

Even in cases where the Greek Courts refrained from explicitly using the language of exceptional circumstances, a more thorough reading reveals that the doctrine permeates judicial reasoning. In order to justify the statutory lower default interest rate paid by the State for outstanding claims as opposed to the ordinary rate paid by individuals, the Greek Special Supreme Court held, in its Judgment 25/2012, that

> throughout its existence the Greek State has been subjected to successive severe finan-
> cial crises, which have lasted for long periods of time and whose impact extend even
> to periods in which the economic situation improved and the circumstances were
> favorable to the country's development.[129]

The Judgment essentially set up an open window of constant exceptional financial circumstances that could conceivably be the basis for invoking any adverse
measure to support the public interest involved.

The use of exceptional circumstances to limit judicial review in economic crisis
cases raises three issues: conceptual; legal; and consistency. The *conceptual* issue
is that it weakens the normativity of the Constitution. Indeed, the Constitution
is not established as a dispute resolution mechanism of normality, but foremost as a superior law providing responses to hard cases arising in political or
other type of crisis and conflict. The Constitution does not vary according to the
factual conditions surrounding each era and is not meant to operate under very
comfortable and undisputed contexts, but is set in place exactly to apply in cases of
heat and intensity as a safeguard for the citizens against any potential authoritarian
regime. Decreasing the normative validity and enforcement of the Constitution
by reducing its scope merely to contextual normality would demoralise and
seriously devaluate it, with all corresponding implications for the welfare of the
people and for the State.

Exceptional circumstances may indeed vary the criteria of judicial review or
the conditions to justify an interference with human rights, but only under very
strict substantive and procedural limitations: as the Hellenic Council of State held,
when it reversed its case law to strike down pension cuts arguing that in cases of
'exceptionally unfavorable financial conditions' and, cumulatively 'if it is reasonably demonstrated that the State is unable to provide adequate funding to social
security organisations',[130] the legislature may decide to reduce social security
benefits, but this is subject to strict judicial review. The rationale of exceptional
circumstances during a financial crisis constitutes a clear misconception of the
functioning of the Constitution, ie that there is an ever-present and ever-dominant

---

[129] Paragraph 10.
[130] Judgments 2287–2290/2015 of the Hellenic Council of State.

escape clause that tacitly abrogates the explicit letter of the Constitution, when a compelling public interest so directs.

Irrespective of this clearly unsustainable syllogism, from the point of view of the doctrine of permissible constitutional interpretation, this attitude constitutes an awkward revival of Cicero's saying, that later became a strong roman doctrine, *salus populi suprema lex esto*. Yet, what this opinion overlooks is that Cicero's expression constituted an advice to future Roman statesmen, not lawyers, let alone judges.

The *legal* issue is that by continuously invoking exceptional circumstances there is a bypass of the constitutional escape clauses through declaration of state of emergency/siege that triggers wide governmental powers and suspends human rights under very strict conditions, normally a substantial danger to the polity. Accordingly, there is a case law parallel process of emergency, outside the constitutional processes. Interestingly, the state of emergency/siege was not officially declared in any European State as a result of the banking and financial crises, since the enactment of those clauses invariably presupposed the existence of a national or physical danger or catastrophe. In this regard, the Constitutional Court of Romania, with reference to Article 93 of the Constitution, essentially broadened the latitude of flexibility and derogation clauses on defence of national security to enhance economic and social security public interests.

Yet, the most striking confession of the exceptionality argument as a parallel stage of constitutional emergency, on a domestic case law level, came in Judgment 693/2011 of the Hellenic Council of State. The majority of four judges (three with decisive vote), based on the unequivocal wording of the Constitution, held that the impugned act, establishing a retroactive tax obligation, violated the non-retroactivity clause of the Constitution (Article 78(2)). Surprisingly, three judges of the Hellenic Council of State (two with decisive vote), without challenging the legal and factual premises that established the retroactivity, held that the Act did not violate the Constitution, because, in their view, the Constitution regulated, in principle, the functioning of the State merely under normal conditions. Although the dissenting view conceded that the Constitution provided a state of emergency on specific grounds – ie war, external dangers, imminent threat against national security, armed coup (Article 48) – the list was not exclusive and other serious grounds, outside the constitutional letter – such as 'full fiscal derailment'[131] – could be invoked to justify retroactive imposition of a *contra constitutionem* measure. Although, this view was a dissent that never expressly became a dominant view in the Hellenic Council of State, it seems ever-existing in crisis case law.

The *consistency* issue refers to a serious contradiction in the judicial rationale on both international and domestic level: although the courts regularly declare that they abstain from any thorough assessment of the impugned policies and

---

[131] Paragraph 7.

measures, they extensively apply counter-factual arguments (usually raised in the meantime from lodging the application of review until the hearing of the case and the judgment of the court) to substantiate the positive effect of austerity programmes or of the bail-in programmes on public revenue. This is, however, contradictory. Self-restraint based on the nature of the case and the surrounding circumstances precisely tends to exclude factual assessment, which by definition touches upon the essence and, arguably, the merits of the case. This is especially true if the argument is based on the technical aspect of the dispute, which by definition suggests that the court does not have the thorough knowledge to enter into an analysis of the specificities of the case. If this is true, the court is not, par excellence, capable of speculating what would be the situation from a technical standpoint, if the impugned measures had not been in place.

There are many examples of this paradox in the crisis case law. On ECHR level, in *Mamatas*, the Court of Strasbourg proceeded to the factual analysis of the economic aspects of the project in three ways:

(1)   It assumed that the PSI was necessary because otherwise there would be no compensation whatsoever for the shareholders anyway, since the State would have, most probably, been unable to honour its obligations under the contractual clauses included in the old bonds.

(2)   It stressed that state interference was justified since it reduced the Greek debt, as ex post evidenced, by approximately 107 billion euros by the end of 2012, 85 per cent of the debt was transferred from individuals to the euro-area States and in 2013 the cost of servicing the debt fell sharply.

(3)   It rendered the collective clause necessary, in that if (reversely) a consensus was needed to be reached among all the bondholders on the plan to restructure the Greek debt or if the operation had been confined exclusively to those having consented, the whole plan would almost certainly have collapsed and a larger cut would have been necessary.

On the EU level, in both *Gauweiler* and *Kotnik* the Court's analysis involved a speculation of the adverse effects in the case, had the impugned decisions not been in place, especially vis-a-vis the economic stability of the euro area and of the Member States. In the latter case, the Court upheld the compatibility of the burden-sharing principle on the ground that, otherwise, distortions of competition could have been caused, since the banks whose shareholders and subordinated creditors had not contributed to the reduction of the capital short-fall would receive state aid of an amount greater than that which would have been sufficient to overcome the residual capital shortfall, thus moral hazard would be cultivated and the financial consequences would be borne by the community as a whole.

On a domestic case law level, in *Dowling*, which contested the Irish bank recapitalisation scheme, the High Court held that, on the balance of probabilities, the Bank in question could not have raised the required amount of capital of four billion euros neither from private investors nor from existing shareholders. In the Court's view, if the Bank had not been recapitalised by the deadline laid down in Implementing Decision 2011/77, that would have led to its failure, due to a number of possible developments, such as a run on deposits held with it, or a call for repayment of various notes, or a cessation of funding under the emergency liquidity assistance scheme, or a combination of some or all of those possibilities. Furthermore, the Court considered that the Bank's failure would not only have led to the complete loss of value of the shares to the shareholders, but would also have had adverse consequences for the country altogether. The Court referred, inter alia, to the possibility of a run on deposits held with the national banks, the subsequent call on the guarantee granted to the Bank by the Irish State and the possibility of full or partial withdrawal of funding to the country under the economic and financial adjustment programme for non-compliance with the terms of that programme. Those adverse consequences for Ireland would, in the Court's view, probably have worsened the threat to the financial stability of other EU Member States and of the EU itself.

Panagiotis Pikrammenos, former president of the Hellenic Council of State, who actually presided in many of the crisis cases heard by that Court, tried in an extra-judicial academic writing to furnish some legitimacy to the insertion of exceptional circumstances – explicitly or, more often, implicitly – in an accurate reflection of reality but in a rather apologetic manner. The extract is of particular value because it presumably reflects the judicial psychology on the deference in the context of exceptional circumstances:

> The main characteristic of the crisis is the sharp and intense manifestation of a deep deregulation. This leads to a violent interruption of the prior status quo and a dominating feeling of discontinuity and anomaly. The crisis can be described in general as a reversal of the status quo and as a moratorium on the rules that ensure the harmony of everyday life in a period of normality. The norms of the social organisation retreat in the face of an imperative need and the existence of a threat that forces the State to rebuild the disturbed stability at all costs. Public authority claims effectiveness of extraordinary measures against the static rules of legality. Conflict is the main, essential element of the crisis, as the general interest requires the abandonment of ordinary regulations and the violation of particular interests ... Thus, the extraordinary circumstances impose a multifaceted action by the State both in the current activity in order to deal with the problems created by the economic crisis and at the organisational and structural level so that the same problems will not be repeated in the future. However, these state actions, which normally should comply with legality ... are imposed almost violently on citizens whose rights and interests are affected, even temporarily ... Things are even more complicated as the political power of our country does not operate in the current circumstances exclusively, but under the supervision of the guidance and, sometimes, the coercion of international organisations, in which it participates, other States and private economic centers of power ... When constitutional and legislative provisions conferring powers, recognising rights or imposing restrictions are unambiguous and specific, no recourse can be made to a theory of

necessity. If, however, these provisions are set in the form of general rules, allowing for a wide margin of discretion, exceptional circumstances may be taken into consideration in order to differentiate their ordinary interpretation.[132]

C. The Instruments of Review

In the pre-crisis case law concerning protection of human rights, especially the right to property, the Courts normally applied a rather holistic interpretation, by entering deeply into the particularities of each dispute, so as to produce a more individualised review. This was made possible, primarily, through the conjunctive reading of the human right concerned with non-discrimination and legitimate expectations, two notions that may be used to establish a case-specific approach to judicial review, and by subjecting the impugned act to a proportionality test, including a strict evaluation of the invoked public interest that allegedly justified the deprivation of or interference with human rights. In the post-crisis case law, the contextual moderation of judicial review because of the mutation of the above vehicles suggests that such interpretation falls back to a more generalised level, eventually a decrease in the level of protection of private property.

i. Non-discrimination

The principle of non-discrimination is also used in the determination of the scope of protection of the right to property. This auxiliary application of equality as a principle is particularly evident in the case law of the Court of Strasbourg, according to which the relevant provision – Article 14 of the Convention – can only be invoked in an auxiliary way, namely only in cases where another right enshrined in the Treaty has been violated. Accordingly, Article 14 complements the other substantive provisions of the Convention and its Protocols and has no independent existence. Discrimination occurs when there is similar treatment of different situations and when there is different treatment of comparable situations. Accordingly, non-discrimination becomes a tool for individualised justice: horizontal restrictions on property cannot be tolerated insofar as they apply equally to a broad range of cases with different characteristics. This sort of proportionate equality, based on similarity and difference, constitutes a commonplace in most constitutional orders as a means to preserve the integrity of the non-discrimination clause.[133] Obviously, establishing what is similar and what is different constitutes a particularly difficult mental and, eventually, legal task. In the context

---

[132] P Pikrammenos, 'Public Law in Extraordinary Circumstances from the Point of View of the Annulment of the Administrative Procedure' (2012) 44 *Theory and Practice of Administrative Law* 97, 98–100 (in Greek).

[133] G Gerapetritis, *Affirmative Action Policies and Judicial Review Worldwide* (Cham, Springer, 2016) 17–20.

of Article 14 ECHR, the Court of Strasbourg applies variable standards using a spectrum ranging from analogous situations to relevantly similar situations. Most importantly, in its pre-crisis case law, the Court insisted on the need of individual-ised justice through a rather inquisitorial mode of judicial review: 'in determining whether there has been a deprivation of possessions... it is necessary not only to consider whether there has been a formal taking or expropriation of property but to look behind the appearances and investigate the realities of the situation complained of'.[134]

On a domestic level, a subtle application of proportionate equality in the crisis case law was furnished in the context of salary cuts of academics and military and public security personnel, when the Hellenic Council of State held that those are special categories that ought to be exempted from the general policy of horizontal cuts in the public sector: in the former case the difference lied with the academ-ics' higher cost of living, the need to safeguard their prestige, their special mission and their high qualifications due to the long postgraduate studies they normally pursue (Judgment 4741/2014); in the latter case, the difference lied with the mili-tants' need for high morale, their increased life risks, the acknowledgment of the importance of their mission and the strict restrictions of their individual rights due to their working conditions (Judgment 2192/2014).

Beyond the above cases, however, judicial review of austerity measures has failed to address the non-discrimination issue in the context of alleged breaches of the right to property by upholding the constitutionality of drastic horizontal measures that treated a very wide range of categories of individu-als and/or entities alike. With the exception of the Cyprus bail-in (which made two categories of immense discrepancy, using the 100,000 euros threshold), cuts on salaries/pensions and bonds were horizontal (pro rata) although no two employees/pensioners/bondholders are in the same position given the difference in their remuneration (for employees/pensioners), life expectancy, micro- v mega-investors, participants v non-participants in the negotiations and professional v private investors (for bondholders, especially since the scheme involved a prolongation of the bonds' maturity), other income, outstanding and forthcoming obligations, social status, possibilities to work further, age, family status and abilities (for all). Reversely, a formal discrimination undeni-ably occurred in favour of the ECB and the ECBS that enjoyed immunity from haircut in the Greek PSI.

In Judgments 3404–3405/2014, the Hellenic Council of State ruled that, regarding the principle of equality, judicial review was restricted to examine the excess of the outer limits of the principle and, therefore, the administration could lawfully make differentiations as long as it took into account general and objec-tive criteria and did not impose unjustified burdens or exculpatory measures.

---

[134] ECtHR Judgment of 28 October 1989, *Brumarescu v Romania*, Application no 28342/95, para 76.

Upholding the 'general and objective criteria' test, the Council easily upheld horizontal deprivations of property, without any breakdown of sub-criteria for diverging categories of people. Essentially, reference to 'general and objective' is, by definition, the exact opposite to individualised justice that precisely suggests paying attention to particularities. Furthermore, in Judgment 1116/2014 on the Greek bail-in, the Council placed emphasis on the unexpected development of credit relations which relieved the State from the obligation to treat certain creditors favourable.

At ECHR level, regarding national measures treating various categories of employees differently, *Fábián* set three criteria of permissible differentiation:

(1)   In order for an issue to arise under Article 14 there must be a difference in the treatment of persons in analogous or relatively similar situations; accordingly, the requirement to demonstrate an analogous position did not require that the comparator groups were purely identical.

(2)   Not every objective difference in treatment amounted to a violation of Article 14: in order for a violation to be accepted there must be difference in treatment based on an identifiable characteristic or 'status' and this difference had no objective and reasonable justification. In assessing the requirement of relevantly similar situation, the Court in *Fábián* added the criterion of 'taking into account the elements that characterise their circumstances in the particular context... in the light of the subject-matter and purpose of the measure which makes the distinction in question'.[135]

(3)   Concerning the allocation of the burden of proof, once the applicant has established a difference in treatment, it is for the Government to show that this was justified.

On the basis of the above criteria, the Grand Chamber made a line of reasoning which essentially minimised the practical effect of the non-discrimination clause in the field of public labour relations. In so doing, the Grand Chamber relied on *Valkov and others v Bulgaria* of 2011.[136] Yet, the reading of this case law was rather inconsistent. As the joint dissenting view of six Judges argued, furthering the reasoning of the Chamber of the Court in the first instance proceedings, only under certain circumstances, and not as a matter of principle, may different treatment of private and public-sector employees be justifiable. The dissenting view accused the majority opinion for 'confusion' as to the relevant circumstances required for the analogy/similarity of situations between private and public-sector employees and concluded that the starting position of public and private employees, prior to the suspension of the applicant's pension payments, was exactly the same. In fact, the Court went beyond the basic premise upon which its prior case law, as well as the case law of the Court of Justice and most administrative law courts in

---

[135] Paragraph 121.
[136] ECtHR Judgment of 25 October 2011, *Valkov and others v Bulgaria*, Application no 2033/04 et al.

Europe, had been developed, namely that the State may legitimately operate different labour standards in the public sector (ie restrictions on appointment and
labour rights) merely ad hoc and with regard to certain public posts that are associated with the exercise of sovereign functions of the State.[137]

At EU level, in *Accorinti*, concerning also the Greek bail-in, the applicants
alleged breach of the principle of equal treatment of private creditors within the
meaning of Articles 20 and 21 of the EU Charter of Fundamental Rights and a
general principle of EU law as a customary principle on international level, ie
that creditors are treated equally in the payout, irrespective of their rank, on the
ground that the ECB and the national central banks had ensured, by implementing the exchange agreement of 15 February 2012, that the bonds held by the ECB
would avoid the restructuring of Greek public debt in application of the collective action clauses and would be immune to a reduction of their value. The ECB
and the national central banks, thus, reserved a status of 'preferential creditor' to
themselves, to the detriment of the private sector, on the pretext of their monetary
policy task. Furthermore, by Decision 2012/153, the ECB made the eligibility of
the Greek bonds subject to the grant to the national central banks of a buy-back
scheme for low-rated bonds in Eurosystem credit transactions.

The Court bluntly refused the equal treatment claim by using an institutional
and a financial argument, both based on non-similarity of the situations. The institutional argument was that the applicants, as investors or savers who acted on
their own behalf and aiming at maximum return on their investments, were in
a different situation compared to the Eurosystem central banks that acted in the
exercise of their basic institutional tasks aiming at maintaining price stability and
the sound administration of monetary policy and within statutory limits, albeit
also creditors of the issuing State. The *financial* argument was that the burden
imposed solely on private investors was not likely to have the same systemic effects
on the European economy (or was not proved so or that the scheme would seriously affect the confidence of investors in the intrinsic value of the Greek bonds
and the reliability of the Greek State as a debtor), as compared to those of the
Eurosystem central banks, whose involvement was likely to affect the financial
integrity of the Eurosystem as a whole and, in particular, its capacity to operate in
the financial markets and to refinance the credit institutions.

A stronger case of multi-layer non-discrimination was raised before the
General Court in cases *Chrysostomides* and *Bourdouvali* relevant to the Cypriot
bail-in, namely:

(a) discrimination of uninsured depositors in Laïki vis-a-vis creditors whose
claims were based on the Emergency Liquidity Assistance (ELA) granted to

---

[137] ECtHR Judgment of 5 May 1986, *K v Germany*, Application no 11203/84; ECtHR Judgment
of 17 May 2001, *Hesse-Anger and Anger v Germany*, Application no 45835/99; ECtHR Judgment of
1 February 2005, *Matheis v Germany*, Application no 73711/01; ECtHR Judgment of 21 July 2011,
Heinisch v Germany, Application no 28274/08; and ECtHR Judgment of 19 April 2007, *Eskelinen and
others v Finland*, Application no 63235/00.

Laïki, insofar as the debt of Laïki resulting from ELA had been transferred to Bank of Cyprus, those creditors could turn to the latter, whereas the debt of Laïki towards uninsured depositors would be extinguished;

(b)   depositors whose deposits exceeded 100,000 euros vis-a-vis depositors whose deposits were below that threshold, in that the latter were entirely covered by the Cypriot Deposit Guarantee Scheme, whereas the former only up to this maximum;

(c)   depositors, shareholders and bondholders of the Cypriot banks in question vis-a-vis their counterparts established in other Member States which had previously benefited from financial assistance because the amount of that assistance was each time greater than that of the financial assistance facility granted to Cyprus but the latter's property remained unaffected;

(d)   depositors, shareholders and bondholders of the Cypriot banks in question vis-a-vis their counterparts in the cooperative banking sector, since the latter were not subject to a bail-in; and

(e)   depositors of the banks in Cyprus vis-a-vis depositors in the Greek branches of the same banks, on the basis of nationality, in that the bail-in conditionality clause for the grant of the financial assistance to Cyprus did not include the branches of those banks in Greece. Regarding the first line of discrimination argument, the Court used the *Accorinti* argument institutionally distinguishing the Central Bank of Cyprus vis-a-vis private operators.

Regarding the second, third and fourth line of discrimination argument, the Court held that those categories of individuals/legal entities were not in comparable situations and, therefore, the principle of equality was not applicable. Regarding the last line of discrimination argument, the Court found the – admittedly different – treatment objectively justified in the light of the legitimate purpose of the authorities to prevent any effect of contagion from the Cypriot banking system to the Greek financial system.

The basic argument of most courts in neglecting to apply standards of individualised justice was the complexity that such an experiment would entail. In fact, the arguments set forth by national courts to justify horizontal restrictions were rather pragmatic, ie such measures were easily applicable and produced immediate results and there were insuperable difficulties in delineating different groups of investors. For example, the Hellenic Council of State in Judgment 668/2012 responded that further delineation of individual/entities would have rendered the state aim to address urgent budgetary needs totally ineffective since a case-by-case determination of the cuts by an administrative authority (instead of general statutory cuts) would require additional time. The Court of Strasbourg in a rather apologetic tone (which is reasonable, given the prior insistence of the Court to requirements of individualised justice) found, in *Mamatas*, that the Greek PSI had not been discriminatory on four grounds:

(1)   There was an inherent difficulty in locating bondholders on such a volatile market, with many bondholders having purchased their securities on the secondary market.

(2) There was a significant difficulty in establishing precise criteria for differentiating between bondholders: some bondholders, albeit private, could not have been classified as small investors since they had allegedly invested sums in excess of 100,000 euros, whereas there were cases of legal entities which had invested a much smaller amount and could not be in a deteriorated position merely because of their legal identity.

(3) An attempt to make justifiable differentiations would potentially jeopardise the whole operation, with disastrous consequences for the economy. Such a treatment would have resulted, prior to the conclusion of the exchange scheme, in a mass transfer of bonds into the exempted categories, which would have reduced the capital required for the restructuring and, in turn, would have entailed more drastic cuts in the nominal value of the non-exempted bonds.

(4) There was an undeniable need to act rapidly in order to restructure the debt, therefore the time to identify the bondholders and discern them into categories might have been in default of the Greek State, which, at the time, had been excluded from the markets and the PSI was part of the conditionality for the external financial assistance.

Yet, what was missing in this argumentation was a sound doctrinal approach to justify collective curtailments of property as a counterbalance to the necessity/ inevitability of deprivation of fundamental rights through the invocation of efficiency arguments and other technical difficulties. In fact, it was only a dissenting block of judges of the Hellenic Council of State that found violation of the principle of equality, between professional investors and ordinary people holding bonds as regular saving accounts. They argued that both in the Greek and in the European legal order, the category of people who were professionally engaged in investment activities was both identifiable and distinguishable and, most importantly, governed by specific provisions, especially secondary EU law, ie an objective and measurable difference triggering the non-discrimination clause. It was further suggested that the PSI was agreed with specific professional investors and not with the applicants, who were not represented by the IIF at the time of agreement. Therefore, in this view, it was apparent that they were in a substantially different status, both legally and factually, compared to the professional investors who had agreed to contribute to the restructuring of the public debt.

ii. Public Interest

The vast majority of the Constitutions contain some reservations especially in the exercise of the right to property. Broadly speaking, they embrace two major restrictions upon property holders in the exercise of their respective right: a public interest and a social restriction, which – to some extent – may overlap. The public interest restriction provides that the right to property shall not be exercised contrary to the public interest, comprising – inter alia – issues related to the national economy, public health and the environment. The social restriction provides that the right to property shall not be exercised to the detriment of the rights of others and/or must respect the social orientation of property.[138]

Furthermore, the European Court of Human Rights has placed particular emphasis on the existence and the quality of public interest as a means for justifying an interference with the enjoyment of property and striking a fair balance with the respective right. According to the ECtHR established case law, such compelling (financial) interests have been the abrupt transition from a state-controlled economy to a market economy, the extreme financial crisis, the sharp devaluation of the national currency, the budgetary priorities in terms of favouring expenditure on pressing social issues, the bankruptcy of state-owned and private banks, the economic instability as well as the considerable inflation. However, the most important aspect of the pre-crisis case law of the Court of Strasbourg was, arguably, that the existence of an admittedly compelling state interest did not per se allow the State to misplace the required fair balance between its pursuit and the protection of the right to property. In this respect, the Court in *Stran* declared that there was no doubt that it was necessary for the post-dictatorship democratic government to terminate a contract considered to be prejudicial to its economic interests, yet this could in no way provide an open-ended escape mechanism from the protection of the right to property.

The public interest mutation with regard to deprivations of or interferences with the right to property constitutes, perhaps, the most outstanding case law evolution in the field of human rights, caused by the economic crisis. It involves two premises in relation to the financial crisis: the predominance of the financial interest of the State as opposed to other state interests (the exclusivity factor) and the upgrade of financial interest, which has been assimilated to the salvation of the country itself (the upgrade factor).

---

[138] A few examples of limitations on private property: the Italian Constitution provides that private property is recognised and guaranteed by law, which prescribes the ways it is acquired and enjoyed, as well as its limitations so as to ensure its 'social function' and make it accessible to all (Art 42) and the law imposes obligations and constraints on private ownership of land, sets limitations to the size of property according to the region and the agricultural area, encourages and imposes land reclamation, the conversion of latifundia and the reorganisation of farm units and assists small and medium-sized properties (Art 44(1)); the Irish Constitution provides that the exercise of the rights stemming thereof ought – in civil society – to be regulated by the principles of social justice and, accordingly, the State may on occasions delimit by law the exercise of the right with a view to reconciling their exercise with the exigencies of the common good (Art 43(2)) and, in particular, shall direct its policy towards securing 'the ownership and control of the material resources of the community may be so distributed amongst private individuals and the various classes as best to subserve the common good' (Art 45(2ii)); the Portuguese Constitution provides that the law shall regulate the resizing of farming units that are excessively large from the point of view of the agricultural policy objectives, the resizing of farming units that are smaller than that which is suitable, particularly by means of legal, fiscal and credit incentives for their structural or merely economic integration, particularly in a cooperative form, or by measures designed to join parcels of land together (Arts 94 and 95 respectively); finally, the Spanish Constitution provides that 'the entire wealth of the country in its different forms, irrespective of ownership, shall be subordinated to the general interest' (s 128(1)).

The *exclusivity* factor safeguards the financial interests of the State against any other state interests. Such financial interests aim exclusively at adducing additional – immediate and riskless – financial resources. In this respect, it follows that in assessing the nature of public interest involved, the courts employ an ordoliberal panacea, which involves self-conclusiveness of and overreliance on financialism.[139] This results in a different economic approach to financial programmes and their respective value for the well-being of the States and the societies. The predominance of financialism in the determination of public interest significantly outweighs the cost–benefit analysis, which means that more social aspects enter into the balancing process for the assessment of the public interest. At the end of the day, it seems that the public interest is only viewed as financial, with a corresponding devaluation of factors relating to the social state and social cohesion. For countries in a financial adjustment programme, this can be attributed to the commitments assumed as conditionality attached to the financial assistance, not necessarily bringing direct financial revenues. Given that such international commitments are assumed by the governments and eventually, according to well-established case law, it is the state authorities that define, within the constitutional limits but in a broad discretionary framework, what constitutes a compelling public interest, the end-result is an overall dominance of financialism against other legitimate state purposes of non-economic nature.

Such predominance of financial public interest is clearly reflected in *Mamatas*, relevant to the Greek bail-in scheme. The European Court of Human Rights has identified the self-evident, ie that the economic crisis has had major repercussions on the Greek economy, that the country was facing an enormous deficit, that it was unable to pay its debts and that the crisis worsened over the ensuing years. Under those circumstances, the Court found that the state authorities should have endeavoured to find legitimate solutions to maintain economic stability and restructure the debt in the general interests of the community. Thus, the Court merely assessed the financial aspects of the public interest, and altogether ignored other relevant public interest considerations that might have been crucial in the context of a cost–benefit analysis.

Such other public interest might be (as raised by a dissenting opinion of the Hellenic Council of State in the same case):

(a) a damage to the country's creditworthiness, in the sense that the conclusion of the PSI would necessarily qualify as a financial incident that would affect the ratings of the State with regard to its ability to take out external loans;

(b) the endangerment of public health, in the sense that hospital medical devices suppliers, who had been granted government bonds in order to settle their

---

[139] See relevant argumentation by the President of the Hellenic Republic Prokopios Pavlopoulos, *An Enemy of Representative Democracy. The Predominance of 'Economics' over 'Public Institutions'* (Athens, Gutenberg, 2018) 101–09.

claims against the hospitals, had a haircut imposed on their bonds and, therefore, they would be rather reluctant to continue to supply the Greek health system; and

(c) increased risks for social security organisations in Greece, which had a significant number of sovereign bonds in the portfolio, meaning that a haircut would necessarily compromise the proper functioning of the national social security system and jeopardise their ability to pay the pensions and meet the expenditure required for medical treatment of employees and pensioners.[140]

Obviously, the aim to restore financial balance and prevent the country's economic default seriously hampered the other three public aims, arguably of equal importance. Yet, this attitude goes against the judicial tradition of many European courts which generally apply a more social-oriented and less financial-exclusive rationale to their respective judicial reasoning. For instance, the French Council of State (*Conseil d'Etat*), whose case law has been a source of inspiration for many supreme administrative courts in Europe, applies, when assessing a technical administrative choice, the cost–benefit balance (*bilan coût-avantages*) test in order to curb state discretion. This technique requires an explicit evaluation of the overall consequences of the measure in question; the advantages expected, on the one hand, and the financial or social inconveniences arising therefrom, on the other. If the inconveniences outweigh the benefit for the public interest then the administrative act shall be quashed.[141] This case law has used the basic components of the bilan as a legal notion that can be traced to the economic notion of a cost–benefit balance, whereby the benefit or the cost of a scheme should not be assessed only in terms of its financial profit but in relation to the overall effects it may have and its global efficiency.

In this way, the Council established a holistic assessment of the public interests involved in governmental choices in order to secure its role as guardian of individual rights. Evidently, the process of assimilating the public interest with

---

[140] Indeed, because of their mandatory participation in the government bond programmes, the social security funds lost 7.3 billion euros and, eventually, 8.8 billion euros of their nominal value (53.5% haircut) or 12 billion euros from their current market price (73% haircut), with significant collateral damages since the State was consequently obliged to make serious money injections to the social security funds to make them sustainable, to increase dramatically the social security contributions for the self-employed and to make further reductions on the pensions.

[141] Judgment of 28 May 1971, *Ministre de l'équipement et du logement v. Fédération de défense des personnes concernées par le projet actuellement dénommé Ville Nouvelle Est,* Rec 409, regarding an expropriation case, where the court held that 'an operation cannot be legally declared of public utility (*utilité publique*) unless the damage to private property, the financial cost and, eventually the inconveniences at a social level are not excessive in view of the interest it presents'. The case concerned the expropriation of a property for the construction of a road needed to facilitate the building of a new town. A group of citizens challenged that scheme on the ground that the benefit of having a road at that spot could not outweigh the financial and social cost of the project. The Council accepted in principle that type of control, but finally held that the disadvantages of the operation did not overcome its usefulness.

the financial interests (and only some aspects of such financial interest, according to the prevailing version of state economics) desocialises the debate, since it excludes all other aspects of public interest involved, a form of privatisation of public interest. One can identify the intrinsic contradictions in the case law of the Cypriot courts dealing with the bank deposit haircut: the financial interest of the State was by definition public, whereas the dispute was proclaimed to be private.

The *upgrade* factor suggests that the financial interest in the context of an economic crisis is not merely a public, or even a compelling, public interest, but is tantamount to the rescue of the country from default. This upgrade reflects the dominance of financialism in the judicial approach to the crisis cases but also served as a necessary tool to get away from rigid requirements of the case law that prohibited curtailment of human rights to serve a merely financial interest of the State. In Greece, for example, prior to the economic crisis, there was a consolidated case law, coming from all three supreme courts of the country, to the effect that the 'revenue interests of the State', did not constitute a legitimate ground for the State to interfere with fundamental rights, especially the right to peaceful enjoyment of property.[142] That meant that the self-evident need of the State to produce public income, be that through taxation, social security fees, monetary sanctions or otherwise, could not be invoked by the state authorities when the purported measures curtailed rights guaranteed by the Constitution. Thus, the Hellenic Council of State could not rely on its precedent to uphold the status of financial public interest in order to justify interferences with the right to property on salary/pensions/bond cuts.

Therefore, in its Judgment No 668/2012, the Hellenic Council of State characterised as compelling the public interest to prevent financial default of the State and not merely to secure more public revenue, in particular:

(a) to deal directly with the severe financial crisis, which made it impossible to meet the country's borrowing needs through the international markets and also rendered the eventuality of state default very possible;

(b) to consolidate the public finances by reducing the budget deficit by approximately 2.5 percentage points of the GDP, at a level which could be sustainable after the three-year period time in which the measures were meant to apply; and

(c) to meet the obligation of budgetary discipline and stability within the euro area.

Furthermore, in its Judgment No 1620/2011, the Council upgraded the public interest involved in the relevant cases to the level of 'financial salvation of the country', entailing the restoration of state budgetary balance of the State, which

---

[142] Judgments of the Hellenic Council of State 1663/2009, 3651/2002, 802/2007, 1151/2006 and 2224/2005; Judgment of the Supreme Civil and Criminal Court of Greece *(Areios Pagos)* 5/2011; and, Judgment of the Court of Audit 513/2009.

had been severely shaken because of the very high level of public deficit and public debt. Finally, in the same line of argumentation, the Special Supreme Court of Greece, in its Judgment No 25/2012, considered financial balance as not merely a requirement to secure public income, but also as a necessary component for the State's welfare. Interestingly, with this Judgment, the Court went against the unequivocal case law of the European Court of Human Rights on exactly the same matter.

In fact, in Judgment of 22 May 2008 *Meidanis v Greece*,[143] the Court of Strasbourg had ruled on an ad hoc basis that the divergence in determining the rate of default interest in favour of a public law entity did not appear necessary in order to ensure the smooth operation of the State, in the light of the basic premise that the mere financial interest could not be equated with the 'public' or 'general' interest and could not justify the breach of the right to respect the creditors' property. Through this upgrade, it was made possible for the courts to uphold the legitimacy of the intended public purpose and the measures that would have been ruled unconstitutional, had they been assessed against a lower-level public interest. More generally, however, the upgrade of financialism as a public interest signalled a totally different approach to the functioning of the State and its relationship vis-a-vis the citizens, since society's welfare became identical to the financial well-being of the State.

a. Proportionality

For a long time, proportionality has been the main instrument to assess the compatibility of a state measure interfering with human rights with the national Constitutions, EU law and the ECHR.[144] It mostly applies as a test of whether austerity measures interfering with human rights, especially the right to property, are suitable, necessary and *stricto sensu* proportionate to the public interest involved. Yet, all parameters of proportionality have been subject to serious qualifications in the post-crisis era.

On EU level, the Court of Justice and the General Court refrained, in all financial crisis cases, from examining in depth the two aspects of proportionality = necessity and *stricto sensu* proportionality – conforming to a simple suitability test, which did not, nevertheless, constitute a serious obstacle to upholding the impugned measures, since they were by definition suitable to serve the purpose of stabilising national economies. A slightly more thorough test was implemented

---

[143] ECtHR Judgment of 22 May 2008, *Meidanis v Greece*, Application no 33977/06, para 30.

[144] On EU level, see T Tridimas, *The General Principles of EU Law*, 2nd edn (Oxford, Oxford University Press, 2006) 193–241; on a comparative level, see G Gerapetritis, *The Application of Proportionality in Administrative Law: Judicial Review in France, Greece, England and in the European Community* (Athens, Ant Sakkoulas, 1997) 59–149.

by the Court of Justice in *Kotnik*. The Court found that the measures for converting subordinate rights or writing down of subordinate creditors' value investment did not exceed what was necessary to overcome the capital shortfall of the bank concerned. Thus, a necessity rationale applied, ie partial, instead of total, conversion or write-down of subordinate rights before the grant of state aid, if this was sufficient to overcome the capital shortfall of the distressed bank; and an escape clause applied, ie where the implementation of measures for converting debt or writing down its principal would endanger financial stability or lead to disproportionate results. Thus, if burdens were imposed upon shareholders, the Member States might provide the bank with a proportionate capital injection and apply burden sharing on a restricted percentage of all subordinated debts.

On ECHR level, there has been a serious downgrade in the assessment of the fair balance requirement between the right to property and the legitimate aim pursued, in that the Court dismissed the necessity test overall. Indeed, in *Koufaki*, the Court held that the possible existence of less restrictive alternatives than salary cuts did not in itself render the contested legislation unjustified, provided that the legislature remained within the bounds of its margin of appreciation, which is, nevertheless a mere tautology. In particular, the Court placed emphasis on the global recovery scheme in the country (including, inter alia, restoring tax equity and tackling tax evasion, reforming the social security system and the public servants' retirement schemes, reviewing the procedures for checking and auditing the public finances, opening up certain closed occupations and placing state-owned companies on a sounder footing) and in some compensatory aspects it contained (such as a flat-rate bonus for those in the lowest income layers to compensate for the abolition of the thirteenth and fourteenth pension payments). Yet, the necessity test was essentially missing. What the Court intimated in *Koufaki* was that the proportionality test becomes significantly stricter when the case in question involves deprivation of property as opposed to the mere peaceful enjoyment of one's possessions, as in that case. Given that the Court merely saw interference, the proportionality test became much looser.

On a domestic level, proportionality seems to be limited to a very basic level of reasonableness without any elaboration upon the necessity of the impugned measures. In its Judgment No 668/2012, the Hellenic Council of State held that salary and pension cuts were suitable for attaining the public interest pursued and that there were no alternatives that were less restrictive for the affected human rights. In relation to the suitability test, the Council noted that the impugned measures, by their very nature, could immediately contribute to the reduction of public expenditure. In this way, the Council of State essentially altered the very nature of the suitability test: by definition this test may merely accommodate a yes/no answer, in the sense that a measure might either be suitable or unsuitable. The court's reasoning that a measure may be more suitable than another (eg because it produces immediate effects) hampers the integrity of suitability and allows for more subjective considerations to creep into that reasoning, thus significantly narrowing the scope of possible options to be assessed by the court. This is so, because all suitable measures should reach the level of the necessity test and be subject to an evaluation of the mildest means for the impaired rights, not merely the 'more' suitable one.

It seems that the Council used the suitability test as an additional factor for the impugned measure to soften the forthcoming necessity and *stricto sensu* proportionality instead of a simple negative barrier. Accordingly, in the necessity test, the Council pursued a rather limited control of less restrictive alternatives and solely placed emphasis on the following:

(a)   the impugned measures were part of a broader plan of fiscal adjustment, which also included other economic, financial and structural measures, the overall coordinated implementation of which had been estimated by the legislator;[145]

(b)   the measures were designed to deal not only with the acute fiscal crisis, but also with the consolidation of public finances in a sustainable manner; and

(c)   the measures were designed as temporary.

In relation to the *stricto sensu* proportionality test, the Council emphasised on some limited compensatory measures in favour of some low-paid public servants and pensioners and, in principle, of pensioners of over 60 years of age.[146] Somewhat more elaborate judicial reasoning on proportionality can be found in the case law of the Council of State on the imposition of outstanding tax burdens and social security contributions. In its Judgments No 1972/2012, 532/2015 and 2563/2015 the Council assessed as relevant considerations: the duration of the imposition of the particular burden (if this is provided for a limited period of time), its amount in relation to the actual tax benchmarking (eg income, real estate), the potential release of the burden for those below a certain taxable threshold as well as whether the impugned measures catered to maintain a tolerable standard of living for the people, which guarantees a fair balance between the general interest pursued and the citizens' rights.

A more thorough proportionality test was applied by the Latvian Constitutional Court in assessing the constitutionality of pension cuts. In that regard, having established that the measures taken to secure the sustainability of the social welfare system and to improve national economics constituted a reasonable and legitimate objective, it assessed the balance between individual rights

---

[145] The Council referred to measures aiming at increasing state revenues (such as increase of the rates of value added tax, of excise duties and of special contributions), restoring fiscal justice and combating tax evasion, reforming the social security system and the retirement scheme for public servants, as well as the public finance monitoring and control mechanisms, and opening certain closed professions and reorganising public enterprises.

[146] At a later stage, holiday allowances were altogether abolished in the public sector, both for public servants and pensioners.

and the benefit of the community as a whole, on the basis of social solidarity that
all citizens owe to the Community. This assessment process was broadly founded
on the criterion of 'socially responsible alternative' and on whether the following
requirements were met:

(a) whether there were adequate expert analyses substantiating the elements
(ie the need, expediency and urgency) justifying recourse to the measures
interfering with social benefits; and

(b) whether there were no less restrictive alternatives to achieve the said purposes.

Two interim conclusions may be drawn on the application of the technique of
proportionality in crisis cases amounting to an overall downgrading of the intensity
of judicial review. First, by allowing a wide margin of discretion to the competent authorities, the courts transform the highly technical proportionality test to
a more empirical rationality test in the conventional *Wednesbury* type of review
of government acts exercised by UK courts, or the *erreur manifeste d'appréciation*
exercised by French administrative courts, which essentially reduces judicial
review merely to cases of flagrant mistakes in the administration of the economic
crisis.[147] Second, on many occasions, the courts applied an existentialist minimum
approach instead of a strict proportionality test of austerity measures. The existential minimum approach suggests that a decline in the people's living standards
cannot go as far as interfering with the core of the constitutional standard of
human dignity, which is essential for the people's dignified existence (*Existenz
minimum*). The main task of this technique is to determine how this subsistence
threshold is determined and whether the austerity measures cumulatively threaten
the core of the existential minimum.

The existential minimum approach has been widely used by the European
Court of Human Rights (in *Koufaki* in the course of the financial crisis) and can
be detected in many domestic judgments assessing austerity measures, essentially
lowering the intensity of judicial review by setting aside a strict judicial search for
less restrictive alternatives that would require the submission of necessary reports
and a thorough balancing assessment, eventually asserting that the applicants
allegedly maintained a dignified standard of life.[148] The extensive use of the human
dignity criterion essentially decreases the level of judicial review, since it introduces a lower threshold, ie a common core, of the property right, instead of placing
emphasis on the possible existence of less restrictive measures, even if those might
be well above the minimum standard of human dignity.

---

[147] Gerapetritis, *Application of Proportionality* (1997) 59–85, 93–98, 136–49.
[148] See *Mamatas* and *Koufaki* on ECtHR level and Judgments 2287–2290/2015, 668/2012 and
3404–3405/2014 of the Hellenic Council of State on a domestic level.

b. Legitimate Expectations

The principle of legitimate expectations applies horizontally to all human rights.

In fact, along with proportionality, the doctrine of legitimate expectations has been the cornerstone for the protection of human rights on a European level.[149] Legitimate expectations are grounded in the conviction that the State consciously and purposively, through legal and/or factual assurances, undertakes, as regards individuals and entities concerned, that their rights will not be frustrated by subsequent state interferences. This doctrine is mostly associated to the right to property, especially in the crisis case law. This aspect goes beyond the general commitment of peaceful enjoyment of property or the commitment towards a contractual obligation, which both refer to the content of the right to property per se. Through the right of legitimate expectations, the right to property acquires a less objective and more subjective character, in that it refers not to the dogmatic approach to interpretation of the property clauses but predominantly to the qualification as to whether, in the light of the particular circumstances of each case, a state authority had conveyed to the individual or entity concerned a reasonable conviction that the right is inclusive of particular features.[150] In that regard, legitimate expectations eventually result in the implementation of the right to property in a different manner from one case to another, while the doctrinal core of the right may remain inalienable. This fluctuation does not compromise the protection of the right overall, insofar as legitimate expectations only operate in favour of the right, thus upgrading the level of protection.[151]

At ECHR level, a rather typical example of the 'jurisprudential bridge' between property and legitimate expectations in the case law of the European Court of Human Rights is the Judgment of 2 December 2010 in Case *Anonymos Touristiki Etairia Xenodocheia Kritis v Greece*. This case concerned the impossibility of developing a hotel complex on the island of Crete, due to building restrictions or prohibitions imposed following the designation of the land in question as part of an environmentally protected area, with no payment of compensation. In particular, in the early 1970s, the applicant company had purchased a plot of land and had been granted a lawful planning permission, given that construction was not prohibited under the legislation in force at that time. Later, the region in question was designated as a full protection zone; this resulted in the prohibition of any construction whatsoever in that area and rendered the building permit practically useless. The applicant company sought to have the property expropriated on the grounds of a de facto deprivation of property. Upon refusal of its application by the competent Ministry and the respective dismissal by the national

---

[149] R Thomas, *Legitimate Expectations and Proportionality in Administrative Law* (Oxford, Hart Publishing, 2000).

[150] On EU level, see T Tridimas, *The General Principles of EU Law*, 2nd edn (Oxford, Oxford University Press, 2006) 280–84.

[151] S Schonberg and SJ Schonberg, *Legitimate Expectations in Administrative Law* (Oxford, Oxford University Press, 2000).

court, the company filed an application before the Court of Strasbourg claiming breach of the right to property due to inability to build.

The Court unanimously found a violation of the Convention relying mostly on the applicant company's legitimate expectation, which arose from prior administrative conduct on the matter in multiple occasions through granting and modification of the planning permit. It held that, compelling as it may be, the legitimate aim to protect archeological sites did not relieve the State of its obligation to compensate those concerned in case of excessive infringement of their property rights. In striking this balance, the Court strongly opposed the rationale of the Hellenic Council of State, according to which a land outside the town planning is not intended to be used for building but for other purposes, on the grounds that this amounted to an irrefutable presumption that ignored the particularities of each land falling in this category; the Court eventually found that the State failed to strike a fair balance between the public interest involved and the individual right to property. This judgment entailed that there should be neither a general nor a collective approach to possible deprivations of property, but rather an individualised approach that ought to take into account the specificities of each particular case and especially the upgraded expectations that were reasonably raised in the context of each case in relation to prior case law.[152]

Apart from the above milestone judgment, numerous ECtHR judgments linked the right to property to legitimate expectations based on a legal provision (such as a judicial decision of domestic courts) or interpretation of a contractual clause (valid or invalid). With regard to legitimate expectations stemming from domestic case law, in the Judgment of 20 November 1995, *Pressos Compania and others v Belgium*, the Court of Strasbourg upheld claims for damages arising from shipping accidents allegedly caused by the negligence of Belgian pilots. The Court classified these claims as 'assets' and accepted the applicants' allegation that, based on numerous judgments of the national Court of Cassation, they had a 'legitimate expectation' that their claims deriving from the accidents in question would be determined in accordance with the general law of tort.

With regard to legitimate expectations stemming from a contractual clause, in the Judgment of 24 June 2003, *Stretch v the United Kingdom*, the applicant had leased land from a local authority for a period of 22 years on payment of an annual ground rent with an option to renew the lease for a further period at the expiry of the term. Relying upon the terms of the lease, the applicant erected – at his own expense – a number of buildings for light industrial use which he had sub-let for rent. The Court found that the applicant had to be viewed as having at least a 'legitimate expectation' of exercising the option to renew and this had to be regarded as 'attached to the property rights granted to him'.

---

[152] In prior case law, especially the Judgment of 29 November 1991, *Pine Valley Developments and others v Ireland*, although also relying on broadly analogous legitimate expectations, the Court also considered that the applicants were engaged in a commercial venture which, by its very nature, involved an element of risk.

In the Judgment of 1 June 2006, *Fedorenko v Ukraine*, the domestic court took the view that the governmental representatives had acted ultra vires and the contract concluded between the State and the applicant was invalid. Neither party had been aware that there was any legal obstacle to this clause. The authority itself, being apparently well aware of the terms of the contract, only raised the problem of its invalidity at a very late stage. The Court considered that the applicant, under these circumstances, must be regarded as having had at least a legitimate expectation of benefiting from the dollar value clause, and this may be regarded as being attached to the property rights due to him under the contract with the State.[153]

The judicial vehicle of legitimate expectations has been moderated in the crisis case law. On ECHR level, in *Mamatas*, the Court of Strasbourg blamed Greek bondholders that they had not acted as careful, well-informed economic operators who could adduce certain legitimate expectations, and they were supposed to be aware of the highly instable economic situation causing fluctuations in the value of the Greek debt instruments. This was so because, in the Court's view, the transactions in question had been conducted on highly volatile markets which were often subject to uncontrollable vagaries and risks in relation to the declining or increasing value of the bonds, which might encourage holders to speculate in order to secure high yield in a very short time. Even supposing that not all applicants had been involved in speculative transactions, they ought to have known of the said vagaries and risks as regards possibly large drops in the value of the bonds purchased. This was especially true as even before the financial crisis in 2009 the Greek State had already faced high debts and a large deficit. Consequently, the Court considered that, by adopting the impugned measures, Greece had not upset the required balance between the public interest and the protection of the applicants' property rights. In that regard, the Court held that forcible participation of non-consenting private investors to the Greek bail-in scheme represented an appropriate and necessary means of reducing the public debt and saving the State from default.

On EU level, the Court of Justice extensively dealt with the plea of legitimate expectations in *Accorinti*. The plea was based on undeniable assurances given by the successive presidents of the ECB, Mr Trichet and Mr Draghi, and also by Members of the ECB's Executive Board. According to those statements:

(a) the Greek bonds held by the ECB would not be subject to a 'voluntary exchange';
(b) there was no risk of payment default on the part of the Hellenic Republic;
(c) a forced restructuring of the Greek public debt was not possible;
(d) the involvement of private creditors in such a restructuring could be envisaged only on a voluntary basis;

---

[153] M Sigron, *Legitimate Expectations under Article 1 of Protocol No 1 to the European Convention on Human Rights* (Cambridge, Intersentia, 2014).

(e) a reduction of the nominal value of those bonds was impossible; and
(f) if such a situation nonetheless arose, the Greek bonds would never be accepted as collateral.

In the applicants' submission, those statements triggered legitimate expectations, which were frustrated by the subsequent unlawful conduct of the ECB, including the exchange agreement of 15 February 2012, in which the ECB actively participated as a member of and a key player in the 'troika'. On the contrary, the ECB contended that it had timely showed and warned that the PSI was not within its powers, that the relevant decisions were taken by the governments and that the sovereign debt crisis in Europe presented significant potential risks linked with investments in Greek bonds. Thus, no credible assurance to that effect was given by the ECB within the limits of its terms of reference to be reasonably understood by any prudent and circumspect reader that a PSI was not one of the possible options and that its adoption did not fall exclusively within the legal and political responsibility of the State.

In this plea, the Court reiterated the right to rely on the principle of legitimate expectations and required four conditions to be cumulatively satisfied:

(a) precise, unconditional and consistent assurances originating from authorised and reliable sources must have been given by the EU authorities;
(b) assurances must be such as to give rise to a legitimate expectation on the part of the person to whom they were addressed;
(c) assurances given must be consistent with the applicable rules;
(d) a prudent and circumspect economic operator would not be able in the factual premises of the exercise of monetary policy to foresee the adoption of an EU measure likely to affect his/her interests and that EU institutions enjoyed wide discretion to adjust their policy according to variations in the economic context.

In applying the above standards to this case, the Court of Justice found that ECB's press releases and public statements produced by the applicants differed significantly in their subject matter and their content. However, they were overall of a general nature, they emphasised that the ECB did not have the power to decide on any restructuring of the public debt of a Member State affected by a selective payment default and that, given the prevailing uncertainty in the financial markets at the time, especially with regard to the Greek economy, they could not be described as precise and unconditional assurances originating from authorised and reliable sources to the effect that the ECB would ultimately oppose a sovereign debt restructuring decided by the Member States or by the competent bodies.

Thus, although the ECB was indeed involved in monitoring developments in the financial situation in Greece, debt restructuring fell mainly, if not exclusively, within the sovereign power and budgetary authority of the Member States and, therefore, no legitimate expectations could possibly have existed. On top of this, the Court made a substantive obiter dictum, upholding a relevant claim made by the ECB, which is of great significance because it was used by subsequent decisions not only of EU adjudicative bodies but also of the ECtHR in *Mamatas*. This dictum concerned the level of investors' certainty with regard to state bonds both in general and in the light of this case. Accordingly, the purchase by an investor of government bonds was by definition a transaction entailing a certain financial risk, because it was subject to the hazards of movements in the capital markets; so, in the light of the uncertainties concerning the economic situation, the investors concerned could not claim to have acted as prudent and circumspect economic operators, who could rely on the existence of legitimate expectations. On the contrary, in the light of the public statements made, those investors were supposed to be aware of the highly unstable economic situation that determined the fluctuation of the value of the Greek bonds which they had acquired and the appreciable risk of at least a selective sovereign default. Thus, a prudent and circumspect economic operator apprised of those public statements could not have ruled out the risk of a restructuring of the Greek public debt, given the differing views prevailing in that regard within the euro-area Member States and the other bodies involved, such as the Commission, the IMF and the ECB.

Concerning the legitimate expectations that the burden-sharing principle would not apply, the Court of Justice in *Kotnik* held that shareholders and the subordinated creditors of the banks concerned were given no precise, unconditional and consistent assurance from the Commission that state aid designed to overcome the capital shortfall of those banks would be approved or that some of the measures enacted would not be liable to be prejudicial to their investments. The fact that, in the first phases of the international financial crisis, the subordinated creditors were not called upon to contribute to the rescue of credit institutions, could not qualify as legitimate expectation in this sense. Moreover, even if there had been admittedly a case of legitimate expectations, an overriding public interest might preclude transitional measures from being adopted in respect of situations which arose before the new rules came into force, but which were still subject to change.

Milestone judgments with regard to the determination of what might be considered as legitimate expectation are *Chrysostomides* and *Bourdouvali* concerning the Cyprus bail-in scheme. The individuals and companies who initiated the actions claimed breach of assurances resulting from three sources. The first source was a letter of 11 February 2013 sent to the executive directors of the banks concerned by the Office Director of the Governor of the Central Bank of Cyprus, on behalf of the Eurosystem. The Court rejected the arguments by holding that:

(a)   nothing in the letter allowed a prudent and circumspect reader to conclude that its contents were attributable to the Eurosystem or to the ECB, although, admittedly, the Central Bank of Cyprus logo was included in the letterhead, followed, below and in capital letters, by the words 'Central Bank of Cyprus' and 'Eurosystem';

(b)   at the time of the facts, the ECB Statute did not mention, among the objectives of the ECB or the ESCB, the determination of the conditions for recapitalisation or the resolution of financial institutions which was, therefore, performed by national central banks and, therefore, a prudent and circumspect reader could not reasonably consider that an approach adopted by the Central Bank of Cyprus concerning the determination of the conditions for recapitalisation or the resolution of financial institutions was attributable to and binding for the Eurosystem.

The second origin was the 21 January 2013 commitment of the Eurogroup regarding the possibility to offer a financial assistance facility on the basis of a political agreement reached in November 2012. The Court rejected the arguments, indicating:

(a)   that in that statement, the Eurogroup in no way committed itself to granting Cyprus the financial assistance requested, but merely described those negotiations in vague and general terms and encouraged the parties concerned to achieve progress in order to finalise the components of the draft MoU; and

(b)   the grant of financial assistance fell within the competence of the ESM.

The third origin was the treatment reserved to other euro-area Member States which benefited from financial assistance prior to Cyprus. The Court rejected the arguments indicating:

(a)   that the mere fact that, during the early phases of the international financial crisis, the grant of financial assistance was not subject to the adoption of measures comparable to the harmful measures, cannot, in itself, be regarded as a precise, unconditional and consistent assurance capable of engendering a legitimate expectation on the part of the shareholders and depositors of the banks concerned that the grant of financial assistance to Cyprus would not be subject to those measures; and

(b)   such rescue measures were likely to differ fundamentally from case to case in the light of experience and of all of the specific circumstances, therefore the applicants could not legitimately expect that the grant of financial assistance would be subject to conditions – identical or even similar – to those under which financial assistance was granted to Ireland, Greece, Spain or Portugal.

Overall, two shortfalls were identified by the Court, namely lack of competence of the authorities allegedly providing the assurances and lack of clear and authoritative assurances.

On a domestic case law level, the general response of national courts to allegations for breach of legitimate expectations broadly focused on the argument that there was no constitutional or other provision that could guarantee a certain amount of public servants' remunerations or pensions but this amount varied in each particular era.[154] In the crisis case law, only incidentally, national courts used

---

[154] Eg Judgment 668/2012 of the Hellenic Council of State.

the principle of legitimate expectations to hold pension cuts[155] or the statutory extension of tax audit deadlines[156] unconstitutional. Most notably, in its judgment No 862/2013, the Portuguese Constitutional Court once again held unconstitutional a further 10 per cent cut on public sector pensions. However, in that case, the Court constitutionally upgraded the issue by declaring that this cut amounted to a violation of the principle of legitimate expectations in breach of Article 2 of the Constitution, guaranteeing, inter alia, the effective implementation of fundamental rights and freedoms.

On top of the above overall downgrading of the principle, there are two particular factual features akin to financial crisis that could reasonably constitute a ground of legitimate expectation but were discarded altogether: the expectations concerning non-default of States; and assessments by credit rating agencies.

With regard to the State insolvency issue, the belief that States do not become insolvent is conceptually based on the concept of sovereignty and financially based on the idea that States enjoy the monopoly of currency and credit, which means they have unlimited financial resources. Under these circumstances, not surprisingly, the States themselves cultivated the conviction that their failure would be inconceivable. In a case referring to the different default interest rates for outstanding claims of the State vis-a-vis individuals and private entities, which was lodged before the economic crisis but issued after the first bail-out programme for Greece, the Council of State in its Judgment No 1611/2011 declared, in a very categorical manner, the creditworthiness of the State:

> The amount of interest is reasonably determined according to the risk of a possible default of debt, either public or private, and therefore the interest rate reasonably varies according to the credibility (creditworthiness) of the debtor. The Greek State is undoubtedly the most reliable debtor when compared to private debtors. Indeed, the Greek State may, due to its poor financial situation, sometimes delay the payment of its debts, but it does pay them, even after the war, with the respective interest. Finally, individual debtors, natural and legal persons, certainly do not enjoy the continuity and duration of a debtor State.[157]

Thus, the Council justified the privileged status of the State as a debtor vis-a-vis individuals and private entities on the ground that claims against the State are rather secured due to its elevated credibility and, arguably eternal, existence. However, in subsequent years the argument of non-default of the State was dismantled. In the bail-in Judgment 1116/2014, the Council of State strongly rejected the view that government bonds did not entail risk for their holders, on the ground that the assumption was grounded upon the false assumption that the State, due to its permanent existence, its unlimited wealth and its creditworthiness, has absolute solvency, ie the ability to always provide the necessary funds for the satisfaction of

---

[155] Judgment 474/2013 of the Portugese Constitutional Court.
[156] Judgment 1738/2017 of the Hellenic Council of State.
[157] Paragraph 6.

its creditors. The issue of non-default of the State was also raised before international courts that dealt with the Greek PSI. On EU level, in *Accorinti*, the General Court, when assessing possible damage caused by EU lawful acts, set an obiter dictum referring to 'a general principle that every creditor must bear the risk of his debtor's insolvency, including a State debtor'.[158]

As rightly put by Advocate General Cruz Villalón in *Gauweiler*,[159] a person who acquires government bonds from an issuing State is, by definition, financing that State, directly or indirectly, and does so for consideration that makes the legal transaction into a sort of loan. The holder of the government bond has a right to seek repayment of a debt from the issuing State, thus becoming its creditor. The State issues the instrument subject to an interest rate initially set at the time of issue and determined on the basis of supply and demand. The transaction entered into by the two parties, therefore, has the same structure as the granting of a loan. On the other hand, the European Court of Human Rights in *Mamatas*, held, in essence, that purchasing government bonds constituted a loan agreement between the bondholder and the State with a high degree of security in the sense that, by definition, States do not become insolvent.

With regard to assessment by *credit rating agencies*, a salient feature of market economy has been the actual significance of the ratings produced therefrom in raising confidence about the state economies. In the pre-crisis era, the misapprehension on the state of European economies was strongly cultivated by positive assessments by the three major credit-rating agencies – Moody's, Standard and Poor's and Fitch – which rendered the circulation of private funding to States very easy. In relation to Greece's debt crisis, on 8 December 2009, Fitch downgraded Greece's credit rating to BBB+ and caused a significant raise in the country's cost of borrowing and a fall of shares worldwide. Interestingly, this was the first time in a decade that Greece did not have an A-rating, irrespective of the huge structural problems of the Greek economy, which were rather commonplace. Only four and a half months later, on 27 April 2010, Standard and Poor's downgraded Greek credit rating to junk status, four days after Greece activated the 45-billion-euro bail-out package in view of a 16-billion-euro debt maturing a month later.

Between the two landmark dates, on 26 February 2010, the – infamous at that time – investment bank Goldman Sachs faced Fed inquiry over the Greek crisis on the accusation of helping to cause the debt crisis by using derivatives contracts to disguise how much Greece was borrowing. The overreliance on the credit-rating companies, which from this viewpoint operated as a convenient substitute reassurance for the smooth operation of the European markets, could reasonably be deemed a de facto legitimate expectation. If Europe itself could not, and did not, see what was coming, it is absolutely unreasonable to blame individual investors for

---

[158] Paragraph 120.
[159] Opinion of Advocate General Cruz Villalón delivered on 14 January 2015, para 122.

being imprudent and risky as regards the overheated economies.[160] Furthermore, the legal assessment of the credit ratings seems to be extremely contradictory, if not hypocritical, on the part of the judicial bodies of the EU.

In *Accortini*, the General Court discarded a claim for damages resulting from an *unlawful* act violating legitimate expectations stemming from a series of acts and statements of the ECB without assessing the role of the credit ratings in establishing the expectations of the investors, whereas at the same time it discarded the claim for damages resulting from a *lawful* act declaring that the damage alleged by the applicants did not exceed the limits of the economic risks inherent in commercial activities in the financial sector, in particular in operations involving negotiable bonds issued by a State, 'especially when that State, like the Hellenic Republic as of the end of 2009, has a low rating'.[161]

---

[160] Below ch 6 section I. Broadly the same happened in the real estate crisis in the US. Prior to Lehman Brothers' default, credit-rating agencies encouraged the housing boom and bubble between 1998 and 2006, through overly optimistic ratings on mortgage-related securities that caused the subprime residential mortgage collapse of 2007–08, since when house prices began to fall, mortgage default rates rose and mortgage bonds and ratings failed.

[161] Paragraph 121.

4

Institutional Impact of New Economic Constitutionalism upon Governance

The economic crisis caused serious turbulence in the balance of the institutions both on national and international level; on the one hand, national legal orders, having faced several crises of similar intensity and persistence in the past, have proved well prepared and more equipped from the viewpoint of institutional stability. On the other hand, European international organisations, mostly operating after World War II, experienced for the first time such an institutional upset and were, accordingly, testing their resilience in uncharted territories. This is especially true for the EU, which has, since its establishment, basically operated in an environment of prosperity beset by continuous growth.

Most importantly, it was the EU structures, which had arguably contributed to its unprecedented success as an international organisation, that were put in challenge. In fact, among the most salient characteristics of the EU legal order is the unique decision-making structures. These structures aim at tackling a double jeopardy: to establish an effective law-making mechanism in a polycentric and pluralistic legal environment, without heavy concessions to a conventional checks and balances system, and, at the same time, to respect the autonomy of the Member States, which remain the ultimate sovereign entities, while conceding essential competences and powers to the EU institutions?

Thus, the community method traditionally awards: legislative initiative competence to the Commission as the most communitarian institution; dominant legislative and monitoring powers to the Council and the Parliament, normally through a qualified majority that secures that an adequate saying is reserved for the Member States; judicial functions to the EU courts; and certain halting powers to the Member States' parliaments in view of the principle of subsidiarity. This amalgam was seriously jeopardised in the course of the financial crisis, primarily due to tensions raised between EU institutions, between Member States, between Member States and EU institutions and between those and external actors, mainly the IMF. These tensions have resulted in an actual reshaping of powers both horizontally, ie between same level institutions within the EU and the Member States (parliament v executive and judiciary), and vertically, ie between EU and the Member States (enhanced EU competences vis-a-vis Member States).

I. Parliamentary Default and Executive Empowerment

In the EU, there are two levels of direct legitimacy: the European Parliament; and the national parliaments. The former is basically engaged in the rule-making on a Union level, whereas the latter enjoy the monopoly of legislative power on domestic level, the control over their respective governments, as well as certain competences stemming from EU law. Thus, within the EU, there are two channels of representation, applying equally albeit with totally different powers and representation mandates, which, at the current stage of development of the EU, are mutually irreplaceable, either as an inter-parliamentary network of representation[1] or as a multilevel parliamentary field.[2] In the management of the financial crisis, the EU Parliament was the least involved institution. On the other hand, national parliaments, mostly of the debtor States, were merely called upon to uphold governmental policies that had been broadly shaped under extreme pressure through intergovernmental processes and with the participation of non-EU institutions. This situation resulted in a serious downgrade of the institutional role of the parliaments with the self-evident correlations for the democratic legitimacy of the respective legal orders and the horizontal balance of powers.

A. EU Structures

The EU ordinary legislative procedure, ie the co-decision procedure, involves three main institutions: the Commission, which has the legislative initiative; and the European Parliament and the Council, which decide, both standing – in principle – on an equal footing in the Union's parliamentary process, although it is argued that the latter's actual legislative capacity in some peripheral aspects is more essential.[3] The horizontal shift of power equilibrium on EU level reflects a double evolution evidenced in the course of dealing with financial emergencies: political intergovernmentalism, on the one hand; and technocratic supranationalism, on the other.[4] Thus, the intergovernmental European Council overshadowed

---

[1] B Kohler-Koch and B Rittberger, 'The "governance turn" in EU studies' (2006) 44 *Journal of Common Market Studies* 27. Also see European Parliament, 'Opinion on CARS 21: A Competitive Automotive Regulatory Framework (2007/2120(INI))', Committee on the Internal Market and Consumer Protection, 13 September 2007, Draftsman: Malcolm Harbour, p 3.

[2] B Crum and JE Fossum, 'The Multilevel Parliamentary Field: A framework for Theorizing Representative Democracy in the EU' (2009) 1 *European Political Science Review* 249, 252.

[3] S Hagemann and B Høyland, 'Bicameral Politics in the European Union' (2010) 48 *Journal of Common Market Studies* 811 present theoretical and empirical evidence to suggest that the Council has conditional agenda-setting power due to a change in the majority thresholds for adopting legislation from the first to the second reading in the Parliament.

[4] A Crespy and G Menz, 'Commission Entrepreneurship and the Debasing of Social Europe Before and After the Eurocrisis' (2015) 53 *Journal of Common Market Studies* 753.

the Parliament and the technocratic Commission, while the Court of Justice assumed further monitoring and reviewing competences.[5]

According to Palonen and Wiesner, the political significance of the creation and institutional acknowledgment of the European Council was undoubtedly a step towards a federal presidency, in particular with regard to the power to set the calendar and the agenda, as well as with regard to its President's double status as both the Union's and the Parliament's president, whereas it serves as a federal congress of ambassadors when it comes to preparing and negotiating key decisions on policies or personnel.[6] Yet, in the course of the financial crisis, the leadership role was in many respects assumed by a Franco-German axis on the highest governmental level, with the implicit approval of all other euro-area Member States, including those receiving the financial rescue packages.

In fact, the major regulations concerning the treatment of the financial crisis and the emergency vehicles to be launched, ie the Fiscal Compact, the European Financial Stability Facility (EFSF) as well as the European Stability Mechanism (ESM), were discussed and decided by the heads of governments of the strongest Member States and then were merely forwarded to the EU institutions and the remaining Member States. In the primary discussions, the Commission was invited, on occasions, to submit various proposals, such as the separation of the activities of general commercial banks and investment banks, and to launch new financial instruments for investment in order to promote growth and development. The Commission and the Council did have a presence in the course of the crisis, mostly to uphold decisions taken by state executives.

In a sense, the EU institutional treatment of the crisis failed to respect the mutual sincere cooperation that EU institutions ought to demonstrate in accordance with Article 13(2) TEU: the financial crisis de facto moved all emergency powers to the intergovernmental institutions of the Union and within them to sub-sections of representatives from powerful governments, at the expense of the supranational institutions, which were marginalised and became mere followers of the policy decisions made in the margin of the community method. There seems to have been a practical necessity to this effect. Since major decisions taken under the community method as well as Treaty amendments required unanimity of all EU Member States, it seemed rather unlikely that such a high threshold could ever be achieved, the UK being the first 'suspect' to decline any bail-out mechanism. Although the intergovernmental method also required unanimity, the number of euro-area Member States was lower and the stakes were higher for them.

---

[5] U Puetter, *The European Council and the Council: New Intergovernmentalism and Institutional Change* (Oxford, Oxford University Press, 2014); MW Bauer, 'The Unexpected Winner of the Crisis: the European Commission's Strengthened Role in Economic Governance' (2014) 36 *Journal of European Integration* 213.

[6] K Palonen and C Wiesner 'Second Chamber, "Congress of Ambassadors" or Federal Presidency. Parliamentary and Non-parliamentary Aspects in the European Council's Rules of Procedure' (2016) 36 *Parliaments, Estates and Representation* 71.

218   *Institutional Impact of New Economic Constitutionalism upon Governance*

In fact, the intergovernmental vehicles introduced to deal with the financial crisis essentially abolished the unanimity requirement for the future, since the entry into force of the Fiscal Compact required the approval of only 12 (out of then 15) euro-area Member States.

Among the European institutions, the European Council has in all aspects proved to be a dominant actor in policy drafting within the Union, even in areas where the supranationalist decision-making seems to prevail; it has acted in a variety of capacities, ie as an allocator of budget funds, a political initiator, an interpreter of the Treaties, a contributor to individual decisions as well as an appeals council.[7] In this context, the Treaty of Lisbon provided for the office of a permanent president of the European Council to strengthen it with further structural power. On the other hand, the Commission came to be the most crucial actor in the monitoring of the financial discipline of the Member States, not merely ex post, as in the pre-crisis era, but also ex ante. This is so not only in terms of monetary policy but also with regard to essentially all aspects of economy, mainly through the enhanced supervision in the context of the European Semester. Furthermore, the Commission's position has been strengthened through the voting process launched by the new economic governance, especially the Six-Pack. Thus, decisions on the majority of sanctions under the Excessive Deficit Procedure are taken by reverse qualified majority voting, which means that fines imposed by the Commission are deemed to be approved by the European Council of Ministers, unless a qualified majority of Member States overturns them.

In addition, the 25 Member States that signed the TSCG have agreed to apply the same voting mechanism even in earlier stages of the process, such as when deciding whether a Member State should be placed under the Excessive Deficit Procedure. Accordingly, a decision is taken by reverse qualified majority voting (launching of the procedure or imposition of sanction) and the minimum number of votes required to reject the Commission recommendation is 255, whereas, in the ordinary process, for a decision to be taken there is a requirement of at least 255 weighted votes (out of a total of 345) representing at least two-thirds of the members of the Council when acting on a recommendation from the Commission. Interestingly, the Commission has been empowered with the monitoring of the Fiscal Pact representing the EU as a whole rather than the euro area and including commissioners from non-Eurozone Member States, ie from the UK and the Czech Republic. In this respect, as Fabbrini argues, legislative measures and new intergovernmental Treaties resulted in a relative transformation of the role of the Commission in the Union and the euro-area structures: its regulatory role in the elaboration and decision-making phase, where it enjoys legislative initiative, was mitigated, while its functional role in the enforcement of intergovernmental decisions and monitoring of the behaviour of

---

[7] F Eggermont, *The Changing Role of the European Council in the Institutional Framework of the European Union: Consequences for the European Integration Process* (Cambridge, Intersentia, 2012).

Member States increased significantly, rendering the Commission a 'watchdog' of intergovernmental decisions.[8]

However, in spite of its enhanced role in financial monitoring and the increase in the level of intergovernmental decision-making over the crisis period, the Commission has remained a key actor in drafting the Union policies, especially through a centralisation of EU executive power and proactive policies in budget surveillance and banking union mechanisms.[9] Finally, the ECB has been significantly upgraded in all respects during and after the financial crisis. Its purchase asset programmes, especially the OMT programme, has arguably been equally important to save the euro as the ESM. In spite of its lack of democratic legitimacy, its independence and high level of technocratic capacity has by all means contributed to the stabilisation of the euro area and the consolidation of a more federal perception of the EU, beyond ordinary intergovernmentalism.

The Council (mainly the ECOFIN) and the Eurogroup of the Finance and Economy Ministers of the euro area took over very significant powers in the implementation of the measures to deal with the financial crisis in the endangered euro-area States. By way of contrast, the European Parliament remained emphatically silent for at least three years after the eruption of the crisis. Although it has indeed matured significantly as an institution since the first direct election of its members in 1971 and it has developed a physiognomy largely resembling that of the national parliaments, in the course of the crisis the EU Parliament demonstrated a very low level of political responsiveness. From a political viewpoint, this might be attributed to the fact that the Parliament represents the entire Union (in fact, the citizens of the Union), whereas the crisis was mainly a euro-area issue.

Since the Parliament, unlike the Commission, the Court of Justice and the ECB, had no monitoring role to perform in the stability mechanism for the euro area, one might say that its involvement would be unwise, if not ultra vires. At any rate, it seems that there was downsizing of the Parliament by both sides: Member States (especially the powerful euro-area States which played a dominant role in the crisis) did not want further institutional involvement of the European Parliament in order to retain control over the handling of the crisis; the other European institutions did not want the European Parliament delaying or even challenging the measures taken to deal with the imminent crisis.

Political dominance of the Member States' governments through intergovernmental processes, on the one hand, along with a notable inaction mainly on the part of the EU Parliament and the Commission, as well as the pending guidance from the European Council and the Eurogroup, on the other, further weakened

---

[8] F Fabbrini, 'The Euro-Crisis and the Courts: Judicial Review and the Political Process in Comparative Perspective' (2014) 32 *Berkeley Journal of International Law* 64.

[9] JD Savage and A Verdun, 'Strengthening the European Commission's Budgetary and Economic Surveillance Capacity since Greece and the Euro Area Crisis: A Study of Five Directorates-General' (2016) 23 *Journal of European Public Policy* 101, 114; M Egeberg, J Trondal and NM Vestland, 'The Quest for Order: Unravelling the Relationship between the European Commission and EU Agencies' (2015) 22 *Journal of European Public Policy* 609, 609–10.

the position of the EU overall. According to Peter Lindseth, the structural deficiencies of the Union, combined with the strictly attributed powers stemming from the proper national Constitutions, rendered the European integration essentially 'administrative', rather than constitutional, in nature, with EU's normative power, like any power of an ultimately administrative character, finding its legitimacy primarily in legal, technocratic and functional claims. In his view, this type of administrative legitimacy has become particularly pertinent to the integration process at times of crisis.[10] Even where some kind of democratic façade was institutionally provided on EU level, it was not materialised, due to the lack of the political will to transform it to applied policy.

By dismantling the equilibrium among the (politically powerful, but not directly representative, and intergovernmental in nature) European Council, the (politically weak, albeit directly representative) Parliament and the (supranational in nature and of high political potential, albeit unrepresentative) Commission, the financial crisis revealed the constitutional limits of the EU. The Union continued to evolve as an imperfect social experiment revealing more and more market failures as well as multilevel governance failures: intergovernmental institutions, mainly the European Council and the Economic and Financial Affairs Council (ECOFIN), placed emphasis on national economic interests, thus creating a fragmental environment where Member States' allies might legitimately overstep the powers of supranational, but mainly executive, EU institutions.[11]

B. Domestic Structures

On a national level, new economic constitutionalism resulted in a strong executive empowerment at the expense of parliaments. In terms of political practice, most States were faced with a situation where the government handled all critical financial situations and took the necessary measures to address them, whereas the national parliament was only involved at a later stage, called to put a mere seal of approval onto measures considered as granted, which were actually already in the course of being implemented. This subversion can be attributed to the technical expertise required to address difficult financial matters, the need for prompt decisions due to the State's pressing financial needs and the requirement for a solid and coherent economic strategy when negotiating in international fora either as a lender or as a debtor. Above all, it is historically proved that in periods of (mostly financial) crises, the executive tends to gather a great amount of power, as it is considered to be the most effective state branch in terms of problem solving.

[10] PL Lindseth, *Power and Legitimacy. Reconciling Europe and the Nation-State* (Oxford, Oxford University Press, 2010) 1–32; PL Lindseth, 'Reflections on the "Administrative, not Constitutional" Character of EU Law in Times of Crisis' (2017) 9 *Perspectives on Federalism* 1.

[11] E-U Petersmann, *International Economic Law in the 21st century. Constitutional Pluralism and Multilevel Governance of Interdependent Public Goods* (Oxford, Hart Publishing, 2012) 36–37, 165–71.

The empowerment of the executive may at times also reflect the composition of both the government and the parliament. In particular, whereas more and more bureaucrats (who are not career politicians) are engaged in the government, resulting in governance through bureaucrats, the quality of members of parliament is in constant decline, and so is the quality of parliamentary debates. The phenomenon of governmental technocracy, blamed by some for the decrease of legitimacy on European level, has resulted in a significant transfer of actual political powers from the parliaments to the governments and the respective administrations.

In the aftermath of the crisis, national parliaments seem to walk a thin line between an upgrade on an EU level and a downgrade on a domestic level. On an EU level, the Protocol on National Parliaments attached to the 1997 Treaty of Amsterdam originally made national parliaments co-partners in the process of European integration, whereas, pursuant to the Treaty of Lisbon, they may object to EU legislation through the early warning mechanism on alleged trespasses of the competences of the Union on the ground of the principle of subsidiarity. This blocking competence of the national parliaments renders them, in the words of Ian Cooper, a virtual collective third chamber for the EU as a policy-influencing body (considering the Council as a second chamber), which gives them the power to influence legislative outcomes at EU level, provides a new channel of representation linking citizens with the EU and creates a new forum for debating the substantive merits of proposed EU legislation.[12] In this way, there is an open institutional channel between the European Parliament and the domestic parliaments so as to justify what Crum and Fossum described as a 'multi-level parliamentary field' in Europe.[13] Yet, on a domestic level, national parliaments were significantly hampered, both in terms of their legislative functions and their actual competence to control the government.

In terms of *legislative function*, domestic parliaments have lost their legislative powers not only towards the EU but also towards the national governments which, in the course of the crisis, activated constitutional clauses allowing them to adopt legislative measures outside parliamentary delegation. For example, the Greek Constitution provides that, under extraordinary circumstances of an urgent and unforeseeable need, the President of the Hellenic Republic may, upon proposal by the Cabinet, adopt legislative orders, without prior parliamentary delegation, that shall be subsequently submitted to the Parliament for ratification; if not ratified, they shall cease to be in force from that moment onwards (Article 44(1)).

---

[12] I Cooper, 'A "Virtual Third Chamber" for the European Union? National Parliaments after the Treaty of Lisbon' (2012) 35 *West European Politics* 441. Also see R Kardasheva, 'The Power to Delay: The European Parliament's Influence in the Consultation Procedure' (2009) 47 *Journal of Common Market Studies* 385; P Kiiver, 'The Early-Warning System for the Principle of Subsidiarity: The National Parliament as a Conseil d'Etat for Europe' (2011) 36 *European Law Review* 98; P Kiiver, 'The Treaty of Lisbon, the National Parliaments and the Principle of Subsidiarity' (2008) 15 *Maastricht Journal of European and Comparative Law* 77.

[13] Crum and Fossum, 'The Multilevel Parliamentary Field' (2009).

In the first years following the sovereign debt crisis in Greece, the number of such instruments has increased significantly as a means for bypassing the rather slow and cumbersome parliamentary process. Given that there is no constitutional court and that those instruments are formally equivalent to statutes, there is no direct remedy against them (except an appeal against an administrative act issued pursuant to the instrument in question); in any case, according to consolidated case law, the courts abstain from controlling whether genuine 'extraordinary circumstances of an urgent and unforeseeable need' are in place to justify such regulation by the executive, because this assessment is considered to be a governmental privilege.[14]

The equivalent in Spain comes in the form of a decree-law, enacted pursuant to a constitutional clause allowing the Government, in cases of extraordinary and urgent need, to adopt such legislative provisions of a temporary nature that must be immediately submitted to Congress for debate and ratification through a special summary procedure provided by the parliamentary standing orders. However, such decree-laws should not interfere with the legal system of the basic State institutions, the rights, duties and freedoms of citizens, the system of Self-governing Communities and the general electoral law (Article 86). In this context, the critical Spanish decree-law 8/2010, which decreased wages by five per cent and suspended the effect of collective bargaining originally providing for a 0.3 per cent increase, was challenged before the Constitutional Court. The Court upheld the constitutionality of the impugned decree-law, ruling that in the Court's view it did not breach the freedom of trade union and the principle of collective bargaining (Articles 28 and 37 respectively).[15] The Court allowed wide discretionary power to the Government by refraining from elaborately analysing the constitutional requirements for the enactment of extraordinary legislation. Most importantly, however, even under ordinary legislative procedures, national parliaments operated under extreme pressure; as a result, the vote of MPs eventually ended up lacking meaningful quality since they were expected to vote on financial assistance packages that could not be altered, at least not significantly, and/or there was indeed very little time for deliberation or very little feedback to make a rational choice.[16]

Regarding their *function to control the government*, domestic Westminster-type parliaments have made significant concessions. Given the extremely pressing

[14] Hellenic Council of State, Judgments 2289/1987, 955/1988, 3636/1989, 5211/1995, 2593/2001, 3612/2002, 1250/2003; Supreme Civil and Criminal Court of Greece (*Areios Pagos*), Judgments 367/1997, 1101/1987.
[15] Spanish Constitutional Tribunal Judgment of 7 June 2011, Auto 85/2011.
[16] Mitigation of the political autonomy of MPs is a widespread contemporary phenomenon in Europe, even in matters not directly associated to financial aspects. This is, for example, the case of the debate in the most historical House in Europe, ie the UK House of Commons, where a lot of discussion took place with regard to the question as to whether MPs would have the opportunity to suggest amendments to the agreement between the UK Government and the EU institutions concerning the exit of the UK from the Union. The campaign on parliamentary meaningful vote exactly resumes the discussion on the devaluation of parliamentary processes and the very little actual political space left to the legitimate Houses to exercise their functions.

circumstances that endangered States normally face, backbenchers are obviously less keen on exercising effective control over the government, since this would undoubtedly hamper the executive power in terms of both time and responsibility, since the measures attached to rescue packages are by definition unpopular and in case of condemnation by the parliament, the members of the government would assume a very high responsibility.

On the other hand, this political power varies in the parliaments of Member States that did not receive rescue packages. Obviously, when the Treaties explicitly establish both the competence of the EU institutions and the means to proceed with the relevant legislation, all Member States have unequivocally conferred this power and have been alienated from such competence. However, on numerous occasions during the financial crisis, the regulatory initiatives to deal with malfunctions or to establish a more solid, well-monitored and disciplined environment have been decided either outside of the Union structures or on the verge of such competence. Although not identical, the situation resembles the general framework of the flexibility clause of Article 352 TFEU, which merely sets out the necessary actions for the attainment of the Union objectives, in case the respective powers have not been granted to the Union.

Broadly speaking, there are countries where either by statute or as a matter of statutory construction through case law, parliamentary intervention is required prior to any major regulation in fields where an explicit power is not conferred to the Union. The issue was raised before the constitutional courts of both Germany and Poland with regard to the approval of the Treaty of Lisbon; these courts ruled that there should be prior formal agreement of the respective Houses. In the remaining Member States, the prevailing view seems to be that the extraordinary powers of the Union, such as the flexibility clause, do not require any consent by national parliaments since the ratification of the Treaty essentially transferred such powers to the EU institutions. Naturally, this does not prevent national executives from taking the relevant regulatory initiative voluntarily before their respective legislatures to increase the level of legitimacy and to operate a burden-sharing policy of responsibility.

Interestingly, national parliaments came out of the crisis rather injured in terms of actual political power and institutional prestige. Two political explanations could be provided for this situation, the first being the subversion of political balance. Although in Westminster-type polities, national parliaments are, in theory, in a superior institutional position by giving their confidence to the government, such institutional mechanics seems to have failed in many respects. In times of crisis, national parliaments seem to be much more inclined to support their governments instead of being critical of them.[17] This results in a subversion of the original mechanism, ie instead of the Parliament being the leader and the

---

[17] Two temporal exceptions could be traced in Europe, ie the Greek Parliament in 2012, which essentially demanded the Prime-Minister Giorgos Papandreou to step down from office and the UK Parliament in the 2018 Brexit process due to the serious split of the governing conservative party.

Government being the follower, the opposite applies. It appears that when there is no dependence between the parliament and the government, such as in the case of the European or the US parliaments, they tend to maintain their political role irrespective of the political context.[18] This political reality is in fact the collateral result of the institutional parliamentary system and requires a strong parliament to overcome such inclinations.

Second, the economic crisis has widely resulted in great losses on the part of the traditional large parties in domestic politics, which broadly paid the price for – seemingly unsuccessfully – handling the crisis. This resulted in compartmentalisation and fragmentation of parliaments without strong governments or strong oppositions. Interestingly, half of the EU Member States were led by coalitions or minority governments. Although this could have conceivably resulted in more powerful parliaments (since it would take internal parliamentary proceedings and bargaining to produce sustainable governments), this did not occur in practice.

II. Judicial Responsiveness (Jureconomy)

In terms of the horizontal shift equilibrium, particular emphasis must be placed on the position of the judiciary. The attitude of the judiciary, both national and international, in the context of new economic constitutionalism is of acute importance (the jureconomy issue). This is because judges are necessarily called upon to rule on the compatibility of economic measures with the domestic Constitutions or the corresponding international treaties. Through this process, irrespective of whether they engage in an exercise of self-restraint or they retain an interventionist role, they inevitably become largely political actors by determining the economic reading of the Constitution. In this respect, most courts have adopted a rather moderate stance, abstaining from any significant involvement with the financial crisis, thus allowing the political branches of government to deal with the effects of the crisis. The fact that the crisis did not widely trigger any constitutional or EU primary law amendments, with the exception of case-specific constitutional amendments enhancing the golden rule and the amendment of Article 136 TFEU, rendered the judiciary a rather crucial actor in new economic constitutionalism, as it was the courts that were called upon to decide whether the new regulations were compatible with the existing clauses of a constitutional ranking.

A. EU and ECHR Structures

The case law on the financial crisis revealed the high level of judicial multiplicity in Europe, including national courts, EU courts and the European Court of

---

[18] KM Johansson and P Zervakis, 'Historical-institutional framework' in K Johansson and P Zervakis (eds), *European Political Parties* (Baden-Baden, Nomos, 2002) 11.

Human Rights. The relationship between national courts and the Court of Strasbourg is mostly defined by the national constitutional orders, yet the actual significance of the ECHR in the field of the protection of human rights is undeniable. On the other hand, the principle of supremacy of EU law seems to arm the Courts of Luxembourg with significant judicial authority vis-a-vis the domestic courts, which today seem to largely accept this principle, expressly or tacitly. Indeed, both the Court of Justice and the General Court, in hearing cases relevant to the financial crisis, took the opportunity to reiterate their exclusive competence to review the compatibility of treaty amendments with EU primary law and the soundness of the aims set forth to justify the legitimacy of the authorities' pursuits. Furthermore, on top of this pre-existing competence, further dispute resolution powers have been conferred upon the Court of Justice in the context of the ESM Treaty and the Fiscal Compact.

In essence, the Court of Justice was involved in determining legal aspects of the euro-area crisis in two respects:

(a) as a *human rights adjudicator*, deciding on cases regarding salary cuts and/or reductions of pensions, benefits, shares, bonds and deposits imposed in the framework of the austerity or restructuring programmes, on the one hand; and

(b) as a *competence arbitrator*, deciding cases where EU authorities were allegedly exceeding their prescribed competences on the other hand. However, the relationship between EU law and the ECHR, as well as the corresponding relationship between their respective adjudicative bodies, still remains the most complex issue at the current stage of development of the EU.

Under Article 6(3) TEU and Articles 52 and 53 of the EU Charter of Fundamental Rights, the Court of Justice and the General Court shall apply the Convention standards as a minimum protection of European citizens within the scope of EU law. Conversely, the Court of Strasbourg, precisely because of the cross-reference to the ECHR in EU law, would normally abstain from any interference with EU case law, except in case of a manifestly deficient judgment, thus establishing a de facto presumption that the Court of Justice adequately protects fundamental rights within its respective scope of application.[19] Thus, irrespective of the current state of failure on the part of the EU to accede the ECHR, there has been a rather significant case law convergence on matters of human rights. When it comes to the crisis case law, given that most of the conditionality measures had involved serious curtailments of existing property rights, the European Court of Human Rights has also ruled on the relevant matters from another perspective that merely involved an interpretation of the property clause, rather than matters of ultra vires. Yet, the outcome remains broadly the same.

---

[19] ECtHR Judgment of 30 June 2005, *Bosphorus Hava Yollari Turizm ve Ticaret AS v Ireland*, Application no 45036/98.

The Court of Strasbourg placed much more emphasis on the exceptional circumstances of the financial crisis that triggered measures to prevent state default, as well as to the technical matter of complex economic issues that allowed wider margin of discretion on the part of state authorities. From this viewpoint, the Strasbourg case law has been more contextual and less strictly legal, although the Courts of Luxembourg made use of counter-factual argumentation, which is also rather contextual. In any case, there seems to be a common core in the rationale of both sets of case law; an informal presumption of validity of state acts in the relevant subject matters. Although one might argue that prior case law in both legal landscapes could substantiate some of the claims raised in the course of the crisis case law, it is undeniable that they both opted for a significant adjustment of key case law concepts instead of allowing for a more generous treatment of the applications, which resulted in a rather unusual statistical outcome: although the applications were very diverse in terms of the nature of the dispute and the grounds of review invoked, neither the Courts of Luxembourg nor the Court of Strasbourg found in favour of the applicants; not in a single case.

From this viewpoint, although there has been an important upgrade on a European level with regard to the protection of human rights, so that one could refer to a 'trialogue', ie EU, ECHR and national Constitutions, as shrewdly put by Tridimas,[20] in the course of the financial crisis the full alignment of EU Courts with the European Court of Human Rights brings us back to a conventional type of dialogue between domestic courts vis-a-vis a single case law bloc of the main international European courts.

Indeed, it is the Court of Justice that has been the major winner in the informal battle for dominance among courts in Europe. Without conceding a significant level of the integrity of its case law, it has become a key actor throughout the period of the crisis by securing the Union's continuity and integration. Accordingly, it upheld the competence of the EU institutions to take measures aiming both at defending the monetary policy of the Union and at stabilising national finances. In both *Pringle* and *Gauweiler*, the Court upheld the validity of the challenged acts by envisaging EU competences in a holistic manner and emphasising that policy and technical decisions should allow a wide margin of appreciation for EU institutions, even if arguably falling outside the EU legal framework. The tone was given, while decision in *Pringle* was pending, by then President of the Court Vassilios Skouris in the following extra-judicial dicta:

> [I]t could indeed be argued that as the law and its interpretation by the Court of Justice constituted the driving force in the advancement of what we could call Europe's political integration, it can play an equally significant role in the process of its fiscal and monetary integration and, consequently, in dealing with the current financial crisis ... [I]n such complex economic policy matters, the law can only provide the instruments

---

[20] T Tridimas, 'The ECJ and the National Courts: Dialogue, Cooperation, and Instability' in D Chalmers and A Arnull (eds), *The Oxford Handbook of European Union Law* (Oxford, Oxford University Press, 2015) 403.

in order to put into action a possible solution but not the solution itself. The role of the law is, in essence, a supporting role. This statement must not be seen as a lessening of the importance of the law within the EU legal order in general. It must be understood as meaning that the law as such cannot conceive and produce policies. Therefore, I am not arguing in favour of a *capitis deminutio* ... I simply believe that the judicial approach in this area must be characterised by two elements: patience and caution. I say patience in the sense that the Courts should not look for legal issues they wish to rule upon where it is not clear that such issues are raised. The body of legislation adopted in response to the financial crisis will take time to develop its full effects and the courts must therefore be patient and deal with the issues only as and when they specifically arise. I say caution because the legal analysis of such matters requires the strictest respect of the boundaries of the respective spheres of competence ... [C]ourts may be tempted to engage in broad interpretations that could amount to a judicial experimentalism without being able to evaluate the consequences both in the short term and long term.[21]

Yet, President Skouris' psychological conditions of 'patience and caution', when a judicial body is dealing with complex issues of economic policy, connotes far more than a simple judicial deference or a wide margin of discretion as regards the possible options of policy-makers. Because on issues of competence, where subsidiarity and proportionality set out a very strict context for the EU institutions, there can be no discretion but merely a legal interpretation of the relevant awarding rules. In fact, the joint reading of the crisis case law coming from Luxembourg seems to employ a presumption of validity of the EU acts that is in practice extremely difficult to overturn. In essence, EU Courts demonstrated a spirit of realism and utilitarianism in order to adjust to contemporary needs, especially when called to decide on the meaning and restrictions imposed by the explicit prohibition of the no-bail-out clause, on the actual meaning of strict conditionality attached to the rescue packages and on the measures taken on the verge of powers conferred to the EU. Furthermore, given that national courts upheld austerity policies with broadly the same reasoning as the respective international courts, one might legitimately support that adversely affected citizens lacked effective judicial remedies and felt exploited by systemic democratic deficiencies in the European constitutional legal orders.[22]

This understandable pro-Union judicial inclination in the post-2008 case law, should, however, also be assessed in conjunction with the attitude of the Court in the 2004 cases of Germany and France, where the Court of Justice arguably had the opportunity, through a more active intervention, to set an effective brake to what was later to be the financial turmoil. From this viewpoint, the Court of Justice has, from the very beginning, been a part of the problem of the adherence of Member States to the EU financial discipline rules; in a sense, it has acted as a political actor itself. This consideration mitigates the force of the argument

---

[21] Vassilios Skouris' (pending decision in *Pringle*) keynote lecture in 2012 at the European Law Institute Project Conference and General Assembly entitled 'The Court of Justice and the Financial Crisis: New Treaties, New Competences, Future Prospects'.
[22] E-U Petersmann, *International Economic Law* (2012) 5.

of patience and caution that was proved to be ineffective judicial policy since it allowed a very loose framework in securing financial discipline that eventually resulted in the 2008 financial crisis.

The EU Courts have, without exception, stood by the other EU institutions at the time of financial crisis, by supporting financialism and – to some extent – by procedurally limiting access to justice for European citizens and entities in cases allegedly involving curtailment of human rights. This relates to:

(a)   the scope of applicable law;
(b)   the procedural prerequisites for challenging an act or applying for damages; and
(c)   the right to invoke grounds of review.

With regard to *the scope of applicable law*, the most striking example is the very limited application of the EU Charter of Fundamental Rights. In the pre-crisis era, the Court of Justice had taken a much more generous stance towards the applicability of the Charter in cases of arguably less direct interest to the EU. In Judgment of 26 February 2013 in Case C-617/10, *Åklagaren v Hans Åkerberg Fransson*, the reference for a preliminary ruling made to the Court of Justice was related to the question of compatibility of the Swedish tax controlling system (which established two separate sets of proceedings – an administrative and a criminal one – to deal with the same breaches of the obligation to declare VAT) with Article 51 of the Charter guaranteeing the *ne bis in idem* principle. The issue of jurisdiction of the Court was related to the lack of EU competence in the respective fields of tax penalties or criminal proceedings and, accordingly, the lack of triggering of Article 51(1) of the Charter; this Article, along with the explanations attached to it, provides that its provisions are addressed to the Member States only when they act in the scope of EU law.

The Court upheld its jurisdiction by using rather loose criteria. Indeed, it made reference to EU law, according to which:

(a)   every Member State is under an obligation to take all legislative and administrative measures appropriate for ensuring collection of all VAT due on its territory and for preventing tax evasion;[23] and
(b)   the Member States ought to counter illegal activities affecting the financial interests of the Union through effective dissuasive measures, equivalent to the domestic processes, in particular to combat fraud affecting the financial interests of the Union (Article 325 TFEU).

Given that the Union's own resources included revenue from application of a uniform rate to the harmonised VAT assessment,[24] the Court found a direct link

---

[23] Articles 2, 250(1) and 273 of Council Dir 2006/112 of 28 November 2006 on the common system of value added tax (OJ 2006 L 347, p 1), which reproduced, inter alia, the provisions of the Sixth Directive (Arts 2 and 22(4)(8), in the version resulting from Art 28h thereof and from Art 4(3) TEU).

[24] Art 2(1) of Council Decision 2007/436/EC, Euratom of 7 June 2007 on the system of the European Communities' own resources (OJ 2007 L 163, p 17).

with EU law. In that regard, the Court concluded that tax penalties and criminal proceedings for tax evasion constituted implementation of EU law for the purposes of Article 51(1) of the Charter, although national legislation upon which those tax penalties and criminal proceedings were founded had not adopted it in transposition of EU law. Presumably, in that case there was no direct link to EU law but merely a matter of general indirect interest. Yet, the interest is not generally tantamount to competence and it is evident that the Court took a very favourable stance towards the expansion of the applicability of the Charter, in spite of the express letter of Article 6(1) TEU, according to which the provisions of the Charter are not to extend in any way the competences of the Union as defined in the Treaties, and of Article 51(2) of the Charter itself that precludes extension of the scope of application of EU law beyond the powers of the Union or establishment of any new relevant power or duty or modification of the powers and duties of the Union as defined in the Treaties.

Arguably, in *Åklagaren*, the mere fact that the extension of the scope of applicability of the Charter would essentially operate to the benefit of the EU, by making the VAT sanction system more effective and, in turn, eventually more profitable for the Union itself, justified the broad interpretation given by the Court. By way of contrast, in the post-crisis case law, where the issue at stake essentially was the conditionality attached to the financial assistance towards the endangered countries, the Court clearly operated in favour of the preservation of the interest of the Union, as generally perceived, although it had to change its mindset in order to reach the opposite conclusion compared to *Åklagaren*. The subsequent judicial approach was that 'it is settled case-law that they bind the Member States in all cases where they are required to apply Union law', without any further elaboration on the matter.[25]

However, the attitude of the Court of Justice is rather contradictory, in its effort to uphold the emergency measures taken to deal with economic crises in Member States. On the one hand, as regards the competences of EU institutions, the Court broadens them by upholding policies not explicitly provided by EU law, such as the OMTs programme by the ECB in *Gauweiler*. On the other hand, concerning substantive limitations imposed upon EU institutions on crafting such policies, the Court limits the level of protection of EU citizens, mainly by excluding the applicability of the EU Charter of Fundamental Rights. Thus, in responding to arguments stemming from Article 47 of the Charter on the right to effective judicial protection, the Court of Justice in *Pringle* concluded that when establishing a stability mechanism such as the ESM, Member States are not implementing Union law, given that the TEU and the TFEU do not confer any specific competence on the Union to establish such a mechanism and, therefore, the Charter is not applicable.

---

[25] eg, CJEU Order of 7 March 2013 in Case C-128/12, *Sindicato dos Bancários do Norte and others*, para 11; CJEU Order of 14 December 2011 in Case C-434/11, *Corpul Naţional al Poliţiştilor v Ministerul Administraţiei şi Internelor (MAI) and others*, para 15; CJEU Order of 10 May 2012 in Case C-134/12, *Corpul Naţional al Poliţiştilor*, para 12.

Yet, just a couple of paragraphs before this ruling, the Court had accepted its own jurisdiction over disputes arising in the context of this financial assistance mechanism, based on Article 273 TFEU, which stipulates that the Court of Justice shall have jurisdiction over any dispute between Member States relating to the subject matter of the Treaties, if such dispute is brought before the Court under a special agreement between the parties. The rationale of the Court was a legalistic sophism: 'since the membership of the ESM consists solely of Member States, a dispute to which the ESM is party may be considered to be a dispute between Member States within the meaning of Article 273 TFEU'. However, even if the ESM Treaty is considered a special agreement within the meaning of this provision, this rationale ignores the most essential premise for submission of the relevant disputes to the jurisdiction of the Court, ie that such disputes are linked to the subject matter of the Treaties.

In spite of the express letter of Article 273, the Court examined the question on a *ratione personae* basis only and set aside the required *ratione materiae* approach. This rationale clearly introduces an irrational contradiction in the judgment of the Court: the ESM qualifies as having the power to instigate the competence of the higher adjudicative EU authority, but does not qualify to fall within the scope of the EU Charter of Fundamental Rights. The result of this line of argumentation is that the Member States may decide, through a special agreement, to submit to the Court's jurisdiction any dispute arising in the domestic legal order, irrespective of its EU relevance, while at the same time the main instrument of protection of EU citizens will not be applicable.

With regard to the *procedural prerequisites* for challenging an act or claiming for damages, the European Court of Human Rights used the tool of Article 35(3)(a) of the Convention allowing the Court to declare inadmissible any application which is 'manifestly ill-founded' to dismiss the applications, in part or in whole, in *Koufaki* and the Hungarian cases *Markovics, Béres* and *Augusztin*. On the other hand, the EU courts also applied the criterion of manifestly ill-founded applications of Article 53(2) of the Rules of Procedure of the Court of Justice (whereby the Court, after hearing the Advocate General, may decide to give a decision by reasoned order concluding the proceedings, where it is clear that it has no jurisdiction to determine a case or where a request or an application is manifestly inadmissible) to requests for a preliminary ruling submitted by Romanian regional Courts (the Court of Justice), and in Cypriot cases *Ledra* and *Mallis* (the General Court, on appeals heard on merits by the Court of Justice).

As a matter of exception rather in peripheral issues unrelated to standing and the proper establishment of the law and facts, in *Associação Sindical dos Juízes Portugueses and others*, concerning salary cuts introduced by the Portuguese Government, the Court of Justice rejected the inadmissibility plea made by the defendant. This was that on 1 October 2016 the impugned Portuguese Law 159-A/2015 totally abolished the salary reductions which had, from 1 October 2014, affected individuals performing duties in the public sector and, therefore, the case had become devoid of purpose. Although the Court accepted that a request for a preliminary ruling might be held inadmissible if the question is unrelated to the actual facts of the main action or its purpose, or where the problem was hypothetical, in the case at hand the interest was still vivid since the amounts withheld from the remuneration of the individuals concerned during the period when salary cuts applied (October 2014 to October 2016) had not been repaid to them.

Furthermore, in *Accorinti*, the defendant (the ECB) claimed inadmissibility of the new application on the grounds that a previous case was at the time pending before the General Court and that it allegedly aimed at circumventing the inadmissibility of the applications for annulment with regard to the same unlawful acts and seeking the same financial outcome. Indeed, on broadly the same factual premises and legal grounds, but with a rather weak reasoning, the General Court issued the Order of 25 June 2014 (Case T-224/12), which found the action inadmissible on the grounds of lack of direct concern to establish *locus standi*. However, in assessing the new application the Court rejected the argument of pending litigation, considering that the wording of that new application set out the essential elements required under Article 44(1)(c) of the Rules of Procedure of the Court, to a sufficient standard and in a coherent and comprehensible manner.

It seems, after all, that the Court of Justice used very pragmatic criteria to deal with procedural issues concerning the crisis case law; when the pending case was of a kind that the Court felt that it deserved a decision on the merits it loosened the admissibility conditions. This was, for example, the case with Judgment of the Full Court of 10 December 2018 in Case C-621/18, *Wightman and others v Secretary of State for Exiting the European Union*, where the Court was asked by the Scottish Court of Session (Inner House, First Division) whether the UK could, after notification to the European Council of its intention to withdraw from the EU in accordance with Article 50 TEU, unilaterally revoke that notification and, if so, subject to what conditions. The decision was not of course strictly related to the financial crisis, but was part of the broader context of the crisis in Europe and the widespread euro-scepticism, caused fundamentally because of the crisis.

The Court, in a decision that attracted huge political attention and was published the day before the House of Commons was called upon to decide on the Agreement concluded between the UK Government and the European Commission (and just 37 days after the publication of the referral judgment by the Scottish court), held that it is permissible for a Member State to unilaterally revoke the notification of the intention to withdraw from the EU pursuant to the UK's own national constitutional requirements. Yet, one might reasonably argue that the judgment trespassed the admissibility criteria set by the Court in Judgment of 26 February 2013 in Case C-399/11, *Melloni v Ministerio Fiscal*, ie that the questions sent by the refereeing national court are not hypothetical. However, in the light of the significance of the case, it was a widespread belief that the Court of Justice could not have refused to take on the case and allow some margin of manoeuvre for the eventual remain of the UK in the EU.

With regard to the *right to invoke grounds of review*, the General Court of the EU took a very restrictive view in *Sotiropoulou*, where it dismissed a claim raised in the course of an action for damages against the EU by individuals on the ground of alleged infringement of the principles of conferral of powers and subsidiarity. The Court had recourse to the scope and nature of those principles and reiterated that they both intend to ensure the Union's institutional balance, ie the division of competences between the Member States and the Union, as well as the exercise of Union competences, rather than the protection of individuals. Consequently, they do not confer rights on individuals and any breach of those principles is not in itself sufficient to establish the non-contractual liability of the EU; therefore, the applicants' argument could not be sustained.

Yet, the rationale of the Court was highly legalistic and doctrinally unsubstantiated. The doctrines of subsidiarity and conferral of powers do determine the division of competences between the Union and the Member States. However, these rules have been set to support state sovereignty against trespasses of powers by the EU institutions. Accordingly, it is rather inappropriate to deprive the actual holder of sovereignty, ie the citizens of the Member States, from the right to invoke those principles in cases of alleged breaches on the part of the Union. It is in this sense rather contradictory that the Treaty of Lisbon designated the national parliaments as the main guardians of adherence to those principles by involving them in the regulatory process of the Union, whereas at the same time the actual source of legitimacy of those parliaments is altogether excluded from invoking those grounds before the judicial bodies of the EU. In this way, the General Court de facto excluded violations of the conferral of powers and subsidiarity altogether from the scope of unlawfulness of the extra-contractual liability of the Union, an immunity that does not stem from any provision of EU law and is contrary to the proper idea of conferral of powers and subsidiarity that are, arguably, cornerstones of the EU architecture.

In the light of the above, one might reasonably argue that the EU courts did not substantially guarantee a fair trial in challenges of conditionality requirements attached to financial assistance packages. In this respect, Hinarejos rightly argues that this judicial approach has been neither sustainable nor coherent and that a more desirable course of action would be for the courts to accept a link to EU law (and, in turn, the admissibility of the grounds raised before them), and then possibly show restraint on the merits of each case.[26] Interestingly, the no-touch approach on the part of the EU courts was complemented by a strong position vis-a-vis domestic courts concerning the former's actual monopoly in interpreting EU or quasi-EU law.

---

[26] A Hinarejos, *The Euro Area Crisis in Constitutional Perspective* (Oxford, Oxord University Press, 2015) 131–36, 152.

For instance, following publication of the Court of Justice's judgment in *Sindicato dos Bancários do Norte*, the referring employment tribunal was called to decide whether it still wished to move forward with its request for a preliminary ruling in the second case, despite the fact that there were no significant factual differences. The response was in the affirmative and the Court of Justice dismissed the new request for a preliminary ruling, on the same grounds, in *Sindicato Nacional dos Profissionais de Seguros e Afins*; indirectly, the Court conveyed some degree of annoyance by declaring that the mere fact that the national court had reworded its request, while adhering to the original questions, was not sufficient to establish the Court's jurisdiction to hear and determine the second request.

Most importantly, in *Gauweiler*, the Court of Justice seized the moment to categorically communicate to the Federal Constitutional Court of Germany (and ultimately to all national courts) that preliminary rulings are binding upon domestic courts and that the Court of Justice remained the ultimate adjudicator of issues relating to the interpretation of EU law and the compatibility of national legislation with that law. The long overdue first request for a preliminary ruling by the Federal Constitutional Court of Germany in *Gauweiler* and that court's relevant observation with regard to the possibility of non-adherence to the Court of Justice's ruling, if that ruling was found in contradiction to the domestic Constitution, did not alter the basic position that national courts are bound by the Luxembourg ruling. Although the Court of Justice prudently refrained from declaring the request for a preliminary ruling inadmissible on the grounds of inappropriate judicial reservations on the part of the German Court (a scenario that could have resulted in an open conflict with unpredictable consequences), the principle of supremacy of EU law and of the exclusive competence of the Court of Justice to uniformly set the applicable judicial rules on matters of EU law and its relationship to domestic law has not been curtailed.

Interestingly, the issue of inadmissibility resulting from to reservations raised by the referring court was raised primarily by the intervening Italian Government, which relied on previous case law of the Court establishing that a decision on a request for a preliminary ruling may only be rendered provided that it is binding upon the national court rather than purely advisory in nature.[27] The Court of Justice reiterated that, since the issue referred by the German Federal Constitutional Court directly concerned the interpretation and application of EU law, the relevant judgment would have definitive consequences on the resolution of the main proceedings. The Court of Justice placed emphasis on the institutional division of competences between national courts and EU courts and essentially ignored the reservation expressed by the Constitutional Court by holding that its own ruling would be firmly binding on the referring court as regards the interpretation or the validity of the acts of the EU institutions in question, for the purposes of the decision to be rendered in the main proceedings.

---

[27] CJEU Judgment of 28 March 1995 in Case C-346/93, *Kleinwort Benson*, paras 23 and 24.

The Court of Justice did, however, make some concessions towards the referring court, in that it ruled that certain safeguards must apply in order for the OMT programme to be compatible with primary EU law – safeguards that were, nevertheless, rather few and of less significance than those brought forward by the Federal Constitutional Court. That national court chose not to carry on the conflict; it accepted the ruling of the Court of Justice, emphasising on the conditionality established by that ruling. This outcome constitutes an undeniable judicial victory for the Court of Luxembourg and for the predominance of EU law altogether. As Tridimas and Xanthoulis rightly put it, the ECB's policy actions within the EMU constitute a transnational matter which cannot be determined unilaterally by a domestic court without risking the fragmentation of EU law: 'In a power-sharing political system, such as the EU, the democratic legitimacy of Germany cannot provide convincing grounds for resisting the ultimate power of the ECJ to determine the legality of an EU act'.[28] Yet, it was proved that allegations for breaches of human rights as a result of the MoUs did not find a place in the judicial scrutiny of EU courts.

B. Domestic Structures

One may come up with a variety of typologies concerning domestic courts based on the responses given to questions relevant to the financial crisis: strong and weak; active and restraint; pro-European and euro-sceptical. Yet, presumably, the most accurate and interesting classification from the point of view of the judicial role in the institutional determination of the crisis is the distinction between sovereignty-oriented versus rights-oriented courts.

Sovereignty-oriented courts are courts mostly defending sovereignty through national constitutionalism and representative democracy. This judicial stance reasonably comes from the courts of lender States, which have had to deal with issues of democratic legitimacy and possible usurpation of parliamentary powers. These courts placed particular emphasis on structural aspects of the polity, such as the relationship between the parliament and the executive (internal balance of powers) and between the State and the EU (external balance of powers). This is par excellence the case of the Federal Constitutional Court of Germany. With regard to the internal balance of powers, the Court took over to protect the competences and the procedural guarantees of the legislature.

In performing this role as guardian of sovereignty, the Court did not hesitate to expressly set out the process that the German Government ought to follow when negotiating with the EU institutions and the governments of other Member States,

---

[28] T Tridimas and N Xanthoulis, 'A Legal Analysis of the Gauweiler Case' in F Fabbrini (ed), *The European Court of Justice, the European Central Bank and the Supremacy of EU Law*, Special Issue (2016) 23 *Maastricht Journal of European & Comparative Law* 1, 36–37.

as well as the exact disclaimers that must be included in the relevant agreements, to impose an effective right of information in favour of the Parliament, to prohibit the transfer of parliamentary competences on relevant matters from the plenary to a parliamentary sub-committee and to emphatically declare that any large amount of financial assistance had to be approved in advance and ad hoc by the Parliament for it to retain its budgetary autonomy.

Finally, in *Gauweiler*, which initiated the dialogue with the Court of Justice, the Constitutional Court requested a delineation of the powers of the ECB, while setting prerequisites for the upheaval of the ruling coming from Luxembourg. Three observations on the crisis case law of the German Federal Constitutional Court are worth mentioning. First, that Court consciously took on the role of protector of national sovereignty and representation not only with respect to Germany but Europe-wise. According to Komárek, the German Constitutional Court's insistence on the meaningful participation of the German Parliament in the political debate concerning the financial crisis and on the adherence to the Union legality should not be seen as a defence of the individual interests of Germans, but as an expression of concern for democracy, which is undermined by the national governments willingly accepting constraints through the new regime of European fiscal governance at supranational level.[29]

Second, while performing its role as guardian of national constitutionalism, the Court also took on considerations on the survival of the European project. Thus, it made a judicial compromise in upholding the emergency measures while imposing specific strict conditions upon Union financial assistance policies. This compromise reflected, albeit not necessarily to a full extent, the general belief in the country that a red line ought to be set in the governmental discretion on grounds of sovereignty and democracy. According to Mattias Wendel, in reference to the ESM and Fiscal Treaty case, the 'conditional yes' judgment (ie permitting the ratification of the challenged reform instruments in general, but demanding certain additional measures to be taken in order to meet constitutional standards) was not unforeseen, yet it stood in sharp contrast to the hope of a considerable part of the German population that the Court would stop the ESM, at least temporarily, or even call for a referendum on the basis of Article 146 of the Basic Law, an expectation which had been nourished not least by some of the judges themselves.[30]

Third, in this judicial compromise, the Court's reasoning suffered, on occasions, from a self-contradictory rationale. Pavlos Eleftheriadis shrewdly criticised the judgment on the First Adjustment Programme for Greece as essentially suffering from false mechanics: it seemingly purported to safeguard the powers

---

[29] J Komárek, 'National Constitutional Courts in the European Constitutional Democracy' (2014) 12 *International Journal of Constitutional Law* 525, 538.

[30] M Wendel, 'Judicial Restraint and the Return to Openness: The Decision of the German Federal Constitutional Court on the ESM and the Fiscal Treaty of 12 September 2012' (2013) 14 *German Law Journal* 22.

of the Parliament but eventually challenged the core of parliamentary choices by suggesting that a higher commitment might have been unconstitutional. What the Court presumably appears to be suggesting to Parliament is that there are certain economic policies that are so risky as to be considered unconstitutional and 'undemocratic', even though they have been drawn by the most legitimate body.[31]

The issue of sovereignty was also raised in other jurisdictions, albeit not with the same force and insistence as in the case of the German Constitutional Court. Both the Estonian Constitutional Court and the Polish Constitutional Tribunal placed emphasis on safeguarding a substantive core of national constitutionalism and representative democracy in the dynamic evolution of the relationship between the EU and the Member States, usually enhancing the legal reasoning under the legal cover of constitutional identity, but did not go as far as to declare unconstitutionality of the provisions of the ESM Treaty introducing, by way of derogation to the ordinary unanimity-based decision-making, the possibility to have recourse to an emergency voting procedure, which weakened national voting share and veto powers.

Interestingly, the Estonian Constitutional Court, in the exact same context of a challenge against the ratification of the ESM Treaty, fell back from the ruling of its German counterpart and upheld the constitutionality of the competence of a parliamentary sub-committee to decide, instead of the plenary, on the relevant matters. Furthermore, the Constitutional Court of Belgium, despite dismissing the complaint against the Fiscal Compact as inadmissible and finding no evident ground of unconstitutionality, stated, in an obiter dictum, that the national constitutional identity, enshrined in representative democracy, cannot be curtailed through a restriction of parliamentary powers. Similarly, the French Constitutional Council found that the Fiscal Compact, especially the budgetary constraints thereof, did not require any constitutional amendments; thus, it validated French accession to the Treaty.

Rights-oriented domestic courts primarily focus on the impact of the crisis on the protection of the human rights. For obvious reasons, this judicial attitude is mostly demonstrated, although with significant variations, in the courts of the States that received financial rescue packages and were called upon to review the constitutionality of the conditionality attached thereto. The most active courts in this respect were the Portuguese ones, which on many occasions set aside statutes involving both salary and pension cuts. The Greek courts were very reluctant, in the first phase of the crisis, to effectively address human rights issues and consistently refused to uphold claims for the submission of a request for a preliminary ruling. Yet again, at some point, well into the crisis, the Hellenic Council of State diversified its case law and assumed the responsibility to declare reductions as violating property rights and the principle of the social state by essentially

---

[31] P Eleftheriadis, 'Democracy in the Eurozone' in W-G Ringe and PM Huber (eds), *Legal Challenges in the Global Financial Crisis: Bail-outs, the Euro and Regulation* (Oxford, Hart Publishing, 2015) 27, 42.

assessing the cumulative effect of consecutive legislative acts interfering with human rights, thereby causing significant budgetary turbulence. Interestingly, the courts of debtor countries were mostly engaged in cases of salary and pension cuts and much less in cases of reconfiguration of taxation and social security burdens. Although in some cases, such as in the case of Greece, tax and social security burdens increased tremendously, resulting in an exorbitant loss of income that was proportionately more onerous in nature than any salary/pension cut, the direct and visible impact of the latter on personal and family status and on the subsequent fall in living standards may explain the different level of attention in those cases.

The rights-oriented judicial approach is, generally speaking, less interventionist than the parliamentary-oriented one. This is so because the judicial role revolves primarily around safeguarding the people's rights as enshrined in the Constitution. The idea of the court as guardian of the fundamental rights is indeed uncontestable and reflects the historic evolution of constitutionalism and the rule of law. This perception of justice as fairness cannot altogether be transferred to the level of safeguarding the polity. In the latter case, what is essentially at stake is the division of competences and the preservation of sovereignty, for which one might reasonably argue that the courts are not the appropriate fora to determine possible conflicts: representative democracy is strictly linked to the parliament and, therefore, it is for the parliament itself to resolve matters pertaining to separation of powers and checks and balances within and beyond the State. This is why most Constitutions acknowledge a certain degree of autonomy to national parliaments and provide immunity of *interna corporis* from external judicial review.

Yet, in the context of the financial crisis, the concept of a powerful, self-reliant and self-determined parliament has been seriously compromised, with regard to both the lender and the debtor States. In the case of lender States, the executives systematically tried to evade parliamentary scrutiny of decisions to grant financial assistance to endangered countries. In the case of debtor States, domestic parliaments were totally absent in the negotiations and were called upon only to confirm executive choices. Accordingly, parliaments proved rather unable to protect themselves against a serious constitutional downgrading of their respective political significance. This is why, on occasions, constitutional courts took over to protect parliamentarism by referring to constitutional concepts that do not often appear in the judicial reasoning, such as democracy and the rights stemming from the citizens' vote. The somewhat political argumentation on these issues, which is, to some extent, unavoidable due to the invocation of concepts closely linked to the polity, resulted in the relevant judgments appearing quite interventionist.

However, not even the German Federal Constitutional Court managed to stand firm against the Court of Justice. In spite of some strong language in the relevant decisions in *Gauweiler*, with regard to the conditions attached to the OMT programme so as to confirm its compatibility with primary EU law, the Constitutional Court eventually accepted the Luxembourg ruling and retracted considerations of unconstitutionality included in the referring judgment.

If taken strictly, those considerations should have led to a revision of the German Basic Law in order to make it compatible with the Union's new legal scenery, whereas in fact there have been no amendments to the German Constitution following the euro crisis.

By way of contrast, most domestic courts of the debtor countries have been particularly self-restrained. Although, technically speaking, the crucial questions were linked to a downgrading of the right to property, in the main relevant cases they were treated as of highly political nature, as demonstrated by oft-repeated statements concerning exceptional circumstances and the wide margin of appreciation allowed to the political branches of government in order to prevent state budgetary default. Therefore, a holistic assessment of domestic crisis case law points to a clear paradox: in cases of a strong political connotation where considerations of democracy, sovereignty and constitutional pluralism were at the forefront, the courts were inclined to be more radical, whereas in cases of a less political nature where the primary legal issue was the interpretation of the constitutional clauses on human rights, the courts were more deferent.[32] Two practical illustrations demonstrate the different approach, in the crisis era, of the lenders' strong domestic courts, which focused on sovereignty, as opposed to the debtors' weak domestic courts, which focused on rights: the procedural prerequisites to file an application for annulment of the relevant acts; and the preliminary reference to the Court of Justice.

As regards the *procedural prerequisites* of the proceedings, domestic courts of the debtor or neutral States were stricter in applying admissibility conditions, in order to avoid entering into the merits of the relevant cases, especially as regards the right to property. On the one hand, some courts dismissed such cases on the grounds of lack of jurisdiction (eg the Cypriot courts, which considered, in the deposit haircut cases, that the legal remedies in question were akin to civil jurisdiction, albeit strong public interest was involved) or legal standing (eg the Constitutional Court of Belgium in the challenge against the TSCG). On the other hand, some national courts on the lenders' side have been rather generous when it comes to such admissibility conditions. In this direction, the German Federal Constitutional Court used the general constitutional right to vote not only as a substantive yardstick of checks and balances and representative democracy but also as a *locus standi* ground for citizens to challenge EU rules in the context of preventive and abstract judicial review.

---

[32] Former President of the Hellenic Council of State Panagiotis Pikrammenos wrote: 'Judicial reasoning … must recognise the wide discretion afforded to political authority as a result of legitimacy thereof … Judges must neither be a sovereign nor absent. They have the highest constitutional mandate to identify and set the limits within which political authority must be exercised in order to exercise its broad decisive powers. This mission is even more important at times of crisis during which there barely is a margin of wrong choices since their consequences may be devastating', P Pikrammenos, 'Public Law in Extraordinary Circumstances from the Point of View of the Annulment of the Administrative Procedure' (2012) 44 *Theory and Practice of Administrative Law* 97, 100 (in Greek).

Thus, in *Gauweiler*, the Court granted standing to all citizens in order to guarantee their ability to influence the European integration process, by ensuring that a transfer of sovereign powers only took place in accordance with the requirements of the German Constitution; otherwise, the EU institutions' ultra vires acts would violate the European integration agenda laid down in the Act of Approval and, consequently, the principle of sovereignty of the German people and the national constitutional identity. The Court's rationale was that legitimacy for such power assignment required more involved citizens and, in judicial terms, this involvement ought to be expressed through an expansion of the scope of the standing to bring challenges against statutes allegedly violating the competences of the Parliament.

An interesting analogy can be found in the UK Supreme Court Brexit Judgment *Miller*, where the application was filed by Gina Miller and Deir dos Santos and supported by a group of people on the ground of their right of residence in the UK under EU law, a group claiming rights of residence from persons permitted to reside in the UK under EU law, including children and carers, a group of mostly UK citizens residing elsewhere in the EU, a group of mostly non-UK EU nationals residing in the UK and the Independent Workers Union of Great Britain, all invoking potential irreversible damage from the initiation of the process. Assessed by reference to the continental standards, such application for annulment would have most probably been found inadmissible. However, the standing issue did not draw the attention of the Supreme Court since, interestingly, the defendants did not raise a relevant allegation or the political nature of the issue at stake. The reason for this evident expansion of standing has to do, as in the case of the German Federal Constitutional Court, with the Supreme Court's judicial predilection to operate as guardian of the sovereignty of Parliament, which of course in the UK has a strong tradition of sovereignty.

As regards the judicial *preliminary reference* policy, the discussion is reasonably dominated by the first ever referral by the German Federal Constitutional Court, which was a gesture of a highly symbolical nature, especially given the circumstances under which that it was made. Interestingly, in almost the same period, the Spanish Constitutional Tribunal also filed, for the first time ever, a request for a preliminary ruling to the Court of Justice[33] on an issue that, albeit non-relevant to the economic crisis, was of akin importance to the European structures, ie the variable levels of protection of fundamental rights on national and EU level with regard to the execution of a European Arrest Warrant, which led to the well-cited *Melloni* case.[34]

Following the ruling of the Court of Justice, the Spanish Constitutional Tribunal unanimously reversed its well-established case law to make sure it aligns, without

---

[33] Spanish Constitutional Court Order of 9 June 2011, ATC 86/2011.
[34] CJEU of 16 February 2013 in Case C-399/11, *Melloni v Ministerio Fiscal*.

any reservations, with the *Melloni* criteria[35] – a remarkable analogy in comparison to the response of the German Federal Constitutional Court on *Gauweiler*. Moreover, national courts of the countries having received financial assistance demonstrated significant variations in their preliminary reference policy, although most of those courts had had a long history of such references in the past. Irish and Portuguese courts did make use of the tool of preliminary reference, mostly as a means of, presumably, providing further legitimacy to their judgments, thus avoiding taking on full responsibility for the outcome thereof. On the other hand, the Hellenic Council of State and the Cypriot High Court have been the most reluctant to address the preliminary reference issues. Yet, both Greek and Cypriot cases eventually reached the EU General Court through direct actions for damages, which nevertheless kept the symbolic relevance of such disputes to a minor level.[36]

Finally, an interesting aspect of the preliminary references in cases relevant to the financial crisis, from the side of the debtor countries, such as Portugal or Romania, is that lower courts took the initiative to refer questions of EU law to the Court of Justice. This can be attributed not only to the personal idiosyncrasy of the judges composing the lower courts (where judicial composition is usually much smaller in numbers), but also to how each instance of justice perceives its role. Thus, on many occasions constitutional or supreme courts also perceive themselves as political actors entrusted not only with the protection of fundamental rights, but also – if not foremost – with the maintenance of an adequate level of sovereignty of the State, especially as regards delegation of powers to international organisations. Obviously, when it comes to the challenge of austerity measures aiming at financial recovery, it takes a truly bold and independent judiciary to decide the annulment of the relevant acts or, less so, to make a reference for a preliminary ruling to the Court of Justice with an obviously unpredictable outcome. Overall, one might argue that the vehicle of preliminary reference to the Court of Justice has, in general, been upgraded in the course of the financial crisis, although there has been no judgment of that Court ruling against EU acts or national austerity measures.

---

[35] Spanish Constitutional Court Judgment of 13 February 2014, STC 26/2014. See, A Torres Pérez, 'Melloni in Three Acts: From Dialogue to Monologue' (2014) 10 *European Constitutional Law Review* 308.

[36] Interestingly, in the PSI cases before the Hellenic Council of State, a well-substantiated dissenting opinion suggested the submission of a request for a preliminary ruling to the Court of Justice, although such claim was not made by the plaintiffs, on ground that there was evidently an issue of EU law and the Council had an obligation to do so as a domestic court of last resort, even on its own motion, in order to safeguard the supremacy of EU law. This dissenting view found that the PSI scheme had a double cross- border element, ie *ratione loci*, since some bondholders had their domicile or official seat in other EU Member States (ie Germany), and *ratione materiae*, for those established in the Greek territory, since bonds were by definition negotiable in the international secondary financial markets, too. In terms of the merits, this dissenting view found that the legal issue was not unquestionable on the grounds of alleged violation of proportionality because of the existence of less restrictive alternatives, thus suggesting a reference for a preliminary ruling.

III. EU Enhanced Competences

In terms of competence, the basic regulatory instruments at EU level are the principles of subsidiarity, proportionality and conferred powers (Article 5 TEU). The first two principles refer to the use of competences, whereas the third principle refers to their limits. The principle of *subsidiarity*, as implemented at EU level, provides that, in areas which do not fall within its exclusive competence, the Union shall act only if and in so far as the objectives of the proposed action cannot be sufficiently achieved by the Member States, either at central level or at regional and local level, but can rather, by reason of the scale or effects of the proposed action, be better achieved at Union level (Preamble and Articles 5(1)(3)(4), 12(b) TEU and Article 352(2) TFEU).

The principle of *proportionality* provides that the content and form of Union action shall not exceed what is necessary to achieve the objectives of the Treaties (Preamble and Articles 5(1)(3)(4), 12(b) TEU). Protocol (No 2) on the application of the principles of subsidiarity and proportionality, annexed to the EU Treaties, specifies the process of adherence of EU institutions to those principles.[37] Accordingly, before proposing European legislative acts, the Commission, unless there is exceptional urgency, consults widely with the relevant stakeholders, taking, where appropriate, into account the regional and local dimension of the action envisaged.

Draft European legislative acts (ie proposals from the Commission, initiatives from a group of Member States, initiatives from the European Parliament, requests from the Court of Justice, recommendations from the ECB and requests from the European Investment Bank for the adoption of a European legislative acts) should:

(a) take account of the need for any burden, whether financial or administrative, falling upon the Union, national governments, regional or local authorities, economic operators and citizens, to be minimised and commensurate with the objective to be achieved;

(b) contain a detailed statement, making it possible to assess compliance with the principles of subsidiarity and proportionality, including assessment of the proposal's financial impact and, in the case of a European framework law, of its implications for the rules to be put in place by Member States, and, where necessary, regional legislation; and

(c) be forwarded to national Parliaments.

Any national Parliament or any chamber of a national Parliament may, within six weeks from the date of transmission of a draft European legislative act, transmit to the Presidents of the European Parliament, the Council and the Commission

---

[37] OJ C 115, 9.5.2008, p 206–09, see T Tridimas, *The General Principles of EU Law, Oxford European Union Law Library*, 2nd edn (Oxford, Oxford University Press, 2006) 175–92.

a reasoned opinion stating the reasons why it considers that the draft in question does not comply with the principle of subsidiarity. Each national Parliament shall have two votes, allocated on the basis of the national parliamentary system; in bicameral systems, each chamber has one vote. Where reasoned opinions on a draft European legislative Act's non-compliance with the principle of subsidiarity represent at least one-third of all the votes allocated to the national Parliaments, the draft must be reviewed. After such review, the initiating bodies may decide to maintain, amend or withdraw the draft by giving reasons for this. The Court of Justice is granted jurisdiction over actions on grounds of infringement of the principle of subsidiarity by a European legislative act.

The principle of *conferred powers* signifies that the EU only enjoys those competences that have been granted to it by the Member States according to their domestic processes and have been incorporated into primary EU law. Under the principle of conferral, the Union can only act within the limits of the competences conferred upon it by the Member States in the Treaties to attain the objectives set out therein, whereas competences not conferred upon the Union in the Treaties remain with the Member States. This principle served to safeguard a core of national sovereignty, in the sense that the Member States retained a substantial veto in relation to the competences to be granted to the Union. Thus, in the absence of such transfer of competences on a primary EU law level, the Member States legitimately exercised the relevant powers.

This aspect clearly reflects the genuine concern of the Member States that the Union is rapidly developing as an autonomous system of law and tends to expand to areas that were previously considered as a sovereign monopoly of the States. Craig and Burca shrewdly put down the EU 'competence problem' to the interaction of four variables: the Member States choice as to the scope of EU competence, as expressed in the Treaty revisions; the Council and European Parliament acceptance of legislation that fleshed out the Treaty Articles; the case law of the EU judicial institutions; and, the decisions taken by the institutions as to how to interpret and to prioritise the power accorded to the EU. An additional feature is, presumably, the competence reservations, more akin in multi-layered EU with different ambits of competences and participants. This partly makes sense: those not participating, as a matter of political choice, in the Schengen agreement or the euro area consider such policies as rather expansionist and, although technically they do not apply to them, the domino effect of creating semi-autonomous subgroups under the Union umbrella cannot but exercise a significant influence upon the totality of the EU structures and, in reflection, upon its Member States. This somewhat psychological adherence to conventional sovereignty became all the more visible in the course of European integration, with the new entries expressing more concerns as to the scope of competences assumed by the EU institutions.

The vertical shift of the equilibrium of power from States to supranational entities at the time of crisis has occurred through enhanced EU competences in four forms: new statutory powers granted to EU institutions; implied powers associated to existing competences; and contractual commitments assumed by the Member States towards the EU.

A. New EU Competences

As regards new EU competences, this mostly refers to new economic governance. Although fiscal policy formally remains with the Member States, a great deal of centralisation has occurred in the EU economic governance both in terms of the processes, including the monitoring of financial policies through extensive supervisory powers for the Commission the ECB and the Court of Justice, and in terms of the substantive restriction basically imposed through the Fiscal Compact. In this way, the original paradox that the monetary union is based on a centralised policy led by the Union and a fiscal policy remaining decentralised to Member States, has been mitigated on the basis of the introduction of stricter rules of discipline that substantially hamper national financial flexibility.

In fact, the procedural surveillance introduced by the European Semester and the substantive standards set out by the Fiscal Compact historically constitute, in my mind, the most violent transfer of economic policy-making powers from a sovereign State, which does, however, retain its sovereignty. Gerda Falkner stresses the EU paradox by wondering how and why these reforms were actually possible in an acute crisis, whereas crucial regulations in the financial markets and economic governance, albeit not a new idea, had been politically blocked for many years preceding the crisis, which is not readily explicable from a behavioural point of view.[38]

The new powers of the EU institutions were confirmed by the Court of Justice in *Pringle*,[39] based on a rather generous statutory interpretation of the relevant provisions of primary EU law. As regards the powers established by the policies of EU institutions, most notably the ECB, which has taken over a series of actions to support the financial stability of the Union and the euro area, the Court of Justice gave its seal of approval with regard to the OMT programme in *Gauweiler*,[40] through a more constructive interpretation of the provisions of the Treaties, given that in that case there was a total lack of a legal basis. In both cases, the Court of Justice seems to uphold EU competences not explicitly prohibited but structurally associated to powers explicitly granted to the institutions. In any case, as Tridimas observes, the most salient feature of the new competences is that they mostly refer to the monitoring, compliance and enforcement of EU law, with regard to financial policies of the Member States, rather than law-generating

---

[38] G Falkner, 'The EU's Problem-Solving Capacity and Legitimacy in a Crisis Context: A Virtuous or Vicious Circle?' (2016) 39 *West European Politics* 953.
[39] Above, ch 3 section I A ii.
[40] Above, ch 3 section I A ii.

powers. In this view, the transition of the EU from law-maker to supervisor signals an upgrade of the integration process, a more advanced form of federalism, and, perhaps, a less romantic and more threatening view of EU integration.[41]

B. Implied EU Powers

'Implied powers' are the powers that are not explicitly granted to the EU but are in some way connected with existing competences and are, therefore, considered as having been conferred upon the Union. Although the doctrine of implied powers has never been used *eo nomine* in the case law of the Court of Justice, it is apparently developing as an escape mechanism from the strict and generally inflexible framework of the requirement of conferred powers.

The principle of conferred powers connotes two significant interpretative issues:

(a) who has the presumption of competence (*Kompetenz-Kompetenz*) within the Union legal landscape (the presumption question); and

(b) whether the Union may assume powers not explicitly but rather implicitly attributed to it (the implicitness question).

As for the presumption question, there is no doubt that the presumption of competence lies with the Member States. This can be deduced not only from the statutory interpretation of the fundamental EU texts, but also from the general understanding of the foundations of the Union. In terms of statutory interpretation, such presumption in favour of the Member States arises from a rather pompous wording:

- the proper establishment of the EU is explicitly based on conferral of competences by the Member States to the Union, in order for the former to attain their common objectives (Article 1(1) TEU);

- the Union pursues its objectives by appropriate means 'commensurate with the competences which are conferred upon it' in the Treaties (Article 3(6) TEU);

- the principle of conferred constitutes the 'limit' of Union competences (Article 5(1) TEU);

- the Union shall act only 'within the limits of the competences conferred' (Article 5(2) TEU);

- competences not conferred upon the Union in the Treaties 'remain' with the Member States (Article 4 TEU and Declaration 18 annexed to the Final Act of the Intergovernmental Conference that adopted the Treaty of Lisbon);

---

[41] T Tridimas, 'The ECJ and the National Courts: Dialogue, Cooperation, and Instability' in D Chalmers and A Arnull (eds), *The Oxford Handbook of European Union Law* (Oxford, Oxford University Press, 2015) 403, 408–10.

- the Union shall ensure consistency between its policies and activities, taking all of its objectives into account and 'in accordance with the principle of conferral of powers' (Article 7 TFEU);

- each Union institution shall act 'within the limits of the powers conferred on it' in the Treaties and in conformity with the procedures, conditions and objectives set out in them (Article 13(2) TEU).

In terms of the general understanding of the Union structure, EU law has been conceived as a limited concession to state sovereignty in specific areas in which the Member States do wish to achieve a higher level of coordination.

As for the implicitness question, the analysis becomes less straightforward. The mere fact that there is a presumption of competence lying with the Member States does not necessarily imply that conferred EU competences cannot conceivably enhance powers not explicitly granted but causally linked with those explicitly conferred. A comparison of the federal systems of governance clearly demonstrates this. In most cases of federal states, the institutional allocation of competences between the federation and the states is beset by the principle that the presumption of competences lies with the states and not with the federation, yet in most such legal systems the case law has developed so as to attribute to the federation (ie the level of governance against which the presumption of governance operates) powers that are connected with those constitutionally attributed to them, albeit not explicitly granted, ie 'implied powers'.[42]

However, there are two significant differences between the EU and federal states; one is legal and the other is structural. Regarding the *legal* difference, unlike some national legal orders, the EU constitutional order does not include any provision that could, even remotely, sustain the doctrine of implied powers.[43] Indeed, EU law, as of its original Treaties, contains a clause of a totally different orientation, which is nevertheless characterised as 'flexibility clause'. Accordingly, Article 352 TFEU stipulates that, should an action by the Union be proved necessary, within the framework of the policies defined in the Treaties, to attain

---

[42] The most notable example in this context is the US polity. Although the Xth Amendment of the Constitution categorically states that the powers not delegated to the federation by the Constitution, nor prohibited by it to the States, are reserved to the States respectively or to the people, the US Federal Supreme Court, as early as 1819, in well-cited case *MucCulloch v Maryland* 17 US 316 (1819) upheld the Congress's competence to incorporate a central federal bank. With this decision, the interpretive principle of 'implied powers' was introduced for the first time, implying, albeit with some case-specific variations, that the Federation includes not only the powers expressly referred to in the Constitution but also all those implicitly associated with these competences, in the sense that the Constitution confers competence on the Congress to enact any 'necessary and proper' law to implement the constitutional powers entrusted to federal bodies. The value of this decision is so important that it could be described as the survival principle of the federal state, given the presumption of competence in favour of the States.

[43] Article I, Section 8 of the US Constitution, for example, stipulates that the Congress shall have the power to make all Laws which shall be 'necessary and proper' for carrying into execution the powers enumerated in the same Art of the Constitution and all other powers vested in the Government or in any department or officer thereof.

one of the objectives set out therein, and the Treaties do not provide for the necessary powers, the Council, acting unanimously on a proposal from the Commission and after obtaining the consent of the European Parliament, shall adopt the appropriate measures.[44] Where the measures in question are adopted by the Council in accordance with a special legislative procedure, it shall also act unanimously on a proposal from the Commission, after obtaining the consent of the European Parliament.

The Court of Justice has been very cautious with the scope of application of this clause. In its notable opinion 2/94 on the accession by the Community to the European Convention on Human Rights,[45] the Court of Justice held that Article 352 TFEU is an integral part of an institutional system based on the principle of conferred powers and, therefore, 'cannot serve as a basis for widening the scope of Community powers beyond the general framework created by the provisions of the Treaty as a whole and, in particular, by those that define the tasks and the activities of the Community';[46] nor could it be used as a means to go around the formal amendment process of the Treaties. The same wording was employed in Declaration No 42 to the TFEU annexed to the Final Act of the Intergovernmental Conference, which adopted the Treaty of Lisbon.[47]

In fact, Article 352 does not apply to any potential policy objective of the EU, such as integration or ever closer Union, but merely to the purposes specifically enshrined within the constitutional texts of the Treaties; said Article ought to be interpreted within the framework of conferred powers, subsidiarity and proportionality. It seems that the Union legislator, through Article 352, aims particularly at excluding any other form of implicit power in favour of the EU. This is why this clause, although conceivably a potential all-embracing institutional weapon at the hands of the EU institutions, has been used on very rare occasions and with extreme self-restraint with regard to issues which, on account of their subject matter, would not raise significant objections on the part of the Member States.[48]

At any rate, the severe procedural requirements for triggering the process – predominantly a unanimous Council – operate rather reversely as regards the envisaged aim, since the intended flexibility clause renders the system of implied powers totally inflexible, in essence. The 'flexibility clause' is actually a rather inflexible formal process, essentially excluding any backdoor enhancement of further implied powers on the Union.

---

[44] Ex Art 308 TEC, ex 235 EEC.

[45] Opinion 2/94, of 28 March 1996, para 30.

[46] The Union competence on the matter was overturned by the Treaty of Lisbon, which explicitly provides that the Union shall accede to the Convention and that this accession shall not affect the Union's competences as defined in the Treaties (Art 6(2) TEU). This is why the Court of Justice did not deal with this specific matter in its later Opinion No 2/13 of 18 December 2014 regarding the same issue.

[47] OJ C 326/339, 26.10.2012.

[48] eg, the adoption of Reg 168/2007 of 15 February 2007 establishing the Agency on Fundamental Rights OJ L53, 22.2.2007, p 1.

In relation to the *structural* difference, most importantly, there is a significant variation between federal states and the EU in terms of their institutional architecture: the former enjoy full sovereignty, whereas the latter lacks sovereignty altogether. In the case of federal states, where the presumption of competence lies with the states, the federation remains the only sovereign and it is, therefore, reasonable that, as a matter of principle, any doubt as to the extent of the competences granted should be seen as proper balancing between sovereignty of the federation and the presumption of competence of the states; in essence, the implied powers doctrine is akin to the federal structure. By way of contrast, such balancing is not possible in the case of the EU. This is so because both sovereignty and the presumption of power lay with the Member States, therefore a generous interpretation concerning the competences of the EU institutions, so as to enhance essential implied powers, would be contrary to the overall architecture of the Union.[49] In the absence of a constitutional transition of the EU, the doctrine of implied powers would appear rather inappropriate.

In theory, the question of the informal extension of EU powers is rather preemptive: to the extent that the principle of conferred powers existed as a cornerstone effectively determining the allocation of powers between the EU and the Member States, in the sense that the competence of the former's institutions could only be materialised through the formal expression of the latter's sovereign will, in the absence of *clear* indications to the opposite a presumption exists in favour of the competence of the Member States. The exclusion of expansion of EU competences through a generous interpretation of the Treaties is conceptually collateral of the convergence at the same level of Union governance, ie the Member States' level, of both sovereignty and the presumption of competence.

Having recourse to arguments of the legal personality of the Union and of the principle of effectiveness of EU law is not, presumably, conclusive. Pursuant to the express letter of Article 47 TEU, legal personality merely connotes specific *external* legal characteristics that are associated with this personality, namely that the Union may negotiate and conclude international agreements in accordance with its external commitments, that it may become a member of international organisations, and that it may join international conventions. The principle of effectiveness, in the broader rubric of Members States' commitment to sincere cooperation, implies a specific interpretation of EU law that will assure an existential minimum level of procedural and substantive guarantee of implementation of EU law, so as to produce effective results.

---

[49] Interestingly, prior to the establishment of the federal state of the United States, the 1787 Articles of Confederation – historically perhaps the most relevant pattern of institutional organisation vis-a-vis the EU as it stands currently – explicitly excluded, in Art 2, incidental or implied powers, arguably because of the very nature of the Confederation, which lacks sovereignty and exists on the basis of the expressed will of the sovereign states. The transition from a confederative legal system lacking sovereignty to a sovereign federal system essentially triggered the expansion of the implied powers doctrine in the US.

Thus, pursuant to Article 4(3) TEU, the Member States ought, in full mutual respect, to assist each other in carrying out tasks which flow from the Treaties, to take any appropriate measure, general or particular, to ensure fulfilment of the obligations arising out of the Treaties or resulting from the acts of the institutions of the Union and to facilitate the achievement of the Union's tasks and to refrain from any measure which could jeopardise the attainment of the Union's objectives. However, neither legal personality nor effectiveness may convincingly provide adequate grounds to trigger the very powerful institutional vehicle of expansion of EU competence outside powers explicitly granted, which would go contrary to the very essence of the operation of the Union as an international organisation, even considering its admittedly very dynamic perspective.

The doctrine of implied powers was not unknown to the EU legal order. Yet, it was restricted to EU external powers, doctrinally linked to the Union's own personality. In this field, the Treaties merely provided for community competences in the field of common commercial policy (Article 3(1)(e) TEU), conclusion with one or more third countries or international organisations of agreements establishing an association involving reciprocal rights and obligations, common action and special procedures (Article 217 TFEU) and some international pursuits complementary with the Member States. The crucial question remained whether the Union could conclude international agreements in other areas, too. In this context, the Court of Justice introduced the doctrine of implied *external* powers, allowing the Union to establish contractual links with third countries not only in areas where this competence was expressly set out by the Treaty, but also over the whole field of EU objectives, under the basic premise that the system of internal community measures might not be separated from that of external relations.[50]

The principle of implied external powers was introduced by Judgment of 14 July 1976 in Joined Cases 3/76, 4/76 and 6/76, *Kramer and others*, concerning the challenge of regulation for the conservation of the biological resources of the sea, founded upon the very nature of things, ie that the rule-making authority of the Union also extended *ratione materiae* to entry into international commitments as a means to ensure effectiveness and equitability: the authority of the EU institutions to enter into international commitments arose not only from an express conferral by the Treaty, but 'may equally flow implicitly from other provisions of the Treaty, from the Act of Accession and from measures adopted, within the framework of those provisions, by the Community institutions'. Thus, the only way to ensure the legitimate objectives of the Community 'both effectively and equitably' was through a system of rules binding on all the States concerned, including non-Member States, therefore 'it follows from the very duties and powers which Community law has established and assigned to the institutions of the Community on the internal level' that the Community had authority to enter into international commitments for the conservation of the resources of the sea.[51]

---

[50] CJEU Judgment of 31 March 1971 in Case 22/70, *Commission v Council* – the AETR case.
[51] Paragraphs 30–33.

Outside the area of EU external powers, the Court of Justice has acknowledged the doctrine of implied powers cautiously and in a rather incidental manner. In Judgment of 14 June 1976 in Case 8/55, *Fédération charbonnière de Belgique v High Authority*, the Court of Justice upheld the High Authority's competence to fix prices in Belgium Coal industry, albeit not explicitly provided in community law. In particular, Article 26 of the Convention on the Transitional Provisions annexed to the 1951 Treaty establishing the European Coal and Steel Community included very extensive provisions establishing powers of the High Authority on the Belgian coal production, such as establishment of forecasts of production, recommendations, consent to production plans, determination of compensations, approval and monitoring of national subsidies and prevention of displacements of production.

In interpreting this statutory framework, the Court substantiated its ruling that there was an implicit fix-pricing competence by means of a general statement that there is an implicit rule-making power without which law would have no meaning or could not be reasonably and usefully applied. Since the High Authority had the duty to ensure that the objectives of the Treaty were attained, it also had the power, 'if not the duty', to adopt measures to reduce the prices of Belgian coal, provided that the proportionality test was satisfied. This rationale was sporadically used by the Court in subsequent cases.[52]

However, in the 2000s, the General Court significantly narrowed the scope and application of the doctrine of implied powers and proved rather reluctant to acknowledge an expansion of EU competence through recourse to this doctrine. The rejection of the European Constitution project and the 2004 enlargement provided a fertile political environment for such self-restraint. In its Judgment of 17 September 2007 in Case T-240/04, *France v Commission*, the Court annulled the Commission Regulation (Euratom) 1352/2003 determining procedures for effecting the investment communications in the nuclear sphere prescribed by the Euratom Treaty on the ground that this Treaty did not confer competence on the Commission for adopting a binding act such as a regulation. In the absence of an explicit provision, the Court engaged into a statutory interpretation of whether implied powers were on that occasion vested to EU institutions.

---

[52] In CJEU Judgment of 9 July 1987 in Joined Cases 281, 283–85 and 287/85, *Germany v Commission*, the Court upheld the Commission's binding Decision 85/381 setting up a prior communication and consultation procedure on migration policies in relation to citizens from non-member countries, not explicitly provided, indicating that where an article of the Treaty confers a specific task on the Commission it must be accepted, if that provision was not to be rendered wholly ineffective, that it confers on the Commission 'necessarily and per se' the powers which were 'indispensable in order to carry out that task'. Furthermore, in CJEU Judgment of 17 October 1995 in Case 478/93, *Netherlands v Commission*, the Court held that, in matters relating to agriculture, the Commission was authorised to adopt all the measures which were necessary or appropriate for the implementation of the basic legislation, provided that they were not contrary to such legislation or to the implementing legislation adopted by the Council. Despite the wording of the judgment, the legal issue in question was essentially a matter of permissible delegation of internal allocation of powers, under the Community system, rather than an issue of the doctrine of implied powers.

The added value of the judgment was that it explicitly delineated the application of the implied powers doctrine by:

(a)   setting the criteria of association to the explicit competence, ie the powers needed to perform the prescribed mission 'usefully and reasonably', otherwise the primary competence would be deprived of all substance; and

(b)   categorically stating that any implicit power derogating from the principle of delegation of powers should be 'assessed strictly' against its substantial provisions, its form and its binding nature, thus such powers could be recognised by case law only exceptionally and in so far as they are 'necessary to ensure the practical effect of the provisions of the Treaty or the basic regulation at issue'.[53]

The strict necessity test proved fatal in practice. In that case, the Court stated that straightforward internal organisation measures, such as guidelines or a communication, would have been sufficient to achieve the Commission's objectives and that the existence of a precedent could not affect the legality of the act adopted since a simple practice could not prevail over Treaty rules and could not modify the delegation of powers between the institutions. Accordingly, by choosing a regulation, the Commission had caused a risk of confusion that undermined legal certainty and, consequently, was ultra vires.

This rationale was essentially reiterated with the same annulment outcome in Judgment of 17 November 2009 in Case T-143/06, *MZT Polyfilms Ltd v Council.* The Court held that when the institutions are determining the export price, their alleged power to carry out prospective analyses was not necessary to ensure the practical effect of the basic antidumping Regulation 384/96, namely entailing that the Council had the power, in an initial review, to use a methodology for the determination of the export price which is incompatible with the requirements set out by Article 11(3) of the Regulation.

In the post-crisis case law, the Court of Justice has gone well beyond the scope of application of implied powers, resulting in serious technical contradictions and deficiencies in the judicial syllogism, especially in *Pringle* and *Gauweiler.* In *Pringle*, the (negative aspect of the) principle of conferred powers upon the EU was at the heart of the judicial reasoning: in the absence of an explicit EU rule awarding such competence, it remained an entitlement of the euro-area Member States to conclude an agreement among themselves for the establishment of a stability mechanism outside the EU framework. Accordingly, there was a reverse EU competence question: whether there was a usurpation of EU exclusive competence by the ESM Contracting States.

The Court essentially employed a hard version of the principle of conferred powers in order to allow a wide margin to Member States, acting autonomously, to conclude agreements which lie in the grey zone of monetary policy. It used a

---

[53] Paragraphs 36–37.

twofold argument. First, monetary policy, upon which there is an exclusive competence of the Union regarding the euro-area Member States, is not strictly defined
in the Treaties: when it comes to monetary policy, the TFEU refers to 'objectives'
rather than 'instruments' to be employed.[54] The objective-oriented definition
of monetary policy clearly broadens the scope of monetary policy compared to
the instruments-oriented definition that would necessarily entail some form of
enlistment. It merely sufficed that the key objective of monetary policy, namely
maintenance of price stability, could be substantiated.

As regards the objective, the Court made a distinction, which appears mostly
as a sophism: the objective pursued by the ESM was 'to safeguard the stability of
the euro area as a whole', whereas the primary objective of the Union's monetary
policy was to 'maintain price stability'. In the Court's view, the two objectives were
'clearly distinct', in the sense that 'an economic policy measure cannot be treated
as equivalent to a monetary policy measure for the sole reason that it may have
indirect effects on the stability of the euro', albeit 'the stability of the euro area
may have repercussions on the stability of the currency used within that area'.[55]
As regards the instruments envisaged in order to attain the objective concerned,
the impugned Decision only stated that the stability mechanism would grant any
financial assistance required, but did not contain any other information on the
operation of that mechanism: 'the grant of financial assistance to a Member State
however clearly does not fall within monetary policy'.[56]

Furthermore, the Court of Justice examined the relationship between the
principle of conferred powers and the flexibility clause of Article 352. The Court
responded to the claim that recourse to that Article should have been made to
launch a stability mechanism comparable to that envisaged by Decision 2011/199
by setting a factual argument, namely that the Union had not actually used its
powers under Article 352, and a regulatory argument, ie that the flexibility
clause did not impose on the Union any obligation to act, but merely granted a
discretion to the Union. This judicial rationale seems to suffer from a variety of
vulnerabilities:

(a) it is axiomatic: reference to a 'clear' interpretation twice, ie in the distinction
     between stability in the euro area as a whole and price stability within the
     euro area and in the legal/economic assessment of the financial assistance to
     endangered countries, is at least problematic, if not flawed – it is, in any case,
     not clear at all;
(b) it constitutes a sophism: structural stability (an ESM objective) relies heavily
     upon price stability (an EU objective with regard to the euro area) and price
     stability primarily aims at structural stability; and
(c) it is self-contradictory: in spite of admitting the predominance of the
     objective-oriented approach to EU competences, the Court of Justice assessed

[54] Paragraph 53.
[55] Paragraph 56.
[56] Paragraph 57.

in an extremely superfluous manner both the objectives and the instruments of the ESM, presumably because the objective rationale was a very weak criterion to leave adequate room for the intervention of the ESM Contracting States.

In *Gauweiler*, the issue at stake was whether EU institutions acted ultra vires. In this case, the Court had to deal with exactly the opposite legal question, namely whether there was a violation of the principle of conferred powers because the ECB action superseded the competence conferred by the Member States. In order to confirm the legality of the OMTs programme, the Court ought to take the exact opposite legal path, ie to be less strict when applying the principle of conferred powers to substantiate either direct or implied powers vested to the ECB. Interestingly, the Court made reference neither to the doctrine of implied powers nor to the flexibility clause of Article 352 TEU. This was, presumably, due to judicial policy grounds: if implied powers were invoked, the Court would essentially open a window with effects that would be very difficult to keep under control in the future; if the flexibility clause had been employed, the Court should have found a procedural violation. Indeed, one might reasonably argue that the OMTs programme was a rather classic example of application of the principle enshrined in Article 352: the action was arguably necessary, it fell within the framework of the policies defined in the Treaties, it aimed at attaining an objective set out in the Treaties and the Treaties had not provided the necessary powers to launch such programme. In other words, the OMTs rationale was within the EU objectives but outside its prescribed statutory powers.

Yet, Article 352 had not been triggered and, presumably, could not possibly have been triggered, given that the unanimity requirement on the part of the Council was impossible to attain under the political discrepancies of the critical period the ECB's decision was taken; arguably, a bypass of the (exclusivity) of the flexibility clause. Under the above conditions, the rationale of the Court was quite generous in the interpretation of the stipulations of the Treaties relating to the EU conferred competences. The Court broadly followed the objectives approach established in *Pringle*, the instruments however being 'also relevant', yet in a wider perspective. Thus, it reiterated that the primary objective of the Union's monetary policy was to maintain price stability, but added the (particular) objectives of the ESCB to support the general economic policies in the Union, with a view to contributing to the achievement of its objectives: 'the Protocol on the ESCB and the ECB is thus characterised by a clear mandate, which is directed primarily at the objective of ensuring price stability'.[57]

The Court confirmed, without any further sincerity test, the OMTs programme purposes set out at the press release of the ECB, ie to safeguard both an appropriate monetary policy transmission and the singleness of the monetary policy. According to the Court, the latter objective contributed to achieving the objectives

---

[57] Paragraphs 43–44 and 46.

of that policy inasmuch as, under Article 119(2) TFEU, monetary policy must be 'single'; the former objective was likely both to preserve the singleness of monetary policy and to contribute to its primary objective of maintaining price stability. The Court once again axiomatically accepted that a monetary policy measure, such as the OMT programme, might also have indirect effects on the enhancement of the stability of the euro area, which is a matter of economic policy, but that does not make it equivalent to such policy.

On this particular issue, Advocate General Villalón's opinion in *Gauweiler* is particularly interesting. His argument was that not only direct purchases on the primary market were prohibited but so were operations on the secondary market whose effect would be to circumvent the primary prohibition. In this view, although the TFEU did not explicitly prohibit operations on the secondary market, it nevertheless required that, when the ECB intervenes on that market, it does so with sufficient safeguards to ensure that its intervention does not fall foul of the prohibition of monetary financing. Thus, the question was whether the OMT programme, under which the ECB intervened on the secondary government bond market, might, despite formally observing the letter of the prohibition to directly purchase debt instruments from the Member, amount to a bypass of the said prohibition. In that respect, Villalón assessed the economic outcome of purchasing government debt in the secondary market.

Interestingly, the application of the principle of conferred powers in *Pringle* and *Gauweiler* led to the exact opposite outcome: in the former case it was invoked so as to trigger the competence of the Member States (in the sense that powers had not been conferred to the EU) whereas in the latter case it was employed to establish the competence of the ECB (in the sense that it includes monetary policy issues within the competence of the ECB). In both cases, the result coincided with the assertions of the EU institutions. Yet, what was generally underestimated was that the ECB and the ESCB do not have objectives of their own that justify taking measures outside the general objectives of the Union. The objectives of the former are subsumed to the objectives of the latter and apply insofar as they are compatible with them: without prejudice to the objective of price stability, the ESCB shall support the general economic policies in the Union with a view to contributing to the achievement of the objectives of the Union (Articles 127(1) and 282(2) TFEU).

Furthermore, on an EU level, the ambiguity about what constitutes conferral of powers to the EU institutions allows some space for potential judicial manipulation. Thus, rather conveniently, in *Mallis*, the General Court abstained from assessment on the merits and dismissed the relevant actions as inadmissible, on the ground that the Eurogroup is not officially enlisted as an EU institution but rather constitutes a 'forum for discussion' for Finance ministers of the euro area. Yet, the political reality of the actual power of the Eurogroup to take on decisions concerning the financial policy of the euro-area Member States and the relationship between the EU and those States, including the use of emergency financing mechanisms, is apparent at first sight.

The web of provisions determining EU competences has been, according to Rosas and Armati, unintelligible, unpredictable and, as far as subsidiarity was concerned, non-justiciable, used to highlight the alleged shortcomings of an ex post judicial control of competence.[58] Not surprisingly, therefore, Article 1(1) TFEU declared that the purpose of the Treaty is to organise the functioning of the Union and determine the areas of delimitation of and arrangements for exercising its competences. However, instead of providing substantive assistance in clarifying the competence of the Union, the relevant Protocol (No 2) on the application of the principles of subsidiarity and proportionality annexed to the EU Treaties merely established a system of ex ante political monitoring of the implementation of subsidiarity (but not proportionality for that matter), based on an early warning process. This stance reflects the original intention to restrict the competences of the Union and to prevent potential broad interpretation of powers already conferred to other domains of activities.

Although their joint reading suggests that the Member States maintain all remaining competences, in realistic terms, given the magnitude of the EU in the global political arena in all matters, it seems that there is a shift of powers towards the Union. In other words, the overriding effect of the economic policies within the context of global economic constitutionalism results in a situation where Member States do not enjoy (full) autonomy on matters pertaining to sovereign policy (such as national security) or principally falling outside the scope of the Union (such as social welfare). However, even those matters are not dealt with as matters of policy by the Member States; they are rather dealt with on intergovernmental conferences. This is particularly true, in the aftermath of the financial crisis, for Member States that have received financial assistance and have, therefore, very little political power to design internal policies without prior consent of the fellow Member States.

From this viewpoint, the principles of conferral of powers, subsidiarity and proportionality did not fulfil the purpose for which they were originally established. However, instead of a rational regulatory transformation of the system so that it would become functional, the Court of Justice essentially changed the constitutional perception of closed EU competences and allowed, through a very generous intra vires interpretation, for the broadening of the powers of the EU institutions. Subsidiarity was not handled as a federal legal tool but mostly as a vehicle of constructivism to secure effective centralisation of powers in emergency circumstances, thus rendering the principle a supple mechanism of convenience. This is to confirm conceptual objections which were timely rose in literature regarding an essentially procrustean mechanism to suit any vision of European integration.[59]

---

[58] A Rosas and L Armati, *EU Constitutional Law: An Introduction*, 2nd edn (Oxford, Hart Publishing, 2012) 21.

[59] J Peterson, 'Subsidiarity: A definition to suit any vision?' (1994) 47 *Parliamentary Affairs* 116.

C. Contractual Commitments Towards the EU

As regards contractual commitments, these are assumed by a Member State receiving financial assistance with the commitment to implement economic adjustment programmes through conditionality that seriously hampers the autonomous exercise of national economic policy and allows for very extensive supervisory and reporting mechanisms both at the time of the programme and as a post-programme surveillance.[60] Obviously, these conditions are not strictly monetary (since the monetary union premises constitute a sine qua non condition for all Member States anyway) but probe very deep into the essence of economic policy, which in theory lies outside the direct competence of the Union.

---

[60] Above ch 2 section II.

5

Factual Impact of New Economic Constitutionalism upon Politics

The financial crisis has had significant consequences for European politics. For the purpose of this analysis such consequences are identified in four groups of politics: power; divisive; cross-border; and delegitimised politics. Obviously, the analysis could not exhaustively cover the political effects of the crisis; this would require an in-depth political analysis with additional references to political history and psychology. The aim of this chapter aims is to present some elements of the interdependence between law and politics in the era of new economic constitutionalism and to suggest that any proposals on the treatment of relevant pathologies must necessarily take both disciplines into serious consideration.

I. Power Politics

Power politics stand for politics primarily based on the use of power as a coercive force, rather than on morality or legitimacy. Such power can be of any source, eg military, but in this case it predominantly refers to economic power. Obviously, power politics based on economic domination is not a contemporary phenomenon. Economic power has traditionally been a serious driving force, both on national and on international level. In domestic politics, financial power determines – to a large extent – the electoral campaign and exercises significant influence upon the constituencies. The financial scale of the electoral campaigns through an outstanding arms race on national and regional level has become so exorbitant that serious concerns are raised as to the quality of democracies and the genuine participation of voters in the electoral process. According to the Center for Responsive Politics, in the 2016 presidential electoral campaign Hilary Clinton spent a total of 768 million and Donald Trump 398 million US dollars (1.4 million and 66 million respectively coming from their personal property).[1] The Center also projected that more than 5.2 billion US dollars would be spent in the 2018 midterm election.[2] In the 2017 parliamentary elections in the UK,

---

[1] www.opensecrets.org/pres16.
[2] www.opensecrets.org/news/2018/10/2018-midterm-record-breaking-5-2-billion.

according to the Electoral Commission, the participating political parties spent almost 40 million pounds, with the Conservative and Unionist Party spending almost half of that amount.[3] In the French Presidential election of 2017, according to the formal expenses review published in the Official Journal, Macron spent 16.8 million,[4] Hamon 15.2 million[5] and Le Pen 12.5 million euros.[6]

Most importantly, however, the cost of democracy on domestic level has been coupled by (economic) power politics in the international arena that poses further dangers for sovereignty, global governance and equality of nations. The split of nations into lenders and debtors essentially underlies economic power politics. The mere dependence established by the financial assistance packages, not only due to obligation for repayment of the funds borrowed but mostly in the form of the conditionality attached to such financial agreements, set up a volatile and variable international environment, where the wealth of a nation becomes the key, if not the sole, criterion for its classification in the world rankings. This is why the programmes attached to all financial assistance packages are broadly similar: although conditionality by definition ought to have reflected the particularities of each close-to-default State and the roots of the pathologies encountered in national finances, there are no significant state-specific variations. In fact, budgetary targets though expenses cuts, bank recapitalisations, restraints upon the public sector and privatisations essentially transcend all conditionality programmes, aiming to address conflicting interests, administrative traditions and cultural norms.[7]

Obviously, persistence on monetarism is not a contemporary phenomenon. Globalisation and transnationalism have greatly contributed to its rise and gradual dominance. One can only think of the G-7 forum of the world's most industrialised economies or the G-20 forum comprising a mix of the world's largest advanced and emerging economies to perceive what the actual power of wealth may mean for the nations. Keohane and Nye historically identified three basic characteristics of complex economic interdependence in an international environment: multiple channels connecting societies, absence of hierarchy among issues; and withdrawal of military force in economic dispute settlement.[8] Yet, what comes as a more intense pathology in the aftermath of the crisis is the formalisation of dependent relations among the nations and the urgent conditions under which interdependence applies to some countries having no essential option to financially survive but to have recourse to fellow Member States.

[3] UK Electoral Commission, 'Political Finance Regulation at the June 2017 UK General Election Report on the UK Parliamentary General Election Held on 8 June 2017' (2017), available at: www.electoralcommission.org.uk/__data/assets/pdf_file/0004/237550/Political-finance-regulation-at-the-June-2017-UK-general-election-PDF.pdf.

[4] www.legifrance.gouv.fr/affichTexte.do?cidTexte=JORFTEXT000036593699.

[5] www.legifrance.gouv.fr/affichTexte.do?cidTexte=JORFTEXT000036593715&categorieLien=id.

[6] www.legifrance.gouv.fr/affichTexte.do?cidTexte=JORFTEXT000036593681&categorieLien=id.

[7] K Featherstone, 'External Conditionality and the Debt Crisis: the "Troika" and Public Administration Reform in Greece' (2015) 22 *Journal of European Public Policy* 295.

[8] R Keohane and J Nye, 'Power and Interdependence' in RK Betts (ed), *Conflict after the Cold War: Arguments on Causes of War and Peace*, 4th edn (Abingdon, Routledge, 2012) 164, 165.

To the extent that States facing economic difficulties cannot reasonably borrow from international markets, the state financial interdependence becomes all the more visible and crucial. Moreover, in the context of the EU, interdependence lies by definition at a higher level, not only due to the concession of part of economic sovereignty to the Union by all Member States, which are, therefore, jointly linked to a common monetary and gradually more economic governance, but also because of the highly intergovernmental function of the EU.

In his seminal analysis of the EU structures, from a liberal intergovernmentalist point of view, Moravcsik normatively suggested a two-stage approach to Union decision-making: first, national preferences are primarily determined by the constraints and opportunities imposed by economic interdependence; and secondly, the outcomes of intergovernmental negotiations are determined by the relative bargaining power of governments and the functional incentives for institutionalisation created by high transaction costs and the desire to control domestic agendas.[9] Even though this analysis was made well before the introduction of the common monetary policy, it shrewdly envisaged the evolution of *interdependence*, with the additional element that after the crisis it has been developed as mere *dependence* of some Member States on others. Yet, one might argue that this is not necessarily a negative aspect of new economic constitutionalism. The transfer of financial dependences from the private sector to the inter-state level could be considered as a safer option for international economics for the stability of global economic governance. Yet, this hypothesis lies on the assumption that state relations operate on an equal footing and that the intervention of the lending States is mostly based on sentiments of genuine solidarity or, at least, of sincere understanding that the global economic community must remain intact.

However, it is rather doubtful that such communitarian considerations prevail in the international economic environment. From this viewpoint, power politics may undermine the basic premise of international community cooperation, ie mutual respect and equality of treatment. As Donnelly explains in the context of the regulatory treatment of the financial crisis in Europe, although some elementary supranationalism emerged to prevent complete collapse, power politics remained the prevailing agenda; power politics, whereby financially powerful Member States coerced and imposed changes on weaker ones, without committing to the financial assistance that the latter require to survive the financial crisis, with negative consequences not only for the States themselves but also for the European financial stability:

> The dominance of power politics ensures that European economic governance not only remains institutionally and financially incapable of properly providing for financial stability, but deliberately so for the foreseeable future, despite strong incentives to Europeanise the institutional and financial environment that supports financial stability.

---

[9] A Moravcsik, 'Preferences and Power in the European Community: A Liberal Intergovernmentalist Approach' (1993) 31 *Journal of Common Market Studies* 473, 517.

This outcome not only preserves, but enhances the mutually dependent relationship between banks and states at the national level, at the expense of the single market, and of its financial stability.[10]

Power politics has, arguably, further cultivated stereotyping and nationalism among peoples of different nations, usually operating in the form of action-reaction. Only few political figures and representatives of the cultural elite have demonstrated a higher level of actual positive solidarity to the nations that have suffered serious financial problems.[11] In the main, people in countries which have not greatly suffered from the crisis and have been called upon to contribute to rescue mechanisms, develop more or less stereotyping attitudes against people of profiting countries, in particular the unproductive PIGS (Portuguese, Irish/ Italians, Greeks and Spaniards). This type of stereotyping is, nevertheless, not only evidently dangerous in terms of the community mentality, but also oversimplistic, self-inflicted and patently mistaken.[12] The counter effect of stereotyping

---

[10] S Donnelly, 'Power Politics and the Undersupply of Financial Stability in Europe' (2014) 21 *Review of International Political Economy* 980, 1005.

[11] A typical such example has been the collective movement *We are all Greeks*, culminating in a special banner-raise event in cities around the world on 18 February 2012 and the 'Support Greece' petition signed by 22 internationally renowned Nobel prize-winners in the fields of science and technology, addressed to Martin Schulz, President of the European Parliament, and the presidents of the European Council and the European Commission; see *Science*, 25 May 2012, 978, available at: http://science.sciencemag.org/content/336/6084/978. Furthermore, a most extraordinary moment of solidarity was given by German Nobel Laureate for Literature, Günter Grass, with the publication of the poem entitled 'Europe's Shame' in *Süddeutsche Zeitung* of 26 May 2012, blaming Europe for its attitude towards Greece.

[12] P Crugman, 'Charlemagne, Empathy in Short Supply. Greece: Not a Simple Fable about Ants and Crickets' *The Economist*, 8 March 2010; P Crugman, 'Whips, Scourges, and Cats' *The New York Times*, 19 June 2012. For example, OECD data show that in 2017, Greeks worked on average 2,018 hours against an OECD average of 1,759 (1,356 in Germany, 1,514 in France and 1,681 in the UK); the only comparable OECD countries are Costa Rica and Korea (2,179 and 2,024 hours respectively), see https://stats.oecd.org/Index.aspx?DataSetCode=ANHRS per cent20. The paid leave entitlement in Greece is on average 23 days, lower than the UK's minimum 28 and Germany's 30 days. At the same time, the public sector in Greece is not statistically above the European average in the overall working structure, as otherwise intimated – this was the ground for the persistent demand of the troika for extensive redundancies in the broader public sector. On the other hand, according to OECD, public expenditure on old-age and survivors' benefits in Greece was, at the peak of its growth in 2007, 12% of GDP as against an OECD-34 of 7.4%, ie 10.8% in Portugal, 12.8% in France, 12.7% in Austria and 12% in Germany; see W Adema and M Ladaique, 'How Expensive is the Welfare State? Gross and Net Indicators in the OECD Social Expenditure Database' OECD Social, Employment and Migration Working Paper no 92 (2009). The overall government social expenditure amounted in Greece for the same year in 21.3% of GDP as against an OECD-total of 19.3% (22.5% in Portugal, 28.4% in France, 26.4% in Austria and 25.2% in Germany). In 2009, the initial salary of upper secondary education teachers in Greece amounted to 27,951 euros per year as against an EU-21 average of 33,553 euros (indicatively, in Portugal 34,296 euros, in Ireland 36,433, in France 35,743 and in Germany 55,743 euros). However, the running expenditure (cost of state administration) in Greece is about 6.5% of GDP, compared to an EU average of 3%. Still, irrespective of the working habits and the expenditure levels, public social services, such as health and education, remain largely ineffective in Greece. For the same expenditure, Greece provides public services that are wasteful and much inferior to other countries due to the systemic irregularities of the Greek labour market. Featherstone shrewdly attributes the country's low competitiveness, trade and investment imbalances and inefficient fiscal mismanagement to the use of the public sector as a substitute for the inadequacies of welfare provision in Greece and the shared

is nationalism. People in endangered countries do not feel that they deserve to undergo such negative attitude and, eventually, such great deterioration of their quality of life. They do not feel guilty for the crisis in the same way that they feel that the crisis randomly hit them and their countries without anyone – expert or politician, within the country or abroad – having timely given proper warning. The imminent reaction was reluctance to proceed with the necessary structural reforms, uprising against measures lowering personal incomes and reducing social benefits and, eventually, a turn to nationalism as a form of defence against external 'conspiracies'. Predictably, long-forgotten diplomatic claims, such as wartime reparations, entered the political agenda as a means of easing the restless public opinion.

II. Divisive Politics

Divisive politics stands for politics that produces actual or, more often, artificial dilemmas in order to set a clear line of distinction from the political opponents. Again, one might argue that divisive politics is not necessarily a negative aspect of public discourse in that it secures political pluralism and contributes to progressive politics that advances those agendas, once it has been tested and survived. Yet, what divisive politics lacks is the deliberative attitude that allows for a reasoned exchange of arguments and an optimisation of the eventual solution based on a genuine predilection of the participants to accept counter-arguments. If these conditions are not met, divisive politics ends up constituting a form of demagogy and misallodoxy that is bound to have an adverse effect on the cohesion of the political community. This divisive and easy populist rhetoric – blaming the 'others', be it the foreign powerful States, or impersonal 'markets', or the immigrants (but never one's own over-consumption habits) – led, not surprisingly, to an increase of extremism, populism and euro-scepticism and allowed far-edge and fringe political parties to gain significant power through organised political participation in national, European and regional elections in both lender and debtor countries.[13] Apart from the eminent danger of extremities becoming more powerful, it is readily apparent that a new type of populism arises in Europe as a result of the distrust of the ideologically moderate political parties.

As regards far-edge parties applying xenophobic and nationalistic agendas, Front National's Marine Le Pen gained a significant 21.3 per cent in the first round, 33.9 per cent in the 2017 French presidential elections and eight seats in the 2017

---

culture of clientelism, see K Featherstone, The Greek Sovereign Debt Crisis and EMU: A Failing State in a Skewed Regime (2011) 49 *Journal of Common Market Studies* 193.

[13] F Hartleb, 'A Thorn in the Side of European Elites: The New Euroscepticism' (2011) 10 *European View* 265; M Goodwin, *Right Response Understanding and Countering Populist Extremism in Europe* (London, Chatham House, 2011); DA Halikiopoulou, 'Right-Wing Populist Momentum? A Review of 2017 Elections across Europe' (2018) 56 *Journal of Common Market Studies* 63.

parliamentary elections, whereas in the last respective parliamentary elections the Front National polled 13 per cent of the popular vote; Swiss People's Party 29 per cent; Freedom Party 26 per cent in Austria (junior partners in coalition government); Danish People's Party 21 per cent; Jobbik 19 per cent in Hungary; the Finns 18 per cent in Finland; the Sweden Democrats 17.6 per cent; the League 17.35 per cent in Italy (senior partners in coalition government); the Freedom Party 13 per cent in the Netherlands; the Alternative for Germany 12.6 per cent; the Freedom and Direct Democracy party 11 per cent in the Czech Republic; United Patriots nine per cent in Bulgaria; Our Slovakia eight per cent; Golden Dawn seven per cent in Greece; and National People's Front 3.7 per cent in Cyprus. These figures normally rise in elections for the European Parliament and upper houses, where applicable.

As regards self-projected 'anti-systemic' alternative political forces, Movimento 5 Stelle in Italy, launched by the popular comedian Beppe Grillo, managed to achieve – with a largely unidentified political agenda – an astonishing 23.8 per cent of the national vote and 54 seats in the 2013 parliamentary elections, as well as 32.7 per cent and 227 seats in the 2018 elections, thus becoming the senior partner of the coalition government. Outside Italy, Pirate Parties International was set up in Brussels in 2010, following the inauguration of the Swedish Pirate Party in 2006, with a view to helping establish, support, promote and maintain communication and cooperation between pirate parties around the world. Its ideology seems to be focusing on digital revolution within the information society and on the mobilisation of people: technology, resources, skills. There are currently as many as 38 registered Pirate Parties around the world.[14] The Icelandic Pirate Party is considered the most successful such party in Europe having reached 14.5 per cent of the popular vote and secured ten out of 63 seats in the 2016 parliamentary elections. Overall, Pirate parties seem to be in decline: in Germany, Piratenpartei Deutschland managed to gain an average of eight per cent of the popular vote and entered four German Länder parliaments (Berlin, North Rhine-Westphalia, Saarland and Schleswig-Holstein), but subsequently lost all their seats.

Not surprisingly, the financial crisis and the austerity policies in Europe brought a tremendous wave of social anxiety and protests in the indebted countries, which on occasions took a pan-European breadth, depending on the specific characteristics of the socio-economic crisis and its consequences in terms of mobilisation potential, on the political reactions to it, ie political opportunities and threat, as well as on the social movement cultures and structures characterizing each country.[15] In fact, concerns on the effectiveness of the Union to deal with the financial crisis were also raised by pro-European political parties and individual politicians, especially in the countries that were hit by the crisis.

---

[14] Information drawn from the official https://pp-international.net/pirate-parties.

[15] D della Porta, 'Late Neoliberalism and its Discontents: A Comparative Conclusion' in D della Porta et al (eds), *Late Neoliberalism and its Discontents in the Economic Crisis: Comparing Social Movements in the European Periphery* (London, Palgrave Macmillan, 2017) 261.

In the 2015 Greek referendum, the citizens voted against a rescue package from the debtors that would most probably have led, if this policy had eventually been implemented, to a withdrawal from the EU, while at the same time all evidence indicated that Greek people, in their vast majority, did not favour the country's exit from the Union. Interestingly, although Greek people at large want the country to remain within the Union, they are at the same time very sceptical, holding the highest ratio of distrust towards the EU (69 per cent). For the fourth successive time (from autumn 2016 to spring 2018) they were the only ones to have a predominantly negative image of the EU (37 per cent), with 36 per cent having a neutral image of the EU and 27 per cent having a positive one. In addition, they were the only Europeans, along with the British, with a majority view of pessimism concerning the future of the EU in Greece, 53 per cent against 42 per cent expressing optimistic views.[16] Ironically, this is not only the view of the people at large.

As Tsirbas and Sotiropoulos very elaborately substantiated, in the course of the financial crisis and while voting in favour of the bail-out programmes, Greek MPs continued to be attached to Europe, but evaluated negatively the role of EU institutions during the economic crisis; they mostly viewed European integration positively while being sceptical about the representativeness of EU institutions.[17] This attitude is not inexplicable. Even in countries which benefited from the financial assistance programmes, there was a strong feeling of victimhood that was conveyed to all layers of citizenship. Thankfully, this was not enough to deter the European orientation of the country, although it allowed for significant space in favour of the populist rhetoric that led to the 2015 coalition government with the basic political motto of imposition of the sovereign will upon the powerful EU Member States and upon the Union itself, simplistically formed as a 'get control back' motto.

In fact, the crisis left politics in Europe sharply divided. On the one hand, there is the stability priority, founded upon the traditional ordoliberal approach praying for financial discipline and entailing severe austerity measures without wide concessions towards the social state, particularly for those countries with immense deficit and loans, and dogmatically opposing inflation. On the other hand, there is the social cohesion priority, an effectuation of social liberalism reshaped in a new social economic progressive politics narrative, emphasising upon partial redistribution of wealth, both among and within the States, arguing in favour of ease of strict measures of financial discipline, of longer adaptation periods for endangered States and of European-centered solutions, such as the Eurobonds and standing

---

[16] According to the findings of the standard Spring 2018 Eurobarometer, http://ec.europa.eu/commfrontoffice/publicopinion/index.cfm/Survey/getSurveyDetail/instruments/STANDARD/surveyKy/2180.

[17] Y Tsirbas and DA Sotiropoulos, 'Europe at the Epicenter of National Politics: The Attitudes of Greek Political Elites towards the European Union and the Economic Crisis' (2016) 41 *Historical Social Research* 86.

against forced austerity in depressed economies. Certain variables that cast light primarily upon the rudiments of western economies, such as the emerging of the discussion on moral and responsible capitalism, part of the rhetoric of the former UK Prime Minister David Cameron, based on ethical economic growth, responsible globalisation and wider responsibilities of entrepreneurs, seem to be easily accommodated within this basic distinction.[18]

Although the above rough sketch seems rather simplistic, it clearly reflects the essence of the new political dialectics in Europe. This is true not only in the case of countries like Greece, where discipline-oriented political parties suffered huge losses, but also in financially healthier States. In the 2018 French presidential election and Italian regional elections, dominating pro-stability political parties lost a significant portion of their power. The major 'stability v cohesion' political debate referred to the most salient feature of the social arena, ie the labour market. The discussion on reduction of labour costs, especially for endangered countries, reasonably triggered an increasing social tension that resulted in public discomfort. The stability proponents persistently argued in favour of serious horizontal cuts that would embrace not only salaries in general but mostly minimum wages. The idea was that in this way competitiveness of the States would rise and investments might be attracted.

The argument may sound reasonable in the context of orthodox liberal economics, but is not beyond challenge. The systemic counter-argument reflects the agony as to how far one might go in order to secure competitiveness (largely following a China-type low-wage producer model), and eventually raises the question of whether there is a single widely acceptable meaning of competitiveness: statistics indicate that economic growth in countries without political freedom is much higher than in countries where rights are respected.[19] As Petersmann notes, rights-based cosmopolitan European constitutionalism differs fundamentally from the constitutional nationalism in most democracies outside Europe.[20] Concessions as to human well-being are of course foreseeable, but the threshold is by definition blurred.

On the other hand, in terms of substance of the argument on fiscal discipline, social economists would raise issues of increase of inequalities and, in turn, of increase of wealth discrepancies, the shift of the labour employment towards high-skilled workers and the potential rise of unemployment of vulnerable categories, such as youth, women, low-level workers, and altogether a reduction in aggregate employment. Crudely put, the dilemma seems to be between inequality and full

---

[18] P Cormack and R Goodman, *Responsible Capitalism: Essays on Morality, Ethics and Business* (London, First, 2009).
[19] K Hassett, 'Does Economic Success Require Democracy? Does Economic Success require Democracy?' *The American Magazine*, May–June 2007, available at: www.american.com/archive/2007/may-june-magazine-contents/does-economic-success-require-democracy.
[20] E-U Petersmann, *International Economic Law in the 21st Century. Constitutional Pluralism and Multilevel Governance of Interdependent Public Goods* (Oxford, Hart Publishing, 2012) 446. The author cites the US example of national constitutionalism and hegemonic and power-oriented foreign policies.

employment – the US labour model in broad terms – as opposed to equality and unemployment, which has been historically the European labour predilection. The above, rather schematic, trade-off is both evidently problematic and largely unsatisfactory. Especially in the case of Europe, the mixture becomes all the more explosive. This is so because of the inherent differences in the labour markets of the Member States and the uneven distribution of product wealth.

Although pluralism and transnationalism seem to interconnect economies, the structure and overall efficiency of a labour market still remain at the discretion of each State. Discrepancies, therefore, cannot be treated on a higher level and that affects not only the labour product but also the attitude of the working forces and of society altogether. It is not, accordingly, inexplicable how the social tension caused by the radical regulatory intervention in labour rights exercises a domino influence upon the psychology and social behaviour of people at large.

The western world seems today to lose its competitive advantages against the developing States. This is mostly true in relation to the growth figures, which spectacularly favour the latter. According to OECD's real GDP forecast for 2019, the global average is estimated at 3.93 per cent, the average of OECD countries at 2.48 per cent and the average of euro-area countries at 2.07 per cent;[21] correspondingly, as regards nominal GDP forecast for 2019, the average of OECD countries is estimated at 4.9 per cent and the average of euro-area countries is estimated at 3.09 per cent. This transfer of wealth is also reflected in the economic literature: Frankel, for instance, provides concrete examples of small-scale reforms that should be drawn from minor countries (both developed and developing), such as, among others: education reforms (Korea); forced saving and traffic congestion pricing (Singapore); standing armies foreswearing (Costa Rica and Mauritius); oil option hedging and conditional cash portfolio with the aim of preserving part of the income from diamond exports for future generations (Botswana); transfers (Mexico); structural budget rules (Chile); and 'Pula Fund' long-term investment (Botswana).[22]

The Arab spring and the Latin American reformists, albeit not radically effective in relation to the aspired redistribution of wealth, seem to transfer dynamic social mobilisation outside Europe. Not unexpectedly, in the 2016 Happy Planet Index of the British New Economics Foundation, using the experienced well-being, life expectancy and ecological footprint as major variables, no European country features in the top ten. Costa Rica, Mexico, Colombia, Vanuatu and Vietnam are the top five countries in the list, whereas the top European country is Albania ranking 13th; Spain ranks 15th, the UK 34th, Cyprus 41st, France 44th, Ireland 48th, Germany 49th, Portugal 79th, Greece 83rd and the US 108th, out of a total of 140 countries.[23]

---

[21] https://data.oecd.org/gdp/real-gdp-forecast.htm.
[22] J Franke, 'What Small Countries can Teach the World' (2012) 47 *Business Economics* 93.
[23] http://happyplanetindex.org.

The divisive politics concerning stability v social cohesion, and the dominance in the relevant discussion of the rhetoric of financialism, can also be seen in the assessment of the policy followed towards the euro-area Member States that came close to default. De Giorgi and Moury set three hypotheses in this respect, which were confirmed by empirical political analysis in the countries that received financial assistance in the post-crisis era:

(1)   First, there has been a decrease in the level of consensus in parliaments, because much of the legislation was salient and dealt with economic and social aspects causing dissension, but also within government coalitions or even within political parties.

(2)   Second, there has been a different legislative behaviour depending on the type of party: mainstream and pro-European integration parties, which usually alternate in government and opposition, are more likely to be led by a sense of responsibility and consequently vote for, or let pass, measures that, no matter how unpopular, could help save the country from the worst effects of the crisis.

(3)   Third, the opposition in parliaments have behaved in a more confrontational way when the government's incumbency is at risk, for instance when it lacks a majority of seats in parliament or its popularity declines dramatically, and in a less confrontational way when it is not, that being when elections have just been held or when technocratic governments, rather than true political competitors, are in charge.

This political phenomenon caused sudden polarisation and fragmentation of the party system, especially in Italy and in Greece.[24] Yet, there was a significant turn even in cases of political parties which strongly opposed any austerity programme before assuming power – most notably, the left-wing SYRIZA Government in Greece; a party which, while in opposition, organised widespread riots against EU financial assistance packages, and when it came to power strongly opposed a (third) rescue package, causing tremendous turbulence in the most critical period of the first half of 2015, when Greece actually came close to exit from the euro area and was further burdened with serious additional debt, and eventually decided to spectacularly reverse its policy and join orthodox ordoliberalism.

III. Cross-Border Politics

Cross-border politics stands for the political phenomenon of de-location of electoral processes in the sense that external actors, representing either foreign nations

---

[24] E de Giorgi and C Moury, 'Conclusions: Great Recession, Great Co-operation?' in E de Giorgi and C Moury (eds), *Government-Opposition in Southern European Countries during the Economic Crisis: Great Recession, Great Cooperation?* (Abingdon, Routledge 2017) 115.

or international organisations, become all the more involved in domestic politics. Electoral extra-territoriality no longer stems from the legitimate interest due to the participation in a common group of nations only, but also from vested interests in the welfare of other States: lender States have an obvious interest in ensuring that the debtor States are progressing smoothly in political and financial terms, so as to prevent default and to be in a position to honour their international contractual commitments. Accordingly, political leaders from all European States as well as EU officeholders become partisan in all European elections.

Chancellor Merkel made extensive statements in favour of then president and presidential candidate Nicolas Sarcozy in France, of the affirmative on the Irish referendum and of the pro-European political parties in favour of financial stability in Greece; she suggested, on 19 May 2012, that a referendum should take place in Greece to confirm the people's will to remain within or leave the Eurozone.[25] A month later, three days before national elections in Greece, *Financial Times Germany* of 14 June 2012 called on Greeks – using Greek language – to cast their vote in favour of conservative New Democracy with the headline:

> Resist the Demagogue: Resist the demagogy of Alexis Tsipras and SYRIZA. Do not trust their promises that the denouncement of the loan agreements is possible without consequences. Your country finally needs a functioning state. For your smooth governance we recommend Nea Dimocratia, even though the recommendation is half-hearted [...] The best option for your country would be a coalition government with Antonis Samaras as leader and not Alexis Tsipras.

In the Greek elections, the same explicit stance was also taken by the IMF Managing Director, Christine Lagarde, the President of the European Council, Herman van Rompuy, and the President of the European Commission, José Manuel Barroso. Prior to the 2018 general elections in Italy, and in view of the predictable victory of anti-European political forces, European Budget Commissioner Guenther Oettinger made a statement to Deutsche Welle to urge financial markets to become so volatile as to persuade voters to turn their backs to non-mainstream parties and advised Italians not to vote for populists.[26] Especially with regard to the IMF intervention, there is an evident dissatisfaction on the part of citizens on the basis that the IMF does not constitute a fellow State, but merely an outsider. Yet, the fact that the IMF has been among the lenders of endangered States renders it a de facto stakeholder.

Overall, the Union and the powerful European States seem to have earned their right to have a word in domestic politics through their legitimate interest to secure the money provided through the rescue mechanisms, but also as a communitarian issue stemming from the EU partnership. Financial dependence seems

---

[25] *Spiegel*, 19 May 2012.
[26] www.dw.com/en/oettinger-warns-italians-against-backing-populists/av-43986499.

to justify interference not only with financial but also with sovereign matters, such as elections or even foreign policy.[27] However, both in the case of Greece and in the case of Italy, external interventions seem to have had the opposite result. People at large reacted negatively to statements coming from abroad, even statements expressed in sensible terms; they were upset and refused to receive instructions. This phenomenon has been described by Olaf Cramme as 'the trend towards the Europeanisation of domestic politics.'[28] Conversely, an 'EU politicization' was also observed during the crisis, with the classical distinction between political left and right division transcending national boundaries and signaling a new perspective in the process of European integration.[29]

More institutionally, an indication of cross-border politics is evident in proceedings before the Court of Justice with regard to requests for a preliminary ruling submitted by national courts, where a true division appeared between the intervening States. In *Pringle*, except for the Irish Government, observations were also submitted by 11 national governments (Belgian, German, Greek, Spanish, French, Italian, Cypriot, Dutch, Austrian, Slovak and British) and three EU institutions (Parliament, Council and the Commission). In *Gauweiler*, except for the German Government, observations were also submitted by ten national governments (Irish, Greek, Spanish, French, Italian, Cypriot, Dutch, Polish, Portuguese and Finish) and three EU institutions (Parliament, Council and ECB). In *Kotnik*, except for the Slovenian Government, observations were also submitted by three national governments (Irish, Spanish and Italian) and the European Commission.

IV. De-Legitimised Politics

De-legitimised politics stands for the dissociation of people with politics. This aberration of the essence of popular sovereignty in a representative democracy has three contemporary reflections: technocratic governments; manipulation of popular referenda; and alienation of people from politics.

With regard to *technocracy*, in the heat of the crisis there was a tendency for countries suffering from financial difficulties to have recourse to non-political

---

[27] In January 2019, shortly before the Greek Parliament ratified the international agreement with Former Yugoslav Republic of Macedonia determining the pending bilateral issue, including the determination of the latter country's name, Chancellor Merkel visited Greece and widely argued in favour of ratification and paying governmental efforts to this effect.

[28] O Cramme, 'The Trend towards the Europeanisation of Domestic Politics is Unstoppable (and Good) but for the Time Being will be Messy and Uneven' London School of Economics European Politics and Policy Blog, available at: http://blogs.lse.ac.uk/europpblog/2012/03/12/europeanisation-eu-domestic-politics.

[29] Ch Rauh and M Zürn, 'Zur Politisierung der EU in der Krise' in M Heidenreich (ed), *Krise der Europäischen Vergesellschaftung?* (Wiesbaden, Springer VS, 2014) 121; P Statham and H-J Trenz, 'Understanding the Mechanisms of EU Politicization: Lessons from the Eurozone Crisis' (2015) 13 *Comparative European Politics* 287.

governments led by experts to handle the situation, whereas parties that signed and supported bail-out rescue packages suffered tremendous losses. This was the case in 2011 in both Greece (with Prime Minister Loukas Papademos, former head of the Central Bank of Greece and vice-President of the ECB, leading the executive for 17.5 months), and Italy (with Prime Minister Mario Monti leading the executive for 17.5 months); both individuals had never been elected politicians. Most significantly, Emmanuel Macron was elected President of France with no back-up from political parties and no parliamentary representation, mostly promoting his technocratic profile.

The phenomenon of technocracy against democracy has not been widely expanded, yet it marked the general distrust of people towards the political system overall and, perhaps, the inability of the latter to respond to over-complicated challenges carrying along a high price in democratic accountability. Yet, neither of the above individuals has had a relaxing political career. Monti was repeatedly obliged to ask for a vote of confidence to ensure adoption of his Government's legislation and was forced to resign a few months before the end of its term when the majority in parliament, People of Freedom Party, withdrew its support to his Government; Papademos stepped down with a dramatic call to the President of the Hellenic Republic stating that the state funds were insufficient to pay the salaries of the public servants. Six years after concluding his duty in office, Papademos underwent surgery for extensive injuries caused after opening a letter bomb addressed to him.

With regard to *referenda* in critical matters of public life, a general conclusion can be drawn that, after 2004, the future of Europe appears to have become an issue that European leaders seem more and more reluctant to take on as a personal responsibility to their respective people and to the future generations, shifting such decision-making responsibility on vital matters to the people. Because of the broader populist and divisive environment those referenda result almost invariably in a more sceptical and anti-European thesis, which is in fact the most readily sustainable position because of the easy emotional rhetoric simplistically formed as 'keeping control' or 'taking back control'. This has happened both in the case of the French and Dutch referenda of 2005 on the Union's constitutional charter, the Irish referendum of 2008 on the Treaty of Lisbon, the Greek referendum of 2015 on the bail-out rescue programme and the Brexit referendum of 2016.

Although turning to people, even in complex issues, can by definition be considered a desirable way to upgrade participatory democracy and partly resolve the legitimacy deficit pathologies, the above referenda were mostly non-deliberative and, especially the last two, constituted serious manipulation of the popular will. As Maria Giannacopoulos critically argues, referenda in situations of crises (not only economic, but also social or cultural ones) are becoming increasingly visible as governance devices mostly to legitimise the global 'colonial power'.[30]

---

[30] M Giannacopoulos, 'Sovereign Debt Crises, Referendums and the Changing Face of Colonial Power' (2017) 31 *Continuum: Journal of Media and Cultural Studies* 21.

Two very uneasy symptoms can be identified in this respect. The first one relates to the false information provided to voters. Although the issue generally relates to any form of popular participation, the situation is more intense in the case of referenda, because of the oversimplistic yes/no type of question, which is very vulnerable to naïve approaches.[31]

The second symptom relates to the reversal of the results of the referendum. In the 2015 Greek referendum, the Government fiercely supported the no-vote to the bail-out conditionality that was attached to a draft agreement with the EU; a few days after the no vote won, it upheld the rescue package, agreeing to conditions arguably stricter than those already rejected by the Greek people. Prior to this, the triggering point for the collapse of the contemporary political system in Greece was the public announcement, on 31 October 2011, by Giorgos Papandreou, the socialist Prime Minister at the time, of his will to hold a referendum, shortly after euro-area leaders had agreed on a second 130-billion-euro financial assistance programme and on a 50 per cent write-down of the country's debt to make it sustainable and a vote of confidence to secure support of his policy for the remainder of the four-year term, set to expire in 2013. The Prime Minister's sentimental vow that 'we trust citizens, we believe in their judgment, we believe in their decision' could not ease huge reaction by most political leaders in Europe, who accused him for being hypocritical and self-destructive. The outcome was barely foreseeable at the time. The referendum was never held; the vote of confidence was given with an unprecedented condition set by the backbenchers that the Prime Minister would shortly afterwards resign; and two (originally three) parties agreed to proceed with a new coalition government to deal with the pressing and pending financial issues led by a non-political figure.

Finally, with regard to the *political alienation*, a more general consequence of the above political symptoms following the financial crisis has been the loss of faith in democratic processes which keeps people away from the natural forum of the representative system, ie elections and participation in the public sphere, mostly through political parties. The history of social reaction towards the austerity measures enacted to treat the financial crisis is very stark. In the first years of the crisis, broadly until 2015, this was evidenced as intense and, occasionally, violent extra-parliamentary popular mobilisation (either self-motivated or through the initiatives of political parties), such as national and transnational strikes, riots and demonstrations. There has since been an overall shift in the people's state of mind, which has led to a significant decrease in the turn-out in the national elections throughout Europe. This demonstrates a general public apathy towards public

---

[31] The case of post-truth propaganda was evident in the period prior to the UK referendum on whether to exit from the EU. A characteristic illustration was the distribution by the Vote Leave campaign of a leaflet bearing the official logo of the National Health Service, supporting Brexit as the sole means for saving the British health system; see http://d3n8a8pro7vhmx.cloudfront.net/themes/55fd82d8ebad646cec000001/attachments/original/1463496002/Why_Vote_Leave.pdf?1463496002.

politics and a fatalism on the part of people, who consider that they cannot, in any way, exercise any significant influence over the process of determination of the state will. From an EU average of just over 60 per cent between 1984 and 1989 (60.56 per cent) and just below this threshold between 1994 and 1999 (56.56 per cent), the projection for the period between 2014 and 2019 is for an average turnout of just over 40 per cent (42.62 per cent).[32] Although this decline is not to be strictly attributed to the financial crisis, it is undeniable that institutions lose dignity and prestige at the expense of a personalised political arena where messianism seems to become the major political issue at stake.

---

[32] Data drawn from: www.politico.eu/interactive/voters-turnout-in-the-european-elections. Relevant and comparable results also available at www.idea.int/data-tools/data/voter-turnout.

6

An EU Recalibration Proposal

I. The Principle: Resilient Institutional Constitutionalism

In a most insightful critique of the current status of the EU, Longo and Murray consider seven options as a solution to the current EU stagnation:

(1) more Europe, especially through a deepened monetary union;
(2) more democracy, especially through the empowerment of its representative character;
(3) development of a public participatory arena, especially through public discourse and narratives;
(4) less European integration;
(5) no European integration, through abolition or wholesale exit;
(6) more cohesion and establishment of cohesion legitimacy;
(7) and development of a communications strategy based on encouraging contestation.[1]

Excluding, as a matter of ideological choice, the options of less or no European integration, I recognise three possible ways of recalibration to treat the financial crisis: an inner-restructuring option advancing societal constitutionalism; an insight cognitive option advancing cognitive constitutionalism; and an outer-resilient option advancing traditional institutional constitutionalism. The question is not one of merely academic interest; depending on the option ultimately selected, institutional change should take a totally different direction.

The *inner-restructuring approach* suggests an internal transformation of the economy, in the form of societal constitutionalism, so as to prevent future crises. Those arguing in favour of this approach mostly consider that the crisis is the result of the economy's bad attitude. Ideologists, such as Naomi Klein, blame the neoliberal economic theology suggesting that the economy should be left entirely alone from any intervention of the State, for economy employs strong self-corrective mechanisms that allow it to find on its own the optimal vehicles to

---

[1] M Longo and Ph Murray, *Europe's Legitimacy Crisis: From Causes to Solutions* (Basingstoke, Palgrave Macmillan, 2015) 111–24.

deal with any relevant crises.[2] The response is that the neoliberal thesis is based upon the false assumption that capitalism can operate on a self-corrective manner. However, this is implausible, given the greediness of profit-making that has no ceiling and responds to no self-restraint. Realists, on the other hand, such as Bruce Alexander with his dislocation addiction theory, begin from a totally different standpoint, thus abandoning pure economic ideology and employing more psychological standards pertaining to individual or collective addictions, which are generated mostly due to contextual factors and produce, in the realm of capitalism, a cumulative effect of overspending and an arms race.[3]

Yet, one could reasonably argue that trying to create an environment of financial security that would anyhow absorb any systemic turbulence is, in fact, pointless. This is because economy is always one step ahead and can always find an effective antidote to any institutional barrier, as securitisations and collective loan sells might prove. A sub-social system, such as economy, that has immensely increased its dynamics, thus becoming semi-autonomous, eventually acquires a natural tendency to develop very powerful and rather self-reflective antibodies against any external compulsion. This is, in fact, the story of the Lehman Brothers crisis, whereby regulatory prohibitions to loans through the establishment of bank loan ceilings were easily bypassed through certain – not necessarily very inventive or ingenious – banking devices.

However, with regard to economy there is always the problem that as soon as regulation is passed, a loophole appears that calls for new regulation; this results in an endless race. Accordingly, only a radical change in the constitutive elements of the economy would make a difference, in that it would change the actual model upon which economy seems to be based, namely a transformation of the 'internal constitution' of the global financial economy.[4] Societal constitutionalists argue that the desired course for social sub-constitutions is in the limitations of the endogenous tendencies towards self-destruction and environmental damage. An external political determination of transnational social sub-constitutions is not feasible, because it is difficult to mutually align the function of a social system with its contribution to the environment at a sufficiently high level, unless this happens through a system of internal reflexion.[5] Since there is no way to foresee evolutions in the subsystem, due to rapidly changing circumstances, 'capital constitution' cannot affect them or prevent destructive tendencies; in Derrida's words, this requires changes to the 'capillary constitution' of the particular subsystem.[6]

---

[2] N Klein, *The Shock Doctrine. The Rise of Disaster Capitalism* (London, Penguin, 2008) 443–66.

[3] B Alexander, *The Globalization of Addiction* (Oxford, Oxford University Press, 2008) 57–84.

[4] G Teubner, 'A Constitutional Moment? The Logics of "Hitting the Bottom"' in PF Kjaer, G Teubner and A Febbrajo (eds), *The Financial Crisis in Constitutional Perspective. The Dark Side of Functional Differentiation* (Oxford, Hart Publishing, 2011) 3.

[5] ibid, 14–15.

[6] J Derrida, *The other Handing: Reflections on Today's Europe* (Bloomington, Indiana University Press, 1992) 34.

The actors of the global economic subsystem can be found not only in the traditional performers of organised economy, such as corporations and banks, but also in its spontaneous spheres.[7] In his works, Teubner suggests three means of inner constitutionalisation of the economy:[8]

(1) The politicisation of the consumers' individual and collective preferences through vehicles such as consumer activism, consumer campaigns, boycotts, product-criticism, eco-labelling, eco-investment, public-interest litigation and expressions of ecologic sustainability. The constitutional reflection of such movement would be to further protect citizens through third-party effect of fundamental rights accompanied by a higher level of freedom of expression, in particular negative criticism.
(2) The ecologisation of corporate governance through transformation of internal company structures oriented to sustainability.
(3) A plain money reform, whereby only central banks have the monopoly of non-cash money, whereas commercial banks would be prohibited from creating money through current account credit, merely limiting themselves to loans based on exiting reserves (this would require amendment to Article 16 of the Statute of the ECB).

Plain money reform has been widely elaborated in modern times, especially by Huber and Robertson, who suggested that the central bank alone should become the sole supplier of any form of money, thus excluding commercial banks from creating non-cash deposits and providing governments with an additional source of funds which would allow them to increase public expenditure or reduce taxation.[9] In essence, plain money reform constitutes a typical example of societal constitutionalism, in that it constitutes a self-limitation mechanism of the economy involving constitutional functions, processes and structures.

The *insight cognitive approach* suggests that emphasis should be placed on enhancing methods for a better understanding of how markets operate, so as to improve learning processes and, thus, reduce the risk of finding someone unprepared against a system fall-down. Those arguing in favour of insight processes focus on the perplexity of economy as a social phenomenon. For them, it is mostly the lack of basic understanding of the processes that results in the incapability of the legal system to respond to irregularities caused by the crisis. Using traditional compulsion to monitor such complex phenomena is ineffective, in that one tries to treat the symptoms without knowledge of the structures that mutate fast and produce extremely complicated situations. The vehicles of such transformation lie primarily with the rapidly evolving knowledge-based and technology-dependent

---

[7] G Teubner, *Constitutional Fragments. Societal Constitutionalism and Globalization* (Oxford, Oxford University Press, 2012).
[8] Teubner, 'A Constitutional Moment?' (2011) 3, 17–35.
[9] J Huber and J Robertson, *Creating New Money – A Monetary Reform for the Information Age* (London, New Economics Foundation, 2000).

society that shakes stability and foreseeability. If this statement is correct, constant evolution does not allow for regulation that requires, by definition, some time to be absorbed and effectively implemented.

In this line of argument, Ladeur considers that the uncertainty produced by the conversion of society into a knowledge-producing network society, the attempt to establish an orthodox normative pattern based on a unitary stabilising public ordering, is an illusion and what is needed is the advancement of cognitive learning processes to mitigate the risk of systemic break-downs. He argues that in technical environments, such as economy, the distinction between legal and factual norms is blurred: when it comes to evaluation of technical risks, a homogenisation and standardisation of the social knowledge infrastructure, ie the factual knowledge basis, can be observed from a public law perspective with regulation referring to practical experience to set the limits on technical industrial production.[10] In this respect, cognitive constitutionalism puts forward a cooperation between private and public actors, on the basis of knowledge and experience, in order to promote awareness and proper risk management practices. Self-regulation processes precisely enhance the discretion granted to social subsystems, especially of highly technical and complex structures, in order to create a fruitful mix of private and public co-existence and an even share of responsibilities and accountability. This pattern essentially results in a new type of constitutionalism based on cognitive processes, which would embrace economy as a key institutional actor with a high degree of liability, but at the same time subject to the principle of legality as any other part of state compulsion.

Traditional public law, based on the concept of legality within a permissible range of discretionary options through formalised administrative and judicial processes, seems rather embarrassed when dealing with issues of a highly technical nature (this explains judicial deference in technical matters). For private economic actors constitutes a synthesis of almost incomprehensible factual analyses that cannot be subject to a thorough in-depth analysis by a traditional state organ. Wide-scale cognitive processes, involving not only the State and public officials but also the societal actors may, thus, contribute to a better understanding of the phenomenon and the mitigation of the possibility of crises, as well as the minimisation of their adverse effects when those occur. In fact, economy should be seen as a collective state actor that ought to operate in the mindset of limited government and be monitored in the manner that any other state organ is constitutionally arranged, with the same gravity as independent administrative authorities. Thus, in the course of *Rechtsstaat*, economy must be subject to law and limited by law. It is exactly in this point that cognitive constitutionalism departs from the rudiments of societal constitutionalism.

---

[10] K-H Ladeur, 'The Financial Market Crisis – a Case of Network Failure?' in Kjaer et al (eds). *The Financial Crisis* (2011) 63–92, 67–68.

Although both theories argue that it is impossible to deal with economic phenomena through traditional external forward-thinking normative orders, because of their rapid evolution and responsiveness to challenges and compulsions, cognitive constitutionalists consider that inner restructuring may also prove to be equally ineffective: if there is always a response to external compulsion, there is no reason why economy could not equally evade structures purporting to introduce self-limitation standards. After all, the difference between internal and external compulsions is rather thin. The plain money policy could be seen in both ways, since it organises but also regulates the economy and it imposes sanctions for possible violations; from this viewpoint, this policy is not substantially different from the bank loan ceilings that did not prevent the US real estate market collapse in 2008.

What is further required is policies that would improve the understanding of how economic phenomena operate; this would, in turn, improve awareness as to the potential risks that any activity in the field (private or professional) would entail. Certain forms of cognitive constitutionalism were developed in the course of the economic constitutionalism era. Renner identifies ethnic networks, professional ethics and reputation mechanisms.[11] One might reasonably add corporate social responsibility, which is a management concept through which companies aims to achieve a proper balance between economic aspirations and social imperatives by integrating social concerns, such as public health, environmental preservation, accessible and quality education, into their business operations and interactions with their stakeholders.

One could also promote activities incorporating large-scale cognitive processes to economy, such as: strengthening of the syllabus in educational institutions of all levels; projects of familiarisation with the operation of economy; detailed information and instructions prior to any transaction of an economic character; multi-level follow-up of economic activities; and lifelong education on the evolution of economy. All these activities are motivated and launched by economic actors acting either on their own or in cooperation with state agencies. In a global world of hyper-complexity and multi-centrality, as described by autopoietic systems social theory, the monopoly of legislative coercion seems to be, in the insight cognitive understanding, at the same time a utopia and a false presumption.

The *outer-resilience approach* suggests that, in order to establish a proper balance between economy and politics/law, interventions ought to be made to strengthen the resilience of institutions to treat foreseeable or less foreseeable events. Proponents of this approach consider that the markets cannot be left alone and that emphasis should be placed on the regulatory subordination of economy to regulation. In that view, economy should not be awarded the status of a constitution as such, for that would amount to a serious obstruction to the logic of

---

[11] M Renner, 'Death by Complexity – The Financial Crisis and the Crisis of Law in World Society' in Kjaer et al (n 4) 93, 99.

representation and sovereignty. In the same way as any other semi-autonomous sectoral constitution, such as domestic or international sports organisations and religions, economy should be subordinate to law and politics. Society must be ready to treat economic malfunctions in the same way it would face any other societal destruction.

The historical fact that economy has gained a very severe and rather irrepressible autonomous status should not allow for a privileged position of economy in the regulatory structure. In that regard, regulatory trespasses should not be seen as systemic malfunctions but mostly as non-institutional behaviours by individual societal actors targeting profit-making. Irrespective of the economy's ability to adjust to regulatory constraints, the successful treatment of financial (or any other type for that matter) crises has to do with the institutional structures, which lie outside economy itself, and provide for the proper resolution mechanisms. Thus, independently of the substantive constraints (be that structural or functional) that are imposed on markets, the essential issue remains how they become constantly supervised and accountable to legitimate state agencies; how the State has been equipped with external enforcement mechanisms; or how the state architecture encourages rational and effective decision-making processes in the field of state economy.

From this viewpoint, fixing the state institutions would necessarily result in a greater capacity to monitor and treat financial crises and would, consequently, make those engaged in economic activities more self-conscious concerning regulatory obedience. Obviously, measures that can be classified in the outer-resilient approach may vary significantly. They can be either of low policy level, such as the OMTs policy, the abolition of bankers' bonuses, enhanced equity funds, quality control of financial products; of medium policy level, such as the introduction of budget discipline rules (eg the Six-Pack or the Two-Pack) and a Tobin tax; or, of high policy level, such as the re-engineering of the balance of state powers (reinforcement of domestic parliaments' supervision competences over hedge funds, capital flows, and stock market transactions, creation of new euro-area assembly, empowering the courts to deal with cases of a financial character). Throughout the crisis, a series of measures were taken in Europe in an attempt both to ease the adverse consequences of the crisis for some euro-area Member States and for Europe as a whole and to set up a new regulatory framework to prevent future crises.

Understandably, this schematic outline of the possible options to deal with financial crises cannot be exhaustive and, to some extent, constitutes an experiment of theoretical abstraction. Furthermore, the suggested responses are not mutually exclusive. Cognitive process can very easily be combined with inner-restructuring and conventional external compulsory measures. In fact, better cognitive understanding in a multi-disciplinary perspective is necessary and may reasonably lead to a more conjunctive solution. For example, issues such as the transformation of private banks to high-maintenance risk-managing institutions when using non-cash money or providing loans or the pre-crisis new financial products, whose effects were broadly underestimated, require a good understanding of the phenomenon and its implications (cognitive process), disciplined internal processes (inner structures) and external resilient regulations (regulatory compulsions).

Perhaps the most illustrative example of low cognisance of complex financial instruments in the pre-crisis era was the operation of credit-rating agencies, which, according to some, have developed into an anathema. Such agencies are a necessary component of contemporary economy as they provide a constant benchmarking for the credibility of both sovereign and private actors, always constituting a relevant consideration in investment decision-making. Yet, their functional basis is merely a modelling of trends and indicators, which by definition cannot prevent inaccuracies. Not surprisingly, the three large global credit-rating agencies were central players in the pre-crisis era.12[12] In fact, at that time, rating agencies essentially operated without extensive regulatory limitations and, paradoxically, they have become more profitable as the quality of their ratings has declined, including during the financial crisis.[13]

In a sense, Europe's inability to safeguard its currency and budgetary structure allowed a wide margin for the private sector to control global economy altogether. Ex post, a series of proposals have been made to deal with this systemic malfunction: the US 2010 financial regulatory reform, also known as the Dodd-Frank Act, authorised a new body to regulate rating agencies and included stricter liability provisions, while authors have also suggested other means, such as state subsidies to rating agencies,[14] less reliance on their ratings,[15] better understanding of how normal market actors think,[16] or even overall prohibition.[17] The truth is, however, that a useful and measurable standard of due diligence in relation to market assessments cannot possibly be established in view of the uncertainty inherent to the economic environment within which the agencies are called to operate. Mostly, rules of procedure, transparency, ethics (conflicts) and accountability are more feasible as measures to restore confidence in these agencies.

Towards this aim, the European Commission published, in December 2015, a Study on the Feasibility of Alternatives to Credit Ratings Final Report,[18] as well

---

[12] Above ch 3 section II C d.

[13] A Darbellay and F Partnoy, 'Credit Rating Agencies and Regulatory Reform' in CA Hill and BH McDonnell (eds), *Research Handbook on the Economics of Corporate Law* (Cheltenham, Elgar, 2012) 273.

[14] RJ Shiller, *The New Financial Order. Risk in the 21st Century* (Princeton, Princeton University Press, 2004) 124.

[15] Financial Stability Board, *Reducing Reliance on Credit Rating Agency (CRA) Ratings Action Plan*, available at: www.fsb.org/wp-content/uploads/c_140429vp.pdf.

[16] CA Hill, 'Why did Anyone Listen to the Rating Agencies after Enron?' (2009) 4 *Journal of Business and Technology Law* 283. Also see CA Hill, 'Regulating the Rating Agencies' (2004) 82 *Washington University Law Quarterly* 43.

[17] M Auerback, 'Ban the Credit Ratings Agencies!' 8 February 2013, www.salon.com/2013/02/08/ban_the_credit_ratings_agencies_partner.

[18] https://ec.europa.eu/info/system/files/alternatives-to-credit-rating-study-01122015_en.pdf.

as, on 1 January 2016, a Study on the State of the Credit Rating Market Final Report,[19] with very elaborate data on the functioning of the agencies and a series of proposals to curb the uncontrollable performance of the rating agencies to amend the existing regulatory framework package, ie Regulation 462/2013 and Directive 2013/14.

> Eventually, the crisis revealed the value of institutions, since cognitive processes do not suffice. Yet, institutions ought to treat the cognitive. At the end of the day, when excesses are produced by semi-autonomous social systems, such as economy, the course of action is either imposition of external limitations or inner-constitutionalisation. The latter would be by all means the greatest concession of orthodox constitutionalism which brought the idea of the monopoly of democratic autonomy through limited governance. For it would necessarily imply that subsystems outside the State are also eligible to an institutional degree of autonomy within which, if the argument stands the integrity test, state regulation is not welcome. In the context of conventional rule of law theory such an evolution would still be unacceptable at the current state of progress. Cognisance is by all means a prerequisite and proper account of internal rules of conduct within the economic structures is welcome, yet the response to excesses by any differentiated social subsystem eventually lies with a legitimate external system of rules, ie a resilient institutional constitutionalism.

Trying to deal with such a multi-level conundrum by simply using tools of economy is entirely unrealistic and vain. The persistence of the EU leadership in the era of new economic constitutionalism to deal with the financial crisis merely through tools of economic governance, which is a clear indication of the predominance of financialism, and neglecting all other aspects of a rational institutional architecture of a very unique structural entity, such as legitimacy, democratic accountability, rational decision-making and governance efficiency, is clearly in vain.[20] As Mark Dawson and Floris de Witteargue argue, the EU constitutional balance has been subverted altogether: the rise of executive control via the European Council, the isolation of smaller Member States and the creation of eternal fiscal rules uncontrollable by national parliaments have set the Union in danger of being desensitised to concerns and interests that need to be accommodated for a stable integration project to continue.[21] What the new economic governance in Europe has failed to address are the actual institutional deficits that, arguably, contributed to the eruption of the financial crisis.

The responsibility-sharing approach to the new model, without clear structures on national and EU level that will effectively create a balanced structural system and will set non-economic considerations at the epicentre of the political

---

[19] MARKT/2014/257/F4/ST/OP, https://ec.europa.eu/info/system/files/state-of-credit-rating-market-study-01012016_en.pdf.

[20] Ch Schweiger, *Exploring the EU's Legitimacy Crisis. The Dark Heart of Europe* (Cheltenham, Elgar, 2016) 257–64.

[21] M Dawson and F de Witte, 'Constitutional Balance in the EU after the Euro-Crisis' (2013) 76 *The Modern Law Review* 817, 818–19.

choices undermines the sustainability of the European project. In that, a restructuring in terms of institutions, as well as the substantive rules to secure sustainable and balanced economic and social growth, is, therefore, required, otherwise there is no way to predict that similar shortfalls risking disintegration will not appear in the future.[22]

New economic constitutionalism brought significant changes in the perception of politics and law. The Constitution, as part of the rule of law and a major institutional tool for political establishment, suffered significant devaluation. It was unable to prevent losses in relation to the rule of law and the social state. This phenomenon raised the call for politics to come back to the front. The call for growth now seems to counterbalance the stability obsession. Monetarism, as the prevailing notion of the 1980s in Europe that outcasted Keynes and his deeply European attributes on income-expenditure models,[23] seems to retreat before a less formalistic and economy-oriented institutionalism. The globality and the extent of the crisis smashed the myth that in developed economies mere financial instruments – banks, bonds, stocks, securities and insurance – may secure human happiness.

An interesting analogy can be drawn from the mid-war US economic crisis. Irrespective of the soundness of the positive analyses of the factual surroundings in the 1920s, the similarities before 2008 in Europe are evident: political stability; a general sense of social prosperity for the middle class; comfortable and wide circulation of money through relaxed bank lending policies; a relatively small part of income coming from labour; weak control over markets due to lack of effective mechanisms; and the lack of institutional means of direct intervention to support Member States at the level of the ECB. The after-effects of the crisis were familiar: a huge expansion of unemployment; elimination of the middle class; and financial depression eventually resulting in psychological depression.[24] However, the way President Roosevelt's administration dealt with the crisis in the US was based not only on fiscal grounds but also on support for a social-democratic welfare state. The essence of the growth strategy of the New Deal programme has not been widely transplanted to Europe.[25]

---

[22] J van Overtveldt, *The End of the Euro: The Uneasy Future of the European Union* (Berkeley, Agate Publishing, 2011) 183–86.

[23] P Kenway, *From Keynesianism to Monetarism: The Evolution of UK Macroeconometric Models* (London, Routledge, 1994). Also see T Congdon, *Keynes, the Keynesians and Monetarism* (Cheltenham, Elgar, 2007) 235–76, where the author re-reads Keynesian and post-Keynesian writings from a different angle, arguing that monetary principles greatly contributed to stability in the last quarter of the twentieth century in Europe. In the US, the most powerful contemporary voice against modern monetarism comes from WH James, *The Monetarists and the Evolving Crisis* (Parker, Outskirts Press, 2011).

[24] JK Galbreith, *The Great Crash 1929* (Wilmington, Mariner Books, 2009) 128–67.

[25] For instance, regulatory interventions for the protection of families with excessive bank loans (Home Owners Loans Act), for the protection of family bank accounts (Federal Deposit Insurance Corporation Act), for the introduction of transitory benefits for unemployed private sector workers (Civilian Conservation Corps), for the employment of redundant workers in large-scale public works (Reconstruction Finance Corporation Act, Public Works Administration Act, Works Progress Administration Act, Civil Works Administration Act) and for the intensification of social security

Today, it is clear that Europe stands before an inevitable crossroads: it shall either move forward with a costly long-vision policy entailing sounder institutions and further solidarity; or it shall remain stagnant, rendering economy a competitive playfield for all European countries. What is in demand is an 'unconventional adaptation', as Bruce Akkerman put it;[26] a New Deal or new Marshal Plan or new Bretton Woods project that would include rules to set up a global system of institutions and procedures to regulate not only the international monetary system and the commercial/financial relations but also the goals for sustainable social growth. But this should occur neither outside democratic legitimacy and accountability, nor by total sacrifice of post-war social democracy, which is the most astonishing achievement of Europe. A system that would embrace the fundamentals of good governance and the re-moralisation of international trade law, as a forum promoting collective good as opposed to an aggregate of individual interests,[27] and would go back to a more conventional concept of property, more of a John Locke idea based on labour and production as opposed to intangible funds.[28] Europe's legitimacy problem cannot be managed solely on grounds of structuralism or utilitarianism. As Habermas rightly put it in his basic legitimacy thesis, market and technocratic systemic structures should not outcast constitutional propriety and deliberative openness, which constitute elements of the European constitutional tradition and the foundation of constitutional legitimacy that is always a target for Europe.29[29]

The question thus remains as to what type of legitimacy should be targeted. Structural reforms concerning the input legitimacy of the Union, deriving from decision-making processes, seem to be more stable and preferable. Output legitimacy, deriving from the effectiveness of a decision, cannot by definition be the means to achieve higher values, but rather the end.[30] In this context, the analysis below refers to ex ante proposals aiming at establishing an institutional environment that could effectively mitigate the risks of any crisis, not only a financial one. The proposal excludes subsequent crisis-resolving measures, aiming at restoring faith and stability.

Although such measures are of obvious usefulness, the main target ought to be the institutional building that would allow for a resilient form of enhanced constitutionalism. In the words of Amartya Sen, the famous Nobel laureate and

---

and public health schemes (Social Security Act); see, CE White, *The Constitution and the New Deal* (Cambridge, MA, Harvard University Press, 2000) 167–97; B Kushman, *Rethinking the New Deal Court. The Structure of a Constitutional Revolution* (Oxford, Oxford University Press, 1998).

[26] B Ackerman, 'Revolution on a Human Scale' (1999) 108 *Yale Law Journal* 2279.

[27] See solid argumentation in A Lang, *World Trade Law after Neoliberalism: Reimagining the Global Economic Order* (Oxford, Oxford University Press, 2011) 345–552.

[28] 'The measure of property nature has well set by the extent of men's labour and the conveniences of life: no man's labour could subdue, or appropriate all ...' J Locke, *Second Treatise of Civil Government* (originally published 1690, Indianapolis, Hackett 1980) ch 5, section 36.

[29] J Habermas, *The Lure of Technocracy* (Cambridge, Polity Press, 2015); J Habermas, *The Crisis of the European Union A Response* (Cambridge, Polity Press, 2013).

[30] F Scarpf, *Governing in Europe: Effective and Democratic?* (Oxford, Oxford University Press, 1999).

professor of economics and philosophy, the intentions of the EU policy-makers have produced 'a world of misery, chaos and confusion', in that the legitimate intention of monetarism conflicted with a more urgent priority, namely the preservation of a democratic Europe that is concerned about societal well-being; 'these are values for which Europe has fought, over many decades'.[31] The legitimacy problem cannot only focus on the Union's economic structure, for the stakes are not only financial, as the major refugee crisis proved in the second half of the 2010s. Interestingly, if someone probes into the literature concerning the treatment of the financial crisis, they would come across a very extensive bulk of economic literature, an adequate quantity of political theory literature and only marginal law and institutional theory. It remains to be seen whether, like mid-war crisis, in David Kennedy's words,[32] the current depression will prove both a disaster and an opportunity for Europe.

A number of theories have tried to set a framework for the advancement of the EU. Theories of social constructivism and neo-functionalism operate mostly as narrative explanations of EU integration. Constructivism fluctuates between rationalism and reflectivism and suggests that reallocations of authority are better explained via changes in actor preferences and, therefore, it is the establishment of norms in the Union environment that is the driving force of integration as opposed to changes as a result of external factors.[33] Neo-functionalism has been suggested to transcend the original theories of federalism, functionalism and transactionalism, and to counter-balance intergovernmentalism.[34] Neo-functionalism is in fact a theory of regional integration aiming at enhancing individual sectors in the hope of achieving spill-over effects, ie the initial sovereign decision to grant specific economic competences to the centralised Community institutions created pressures and dynamics to extend their powers to interrelated policy areas, such as taxation, labour and environment.[35]

Although, neo-functionalism did indeed find adequate narrative support in the expanding dynamics of the Union until the 2000s, the increasing euroscepticism in the new millennium and the financial crisis have seriously hampered the spill-over effect, raising serious concerns regarding the actual roots of EU

---

[31] A Sen, 'The Crisis of European democracy' *New York Times*, 22 May 2012.

[32] DM Kennedy, *Freedom from Fear: The American People in Depression and War 1929–1945* (Oxford, Oxford University Press, 1999) 852–58.

[33] JT Checkel, 'Social Constructivism and European Integration' in T Christiansen, K Jorgensen and A Wiener (eds), *The Social Construction of Europe* (London, Sage, 2001); J Jupille, JA Caporaso and JT Checkel, 'Intergration Institutions: Rationalism, Constructivism, and the Study of the European Union' (2003) 36 *Comparative Political Studies* 7; R Koslowski, 'A Constructivist to Understanding the European Union as a Federal Polity' (1999) 6 *Journal of European Public Policy* 561; A Moravcsik, 'Is Something Rotten in the State of Denmark? Constructivism and European Integration' (1999) 6 *Journal of European Public Policy* 669.

[34] B Rosamond, *Theories of European Union Integration* (Basingstoke, Macmillan 2000) 20–73.

[35] M Eilstrup-Sangiovanni, 'Introduction. Neo-Functionalism and its Critiques' in M Eilstrup-Sangiovanni, (ed), *Debates on European Integration* (Basingstoke, Palgrave Macmillan, 2006) 89–104.

functionalism; this is why academics argue for a post-functional era[36] or, as a counter-theory, a post-democratic executive federalism.[37] All these theories, however, seem to rely on the preconception that the EU constitutes a single project which operates as a magnet to bring in the Member States. Yet, as previously demonstrated, there was neither a single perception of the project nor a common core of interest.[38]

Overall, an outer-resilience approach might conceivably adopt a top-down approach (aiming at structuring key institutions and the overall architecture of the State) or a bottom-up approach (aiming at bringing people and their rights at the epicentre of state policies). The proposal hereinafter puts forward an amalgam of three propositions: multi-level representative governance, holistic deliberativism and global solidarity/intergenerational sustainability.

II. Multi-Level Representative Governance

The current structure of the EU is essentially the reflection of continuous transformations of the integration project: from peace and prosperity in the 1950s and 1960s, to free market in the 1970s and 1980s, to political union with centralised monetary and fiscal management of the constituent Member States in the 2000s and 2010s. Obviously, such continuous transformations resulted in consecutive changes in the constitutional mix of the supranational entity with a view to adjusting to the requirements of each era. Market management and monetary union mostly required a more cognitive and technocratic approach, whereas the political union called for an elevated level of constitutional arrangement and legitimacy.

These temporal developments, along with the different perspectives of Member States on key issues concerning the physiognomy of the Union, with compromises and opt-outs rendering the institutional architecture a difficult puzzle, have resulted in a rather peculiar system that tries to accommodate seemingly antithetical poles:

(a) to upgrade the Union legitimacy through the involvement of both the European Parliament and – to a more limited extent – national parliaments;

(b) to reserve major policy decisions for the Council and, through the Council to the (most powerful) Member States;

(c) to maintain the European-oriented character of the Commission, and render it – to some extent – accountable to the Parliament; and

---

[36] L Hooghe and G Marks, 'A Postfunctionalist Theory of European Integration: From Permissive Consensus to Constraining Dissensus' (2009) 39 *British Journal of Political Science* 1.

[37] A Borriello and A Crespy, 'How to not Speak the 'F-Word': Federalism between Mirage and Imperative in the Euro Crisis (2015) 54 *European Journal of Political Research* 502, 519–20.

[38] Above ch 1 section III C.

(d)   to effectively deal with the very high institutional heterogeneity and diversification of EU Member States.

However, this complicated scheme, precisely because it purports to employ a number of characteristics that are hardly compatible with each other, presumably fails and is vulnerable in many respects. Not surprisingly, the issue of EU 'institutional balance' within the EU attracts significant attention both in literature and in the case law of the Court of Justice.[39] The inadequacy of the system both in terms of legitimacy and accountability, as well as in terms of effectiveness, was demonstrated in the first phase of the financial crisis.[40]

Given the complexity of the EU structures, the continuing effort to deal with questions of representation, legitimacy and the separation of powers, which undermine the development of the Union as an integral constitutional order, and the strong claims of renationalisation (especially after the 2004 enlargement of the Union), many tailor-made theories of governance might be applicable:

- various types of classic federalism;[41]

- multi-level quasi-federalism within Europe;[42]

- multi-level governance, ie a system produced through continuous negotiation among nested governments at supranational, national, regional and local level as a result of the institutional reallocation of powers;[43]

[39] On the issue of institutional balance within EU see K Lenaerts and A Verhoeven, 'Institutional Balance as a Guarantee for Democracy' in Ch Joerges and R Dehousse (eds), *Good Governance in Europe's Integrated Market* (Oxford, Oxford University Press, 2002) 35.

[40] B Crum and D Curtin, 'The Challenge of Making European Union Executive Power Accountable' in S. Piattoni (ed), *The European Union: Democratic Principles and Institutional Architectures in Times of Crisis* (Oxford, Oxford University Press, 2015) 63–87.

[41] Most importantly, constitutional federalism for the EU has been supported as a liberal emancipatory project in the 1941 *Ventotene* manifesto by anti-Fascist activists Ernesto Rossi and Altiero Spinelli; see A Spinelli and E Rossi, *The Ventotene Manifest* (The Altiero Spinelli Institute for Federalist Studies, 1988), 75. Also see, M Burgess, *Federalism and the European Union: The Building of Europe 1950–2000* (London, Routledge, 2000); A Glencross and AH Trechsel (eds), *EU Federalism and Constitutionalism – The Legacy of Altiero Spinelli* (Lanham, Lexington, 2010); RD Kelemen, *The Rules of Federalism: Institutions and Regulatory Politics in the EU and Beyond* (Cambridge, MA, Harvard University Press, 2004); JE Fossum and M Jachtenfuchs 'Federal Challenges and Challenges to Federalism. Insights from the EU and Federal States' (2017) 24 *Journal of European Public Policy* 467; R Koslowski, 'Understanding the European Union as a Federal Polity' in T Christiansen, KE Jørgensen and A Wiener (eds), *The Social Construction of Europe* (London, Sage, 2001).

[42] The Belgian ex-Prime Minister Guy Verhofstadt suggested in this respect 'United States of Europe', ie a core federal Europe composed of pro-federation Member States subsumed into the current Union, which would additionally take on specific common competences, namely social-economic policy, technology cooperation, justice and security policy, diplomacy and a European army. See, G Verhofstadt, *Verenigde Staten van Europa* (Antwerpen, Uitgeverij Houtekiet, 2006), translated into English under the title *The United States of Europe* (London, The Federal Trust, 2006).

[43] N Bernard, *Multilevel Governance in the European Union*, European Monographs Series Set no 35 (The Hague, Kluwer Law International, 2002); G Pagoulatos and L Tsoukalis 'Multilevel Governance in the European Union' in E Jones, A Menon and S Weatherill (eds), *Handbook on the European Union* (Oxford, Oxford University Press, 2012) 62; G Marks, 'Structural Policy and Multi-Level Governance in the EC' in A Cafruny and G Rosenthal (eds), *The State of the European Community: The Maastricht Debate and Beyond* (Boulder, Lynne Rienner, 1993) 391, 392. See also, G Marks and L Hooghe,

- polycentricity, ie governance through a multiplicity of decision-making actors that are formally independent of and competitive to each other and function coherently through contractual and cooperative undertakings and central mechanisms to resolve conflicts without a single collective institution controlling those actors altogether;[44] and

- functional overlapping competing jurisdictions arguing for autonomous communities and direct access to federal level courts for all citizens.[45]

In an effort to reconcile the seemingly antithetical poles advanced within the Union, various combinations have been proposed, from Weiler's progressive approach of an effective mix of legal supranationalism and political intergovernmentalism[46] to Majone's critical theory of Europe as a regulatory state which needs to remain within strict regulatory boundaries so as not to conflict with the lack of effectiveness and legitimacy.[47] Early enough, in 2001, the European Commission issued a White Paper on European Governance,[48] where it stressed the need for democratic institutions and the representatives of the people, both at national and European level, to try to connect Europe with its citizens as a starting condition for more effective and relevant policies through opening up the policy-making process to get more people and organisations involved in shaping and delivering EU policy to promote greater openness, accountability and responsibility for all those involved. Certainly, the response is not merely a matter of political choice but also an issue of institutional structures. Eventually, the political question still revolves around bargaining between federalism/supranationalism and national sovereignty/intergovernmentalism, between a relative halt through nationalisation of Europe, in the original British perception, and a deeper political unity through europeanisation of domestic politics towards an ever closer union, in the continental – mainly German – thinking.[49]

(2004) 'Contrasting Visions of Multi-Level Governance' in I Bache and M Flinders (eds), *Multi-Level Governance* (Oxford, Oxford University Press) 15–30; H Enderlein, S Wälti and M Zürn, *Handbook on Multi-Level Governance* (Cheltenham, Elgar, 2010); T Conzelmann and R Smith (eds), *Multi-Level Governance in the European Union: Taking Stock and Looking Ahead* (Baden Baden, Nomos, 2008); S Piattoni, 'Multi-Level Governance: A Historical and Conceptual Analysis' (2009) 31 *Journal of European Public Policy* 163.

[44] C Ostrom, M Tiebout and R Warren, 'The Organization of Government in Metropolitan Areas: A Theoretical Inquiry' (1961) 55 *The American Political Science Review* 831.

[45] R Eichenberger and BS Frey, 'Functional, Overlapping and Competing Jurisdictions: A Complement and Alternative to Today's Federalism' in A Ehtisham und G Brosio (eds), *Handbook of Fiscal Federalism* (Cheltenham, Elgar, 2006) 154–81.

[46] JHH Weiler, 'The Community System: the Dual Character of Supranationalism', (1981) 1 *Yearbook of European Law* 257; JHH Weiler, 'Transformation of Europe' (1991) 100 *Yale Law Journal* 2403.

[47] G Majone, *Dilemmas of European Integration: The Ambiguities and Pitfalls of Integration by Stealth* (Oxford, Oxford University Press, 2005).

[48] *European Governance. A White Paper* 25.7.2001 COM(2001) 428, http://europa.eu/rapid/press-release_DOC-01-10_en.htm.

[49] V Schmidt, 'The "New" EU Governance: "New" Intergovernmentalism Versus "New" Supranationalism plus "New" Parliamentarism' in *Cahiers du CEVIPOL* 5/2016 (Bruxelles, Université Libre de Bruxelles, 2016) 5; J Lacroix, *Communautarisme Versus Libéralisme: quel Modèle d'Intégration*

Although the need for Union restructuring has been evident and prominent, three paradoxes akin to new economic constitutionalism in the aftermath of the financial crisis have blurred the relevant debate, thus making any effort to doctrinally suggest a new model of political governance even more complicated. The first paradox is that while the financial crisis revealed all sorts of deficiencies in the structure of the euro area, which gave rise to serious concerns regarding the actual feasibility of the euro project, there was no substantiated debate on whether the monetary union should be abandoned or at least become looser. Instead, a more disciplined policy was projected as the only way out of the crisis. The second paradox is that the monitoring of fiscal commitments was centralised and entrusted to the EU institutions rather than the Member States, which is something not akin to federal layers of government where balanced budget rules apply but it is mostly for the States to ensure compliance. As Fabbrini argues, although in crafting the institutional response to the euro-area crisis state governments have repeatedly discarded a US-like federal model as being too centralised and centripetal for the EU, they have ended up establishing a regime that is much less respectful of state sovereignty than the US federal system.[50]

The third paradox relates to the gap between the high level of interdependence between EU Member States in the context of the monetary union and the ever closer fiscal union, on the one hand, and the increasing actual discrepancies among the States both in terms of their financial status and their relevant political strength in the European decision-making process, on the other. According to Joerges, although the EU Member States are no longer autonomous but are, in many ways, interdependent and, hence, dependent upon co-operation, this interdependence strikingly contrasts with an ever greater socio-economic diversity, new schisms between euro area countries and other EU Member States, conflicts between north and south, creditors and debtors.[51]

The task of multi-level representative governance must primarily address three main concerns: to strengthen the level of direct legitimacy of key EU institutions (legitimisation); to actively involve European territories into the Union governance (regionalisation); and to establish a functional constitutional ratio of checks and balances between EU institutions as well as between the community and the intergovernmental methods of decision-making (europeanisation).[52]

Politique? Les Présupposés Normatifs d'une Union Politique Européenne à la Lumière des Débats Intellectuels Contemporains, PhD Thesis (Université de Bruxelles, 2003).

[50] F Fabbrini, 'The Fiscal Compact, the "Golden Rule", and the Paradox of European Federalism' (2013) 36 *Boston College International and Comparative Law Review* 1; F Fabbrini, *Economic Governance in Europe. Comparative Paradoxes and Constitutional Challenges* (Oxford, Oxford University Press) 23–61.

[51] C Glinski and Ch Joerges, 'European Unity in Diversity?! A Conflicts-Law Re-construction of Controversial Current Developments' in K Purnhagen and P Rott (eds), *Varieties of European Economic Law and Regulation. Liber Amicorum for Hans Micklitz* (Cham, Springer, 2014) 285.

[52] P Stephenson, 'Twenty Years of Multi-Level Governance: Where does it Come from? What is it? Where is it Going?' (2013) 20 *Journal of European Public Policy* 817, 821–22.

Many structural suggestions are conceivable and have indeed been set in this respect both by academics and politicians. For instance, Habermas suggested multi-layer EU with more federation-friendly EU Member States in the first core layer, whereas former Commissioner and member of the European Parliament Vivian Reading suggested that the Commission be directly elected by the Parliament, be controlled by the Parliament by means of a Westminster-type control, and be granted the competence to dissolve the Parliament, as well as that the President of the Commission preside over the European Council.[53]

Clearly, most of the institutional proposals focus on the strengthening of the parliamentary model, not the presidential aspects of the EU polity, ie increasing the powers and control of the already directly legitimate Parliament vis-a-vis the Commission and the Council. This may be attributed, according to Decker and Sonnicksen, to familiarisation of the heads of European governments with the parliamentary system and the widespread idea that the political system of the EU already 'leans' toward a parliamentary system. However, in the authors' view, the deficient consolidation of the EU party system poses an insurmountable hurdle for its democratisation; in the EU context, a prerequisite for true parliamentarisation would be the europeanisation of the European Parliament elections, ie transnational elections on the basis of a single and united electoral system, cross-border political entities participating in the elections and a wide European political agenda.[54]

The thesis of the book aims at a symmetrical strengthening of democratic processes and correlating input legitimacy within the EU, through a fusion of federal and presidential characteristics, closer to Hig's idea of 'limited democratic politics',[55] which would respect concerns of both the Member States and the people and could provide some mobilising force to the European project: direct election of the Commission through an alternative vote system and a second chamber equally representing the Member States and the European territories thereof.

As regards *direct election of the Commission through an alternative vote system*, there has been a constant effort by the Union to furnish the process with some elements of legitimacy. In fact, since the pre-1994 era, when the Commission president was appointed by common accord of the governments of the Member States, the process has undergone six changes towards a more democratic vision.[56] Eventually, the Treaty of Lisbon stipulated that the results of the European elections have to be taken into account when the Council, after appropriate consultations

---

[53] V Reding, 'Mit einer Vision aus der Krise Finden' *Frankfurter Allgemeine Zeitung*, 9 March 2012.

[54] F Decker and J Sonnicksen, 'The Direct Election of the Commission President. A Presidential Approach to Democratising the European Union', Centre for European Integration Studies, ZEI Discussion Paper C 192 (2009) 5–7, 14.

[55] S Hix, *What's Wwrong with the European Union and How to Fix it?* (Cambridge, Polity Press, 2008).

[56] F Decker and J Sonnicksen, 'An Alternative Approach to European Union Democratization: Re-examining the Direct Election of the Commission President' (2011) 46 *Government and Opposition* 168.

and acting by a qualified majority, proposes to the Parliament the candidate for Commission President (Declaration 11 on Article 17(6) and (7) TEU annexed to the Treaty). The candidate for President is subject to a vote of consent by the Parliament and is then appointed by the Council, acting by a qualified majority (Article 17(7) TEU). The Council, acting by a qualified majority and by common accord with the President-elect, adopts the list of candidates for Commissioners, on the basis of the suggestions made for one candidate by all Member States.

Although the Treaty does not involve the European Parliament in the proposal made by the Council ex ante, prior to the 2014 elections, the main political parties in the Parliament nominated a candidate, who would become President of the Commission in case of electoral victory of the respective party in the elections, a system prescribed as *Spitzenkandidat*. In this context, there was a clear electoral campaign on the part of the candidates for the presidency of the Commission, which, although not institutionalised, did not raise any objections but was merely considered as a normal development of European politics. The same practice was also observed in the way towards the 2019 elections with the major parties having made public their choices for the candidate for the presidency of the Commission.

Technically, if the Council does not propose the candidate among the European party that won the elections, there will be a significant political crisis since the Parliament eventually retains the power to veto the Council's proposal. The Commission is collectively accountable to the Parliament, which may adopt a motion of censure against its members; this requires a two-thirds majority representing a majority of Parliament's component members, in which case the members of the Commission, including the High Representative of the Union for Foreign Affairs and Security Policy (Article 17(8) TEU and in Article 234 TFEU), are required to resign. The members of the Commission must be completely independent in the performance of their duties, in the general interest of the Union (Article 245 TFEU) and may be compulsorily retired by the Court of Justice, at the request of either the Council or the Commission itself, in case they breach any Treaty obligations or are found guilty of serious misconduct (Article 247 TFEU).

The proposal for direct election of the President of the Commission, and not the Commission as a whole, has been sporadically brought up, with some variations, by political theorists[57] and politicians.[58] Yet, the whole debate about the

[57] V Bogdanor, 'The Future of the European Community: Two Models of Democracy' (1986) 21 *Government and Opposition* 161; S Hix, 'Elections, Parties, and Institutional Design. A Comparative Perspective on European Union Democracy' (1998) 21 *West European Politics* 19; F Decker, 'Governance beyond the Nation-State: Reflections on the Democratic Deficit of the European Union', (2002) 9 *Journal of European Public Policy* 256; M Gallagher, M Laver, M Marsh, R Singh and B Tonra, 'Electing the President of the European Commission', Trinity Blue Papers in Public Policy 1, Trinity College (1995).
[58] J Fischer, 'Vom Staatenbund zur Föderation. Rede am 12. Mai 2000 in der Humboldt-Universität in Berlin am 12. Mai 2000', in C Joerges, Y Mény and JHH Weiler (eds), *What Kind of Constitution for what Kind of Polity? Responses to Joschka Fischer* (Cambridge, MA, Harvard Law School, 2000) 5–17;

democratisation of the EU seems to favour democratic injunctions in the parliamentary structures as opposed to executive structures. The basic characteristics of the proposal set forth in this book for direct election of the Commission as a means to enhance democratic legitimacy are:

(a) Single ballot, including the President of the Commission and the candidates for Commissioners. In the course of the term in office, the President of the Commission may release a Commissioner from office, but in this case the new Commissioner is subject to the consent of the Houses. Until the new appointment process is confirmed, the President of the Commission exercises the competences of the vacant Commissioner's office.

(b) Alternative vote system so that the voter may put a number of preference by each candidate; if there is an absolute majority of first options in favour of a candidate, that candidate is elected President, otherwise the last candidate in number of votes is discarded and the second round is automatically calculated with the second choices of those who voted for the eliminated candidate. This process goes on for as many rounds as needed until one candidate gets the absolute majority of votes.

   This system is used in Australia for the House of Representatives and in Ireland for the President, but it was not upheld in the British election reform referendum in 2012. It combines: *legitimacy*, since the elected President will by definition have more than 50 per cent of the popular vote among the last two candidates and all votes eventually count; *convenience*, since it precludes multiple actual electoral rounds or run-off votes; and *political convergence*, since it substantially reduces the chances of extreme or marginal political figures from being elected in office.

(c) The elected President, and all Commissioners for that matter, would neither be dependent on a vote of confidence nor be subject to a motion of censure by the Parliament. Since the President would enjoy legitimacy of his/her own, he/she could not be removed from office, but could only be impeached, as any other member of the Commission, by a qualified majority of two-thirds of the members of the Parliament in case of gross misconduct or a criminal conviction.

(d) The Commission retains its existing competences; no competence to dissolve the Parliament is granted. However, the President of the Commission would also preside over the European Council.

(e) The European Council retains a role as a general policy orientation forum and a veto power in the amendment of the Treaties.

The political consequences of this structural reform would be rather significant. First, the European electorate would obviously have a more direct say in the

J Bruton, 'A Proposal for the Appointment of the President of the Commission as Provided for in Art 18.bis of the Draft Constitutional Treaty', Contribution from J Bruton, Member of the Convention on the Future of Europe, for Consideration by the Convention, 6 January 2003, CONV 476/03.

formation of EU policies, given that the elections would inevitably take place both on the basis of policy agendas presented by the candidates and of European party politics, through the establishment of pan-European political parties, campaigning as such in favour of a particular candidate, not merely through the current *Spitzenkandidat*, but mostly as a matter of institutionalised process of direct representation. Second, the new architecture would render the governance system more presidential, since the Commission would now enjoy direct legitimacy along with the Parliament. This legitimacy upgrade would arguably result in a stronger political role for the Commission. Third, an increased level of political cooperation between the executive, having the power to initiate legislation, (here, the Commission) and the legislature (here, the Parliament) would by definition be required in order to implement Union policies.

As regards a *second chamber*, the proposal is not presented for the first time. In fact, it goes even before the launching of the European Economic Community. In 1952, an ad hoc Constitutional Committee, appointed by the Common Assembly of the European Coal and Steel Community upon initiative of France, Germany and Italy, and chaired by Heinrich von Brentano, drafted a European Political Community treaty, the envisaged predecessor of the European Economic Community. The draft treaty provided for a bicameral parliament, comprising a directly elected Chamber of the Peoples and a European Senate appointed by the national parliaments; these would jointly have legislative powers and control over the executive determining the policy of the future European army. Furthermore, the Senate would elect the president of the executive council, who would be responsible for the administration of the community and accountable to the Chamber of the Peoples. The draft treaty was rejected by the Foreign Ministers of the six Member States of the European Coal and Steel Community, because it was considered to be very federalist in nature.[59]

Indeed, in such state structures, sub-federal entities are directly represented in federal decision-making through a second chamber of state representatives, which, therefore, establishes a vertical system of separation of powers and a dual level of legitimacy. This is mostly because of the multiplicity of authorities that are external to the constitutional personality of the Union itself and refer to the Member States (essentially the European Council and the Council) and the domestic parliaments, which also operate on an EU level as external institutional actors. Accordingly, Member States operate on a sub-level and directly through the Council, which contributes to the ordinary legislative process on equal terms with the European Parliament. One might also add the European Council in the federal framework: the most fitting interpretation in this respect is, according to Palonen and Wiesner, to view the European Council and the Council as

---

[59] DW Urwin, *The Community of Europe: A History of European Integration since 1945*, 2nd edn (Abingdon, Routledge, 1995) 58.

'two distinct configurations or two parts of the second parliamentary chamber',[60] or, according to Hueglin and Fenna, as 'second-chamber governance'.[61] Interestingly, in the course of the evolution of the EU, a number of European politicians, routed in divergent political backgrounds, such as Tony Blair, Valéry Giscard d'Estaing, François Mitterrand and Gerhard Schröder, revisited the original idea of a second chamber. On the other hand, Chancellor Angela Merkel argued, on 14 December 2012, that, in the process of a fully fledged EU, the Commission should develop as a Union government body and the Council should become something like a second chamber.[62]

The basic characteristics of the proposal regarding a second chamber are as follows:

(a) As regards its composition, Member States would be represented on an equal standing, ie with the same number of representatives (indicatively 10), irrespective of the population and the relevant power of each Member State, after the model of the US Senate. The members of the chamber would be appointees of the Member States' national parliaments (jointly in case of bicameral parliaments). A further strict EU law obligation for even representation of the European regions would apply, in the sense that the appointees must be geographically dispersed to domestic territories in order for the chamber to eventually reflect the regions of Europe. Once appointed, the member of the second chamber would not be removed from office at the discretion of the appointing Member States.

(b) As regards its term in office, this should be rather limited (indicatively two years), in order to reflect the contemporary political power in the appointing Member States as closely as possible.

(c) As regards its competences, the second chamber would participate in the legislative process on an equal footing with the European Parliament, but it would not have the competence to control the Commission; this would remain with the Lower House. Amendment to the Treaties must be decided by a qualified majority in both Houses, with the consensus of the European Council. Finally, the second chamber would also assume the competence to initiate, alongside the Commission, legislation on its own motion, to deal with the current state of imperfect parliamentarism reflecting the reluctance of the Member States to grant such a significant power that could lead the Parliament to develop a rather autonomous policy. Yet, given the composition of the second chamber, such relative empowerment would not result in an abrupt change in the parliamentary process.

---

[60] K Palonen and C Wiesner 'Second Chamber, "Congress of Ambassadors" or Federal Presidency. Parliamentary and Non-Parliamentary Aspects in the European Council's Rules of Procedure' (2016) 36 *Parliaments, Estates and Representation* 71, 88.

[61] ThO Hueglin and A Fenna, *Comparative Federalism: A Systematic Inquiry*, 2nd edn (Toronto, University of Toronto Press, 2015) 208, 225–30.

[62] Borriello and Crespy, 'How to not Speak the 'F-word' (2015) 515.

(d) As regards collateral institutional effects, since the second chamber would essentially take over the legislative powers of the Council, the latter would turn to a body of national experts (not necessarily the ministers of the respective fields of legislation) that could be part of the legislative process through filing a report on the matter or requesting the Commission for a legislative initiative.

Obviously, the political consequences of launching a second chamber would be equally substantial, especially from the point of view of the federal elements that would be introduced as a result of an almost perfect bicameralism. First, from the point of view of the Union's polity, there would be a federal element of two-level representation, ie by population (the European Parliament) and by Member States (the second chamber). Second, from the point of view of institutional checks and balances, the new legislative player would arguably bring a more rational regulatory decision-making process. This is predominantly due to the replacement of the politically dominant Council by a second chamber with different political characteristics and institutional idiosyncrasy that would reflect not only the national interests but also the Union's interest. This would amount to an overall upgrade of the legislative process and, by reflection, of the Lower House. Obviously, the two Houses would have to develop a *modus vivendi* in the American bicameralism style of political co-habitation, which would conceivably be more feasible and effective without the externalities of the Council. Third, from the point of view of vertical organisation of the Union, the second chamber would reflect a federalist element in a double manner: first, on a state level, due to the equal representation of the Member States, supplementing the European Parliament's proportionate representation; and second, on a regional level, since European sub-state regions would be represented in their capacity as genuine EU regions. With regard to regional representation, currently, only EU primary law gives regions the possibility to become stakeholders in the process of European integration only indirectly, through the Committee of Regions and its jurisdictional standing before the Court of Justice in actions on alleged infringement of the principle of subsidiarity of a legislative act.[63]

The proposal for direct election of the Commission and for a second chamber constitutes an amalgam of supranational and intergovernmental elements, leaning mostly towards the former in a more presidential and federal perception of governance. Obviously, this proposal amounts to a more complex system of checks and balances that would altogether improve the cumulative state of the Union's legitimacy and, arguably, result in a more functional system of governance. Two objections could be raised in relation to the plausibility of the above scheme: a normative one and a factual one.

---

[63] Article 8 of Protocol (No 2) on the application of the principles of subsidiarity and proportionality, annexed to the Treaties by the Treaty of Lisbon.

The normative objection is based on the assumption that direct election for the Commission runs an implicit risk that this branch of Union government would opt for an upgrade of its political role within the EU structures, thus causing further turbulence in the Union's architecture. This objection is by definition invalid. Direct election of the Commission might politically connote its more active involvement in defining the Union policies but would not institutionally expand its competences, especially in the light of the doctrines of conferred powers and subsidiarity. The example of the European Parliament is, in this respect, illustrative. It was not the launching of direct elections of its members in 1979, replacing the pre-existing system of delegated national parliamentarians, but the actual changes introduced in the Treaties that steadily enhanced its competences as co-legislator of equal standing with the Council and as a controller of the actions of the Commission. It seems that, in the light of the current institutional and factual surroundings, there can be no executive EU power, equivalent to Charles de Gaulle's power in 1958, to significantly transform the political system of the Union.

The factual objection contests the actual willingness of the Member States to proceed to an institutional restructuring that would obviously curtail the intergovernmental aspects of Union governance by downgrading the European Council and the Council. This political objection is in principle valid, irrespective of the soundness of the normative objection. The history of the Member States' policies on deepening the European project, especially after Nice, does not leave ample space for optimism when it comes to the strengthening of the supranational institutions of the Union. This reflects what has been described by Borriello and Crespy as a 'double discourse' of leaders of influential Member States rendering the federalism question both a taboo and a pervasive issue: constitutional federalism is at the same time elusive, ineluctable and unreachable, whereas functional (economic) federalism has become an ubiquitous imperative justifying further integration (the 'elephant in the room' pathology).[64]

Yet, some improvement has been made. As of 1979, political parliamentarism seems to rise in the European Parliament as a matter of increased power for transnational parties. As supported by extensive empirical data, there has been growing party cohesion, despite growing internal national and ideological diversity within the European party groups.[65] After Lisbon, the *Spitzenkandidat* method, upon which all EU Member States agreed in the drafting of the Treaty, none objecting in the pre-electoral period for the 2014 European Parliament elections, clearly stands for a strong move towards politicisation of the Commission

[64] Borriello and Crespy (n 37) 504; A Borriello and A Crespy, 'Less and More Europe: The EU at a Crossroads between Federalism and Political Disintegration', London School of Economics European Politics and Policy blog (2016), http://blogs.lse.ac.uk/europpblog/2016/01/14/less-and-more-europe-the-eu-at-a-crossroads-between-federalism-and-political-disintegration.

[65] S Hix, A Noury and G Roland, 'Power to the Parties: Cohesion and Competition in the European Parliament, 1979–2001' (2005) 35 *British Journal of Political Science* 209.

on the grounds of its upgraded legitimacy. This is clearly reflected in Juncker's presidency, the first one under the new system, which could be reasonably characterised as a strongly 'political' Commission, within, nonetheless, the competences awarded to the Commission.[66] Besides, in political practice the European Parliament does not behave as a typical House in a parliamentary system, ie through party discipline and strong political alliances, but mostly with a rather loose affiliation of members with their respective parties. In this context, the current Union structure already 'behaves' like a presidential system.[67] However, this system has failed to boost democratic legitimacy and accountability of the Commission and, most importantly, did not bring European people closer to EU politics, since the whole process was properly understood by a limited number of political circles and academics, creating, therefore, no added value for European politics.[68]

Thus, the situation remains that the Parliament neither controls the European executive nor determines its political agenda, which, in turn, deprives citizens from the possibility to directly influence policy-making and choose their political leadership. At any rate, the Commission has already been granted the competence of initiating new EU legislation, which is not an insignificant power. The diminution of the actual power of the intergovernmental European Council and, especially, the Council as a result of the second chamber and the legitimation of the Commission would most probably trigger negative reflexes on the part of the Member States. Yet, both institutions would retain some core competences of general policy orientation (the European Council) and as expert advice (the Council). In any case, Member States maintain the crucial power to appoint members of the second chamber, which could ease relevant concerns and act as a counterbalance mechanism to the possible reinforcement of a majoritarian element due to the direct election of the Commission by the European people, that could arguably dilute the relative power of the smaller States against the larger and more powerful ones.

III. Holistic Deliberativism

Deliberative decision-making has been a key element in the discussion concerning a new and enriched vision of democracy. David Held considered deliberative democracy as a new (ninth) version of democracy in the third edition of his authoritative *Models of Democracy*.[69] As a term, it first appeared in 1980 in

---

[66] J Peterson, 'Juncker's Political European Commission and an EU in Crisis' (2017) 55 *Journal of Common Market Studies* 349.

[67] Decker and Sonnicksen, 'The Direct Election of the Commission President' (2011) 28.

[68] Schweiger, *Exploring the EU's Legitimacy Crisis* (2016) 189–207.

[69] D Held, *Models of Democracy*, 3rd edn (Cambridge, Polity Press, 2006) 231–58.

Bessett's work and was expanded in his later works.[70] Distinguished scholars worldwide, such as Joshua Cohen, Claus Offe and Ulrich Preuss, James Fishkin, Jon Elster, John Dryzek, Philip Petit and James Bohman, have ever since elaborated upon this topic. Furthermore, fundamental aspects of deliberativism in democratic decision-making have been dealt with by leading figures of political philosophy, such as Jürgen Habermas, John Rawls, James Madison, Karl Marx and Plato.

Deliberative decision-making stands for the process of opinion-convergence through wide and equal participation and reasoned and elaborate exchange of arguments so as to produce legitimate outcomes, ie ethical and justifiable grounds for regular obedience to power. According to the orthodox deliberative theory, when decision-making complies with the required standards, the outcome is bound to be reasoned, and there is no need to have recourse to substantive criteria in order to assess the outcome itself. By way of contrast, if no deliberative process is followed, the outcome may still be, as a matter of coincidence, reasonable, or even optimal, but it cannot be reasoned. It is, in that view, the deliberative process that will adduce reason and not the opposite. In that abstract sense, the deliberative process resembles Rawls' 'pure procedural justice' (as opposed to perfect and imperfect procedural justice), in which, if there is a correct or fair procedure, the outcome is likewise correct or fair, whatever that outcome is.[71] It also resembles Habermas's idea of the public sphere as a (virtual) community beset by the 'ideal speech situation', where everyone should be allowed to take part in a discourse, to introduce and question any assertion whatsoever and to express their attitudes, desires and needs; on the other hand, no one should be prevented, by internal or external coercion, from exercising the above rights and there is no oppression in the decision-making apart from that of the optimal solution, which cannot be rationally refuted.[72]

In a multi-layer environment, deliberative decision-making approaches Maduro's interpretive pluralism, in that it suggests and presupposes a common basis for discourse between institutional actors from various legal orders (in deliberative processes this is tantamount to reason), that must be shared by all of them, while respecting their competing interests and claims for authority.[73] Furthermore, building upon the premises of a divided world and divided societies (the concept of the clash of civilisations, originally conceived by Lewis and developed and diffused by Huntington, arguing that on an international level cultural disputes

[70] J Bessett, 'Deliberative Democracy: The Majority Principle in Republican Government' in L Goldwin and D Shambra (eds), *How Democratic is the Constitution?* (Washington DC, American Enterprise Institute, 1980).

[71] J Rawls, *A Theory of Justice* (Cambridge, MA, Harvard University Press, 1971) 118–41.

[72] J Habermas, *Strukturwandel der Öffentlichkeit. Untersuchungen zu einer Kategorie der Bürgerlichen Gesellschaft*, 5 Auflage (Darmstadt, Luchterhand, 1962) 176–85; translated into English, The Structural Transformation of the Public Sphere: An Inquiry into a Category of Bourgeois Society (Boston, MA, Massachusetts Institute of Technology Press, 1989).

[73] M Maduro, 'Contrapunctual Law: Europe's Constitutional Pluralism in Action' in N Walker (ed), *Sovereignty in Transition* (Oxford, Hart Publishing, 2003) 501, 523–29.

would constitute the starting point of world crises in the future), and discarding the restrictive vision of neoconservativism and cosmopolitanism, Dryzek suggests that global deliberative politics constitutes the most reliable model of thorough democratic government.[74]

Deliberative processes serve three types of purposes: the dogmatic purpose of legitimacy; the instrumental purpose of participation; and the substantive purpose of reason. The *dogmatic* purpose of legitimacy suggests that deliberative processes invest with legitimacy the decisions taken by authorities, especially those which do not enjoy direct legitimacy, thus bridging through rational processes the potential gap between legality and legitimacy. The underlying idea of the legitimacy factor is that, as Dryzek sees it, the outcomes are legitimate to the extent that they receive reflective assent through participation in authentic deliberation by all those subject to the decision in question.[75]

The *instrumental* purpose of participation suggests that deliberativism improves the level of citizens' involvement. Deliberation semantically surpasses reflection, dialogue and participation. It surpasses reflection, which is a solipsistic exercise, by involving at least two people or deliberative bodies or entities; one person, irrespective of the level of his/her intelligence, is not in a position to enter into a deliberative process of argumentation and exchange.[76] It also surpasses dialogue, in that it emphasises not only the procedural mechanics of speech-making, to which dialogue is basically restricted, but also the scope of participation (the maximum possible of all stakeholders) and the actual outcome of the deliberative process, ie the achievement of an optimum result for the political community. Finally, it surpasses participation and participatory democracy, which reflect a formal procedure without any guarantees towards a reasoned exchange of arguments. As Fishkin puts it, contemporary democracy appears as a forced choice between politically equal but relatively incompetent masses and politically unequal but powerful elites; in either case people are uninterested, debate is superficial and dominated by personalities as opposed to reason, and politics is dominated by a media-saturated world.[77] For deliberative purposes, it is not crucial to broaden participation, although this is as a desirable matter of principle, but to introduce added-value procedures resulting in the formulation of carefully considered, consistent, and reasoned choices.

The *substantive* purpose of deliberativism is to implement a democracy of reason that necessarily involves all potential arguments and all sustainable solutions. Reason, including beliefs about the means and the ends, is a salient

---

[74] JS Dryzek, *Deliberative Global Politics. Discourse and Democracy in a Divided World* (Cambridge: Polity Press 2006) 148–64.

[75] JS Dryzek, *Deliberative Democracy and Beyond: Liberals, Critics, Contestations* (Oxford, Oxford University Press, 2000) 651.

[76] I Shapiro, 'Optimal Deliberation?' (2002) 10 *Journal of Political Philosophy* 196, 196–97.

[77] JS Fishkin, *Democracy and Deliberation: New Directions for Democratic Reform* (New Haven, Yale University Press, 1991) 1–3.

feature in collective decision-making, serving to eliminate the force of other hidden or revealed incentives, such as interest and passion.[78] Most importantly, reason operates as a counterbalance to majoritarianism, which, within the boundaries of the constitutional restraints upon government, is somehow indifferent towards the achievement of optimal outcomes. This is so because there is a presumption that either the majority holds the wisdom to advance what is best for the political community (and, therefore, for the majority itself) or that the interests of the majority are equivalent to the interest of the political community as a whole.

Irrespective of the obvious counter-arguments that one may raise against these premises, either on the basis of political ideology or on the basis that such collective wisdom can never exist, the argument that optimal outcomes stem from majoritarian processes is challenged on a variety of narrative grounds. The majority outcome is not necessarily tested against any other alternative, either because all the arguments may not be in place (due to a lack of information), or because arguments might not have been given their relative value (due to inadequate or false procedures), or because those suggesting arguments are not on an equal footing when it comes to the formation of the majority will (due to the influential role of political elites and the media or to people's apathy towards issues affecting the political community). By bringing reason into the discussion, deliberativism departs from the arena of market-oriented political competition and adopts a forum-oriented approach where reason dominates public discourse.

Given that deliberativism suggests a specific technique of decision-making process, any procedure before a collective body (eg the parliament, the council of ministers, a court) can qualify as deliberative. Yet, the most ordinary vehicles of deliberativism are polls, juries and assemblies. Polls indicate the process where emphasis is placed on the evidence provided to substantiate various approaches to the issue in question and not to the actual interplay between members of a voting body (an assembly in a proper sense), provided that this body is constituted properly, the process is transparent and the electors support the process and possess a retraction predilection. Juries indicate the process where emphasis is placed on the actual interplay of members of a voting body with a view to achieving unanimity, provided that the evidence furnished to substantiate various approaches to the issue in question is at an appropriate level, the body is constituted properly and the electors support the process and are open to other reasoned options. Assemblies broadly resemble juries, the only difference being that no unanimity is required as a matter of principle, but the outcome is legitimate if an adequate majority is achieved. In order to qualify as deliberative, polls and assemblies must abide by the basic rules of deliberativism. Global polls and assemblies operate at the present time in Switzerland, whereas experiments of deliberative micro-bodies at a representative level have been launched in many parts of the world, especially at regional and local levels, with diverse results.

---

[78] C Offe and U Preuss, 'Democracy Institutions and Moral Resources' in D Held (ed), *Political Theory Today* (Cambridge, Polity, 1991) 156–57, 167.

Holistic deliberativism proposed hereinafter constitutes a fully fledged deliberative model of decision-making, as a set of applied principles to supplement existing institutional safeguards at all levels of governance, including international, central, regional and local government. Decentralised layers of government are essential in the implementation of an effective model of deliberative democracy. This is so, on a practical level, primarily because the size of regional and local authorities allows for a more substantial involvement of participants and an interaction of arguments on particular issues and eases the basic scale problem encountered by all proponents of deliberativist theories. Following the economic model of voter participation, which has been developed with extreme mathematical rigour by Riker and Ordeshook, it appears that the level of voter participation in any voting procedure is largely determined by the subjective probability of affecting the election results, ie the closer the citizens believe the election will be.[79] Therefore, it is of acute importance that the electors believe that their opinion can be effective; that it might succeed in overturning a prevailing view or that it might be a crucial one. On a theoretical level, decision-making at a level closer to the citizens provides further input legitimacy, especially when the issues in question relate mostly to matters of local interest. In order for a decision-making process to qualify as deliberative, five conditions ought in principle to apply cumulatively: inclusiveness, endorsement, evidence, interplay/fair play and transparency.[80]

The first condition of deliberativism is *inclusiveness*. It calls for the enhancement of all interests involved in or affected by the outcome of the decision-making. In global participatory processes the condition of inclusiveness does not, by definition, apply, since everyone is entitled to participate and to express an opinion. This is the case, for example, in large-scale or local – physical or electronic – referenda, where all citizens participate in the voting process. Obviously, if not all interests are represented, there will most likely be a shortage in the arguments presented to the deliberative body. Furthermore, the arguments set out in the course of the deliberative process need not only be presented but also elaborated, refined and enriched when interacting with other contrary or concurring – in part or in whole – arguments, so that all participants may reflect on the qualities of each argument and reach a reasoned conclusion. Therefore, both the arguments and those originally advancing each set of arguments ought to be present and active in the deliberative process.

Of course, the need to embrace all arguments in the deliberative process does not imply that there must be an algorithm securing proportionate representation of all those affected by the prospective decision, which is an issue relating to

---

[79] WH Riker and PC Ordeshook, 'A Theory of the Calculus of Voting' (1968) 62 *The American Political Science Review* 25.

[80] G Gerapetritis, 'Deliberative Democracy Within and Beyond the State' in L Papadopoulou, I Pernice and JHH Weiler (eds), *Legitimacy Issues of the European Union in the Face of Crisis. Dimitris Tsatsos in Memoriam*, 2nd edm (Baden Baden, Nomos, 2018) 25, 32–50.

the diversity question. It suffices that the arguments be set in place and open to authentic deliberation. For this purpose, it is not necessary for a deliberative body to be composed of experts in the respective field. Dryzek effectively dismisses such instrumental rationality and objectivism in political institutions and public policy through technocracies and experts, claiming that they are not well equipped to deal with complex social problems.[81] Furthermore, although not all stakeholders need to be present, all stakeholders' arguments should be present in order to achieve genuine diversity, irrespective of how proportionate representation might be, with a special emphasis on group membership's entitativity (ie the mode and degree to which groups are perceived as having the interest to constitute an entity) and similarity (the issue of the arguably common interests of a group's specific members).[82]

The second condition of deliberativism is *readiness* and it refers to the basic procedural ground rules that ought to apply in order to accommodate the implications of disagreement in public discourse and to render them constructive. As Popper convincingly suggests in the context of critical rationalism, seeking to replace allegedly justificatory methods with critical ones, disagreement goes hand in hand with open societies.[83] In this, it presupposes two subjective perceptions of the participants. First, all solutions and arguments must be presumed and treated by the participants as valid, without any prejudice as to their sustainability (unconditional validity). Second, the participants in the deliberative process must be ready and inclined to accept the validity and soundness of any view or argument and retract from their original position (retraction predilection). Unconditional validity and retraction predilection jointly constitute the normative psychological aspect of what Offe and Preuss more objectively suggest as 'reflecting preferences', namely end results based on the conscious confrontation of one's own point of view with an opposing point of view or multiplicity of viewpoints, in contrast to spontaneous and context-contingent choices.[84] Both unconditional validity and retraction predilection reflect the participants' readiness to uphold the validity of propositions and change their primary view on the matter; deliberative process does not imply a forum of negotiation or bargaining where rival interests compete and a fair balance is sought.[85]

---

[81] J Dryzek, *Discursive Democracy: Politics, Policy, and Political Science* (Cambridge, Cambridge University Press, 1990) 151–200.

[82] G Gerapetritis, *Affirmative Action Policies and Judicial Review Worldwide* (Cham, Springer, 2016) 66.

[83] K Popper, 'The Logic of the Social Sciences' in T Adorno (ed), *The Positivist Dispute in German Sociology* (New York, Harper and Row, 1976) 87.

[84] Offe and Preuss, 'Democracy institutions' (1991) 169–70.

[85] Gutmann and Thompson claim that the key factors determining a deliberative process are justification and reciprocity of the furnished grounds, together meaning a reason-giving process based on premises mutually accepted by the participants. The authors, thus, limit the ambit of the grounds that are permissible in a deliberative process in that not all reasons are reciprocal, but merely those founded upon basic democratic principles, see A Gutmann and D Thompson, *Why Deliberative Democracy?* (Princeton, Princeton University Press, 2004) 95–124.

Obviously, a type of Rawlsian veil of ignorance cannot in practice exist in a society of multi-complex interests and abundant information, which renders reflective equilibrium an implausible solipsistic experiment. Instead, it is more plausible and arguably more expedient to try and curb potential partiality by allowing all interested parties to appeal to their respective self-interests.[86] Participants in deliberative bodies ought to be directly involved in the process, not simply as outsiders to the issue in question (eg as a jury member) or as arbitrators, but rather as stakeholders. In this, the members of deliberative assemblies must be eager to reach the optimal result by means of reasoned discourse. In a political community where people tend to imagine themselves in the position of various other people and take decisions on the presumption of what they would do, Goodin suggests a model of 'democratic deliberation within' where, through provided evidence, people are reflective by themselves and expansive across time and distance.[87]

The third condition of deliberativism is *evidence*, ie a critical mass of feedback that ought to be produced in the decision-making process to allow people to make rational choices.[88] A decision taken in the absence of such evidence might eventually be the correct decision. On the other hand, if all the relevant information is produced before the deliberative body, the decision might still be mistaken, but this will not be a fault of the deliberative process but ought to be attributed mainly to the inability of the members of the deliberative body properly to assess the evidence adduced. Micro-assemblies might be better at acquiring information, whereas larger assemblies might be better at processing information; yet, there is no stable point between the underproduction of information, leading to bad decisions, and the overproduction of information, leading to costly redundancy.[89]

The fourth condition of deliberativism is *interplay/fair play*, essentially reflecting the maxim *audi altera partem*. This requirement does not follow as a matter of moral or divine obligation, as early criminal case law in England might suggest.[90] It is a reflection of the rationalism that substantiates the legitimising factor of reason in the deliberative process. Fair play requires a set of rules securing equality of arms among the participants so that all participants may have an

[86] J Mansbridge, 'The Place of Self-Interest and the Role of Power in Deliberative Democracy' (2010) 18 *Journal of Political Philosophy* 64.

[87] RE Goodin, 'Democratic Deliberation Within' (2000) 29 *Philosophy and Public Affairs* 81.

[88] J Rawls, *The Law of Peoples with the Idea of Public Reason Revisited* (Cambridge, MA, Harvard University Press, 1999) 49.

[89] J Elster, 'Forces and Mechanisms in the Constitution-Making Process' (1995) 45 *Duke Law Journal* 364.

[90] "The laws of God and man both give the party an opportunity to make his defense, if he has any. I remember to have heard it observed by a very learned man, upon such an occasion, that even God himself did not pass sentence upon Adam before he was called upon to make his defense', Justice Fortescue in *The King v The Chancellor, Master and Scholars of the University of Cambridge*, 1 Str 557 at 567, [1748] EngR 223, (1748 Fort 202, 92 ER 818).

equal chance to exercise influence upon the body and be influenced by other fellow members; interplay requires an adversarial flow of arguments by all participants. The ideal of deliberative processes is that reason would eventually result in a unanimous body. When deliberative bodies, having completed proper deliberative processes, are still divided, it harms the general persuasiveness of the process itself.

In cases where no unanimity is required, participants in the collective bodies are less likely to moderate their views and eventually shift positions. By way of contrast, consensus seems to be at odds with the conventional concept of democracy where disagreement is essential to the opposition and excessive agreement may hamper the envisaged democratic discourse,[91] while it may also be at odds with the relativist objection that there is not a single, let alone manifest, truth.[92] A strict requirement for unanimity would, in any case, necessarily be a micro-sample, as opposed to a mega-sample, since in the latter case the process would probably end up being unsuccessful and potentially frustrating, as well as very time-consuming.

The fifth condition of deliberativism is *transparency*, which provides the setting for an appropriate testing of the degree of persuasion involved in the relevant argumentative process (so as to satisfy the substantive test of reason) and provides the decision with the necessary persuasiveness that elicits regular obedience (the institutional test of legitimacy).[93]

In the light of the above, decision-making in Europe, both in the EU and in the Member States can hardly qualify as employing deliberative processes. However, this assertion does not lead to the conclusion that all legal orders are illegitimate and lack ethical and justifiable grounds for obedience, since there is a formal standpoint of legitimacy (more so in national States). There is no doubt that European regimes are genuine democracies; what remains strongly questionable is whether they can qualify as *deliberative* democracies.

This is especially true for the EU legal order, because of its very nature. First, there is no conventional *demos* which makes a single optimal solution more feasible. Second, there is a largely contradictory target of integration while respecting the national (constitutional) identities of the Member States. Third, complicated internal structures, ie shared competences, political subordination of the executive (Commission) and the legislature (Parliament and Council) to the European Council, constitute an early warning subsidiarity system in favour of national parliaments.

---

[91] FM Watkins, *The Political Tradition of the West: A Study in the Development of Modern Liberalism* (Cambridge, MA, Harvard University Press, 1948).

[92] On the institutional role of the opposition in parliament as a forum of democratic disagreement, see the 2010 Report of the Council of Europe's European Commission for Democracy through Law (Venice Commission) to the Parliamentary Assembly, CDL-AD(2010)025, at www.venice.coe.int/webforms/documents/?pdf=CDL-AD(2010)025-e.

[93] A Gutmann and D Thompson, *Democracy and Dsagreement* (Cambridge, MA, Harvard University Press, 1996) 105–27.

On the national level, it seems that there is a decrease in the level of deliberativeness, mostly with regard to participatory processes. Thus, national referenda
have mostly operated on a purely non-deliberative manner, since not all related
evidence was adduced and numerous totally false statements were set in place
(in violation of the evidence requirement), the opposing views were expressed
in a dogmatic manner that does not allow any space for retraction on the basis
of a rational choice approach (in violation of the endorsement requirement)
and there was no genuine and on an equal footing exchange of argumentation
(in violation of the interplay and fair play requirement).[94] Quality deliberative
techniques obviously require additional time to adduce evidence and enter into
a genuine process of deliberation on all the relevant arguments, yet one might
reasonably argue in favour of a positive-sum gain in relation to the legitimacy
and accountability versus efficiency debate, where democratic and managerial
concepts become complementary and mutually reinforcing.[95]

A critical approach to deliberativism in decision-making would be that it is
very theoretical and lacks an objective benchmarking against which it should
be measured, as well as a monitoring mechanism to render it actually applicable. Yet, deliberativism, as any other model of democracy, mostly operates on a
normative level. It essentially serves to improve the actual functioning of democratic decision-making processes and to optimise the results thereof. Specific
aspects associated with deliberativeness are already part of the judicial review
of administrative action: the obligation to state reasons for individual executive
decisions; prior hearing; and publicity of acts. Indeed, deliberative democracy
pattern cannot altogether become a justiciable issue. It mostly serves as a yardstick to assess the quality of democratic governance without any judicial sanctions
whatsoever. One can say that the sufficiency of the conditions of parliamentary
deliberation ought to be reviewable by a court following the deliberative theory
of legitimacy. This does not result in a curtailment of the level of the rule of law,
because it reflects representative democracy and, at the end of the day, it is the electorate itself that will approve or disapprove of an applicable model of democracy.
Nonetheless, deliberativism could genuinely restore reason into politics, which at
times of crises is very often lacking in policy-making.

For that matter, the establishment of a deliberative culture is imperative for
the constructive implementation of any deliberative technique. Deliberative
processes ought to be supplemented by a long vision of deliberative education that
could raise the level of awareness, whereas extensive use of distant technologies
must be ensured in order to promote the advantages of deliberative democracy,
to call for the broader participation of citizens through experimental polls and to
disseminate information concerning issues of public interest. The project obviously

[94] Above ch 5 section IV.
[95] I Bache and M Flinders, 'Multi-Level Governance: Conclusions and Implications' in I Bache and
M Flinders (eds), *Multi-Level Governance* (Oxford, Oxford University Press, 2004) 195, 206; B Jessop,
'The Rise of Governance and the Risk of Failure' (1998) 50 *International Social Science Journal* 29, 42.

entails financing deliberative education projects, originating both from the States and international organisations and from civic societies through private entities, aiming at a more efficient participation of citizens in public life.[96]

IV. Global Solidarity and Intergenerational Sustainability

Global solidarity and intergenerational sustainability are not rights enshrined in the traditional perception of legal liberalism, but mostly aim at establishing a set of relevant ethical obligations in policy-making. The concrete character-istics of the two doctrines have been shaped distinctively by literature, the law and case law. Yet, the present analysis suggests a joint reading and application of the two doctrines (the 'combined standard') in order to maximise the results thereof.

Global solidarity reflects the basic consideration that decision-making ought to enhance and demand the solidarity owed by every individual towards the globe. It lies on two premises:

(a) the existence of actual divisions, in terms of wealth, resources and secu-rity, which solidarity aims to ease by a redistribution of common goods or common efforts to bring the globe to the equilibrium of a less unequal world, an idea close to Brunkhorst's universal solidarity;[97] and

(b) the feeling of a joint responsibility of people and nations not on the level of individuals, groups or nations but vis-a-vis the world at large, an idea that comes closer to Hegel's and Habermas' assumptions of reciprocity of recogni-tion in the foundation of solidarity or Lock's notion of community property.

Accordingly, global solidarity transcends the conventional ideas of general or community solidarity in two ways. First, as regards the duty bearer: the obliga-tion should be imposed on anyone, be it an international organisation, a State, a public or private entity or an individual, irrespective of the relative power each of those may possess. In this way, global solidarity discards the outdated typology based on class and nation and goes beyond Durkheim's objective idea of organic solidarity based on formal membership to the same community,[98] Gould's subjec-tive theory based on common interests created through a feeling of bonding with

---

[96] JA Flammang, 'Democracy: Direct, Representative, and Deliberative' (2001) 41 *Santa Clara Law Review* 1085, 1091.

[97] H Brunkhorst, *Solidarity: From Civic Friendship to a Global Legal Community*. Studies in Contem-porary German Social Thought (Cambridge, MA, Massachusetts Institute of Technology Press, 2005); H Brunkhorst, 'Collective Bonapartism – Democracy in the European Crisis' (2014) 15 *German Law Journal* 1177.

[98] E Durkheim, *The Division of Labor in Society* (Detroit, Free Press, 1964).

members of the group,[99] or Scholz's idea of political solidarity, founded upon common interests shared as a matter of ethical or political beliefs,[100] because all these theories lie on the assumption of sectoral interests that ought to be preserved *against* other sectoral interests and, therefore, lack universality.

Although global solidarity comes closer to ideas reflecting cosmopolitan solidarity, such as Kantian universalist morality or Aristotelian virtue ethics, it still differs in that those theories mostly apply as an extension of or alternative to the kind of solidarity that once existed at the level of class and nation.[101] Although group solidarity is indeed a sine qua non factor for the establishment of an entity of common interests, eg a labour union or a religious community, any segmental material interest cannot outweigh the universality of the solidarity owed to the globe.

Second, as to the scope of solidarity, the beneficiary is not a political community or a society but the world as a whole. It is neither the State that is entitled to claim of all citizens to fulfil the duty of social and national solidarity, a provision contained in the Greek Constitution (Article 25), nor an international organisation that may request the contracting States to demonstrate solidarity towards their fellow contracting States, such as in the case of the EU (Article 222 of the TFEU). Solidarity does not entail the idea of charity, altruism or compassion from the powerful to the weak and the oppressed, but rather the conscious effort to soften social and economic discrepancies with the understanding that this aim would positively contribute to the global common good, namely both to the givers and the receivers: the complementary point of view of equal treatment is not benevolence but the experience of one person having to stand for the other because, as associates, all must take the same interest in the integrity of their common life context.[102]

From this viewpoint, global solidarity praises democratic citizenship through 'solidarity between strangers', in Habermas's worlds,[103] and presupposes seeing the world in a different manner, ie more tolerant, understandable and equal, as well as realising oneself in a more external manner, namely not within the boundaries of personal, group or national interests, but rather as a member of an international community with responsibility towards all other fellow members on

---

[99] CC Gould, *Globalizing Democracy and Human Rights* (Cambridge, Cambridge University Press, 2004) 118–38.

[100] SJ Scholz, *Political Solidarity* (Pennsylvania, Penn State University Press, 2012).

[101] R Fine, 'The Idea of Cosmopolitan Solidarity' in G Delanty (ed), *Routledge Handbook of Cosmopolitanism Studies* (London, Routledge, 2012); P Niesen, 'Volk-von-Teufeln-Republikanismus: Zur Frage nach den Moralischen Ressourcen der Liberalen Demokratie' in K Günther and L Wingert (eds), *Die Öffentlichkeit der Vernunft und die Vernunft der Öffentlichkeit. Festschrift für Jürgen Habermas,* (Frankfurt, Suhrkamp, 2001) 568.

[102] J Habermas, 'Justice and Solidarity: On the Discussion Concerning "Stage 6"' (1989) 21 *Philosophical Forum* 32, 47.

[103] J Habermas, 'The European Nation-State: On the Past and Future of Sovereignty and Citizenship' in CP Cronin and P de Greiff (eds), *The Inclusion of the Other* (Cambridge, MA, Massachusetts Institute of Technology Press, 1999) 105, 119.

grounds, as Ferrera set it, of 'neighbourhood', 'hospitality' and 'pardon/promise' principles, along with leaders capable of far-sighted, competent, principled and responsible choices for a *neuegeordnete Europa*.[104] The eventual aim is a re-engineering of decision-making structures and principles so as to ensure that everyone sees all interests (which might originally seem as mutually conflicting) as compatible and worth protecting. In that respect, Habermas set the seminal notion of a morally rooted communicative-theoretic account of solidarity vis-a-vis justice, ie that solidarity is the 'reverse side' of deontological justice. Alongside solidarity, he also views human dignity, self-realisation and autonomy as fundamental deontological principles.[105]

Yet, in the aftermath of the European economic crisis, Habermas devaluated the moral ground of solidarity as an intrinsic part of justice and turned to a more realistic approach with regard to the notion. This new approach involves a political-realist approach to the principle that is disassociated from his moral-theoretic pre-crisis account. Under this new perception, solidarity becomes a political act and loses the false appearance of being unpolitical; thus obligations to show solidarity are distinguishable from both moral and legal obligations and are no longer synonymous with justice. Through this new approach, Habermas essentially blamed the lack of solidarity as partially responsible for the financial crisis and the strengthening of solidarity as the treatment of the injuries caused to the Union in the post-2008 era.[106]

Intergenerational sustainability reflects the basic consideration that decision-making ought to provide for the ability to continue behaviour for an indefinite period of time by introducing the rights of future generations as of distinctive and equal value to the rights of the present generation. This type of sustainability reflects the pursuit of intergenerational equity, by taking into account not only the future but also the past, through remedying past injustices that remain embedded in the social, economic and ecological fabrics of present-day society, ie a form of restorative justice and safeguarding adequate resources for the future.[107] Indeed, Wade-Benzoni used historical examples to confirm that in situations where a present generation must give up benefits or take on burdens to act on behalf of future generations, there is in fact an 'intergenerational reciprocity', in that the behaviour of previous generations influences the way a present generation treats future generations.[108] In this line, Beckerman discards the idea of intergenerational egalitarianism and, instead, favours an 'extended humanitarianism' that would

[104] M Ferrera, 'Solidarity in Europe after the Crisis' (2014) 21 *Constellations* 222, 235.

[105] J Habermas, *Between Facts and Nouns* (Cambridge MA, MIT Press, 1996) 244–57.

[106] G Carrabregu, 'Habermas on Solidarity: An Immanent Critique' (2016) 23 *Constellations* 507, 512.

[107] A Golub, M Mahoney and J Harlow, 'Sustainability and Intergenerational Equity: Do Past Injustices Matter?' (2013) 8 *Sustainability Science* 269.

[108] KA Wade-Benzoni and LP Tost, 'The Egoism and Altruism of Intergenerational Behavior' (2009) 13 *Personality and Social Psychology Review* 165.

take the suffering of the poor of the present into serious consideration and would entail concern for future generations, ie of all living creatures of the planet.[109]

As a technical term in policy-making, sustainable development is, according to the 1987 report *Our Common Future* of the World Commission on Environment and Development, established in 1983 by the UN General Assembly, 'a process of change in which the exploitation of resources, the direction of investments, the orientation of technological developments and institutional change are all in harmony and enhance both current and future potential to meet human needs and aspirations'.[110]

Furthermore, according to the 1992 *World Development Report* of the World Bank, sustainability reflects a key policy that contemporary development does not compromise or jeopardise the ability of future generations to meet their own needs.[111] Sustainable development may conceivably enhance various aspects, such as social inclusion, lift of social and economic inequalities, fight against poverty, tolerance, equality and positive action in favour of minorities and vulnerable categories, diversity, quality of life, dignity and integrity and environmental responsibility, that need to be relevant considerations when drafting public policies as well as to be in a state of a fair balance with economic growth and technical evolution. Generally speaking, as Goodland suggests, drawing inspiration from the sociological findings in the EU, there are three pillars of sustainability in the EU context: economic; social; and environmental.[112] Evidently, there is interdependence among those forms of sustainability: environmental sustainability is a prerequisite for both social and economic sustainability and both environmental and social sustainability operate as restrictions upon the economic growth and to some extent qualify economic sustainability. The interaction of the three essentially determines the level and quality of social development as a community good.

Economic sustainability suggests the ability to support a predetermined adequate level of economic production indefinitely. It is arguably the most fluid indicator since there is no uniformly applied benchmarking to determine what adequate level stands for and reasonable contradictions may exist. One criterion might be the domestic GDP, yet in current economic terms flat GDP is not considered growth but stagnation (unless an economy exits recession), thus economic sustainability could be met on a level about two per cent GDP per year. Yet, the application of the GDP criterion is neither necessary nor adequate to satisfy the goal of economic sustainability. Non-discrimination, transparency and removal

---

[109] W Beckerman, 'Sustainable Development and our Obligations to Future Generations' in A Dobson (ed), *Fairness and Futurity: Essays on Environmental Sustainability and Social Justice* (New York, Oxford University Press, 1999) 71.

[110] *The Brundtland Report*, 46.

[111] See p 8.

[112] R Goodland, 'The Concept of Environmental Sustainability' (1995) 26 *Annual Review of Ecology and Systematics* 1, 1–2.

of anti-competitive hindrances also constitute in a sense salient standards of economic sustainability.

Accordingly, the Court of Justice has used the conjunctive wording of 'harmonious, balanced and sustainable economic development throughout the European Union' to interpret the provisions of Directive 91/308 laying down harmonised rules for the control of cash entering or leaving the EU, thus providing some sort of moral justification to the internal market.[113] Most importantly, one might consider as the most striking element of EU economic sustainability the golden budgetary rule imposed upon the Member States and aiming at full economic balance in order not to undermine the future generations through debts assumed by their predecessors. Yet, this is not the only and, arguably, not the correct academic meaning of the golden rule in a sustainability environment. What the rule actually implies is that deficits are not by definition discarded and blamed, but they can and should be used to finance investments that are to the benefit of future generations. This is so because the present generations overexploit resources in every possible way, just like previous generations did before them, and budgetary balance does not suffice to restore intergenerational stability. It takes positive measures (that require investments, thus deficits) in order to achieve proper intergenerational sustainability.

Strictly speaking, sustainability may call for financial deficits, with the extra financial resources used to finance investments that are to the benefit of future generations. In that regard, balanced budget and the commitment to reducing sovereign debt is not necessarily a sustainable policy.[114] Although the EU fiscal pact set the benchmarking on structural deficit that leaves some margin for manoeuver in favour of sustainability goals, no strict requirement applies to allow, or even encourage, action for the advancement of sustainability, especially if this might entail public over-expenditure. The Fiscal Compact requirements could conceivably set at risk sustainability public investments aiming at long-term challenges concerning combatting social exclusion, poverty and the destruction of the environment.

Social sustainability intimates existence of structures, processes and principles which abstain from taking risks of devaluation of the existing social cohesion and welfare of the community and the people and positively aim at securing such cohesion for the future generations. In their social-oriented definition, Vallance, Perkins and Dixon embrace the terms 'development sustainability', addressing basic needs, the creation of social capital, justice and so on, 'bridge sustainability' concerning changes in behaviour so as to achieve bio-physical environmental goals, and 'maintenance sustainability' referring to the preservation

---

[113] CJEU Judgment of 16 July 2015 in Case C-255/14, *Chmielewski*, para 17; CJEU Judgment of 4 May 2017 in Case C-17/16, *Oussama El Dakkak and Intercontinental SARL v Administration des douanes et droits indirects*, para 31.

[114] M Artis, 'The Stability and Growth Pact: Fiscal Policy in the EMU' in F Breuss, G Fink and S Griller (eds), *Institutional, Legal and Economic Aspects of the EMU* (Vienna, Springer, 2002) 101.

of socio-cultural characteristics in the face of change.[115] At any rate, there could be a lot of variables in determining the social sustainability standards. The World Happiness Report includes GDP, life expectancy, generosity, social support, freedom and corruption; the Human Development Index comprises life expectancy, education and per capita income indicators. One might set as primary criteria the poverty index of the country, ie what percentage of the population lives below a minimum level of income deemed necessary to achieve an adequate standard of living per country or the levels of unemployment in each country.

Environmental sustainability argues for an increased level of protection of the environment through sustainable resource management. In technical terms, this means an amalgam of rates of renewable resource harvest, pollution creation and non-renewable resource depletion that allows for an indefinite coexistence of the human community.[116] In this field, there is a very large bulk of EU case law:

(a) emphasising on the principle of precaution and the requirement for preventive action requiring the Union and the Member States to avert, reduce, and, in so far as is possible, eliminate from the outset the sources of pollution or nuisance, by adopting measures of a nature such as to eliminate recognised risks;[117] and

(b) upholding the preservation of the environment as a possible criterion for the contracting authorities, when assessing the economically most advantageous tender in the context of the EU procurement directives.[118]

Both national and EU law widely enhance elements of sustainability. On an EU level in particular, in spite of the economic orientation of the original Treaties of the European Communities, sustainability features prominently in the Preamble of the Treaty of Rome: it affirms the essential objective of constant improvement of the living and working conditions of the peoples of the Member States and declares the anxiety to strengthen the unity of their economies and to ensure their harmonious development. The Treaty on European Union explicitly provides for sustainable development elements in a rather pompous manner:

- protection and improvement of the quality of the environment and of the sustainable development of the Earth;

- pursuit of a highly competitive social market economy and of balanced economic growth and price stability;

---

[115] S Vallance, HC Perkins and J Dixon, 'What is Social Sustainability? A Clarification of Concepts' (2011) 42 *Geoforum* 342.

[116] HE Daly, 'Commentary: Toward some Operational Principles of Sustainable Development' (1990) 2 *Ecological Economics* 1.

[117] CJEU Judgments of 5 October 1999 in Joined Cases C-175/98 *Lirussi* and C-177/98 *Francesca Bizzaro*, para 51, on the definition of temporary storage, pending collection, on the site where it is produced, and of waste management; CJEU Judgment of 22 June 2000 in Case C-318/98, *Fornasar and others*, para 37, on stringent measures of protection of hazardous waste.

[118] CJEU Judgment of 17 September 2002 in Case C-513/99 *Concordia Bus Finland Oy Ab v Helsingin kaupunki and HKL-Bussiliikenne*, para 57, under then applicable Dir 92/50.

- pursuit of a full employment;
- promotion of economic, social and territorial cohesion and social progress through combat of social exclusion and promotion of social justice and protection;
- eradication of poverty; and
- respect for solidarity between generations, among peoples and among Member States (Articles 2 and 3).

In interpreting these clauses, the Court of Justice has emphatically stated that 'the Community has thus not only an economic but also a social purpose' and the basic freedoms stemming therefrom must be balanced against the objectives pursued by social policy.[119] Furthermore, primary law instruments apply for the protection of the environment, entailing that 'a high level of environmental protection and the improvement of the quality of the environment must be integrated into the policies of the Union and ensured in accordance with the principle of sustainable development' (Article 37 EU Charter of Fundamental Rights) and that 'environmental protection requirements must be integrated into the definition and implementation of the Union's policies and activities, in particular with a view to promoting sustainable development' (Article 1 TFEU).

Especially in its external action, the Union shall define and pursue common policies and actions, and work for a high degree of cooperation in all fields of international relations, in order, inter alia, to preserve and improve the quality of the environment and the sustainable management of global natural resources and to ensure sustainable development (Article 21(2)(d) and (f) TFEU).[120] Moreover, basic instruments of EU policy – such as the EU Sustainable Development Strategies, the EU 2020 Strategy, the EU's Better Regulation Agenda and the 7th Environment Action Programme – have employed the principles of sustainable development. Furthermore, the Union was a key factor in the global 2030 Agenda broadly embodying global sustainable development, acknowledging that it involves eradicating poverty in all its forms and dimensions, combatting inequality within and among countries, preserving the planet, creating sustained, inclusive and sustainable economic growth and fostering social inclusion, which are linked to each other and are interdependent, and employing 17 Sustainable Development Goals and 169 targets for people, planet and prosperity. In terms of secondary EU law, Recital 2 of Regulation 1889/2005 reads that the

---

[119] CJEU Judgment of 18 December 2007 in Case C-341/05 *Laval un Partneri Ltd v Svenska Byggnadsarbetareförbundet, avdelning 1, Byggettan and Svenska Elektrikerförbundet*, para 105.

[120] This stipulation has in fact been used by the EU institutions either positively to determine the goal of agreements concluded between the Union and third countries to promote sustainable social and economic development (see Preamble and Arts 1, 29 and 34 of Council Decision 2012/272 of 14 May 2012, concerning Philippines) or negatively to impose restrictive measures against those third-party nationals that were responsible for depriving their nations from the benefits of the sustainable development of their economy and society (Recitals 1 and 2 in the Preamble to Decision 2011/172 of 21 March 2011, concerning Egypt).

introduction of the proceeds of illegal activities into the financial system and their investment after laundering are detrimental to 'sound and sustainable economic development'.

Global solidarity and intergenerational sustainability can apply as a combined standard in that they aim at treating the same institutional pathologies and share a critical doctrinal core to treat such pathologies: first, against the pathology of limited legitimacy of political judgements, the response of the combined standard is reliance on equity and reason; and second, against the pathology of a restricted vision of human rights, the response of the combined standard is trespass in space-time.

(a) Against the pathology of limited legitimacy of political judgements, the combined standard, as an expression of equity and justice, aims at strengthening the substantive reasoning of policy choices. In Habermas's words, reasons that are convenient for the legitimation of law must, on pain of cognitive dissonances, harmonise with the moral principles of universal justice and solidarity.[121] Given the global structure of economics and politics, as Agyeman, Bullard and Evans argue, a sustainable society must also be an equitable society, locally, nationally and internationally, both within and between generations and between species.[122] The target is, according to Petersmann, a search for cosmopolitan public reason, focusing on legal and judicial protection of the individual human rights, therefore justifying and promoting constitutional reforms in a domain, such as international economic law, which does not widely acknowledge individuals as its primary legal subjects and its democratic owners.[123]

Democratic deliberative ownership seems to lay also at the heart of Habermas's theory: since law admittedly preserves its socially integrating force only insofar as the addressees of legal norms may at the same time understand themselves as having been the rational authors of those norms, it lives off a solidarity concentrated in the value orientations of citizens and ultimately issuing from communicative action and deliberation.[124] Indeed, deliberativeness, global solidarity and intergenerational sustainability all constitute grounds of substantive legitimacy based on reason; such doctrinal bridge is obvious when Offe and Preuss suggest that decision-making processes must be future- and others-regarding,[125] which are the functional equivalents to sustainability and solidarity respectively.

---

[121] Habermas, *Between Facts and Norms* (1996) 99.
[122] J Agyeman, R Bullard and B Evans, 'Conclusion: Towards just Sustainabilities. Perspectives and Possibilities' in J Agyeman, R Bullard and B Evans (eds), *Just Sustainabilities: Development in an Unequal World* (Cambridge, Massachusetts Institute of Technology Press, 2003) 323.
[123] E-U Petersmann, *International Economic Law in the 21st Century*, 36, 160–209.
[124] Habermas, (n 105) 30.
[125] C Offe and U Preuss, 'Democracy Institutions and Moral Resources' in D Held (ed), *Political Theory Today* (Cambridge, Polity, 1991) 156–57.

(b) Against the pathology of a restricted vision of human rights, the main doctrinal core of the combined standard is that decision-making ought to trespass
space and time, by enhancing as distinctive elements those locally outside
immediate stakeholders (the non-space factor) and those timely outside
current stakeholders (the non-time factor). In the conventional understanding of constitutionalism, beneficiaries of human rights are merely those
present and active in the political community and in shaping public policies
predominantly national and ephemeral considerations apply. In Brian Barry's
worlds, we are accustomed to thinking about relations among contemporar-
ies and we have developed a quite sophisticated apparatus to help us in doing
so, whereas we have no similar apparatus to aid our thoughts about relations
between people living at different times.[126]

Yet, future generations have the right to non-deteriorated ecological and
economic capacity and this ought to be part of the constitutional reading
of human rights.[127] In essence, what the combined standard intimates is
the – basically moral – perception that in any contemporary decision there
is an element of choice also on behalf of the globe and of future generations. Accordingly, both on constitutional and legislative level, drafting and
policy-making must be forward-thinking.[128] Especially with regard to the
constitution-drafting, an upgrade of the rights of the future generations is of
acute importance for the sake of the Constitution itself.[129]

According to Acemoglou, Egorov and Sonin, when a society chooses its
constitution, naturally, the current rewards from adopting a specific constitution will influence this decision; but, as long as the members of the society
are forward-looking and patient, the future implications of the Constitution may be even more important and can guarantee a dynamically stable
state: under natural acyclicity assumptions, a constitution is made stable
not by the absence of a powerful set of players that prefer another alternative, but because of the absence of an alternative stable arrangement that is

---

[126] B Barry 'Sustainability and Intergenerational Justice' in A Dobson (ed), *Fairness and Futurity:
Essays on Environmental Sustainability and Social Justice* (New York, Oxford University Press, 1999)
93. Also see, A Gosseries, *Intergenerational Justice: Probing the Assumptions, Exploring the Implications*,
PhD thesis (Louvain-la-Neuve, Université Catholique de Louvain, 2000).

[127] E Padilla, 'Intergenerational Equity and Sustainability' (2002) 41 *Ecological Economics* 69, 75–76.

[128] A rights-oriented constitutional reading based on an enforceable doctrine of sustainability was
also made in the UK Supreme Court Judgment *Miller*, concerning the 2016 Brexit referendum. Indeed,
in determining whether the British Government could as a matter of prerogative trigger Article 50
of the TFEU to withdraw from EU, the Court took account of the rights that have been granted
because of the accession to the Union directly to the British citizens, obviously including future generations: 'the continued existence of the rights and other legal incidents which flow therefrom, cannot as
a matter of UK law depend on the fact that to date ministers have refrained from having recourse to
the Royal prerogative to eliminate that source and those rights and other incidents', [2017] UKSC 5,
para 93.

[129] J Tremmel, 'Establishment of the Rights of Future Generations in National Constitutions' in
J Tremmel (ed), *Handbook of Intergenerational Justice* (Cheltenham, Elgar, 2006) 187.

preferred by a sufficiently powerful constituency.[130] Only through taking into account non-space and non-time considerations can long-term stability of the community be secured.

Yet, there is in this respect a rather unfortunate paradox in contemporary social communities: in spite of the current state of economic globalisation and the institutional internationalisation, decision-making seems more and more to ignore non-space and non-time factors. According to anthropologist David Harvey, there is a time–space compression: in a globalised social environment, the broadening of space goes hand in hand with the acceleration of time, which at the same time abolishes the distance and reduces the time needed to perform any form of social activity or interaction. By bringing time ahead, what happens is that decision-making (be that of an economic or policy choice or regulation drafting) subsumes considerations of the future into the current context, which are therefore merged with contemporary needs and priorities. This is, however, the exact opposite of what normatively ought to apply, ie to consider the rights and interests of other communities and of future generations as distinct and disassociated from any contemporary and local, potentially conflicting, interest, instead of being merged with them. Thus, instead of forward thinking, the process in evolving capitalism largely becomes backwards pre-emptive.[131]

Global solidarity and intergenerational sustainability go beyond the Kantian notion of cosmopolitan constitutionalism in the field of human rights protection, in that it appeals to future generations and calls not only for a passive global protection of human rights, but rather for a proactive solidarity in the distribution of public wealth. The multi-layer structures of domestic and international economic law (including both private and public actors) call not only for a homogenous interpretation of regulatory tools but also for a clear vision as to the purpose of global constitutionalism and its constraints. Accordingly, the Ralwsian hypothesis that domestic economic and social welfare basically depends on national regulation and not on the morally arbitrary distribution of natural resources among the States is a necessary but not adequate moderation of financialism. A transnational approach that aims at securing equal economic liberty, such as the Bretton Woods Agreements, the WTO, the GATT, the ILO and the Financial Action Task Force, might be equally inadequate because all these instruments aim essentially at preserving the existing economic foundations and do not guarantee welfare for the people.

---

[130] D Acemoglou, G Egorov and K Sonin, 'Dynamics and Stability of Constitutions, Coalitions, and Clubs' (2012) 102 *American Economic Review* 1446, 1446–48.

[131] D Harvey, *The Condition of Post-Modernity: An Enquiry into the Origins of Cultural Change* (Cambridge, Wiley-Blackwell, 1989) 239–40; D Harvey, 'Between Space and Time: Reflections on the Geographical Imagination' (1990) 80:3 *Annals of the Association of American Geographers* 418.

The combined standard has on limited occasions emerged both in law and politics. In relation to law, the closest constitutional paradigm, due to its reference both to solidarity and sustainability and to its horizontal effect, comes from Belgium, whose Constitution provides that in the exercise of their competences, state authorities of all layers pursue the objectives of sustainable development in its social, economic and environmental aspects, taking into account the solidarity between generations (Article 7bis). In relation to politics, the most striking such example was John Maynard Keynes' proposal at Bretton Woods, as delegate of the British Government, to set up a world central bank which could issue its own currency (the 'bancor') to help reflate the world economy by expanding the money supply, whereby the cost of adjustment would be shared pro rata, so that countries with big surpluses would have to revalue their currencies, while deficit countries would be forced to devalue. The idea was that a global fund should be established to guarantee equilibrium in the distribution of wealth, through policies by surplus States to donate to debtor nations or import from them or build infrastructures in their territory.

In recent history, the most vivid policy example is the 2015 UN Climate Change Conference.[132] The Conference concluded the Paris Agreement, by consensus of the representatives of 196 parties, which would become legally binding if joined by at least 55 countries representing at least 55 per cent of global greenhouse emissions. The Paris Agreement brought together long-divided actors from both the developing and developed world, with largely conflicting interests, in a rather deliberative and global discussion about environmental sustainability of the climate. Its most astonishing success was in the agreement to limit global warming to less than two degrees Celsius compared to pre-industrial levels (intergenerational sustainability) and to an agreement that developed countries agreed would help underdeveloped countries to achieve their emissions targets by contributing 100 billion US dollars per year by 2020 (global solidarity).

Yet, in relation to the latter accord, the US, Japan and Australia proposed a rearrangement of that contribution during negotiations at a climate summit in Bangkok in 2018, which was a considerable setback. Unfortunately, it seems that global solidarity is some way off, in the sense that dominant countries in the respective arena (ie the US) do not share common interests and attitudes towards this goal.[133] This is probably why although a total of 28 countries ratified the Paris Agreement as of 9 September 2016, accounting for 39.08 per cent of global greenhouse gas emissions, the ratification process has essentially been stagnant.

---

[132] It was the 21st yearly session of the Conference of the Parties (COP 21) to the 1992 United Nations Framework Convention on Climate Change (UNFCCC) and the 11th session of the Meeting of the Parties to the 1997 Kyoto Protocol (CMP 11).

[133] ChF Parker and Ch Karlsson, 'The UN Climate Change Negotiations and the Role of the United States: Assessing American Leadership from Copenhagen to Paris' (2018) 27 *Environmental Politics* 519.

Two crucial questions remain unanswered concerning the efficacy of the combined standard:

(a) *How compelling can it be?*

With regard to the issue of the compelling, basically justiciable, character of the combined standard, admittedly, both intergenerational sustainability and global solidarity are mostly normative propositions that ought to apply as substantive principles in decision-making of the political community and, currently, remain broadly in the realm of deontology. This is not necessarily linked to the perception of solidarity itself as a charitable contribution to the restoration of normality or fairness. Mostly, it is associated with the predominance of the new economic constitutionalism that places moral hazard on top of the political and institutional stakes. The EU no-bail-out clause obviously constitutes the epitome of this stance.

In this context, not surprisingly, financial assistance to the euro-area Member States was considered not as an institutional act of solidarity but mostly as an optional and charitable gesture of necessity to prevent contagion – eventually as a self-protection mechanism. Although the give and take of financial rescue packages took a strict legal form with the drafting of multiple legal instruments that determined in a considerable level of analysis the rights and obligations of all parties, the underlying rationale seems even today to focus on the voluntary aspect of the transaction and much less so on an institutional obligation stemming from the rule of solidarity.

Eleftheriadis argues that it should not be this way. He considers that corrective justice that applies to cooperative arrangements between States and creates a principle of symmetry of risks and opportunities requires that those who have been unfairly burdened by an agreement have to be compensated by those who were not, even if the unfair agreement was entirely voluntary. He then goes on to establish that, regardless of their own respective financial inadequacies or trespasses, States that were unfairly burdened by the euro area's flawed architecture and suffered economic loss as a result, have some claim of redress against the others. This flawed architecture – today a commonplace in European literature – was based from the outset on the asymmetrical risks for several disadvantaged States, either through sovereign debt or through the banking system, because it created a monetary union without a commensurate fiscal union, that set up a case of 'structural responsibility' burdening all the original euro-area Member States. From this viewpoint, Eleftheriadis concludes that the programmes of financial assistance towards the Eurozone's periphery were not merely actions of self-preservation, prudence, or charity but were discharging existing obligations of solidarity among the Member States.[134]

---

[134] P Eleftheriadis, 'Solidarity in the Eurozone' Working Paper Series of the Bank of Greece (2019, unpublished, cited with permission).

Similarly, Habermas sees solidarity in a more coercive way, as a condition of survival in a multi-dependent financial environment to promote growth and competitiveness in the euro area as a whole, given the uncontrolled systemic contingencies of a form of capitalism driven by unrestrained financial markets creating tensions between euro-area Member States.[135] Concerning the justiciability of the combined standard, the dominance of financialism in constitutional drafting and reading during the economic crisis seems to have seriously hampered other concerns. Even solidarity, which is explicitly provided in primary EU law, is not an all-encompassing principle, value, or concept in absolute terms, and there are specific limits that make it 'questionable in law'.[136] This is particularly evident with regard to social sustainability, which was in fact greatly affected by the widespread austerity measures as collateral to financial assistance conditionality. The curtailment of social sustainability is evidenced both in the way the public interest justifying interference with human rights is determined, where there is a unilateral upheaval of the monetary aspects of public needs, and at the eventual balancing between the compelling public interest of holding the public economics within strict financial boundaries and the level of normative decrease of the right to property.

Ordoliberalism set a specific version of economic sustainability on the top of the political agenda. Although the idea remains that economic growth should be achieved without negatively impacting social, environmental, and cultural aspects of the community, it is of primary importance to prevent or treat recession or stagnation of the economy. This, as matter of principle, strongly misapprehends social sustainability and results in an overturn of the original conception of the three pillars of sustainability: instead of having social and environmental sustainability setting substantive restrictions upon economic sustainability, economic sustainability largely determines the level of environmental consumption and of social protection. As a matter of logic, nevertheless, the degree to which considerations of sustainability or solidarity may or may not become justiciable issues broadly remains within the discretion of the judicial authorities that will decide on relevant cases. In particular sustainability aspects, namely environmental sustainability, the EU courts have maintained, in spite of the economic crisis, a relatively strong judicial position which also entails technical judgements and assessment of the discretion exercised by the national authorities.[137]

---

[135] Habermas, *The Crisis of the European Union* (2013) 10.

[136] G Butler, 'Solidarity and its Limits for Economic Integration in the European Union's Internal Market' (2018) 25 *Maastricht Journal of European and Comparative Law* 310, 331.

[137] JR May and E Daly, *Global Environmental Constitutionalism* (New York, Cambridge University Press, 2015) 85–172. Indeed, the Court of Justice and the General Court, in spite of the economic crisis, have in the 2010s maintained the adherence to the principle of precaution and the requirement for preventive action by strictly implementing EU environmental legislation towards the aim of

(b)   *What benchmark applies?*

With regard to the issue of the applicable benchmark for the combined standard, it is obviously an extremely different task to set up actual measureable indicators due to the inherent fluidity of the two constitutive elements of the standard. The most difficult experiment is to determine what is at any given time and place the proportion of all sort of natural consumption of people (individually or in groups) for a policy to qualify as sustainable or as globally solidary. In a very elaborate work, Endress, Pongkijvorasin, Roumasset and Pitafi drafted a series of mathematical formulations to quantify data that would assess intergenerational equity through a model of optimal and sustainable growth that accommodated distinct intragenerational and intergenerational discount rates: in their findings, under the assumption of constant elasticity of marginal utility, the optimum trajectory of aggregate consumption is governed at each time by the relationships among aggregate quantities and the generational discount rate but not the personal discount rate; as the personal discount rate increases, each generation allocates a higher share of its lifetime consumption to earlier stages of life, yet an increase in the personal discount rate does not affect the trajectory of aggregate consumption.[138]

Nonetheless, establishing such a global intergenerational index is merely a utopia given the perplexities of the global economy and governance and the multiplicity of interests involved. This does not mean, however, that those considerations can legitimately be absent from any type of major decision that affects the community, be it global or local. The economic crisis has proved that mere financial considerations of the contemporary era are bound to result in an inadequate, if not altogether false, assessment. The landscape becomes even more complex if one adds to the contemporary polycentric institutional labyrinth the fragile social and economic conditions and the sharp divisions between nations. Obviously, global problems by all means require global solutions, thus to a great extent global governance. Emilio Padilla rightly argues that the rights of future generations ought to be incorporated into economic evaluation and management through an appropriate and enforceable institutional network with an appropriate design and function to be able to employ such principles and to enforce its decisions.[139]

---

environmental sustainability, see among a bulk of relevant cases, see recent CJEU Judgment of 17 April 2018 in Case C-441/17, *Commission v Poland*, concerning conservation of natural habitats and of wild fauna and flora pursuant to Dir 2009/147; CJEU Judgment of 18 January 2018 in Case C-58/17, *INEOS Köln GmbH v Bundesrepublik Deutschland*, concerning a scheme for greenhouse gas emission allowance trading within the EU pursuant to Dir 2003/87; CJEU Judgment of 12 July 2018 in Case C-540/16, *UAB 'Spika' and othersv Žuvininkystės tarnyba prie Lietuvos Respublikos žemės ūkio ministerijos*, concerning allocation of fishing opportunities pursuant to Reg 1380/2013.

[138] L Endress, S Pongkijvorasin, J Roumasset and B Pitafi, 'Impatience and intergenerational equity in a model of sustainable growth' Working Paper No 09-6. University of Hawaii at Manoa, Department of Economics (2009), www.economics.hawaii.edu/research/workingpapers/WP_09-6.pd, 12.

[139] Padilla, 'Intergenerational equity' (2002) 78–80.

New economic constitutionalism and the corresponding dominance in many respects of financialism over human rights seriously undermines both the rights of future generations (by consuming a disproportionately high natural capital and alienating natural conditions for the future) and the social solidarity owed to less privileged individuals and groups, especially from less favoured regions. As a mode of defence towards potential extremities, any capital decision-making process ought to consider both intergenerational sustainability, as a form of existing and not merely a prospective right of future generations, and due solidarity, not only towards the citizens within the territory where a regulation applies or an economic activity is implemented, but also on a global basis. Obviously, ephemeral prosperity should not undermine the right of all individuals, including future generations, to enjoy an adequate level of wealth.

Conclusions

There are six conclusions that summarise the research outcomes of this book.

(1) The economic crisis undeniably signalled a new era in the rapport between Constitution and economy that is readily discernable from prior stages of constitutionalism and can be qualified as new economic constitutionalism.

The era of new economic constitutionalism has elevated economy to an equal status with politics/law and has prompted significant constitutional change throughout Europe. This process of change has been greatly facilitated by a fundamental convergence of both EU and the European States in a single economic constitutional identity, ie financialism, which calls for priority of economic provisions over other constitutional clauses and principles and, accordingly, an interpretative transformation of key constitutional notions, such as competence, sustainability and property.

This convergence was the outcome of a parallel evolution process in national States and international entities: the former seeking for functionality, which conventional constitutionalism failed effectively to establish in order to prevent the break-out of the economic crisis; the latter seeking for legitimacy, which still remains their basic shortfall in relation to sovereign States and inhibits them from gaining a genuine constitutional status equivalent to them. Transition to new economic constitutionalism and the predominance of financialism were facilitated by a number of factual surroundings, such as transnationalism of economic governance, transformation of the classical ordoliberal perception, larger intangibility of financial assets, dismantling between politics and law and osmosis of public and private spheres.

In spite of non-institutional explanations of the economic crisis set forth by the relevant literature (political, psychological, sociological), the main causes for the new economic constitutionalism and financialism have presumably been the structural asymmetries of the European project, especially the lack of EU constitutional foundation, the lack of fiscal convergence of the euro area, the economic divergences of euro-area Member States and the limited monitoring for financial trespasses. Those asymmetries resulted in a twofold type of overreliance within the EU, ie conceptual overreliance on monetarism and structural overreliance on sincere cooperation among the euro-area Member States.

(2) New economic constitutionalism produced significant consequences on the drafting and reading of the Constitution, through plethoric regulation of purely

economic nature and economic-oriented constitutional interpretation that brought economic considerations to the forefront of constitutionalism.

Constitutional adaptation to the era of new economic constitutionalism was made without wide constitutional revisions (apart from specific balanced budget and debt brake amendments) or EU Treaties' amendments (except for Article 136 TFEU) but essentially through ordinary tools of legislation and judicial decisions ruling on the compatibility of such legislation with the higher norms of the respective legal orders. This adaptation was almost exclusively made on the basis of economic considerations putting financialism to the forefront of the constitutional drafting and reading.

First, the regulation produced was merely economic, predominantly stabilisation and stability rules, economic governance processes, financial rescue tools and banking regulation. This may sound reasonable given the nature of the crisis. Yet, treating the crisis on merely economic grounds without the corresponding structural measures safeguarding institutional resilience and a minimum level of social protection and cohesion, which was the case in the equivalent example of the US mid-war crisis, might prove detrimental.

Second, the need for emergency measures in order to effectively deal with the immediate consequences of the crisis was to some extent detrimental to the rule of law, either because they were arguably introduced outside the framework of formal legality or because it took a very generous judicial interpretation, often abstaining from prior consolidated doctrines and principles, in order to provide some legitimacy for the treatment of the crisis.

Third, the new economic regulation created an over-complicated technical mix, with the EU and the powerful European States largely determining the economic policies upon all euro-area Member States – more intensely upon debtor States. These relationships have been largely determined on the ground of financial dependencies, with significant retreat of more communitarian principles, such as solidarity. This is indicated by the ex ante tool of prudency in all aspects of financial and banking regulation, with the corresponding obligation of sovereign States to enhance financial restraints in their respective Constitutions and the ex post, essentially non-negotiable and not tailor-crafted, conditionality clauses in the financial assistance agreements. Not surprisingly, national constitutional orders seem to be in a process of overall convergence based on a single model of economic constitution.

Fourth, with only few variations, both international and national courts alike adopted an economic-oriented reading of constitutional clauses as well as of new economic rules in order to confirm priority of economic considerations against other principles of constitutional ranking. In most cases, this process required a transformation of key concepts upon which the EU and the ECHR projects were built. Thus, the EU principles of conferred powers and subsidiarity were essentially revisited so as to accommodate policies enhanced on the verge of Union legitimacy, the social rights suffered serious downgrading both on domestic and international level and bondholders', bank depositors' and shareholders' rights were substantially sacrificed in order to prevent systemic default. Most strikingly, the right to property, a cornerstone of the contemporary liberal state, was subject to a tremendous adjustment concerning its scope (intangible assets being essentially excluded from the domain of constitutional protection) and the intensity of judicial review that allowed very wide discretion on the part of the state authorities by invoking exceptional circumstances and the political and/or technical nature of the impugned measures. Alongside property, a number of relevant principles, such as non-discrimination, public interest, proportionality and legitimate expectations, were subject to qualifications in order to fit, in a rather procrustean manner, to the need to deal with the imminent crisis. The change of the constitutional interpretation was so evident that, on occasion, conjunctive reading of pre- and post-crisis case law is rather striking for the opposite judicial reasoning. This resulted in a case law paradox on a domestic level, namely that in cases of balance of powers of state institutions, where considerations of democracy, sovereignty and constitutional pluralism came into play more strongly, national courts were inclined to be more interventionist, in order to safeguard the parliamentary nature of the polity and national constitutionalism, whereas in cases involving interferences with human rights judges were significantly more self-restrained.

(3) New economic constitutionalism has altogether changed the institutional balance between the internal organs, both in the EU and domestic orders, and the balance of power between the EU and its Member States, resulting internally in the empowerment of the executive branch and of powerful euro-area Member States and the EU itself.

The fundamental principles of representation, legitimacy, accountability, separation of powers and subsidiarity that have for a long time consolidated an effective mix of competences among the legislature, the executive and the judiciary have been subject to transformation in the course of the economic crisis. With the exception of the EU, where new rules of economic governance have granted new monitoring and supervising powers to the Commission and the Court of Justice, in all other cases the reshaping of the institutional balance has occurred de facto as a matter of actual political imposition. Thus, in the main, the national executives have gained significant political dominance over the respective parliaments, with the latter becoming mostly legitimising fora for decisions taken by the governments.

In fact, on very few occasions national parliaments demonstrated a high level of political resilience to executive decisions. Interestingly, in some domestic legal orders of the lending States with a strong tradition of constitutional justice, it was the respective constitutional court that took over to protect the parliamentary character of the polity and demand that the legislature in plenum (and not as a subsection) had adequate feedback upon which to decide on matters pertaining to EU and euro-area financial policy and to prevent executive decisions taken without prior consent of the parliament. By way of contrast, most of the debtors' national courts, as well as the European Court of Human Rights, normally upheld austerity measures entailing salary and pension cuts and hampering property rights associated to bonds, deposits and shares. Thus, given that in all crisis cases brought before them the EU courts upheld the validity of the acts of the EU institutions and rejected any claims raised by citizens against those institutions, more often as inadmissible, jureconomy in Europe seems to overwhelmingly uphold financialism and all concessions made on rights in order to make this model functional and sustainable.

Finally, in the course of the management of the crisis, there has been a serious transfer of powers from national States to supranational entities, especially the EU, through new statutory powers awarded to the EU institutions, through implied powers associated to existing competences and through contractual commitments assumed by the Member States. Irrespective of the expediency of such transfer of competence and the legitimacy and sovereignty concerns thereof, the EU has been de jure and de facto armed at the expense of its Member States.

(4) New economic constitutionalism has significantly changed the perception of politics and the terms of political debate in Europe towards less deliberate, representative and participatory processes.

First, the pre-existing interdependence of sovereign States in an environment of global economy and constitutional pluralism has essentially turned in the course of the crisis to mere dependence of some Member States upon others. This is due to contractual obligations assumed in order to receive the necessary financial assistance, and has resulted in a state of power politics much more intense than before.

Second, the economic crisis left politics in Europe sharply divided between those arguing in favour of financial stability and those setting social cohesion at the top of their political agenda, with a total lack of a deliberative spirit on either side. This division amounted to a decrease in the level of consensus in national politics, which brought in easy populist rhetoric and resulted in strongly divisive politics.

Third, national politics concern a much wider spectrum of interested parties apart from domestic political actors, such as international organisations and other States, which become stakeholders through multilateral loan agreements in which they participate as contracting parties, thus resulting in overall cross-border politics.

Fourth, in the post-crisis political arena there was a tendency to depart from salient features of representative democracy. Thus, technocratic governments took over on some occasions to treat the over-complicated issues stemming from the economic default, referenda were declared which were largely manipulated (through misleading questions, or widespread false information on the issues involved, or unidentified consequences that the results might have, or by changing their outcome altogether) and strong deference of the people was marked towards their participation in the public sphere, predominantly in the national elections and in spite of the divisive political climate that could have conceivably led to greater popular turnout.

(5) The post-crisis EU regulatory strategy has failed to address the challenges of new economic constitutionalism, in that it has been restricted to economic governance rules instead of launching institutional reforms aiming at the roots of systemic pathologies.

In that regard this book suggests an EU recalibration proposal of three elements. In terms of structures, multi-level representative governance is suggested, purporting to strengthen legitimisation, regionalisation and european-isation through enhanced presidentialist and federalist elements, ie direct election of the European Commission through an alternative vote system and not subject to a parliamentary vote of confidence and establishment of a second EU legislative body. In terms of decision-making processes, a vision of holistic deliberativism is envisaged, entailing inclusiveness of stakeholders, endorsement through uncon-ditional validity of all arguments and retraction predilection of the participants, consideration of full evidence, interplay/fair play of procedures and transparency. In terms of policy choices, global solidarity and intergenerational sustainability are suggested, jointly bringing time ahead by incorporating the benefits of future generations at the forefront of policy-making and transcending locality by intro-ducing universal solidarity in order to see human rights, whose protection has beyond any doubt been curtailed in the crisis era, from a different standpoint, promoting a broader community spirit.

(6) New economic constitutionalism is neither conservative nor progressive, neither a constitutional theocracy nor a democratic anathema.

The upgrade of economy in the constitutional drafting and reading in the post-crisis era and the corresponding dominance of financialism as a key inter-pretative principle vis-a-vis other principles of constitutional order is not in itself a benevolent or a detrimental status, but rather a reality that calls for specific institutional management. The critical view adopted in this book does not reflect the expediency of the new level of interrelationship between economy and the Constitution. It is mostly aimed at identifying the deficiencies in treating a phenomenon which, even today, after the extensive load of economic regulation, seems to suffer from serious shortfalls. Given the cognitive complexity of econ-omy, which has allowed economic actors to be readily responsive to political/legal interventions to curb its autonomy, legal discourse must turn to a readjustment of constitutional mechanics in order to address new challenges. The institutional power lies with the basics of the constitutional doctrine: instead of chasing a chimera of subordination of economy, it is more expedient and wise to enter into a project of resilient institution-building in Europe. After all, in the course of political history, there has been no prosperity without sound institutions.

BIBLIOGRAPHY

D Acemoglou, G Egorov and K Sonin, 'Dynamics and Stability of Constitutions, Coalitions, and Clubs' (2012) 102 *American Economic Review* 1446.

B Ackerman, 'Revolution in a Human Scale' (1999) 108 *Yale Law Journal* 2279.

W Adema and M Ladaique, 'How Expensive is the Welfare State? Gross and Net Indicators in the OECD Social Expenditure Database' OECD Social, Employment and Migration Working Paper no 92 (2009).

J Agyeman, R Bullard and B Evans, 'Conclusion: Towards Just Sustainabilities. Perspectives and Possibilities' in J Agyeman, R Bullard and B Evans (eds), *Just Sustainabilities: Development in an Unequal World* (Cambridge, Massachusetts Institute of Technology Press, 2003) 323.

EF Albertsworth, 'The New Constitutionalism' (1940) 26 *American Bar Association Journal* 865.

—— 'The Mirage of Constitutionalism' (1935) 29 *Illinois Law Review* 608.

B Alexander, *The Globalization of Addiction* (Oxford, Oxford University Press, 2008).

C Altavilla, D Giannone and M Lenza, 'The Financial and Macroeconomic Effects of OMT Announcements' (2016) 12 *International Journal of Central Banking* 29.

SS Andersen and KA Eliassen, *The European Union: How Democratic is it?* (London, Sage, 1996).

MG Arghyrou, 'From the Euro-Crisis to a new European Economic Architecture' in DD Thomakos, P Monokrousos and K Nikolopoulos (eds), *A Financial Crisis Management: Reflexions and the Road Ahead* (Basingstoke, Palgrave Macmillan, 2015) 308.

MG Arghyrou and J Tsoukalas, 'The Greek Debt Crisis: Likely Causes, Mechanics and Outcomes' (2011) 34 *The World Economy* 173.

M Artis, 'The Stability and Growth Pact: Fiscal Policy in the EMU' in F Breuss, G Fink and S Griller (eds), *Institutional, Legal and Economic Aspects of the EMU* (Vienna, Springer, 2002) 101.

M Auerback, 'Ban the Credit Ratings Agencies!' 8 February 2013, available at: www.salon. com/2013/02/08/ban_the_credit_ratings_agencies_partner.

JL Austin, *The Province of Jurisprudence Determined* (Cambridge, Cambridge University Press, 1995).

M Avbelj and J Komarek, *Constitutional Pluralism in the European Union and Beyond* (Oxford, Hart Publishing, 2012).

M Avbelj, 'Differentiated Integration – Farewell to the EU-27' (2014) *German Law Journal* 191.

V Babis, 'State Helps those who Help Themselves: State Aid and Burden-Sharing' University of Cambridge Faculty of Law Research Paper no 62/2016 (2016).

I Bache and M Flinders, 'Multi-Level Governance: Conclusions and Implications' in I Bache and M Flinders (eds), *Multi-Level Governance* (Oxford, Oxford University Press, 2004) 195.

A Baglioni, *The European Banking Union: A Critical Assessment* (London, Palgrave Macmillan, 2016).

R Balodis and J Pleps, 'Financial Crisis and the Constitution in Latvia' in X Contiades (ed), *Constitutions in the Global Financial Crisis. A Comparative Analysis* (Farnham, Ashgate, 2013) 115.

B Barry 'Sustainability and Intergenerational Justice' in A Dobson (ed), *Fairness and Futurity: Essays on Environmental Sustainability and Social Justice* (New York, Oxford University Press, 1999) 93.

J Bast, 'Don't Act beyond your Powers: The Perils and Pitfalls of the German Constitutional Court's Ultra Vires Review' (2014) 15 *German Law Journal* 167.

MW Bauer, 'The Unexpected Winner of the Crisis: The European Commission's Strengthened Role in Economic Governance' (2014) 36 *Journal of European Integration* 213.

W Beckerman, 'Sustainable Development and our Obligations to Future Generations' in A Dobson (ed), *Fairness and Futurity: Essays on Environmental Sustainability and Social Justice* (New York, Oxford University Press, 1999) 71.

S Bekker, 'Flexicurity in the European Semester: Still a Relevant Policy Concept?' (2018) 25 *Journal of European Public Policy* 175.

R Bellamy, *Political Constitutionalism. A Republican Defence of the Constitutionality of Democracy* (Cambridge, Cambridge University Press, 2009).

J Bengoetxea, 'Rethinking EU Law in the Light of Pluralism and Practical Reason' in M Maduro, K Tuori and S Sankari (eds), *Transnational Law: Rethinking European Law and Legal Thinking* (Cambridge, Cambridge University Press, 2014) 145.

N Bernard, *Multilevel Governance in the European Union* (The Hague, Kluwer Law International, 2002).

J Bessett, 'Deliberative Democracy: The Majority Principle in Republican Government' in L Goldwin and D Shambra (eds), *How Democratic is the Constitution?* (Washington DC, American Enterprise Institute, 1980).

S Bilakovics, *Democracy without Politics* (Cambridge MA, Harvard University Press, 2012).

J-H Binder and ChV Gortsos, *The European Banking Union: A Compendium* (Baden-Baden, Beck – Hart – Nomos, 2016).

O Blanchard, 'Adjustment within the Euro: The Difficult Case of Portugal' (2007) *Portuguese Economic Journal* 1.

S Blavoukos and G Pagoulatos, 'The Limits of EMU Conditionality: Fiscal Adjustment in Southern Europe' (2008) 28 *Journal of Public Policy* 229.

Bloomberg Editorial Board, 'Hey, Germany: You got a Bail-out, Too' 24 May 2012, available at: www.bloomberg.com/opinion/articles/2012-05-23/merkel-should-know-her-country-has-been-bailed-out-too.

G Boccuzzi, *The European Banking Union: Supervision and Rsolution* (London, Palgrave Macmillan, 2015).

M Bogaards, 'De-Democratization in Hungary: Diffusely Defective Democracy' (2018) 25 *Democratization* 1481.

V Bogdanor, 'The Future of the European Community: Two Models of Democracy' (1986) 21 *Government and Opposition* 161.

A Borriello and A Crespy, 'How to not speak the 'F-word': Federalism between Mirage and Imperative in the Euro Crisis (2015) 54 *European Journal of Political Research* 502.

—— 'Less and More Europe: The EU at a Crossroads between Federalism and Political Disintegration', London School of Economics European Politics and Policy blog: http://blogs.lse.ac.uk/europpblog/2016/01/14/less-and-more-europe-the-eu-at-a-crossroads-between-federalism-and-political-disintegration (2016).

H Brunkhorst, *Solidarity: From Civic Friendship to a Global Legal Community* (Cambridge MA, Massachusetts Institute of Technology Press, 2005).

—— 'Collective Bonapartism – Democracy in the European Crisis' (2014) 15 *German Law Journal* 1177.

K Budziło (ed), *Selected Rulings of the Polish Constitutional Tribunal Concerning the Law of the European Union – 2003–2014* (Warsaw, Biuro Trybunału Konstytucyjnego, 2014).

M Burgess, *Federalism and the European Union: The Building of Europe 1950–2000* (London, Routledge, 2000).

D Busch, 'Governance of the Single Revolution Mechanism' in D Busch and G Ferrarini (eds) *European Banking Union* (Oxford, Oxford University Press 2015) 9.01.

G Butler, 'Solidarity and its Limits for Economic Integration in the European Union's Internal Market' (2018) 25 *Maastricht Journal of European and Comparative Law* 310.

CM Cantore and G Martinico, 'Asymmetry or Dis-integration? A Few Considerations on the New "Treaty on Stability, Coordination and Governance in the Economic and Monetary Union"' (2013) 19 *European Public Law* 463.

F Carballo-Cruz, 'Causes and Consequences of the Spanish Economic Crisis: Why the Recovery is Taken so Long?' (2011) 3 *Panoeconomicus* 309.

K Cardiff, *Recap: Inside Ireland's Financial Crisis* (Dublin, The Liffey Press, 2016).

G Carrabregu, 'Habermas on Solidarity: An Immanent Critique' (2016) 23 *Constellations* 507.

M Chang, *Economic and Monetary Union* (London, Palgrave Macmillan, 2016).

JT Checkel, 'Social Constructivism and European Integration' in T Christiansen, K Jorgensen and A Wiener (eds), *The Social Construction of Europe* (London, Sage, 2001).

N Chronowski and G-O Fruzsina, 'The Hungarian Constitutional Court and the Financial Crisis' (2017) 58 *Hungarian Journal of Legal Studies* 139.

D Chryssochoou, *Democracy in the European Union* (London, Tauris, 2000).

AR Coban, *Protection of Property Rights within the European Convention on Human Rights* (Aldershot, Ashgate, 2004).

T Congdon, *Keynes, the Keynesians and Monetarism* (Cheltenham, Elgar, 2007).

X Contiades and IA Tassopoulos, 'The Impact of the Financial Crisis on the Greek Constitution' in X Contiades (ed), *Constitutions in the Global Financial Crisis. A Comparative Analysis* (Farnham, Ashgate, 2013) 195.

T Conzelmann and R Smith (eds), *Multi-Level Governance in the European Union: Taking Sstock and Looking Ahead* (Baden Baden, Nomos, 2008).

I Cooper, 'A "Virtual Third Chamber" for the European Union? National Parliaments after the Treaty of Lisbon' (2012) 35 *West European Politics* 441.

P Cormack and R Goodman, *Responsible Capitalism: Essays on Morality, Ethics and Business* (London, First, 2009).

S Coutts, 'Ireland: Traditional Procedures Aadapted for Economic Emergency' in T Beukers, B de Witte and C Kilpatrick (eds), *Constitutional Change through Euro-Crisis Law* (Cambridge, Cambridge University Press, 2017) 230.

P Craig, 'Pringle and Use of EU Institutions outside the EU Legal Framework: Foundation, Procedure and Substance" (2013) 9 *European Constitutional Law Review* 263.

—— 'Gauweiler and the Legality of Outright Monetary Transactions' (2016) 41 *European Law Review* 1.

—— 'Pringle: Legal Reasoning, Text, Purpose and Teleology' (2013) *Maastricht Journal of European and Comparative Law* 14.

—— 'The Stability, Coordination and Governance Treaty: Principle, Politics and Pragmatism' (2012) 37 *European Law Review* 231.

O Cramme, 'The Trend towards the Europeanisation of Domestic Politics is Unstoppable (and Good) but for the Time Being will be Messy and Uneven' London School of Economics European Politics and Policy Blog (2012), available at: http://blogs.lse.ac.uk/europpblog/2012/03/12/europeanisation-eu-domestic-politics.

A Crespy and G Menz, 'Commission Entrepreneurship and the Debasing of Social Europe before and after the Eurocrisis' (2015) 53 *Journal of Common Market Studies* 753.

P Crugman, 'Charlemagne, Empathy in Short Supply. Greece: not a Simple Fable about Ants and Crickets' *The Economist*, 8 March 2010.

—— 'Whips, Scourges, and Cats' *The New York Times*, 19 June 2012.

B Crum and D Curtin, 'The Challenge of Making European Union Executive Power Accountable' in S Piattoni (ed.), *The European Union: Democratic Principles and Institutional Architectures in Times of Crisis* (Oxford, Oxford University Press, 2015) 63.

B Crum and JE Fossum, 'The Multilevel Parliamentary Field'. A Framework for Theorizing Representative Democracy in the EU' (2009) 1 *European Political Science Review* 249.

T Daintith, 'The Constitutional Protection of Economic Rights' (2004) 2 *International Journal of Constitutional Law* 56.

HE Daly, 'Commentary: Toward some Operational Principles of Sustainable Development' (1990) 2 *Ecological Economics* 1.

A Darbellay and F Partnoy, 'Credit Rating Agencies and Regulatory Eeform' in CA Hill and BH McDonnell (eds), *Research Handbook on the Economics of Corporate Law, Research Handbooks in Law and Economics Series* (Cheltenham, Elgar, 2012) 273.

ZM Darvas, and Á Leandro, 'The Limitations of Policy Coordination in the Euro Area under the European Semester' (2015) 19 *Bruegel Policy Contribution* 1.

M Dawson and F de Witte, 'Constitutional Balance in the EU after the Euro-Crisis' (2013) 76 *The Modern Law Review* 817.

F Decker and J Sonnicksen, 'The Direct Election of the Commission President. A Presidential Approach to Democratising the European Union', Centre for European Integration Studies, ZEI Discussion Paper C 192 (2009).

—— 'Governance beyond the Nation-State: Reflections on the Democratic Deficit of the European Union', (2002) 9:2 *Journal of European Public Policy* 256.

—— 'An Alternative Approach to European Union Democratization: Re-examining the Direct Election of the Commission President' (2011) 46 *Government and Opposition* 168.

P Demetriades, *Diary of the Euro Crisis in Cyprus: Lessons for Bank Recovery and Resolution* (Cham, Springer, 2017).

J Derrida, *The other Handing: Reflections on Today's Europe* (Bloomington, Indiana University Press, 1992).

K Dilek Azman, *The Problem of Democratic Deficit in the European Union: The Democratic Deficit Issue with Reference to the Acquis* (Saarbrücken, Lap Lambert Academic Publishing, 2011).

S Donnelly, 'Power Politics and the Undersupply of Financial Stability in Europe' (2014) 21 *Review of International Political Economy* 980.

YZ Drossos, 'Yesterday' (2012), available at: www.constitutionalism.gr/site/2352-yesterday.

JS Dryzek, *Discursive Democracy: Politics, Policy, and Political Science* (Cambridge, Cambridge University Press, 1990).

—— *Deliberative Democracy and Beyond: Liberals, Critics, Contestations* (Oxford, Oxford University Press, 2000).

—— *Deliberative Global Politics. Discourse and Democracy in a Divided World* (Cambridge, Polity Press, 2006).

E Durkheim, *The Division of Labor in Society* (Detroit, Free Press, 1964).

B Dutzler and A Hable, 'The European Court of Justice and the Stability and Growth Pact – Just the Beginning?', European Integration Online Papers (EIoP), vol 9, no 5 (2005).

K Efstathiou and GB Wolff, 'Is the European Semester Effective and Useful?' (2018) 9 *Policy Contribution* Issue 1.

M Egeberg, J Trondal and NM Vestland, 'The Quest for Order: Unravelling the Relationship between the European Commission and EU Agencies' (2015) 22 *Journal of European Public Policy* 609.

F Eggermont, *The Changing Role of the European Council in the Institutional Framework of the European Union: Consequences for the European Integration Process* (Cambridge, Intersentia, 2012).

R Eichenberger and BS Frey, 'Functional, Overlapping and Competing Jurisdictions: A Complement and Alternative to Today's Federalism' in A Ehtisham und G Brosio (eds), *Handbook of Fiscal Federalism* (Cheltenham, Elgar, 2006) 154.

A Eide, C Krause and A Rosas (eds), *Economic, Social and Cultural Rights: A Textbook*, 2nd edn (Leiden, Brill, 2001).

M Eilstrup-Sangiovanni, 'Introduction. Neo-Functionalism and its Critiques' in M Eilstrup-Sangiovanni, (ed), *Debates on European Integration* (Basingstoke, Palgrave Macmillan, 2006) 89.

P Eleftheriadis, 'Democracy in the Eurozone' in W-G Ringe and PM Huber (eds), *Legal Challenges in the Global Financial Crisis: Bail-outs, the Euro and Regulation* (Oxford, Hart Publishing, 2015) 27.

—— 'Solidarity in the Eurozone' Working Paper Series of the Bank of Greece (2019, forthcoming).

—— 'The Euro and the German Courts' (2012) 128 *Law Quarterly Review* 216.

J Elster, 'Forces and Mechanisms in the Constitution-Making Process' (1995) 45 *Duke Law Journal* 364.

H Enderlein, S Wälti and M Zürn, *Handbook on Multi-Level Governance* (Cheltenham, Elgar, 2010).

L Endress, S Pongkijvorasin, J Roumasset and B Pitafi, 'Impatience and Intergenerational Equity in a Model of Sustainable Growth' Working Paper No 09-6. University of Hawaii at Manoa, Department of Economics (2009).

M Everson and Ch Joerges, 'Who is the Guardian for Constitutionalism in Europe after the Financial Crisis?' London School of Economics 'Europe in Question' Discussion Paper Series no 63/2013.

S Fabbrini, *Which European Union? Europe after the Euro Crisis* (Cambridge, Cambridge University Press, 2015).

—— *Economic Governance in Europe. Comparative Paradoxes and Constitutional Challenges*, Oxford Studies in European Law (Oxford, Oxford University Press).

—— 'The Euro-Crisis and the Courts: Judicial Review and the Political Process in Comparative Perspective' (2014) 32:1 *Berkeley Journal of International Law* 64.

—— 'The Fiscal Compact, the "Golden Rule", and the paradox of European Federalism' (2013) 36 *Boston College International and Comparative Law Review* 1.

—— 'After the OMT Case: The Supremacy of EU Law as the Guarantee of the Equality of the Member States' (2015) 16:4 *German Law Journal* 1003.

G Falkner, 'The EU's Problem-Solving Capacity and Legitimacy in a Crisis Context: A Virtuous or Vicious Circle?' (2016) 39:5 *West European Politics* 953.

K Featherstone, 'External Conditionality and the Debt Crisis: the "Troika" and Public Administration Reform in Greece' (2015) 22:3 *Journal of European Public Policy* 295.

—— 'The Greek Sovereign Debt Crisis and EMU: A Failing State in a Skewed Regime' (2011) 49 *Journal of Common Market Studies* 193.

N Ferguson, *The Ascent of Money: A Financial History of the World* (New York, Penguin, 2009).

Ó Fernández, *The Democratic Deficit of the European Union* (Saarbrücken, Lap Lambert Academic Publishing, 2013).

G Ferrarini and F Recine, 'The Single Rulebook and the SSM: Should the ECB have more Say in Prudential Rule-Making?' in D Busch and G Ferrarini (eds) *European Banking Union* (Oxford, Oxford University Press, 2015) 5.01.

M Ferrera, 'Solidarity in Europe after the Crisis' (2014) 21 *Constellations* 222.

R Fine, 'The Idea of Cosmopolitan Solidarity' in G Delanty (ed), *Routledge Handbook of Cosmopolitanism Studies* (London, Routledge, 2012).

J Fischer, 'Vom Staatenbund zur Föderation. Rede am 12.Mai 2000 in der Humboldt-Universität in Berlin am 12. Mai 2000' in C Joerges, Y Mény and JHH Weiler (eds), *What Kind of Constitution for what Kind of Polity? Responses to Joschka Fischer* (Cambridge, MA, Harvard Law School, 2000) 5.

JS Fishkin, *Democracy and Deliberation: New Directions for Democratic Reform* (New Haven, Yale University Press, 1991).

JA Flammang, 'Democracy: Direct, Representative, and Deliberative' (2001) 41 *Santa Clara Law Review* 1085.

JE Fossum and M Jachtenfuchs 'Federal Challenges and Challenges to Federalism. Insights from the EU and Federal Sates' (2017) 24 *Journal of European Public Policy* 467.

J Frankel 'Causes of Eurozone Crises' in R Baldwin and F Giavazzi (eds), *The Eurozone Crisis: A Consensus View of the Causes and a Few Possible Solutions* (London, CEPR Press, 2015) 109.

—— 'What Small Countries can Teach the World' (2012) 47 *Business Economics* 93.

M Friedman (ed), *The Optimum Quantity of Money and other Essays* (Chicago, Aldine, 1969).

H Gabrisch and K Staehr, 'The Euro Plus Pact: Competitiveness and External Capital Flows in the EU Countries' (2014) 53 *Journal of Common Market Studies* 558.

JK Galbreith, *The Great Crash 1929* (Wilmington, Mariner Books, 2009).

M Gallagher, M Laver, M Marsh, R Singh and B Tonra, 'Electing the President of the European Commission', Trinity Blue Papers in Public Policy 1, Trinity College (1995).

A Gardella, 'Bail-In and the Financing of Resolution within the SRM Framework' in D Busch and G Ferrarini (eds), *European Banking Union* (Oxford, Oxford University Press 2015) 11.01.

G Gee and GCN Webber, 'What is a Political Constitution?' (2010) 30 *Oxford Journal of Legal Studies* 273.

N Georgikopoulos and T Efthimiadis, 'The Development of the Greek–German Government Bond Spreads' *European Business Review* 4 February 2010.

G Gerapetritis, *The Application of Proportionality in Administrative Law. Judicial Review in France, Greece, England and in the European Community* (Athens, Ant. Sakkoulas, 1997).

—— *Affirmative Action Policies and Judicial Review Worldwide* (Cham, Springer, 2016).

—— 'Europe's New Deal: a New Version of an Expiring Deal' (2014) 38 *European Journal of Law and Economics* 91.

—— 'Deliberative Democracy within and beyond the State' in L Papadopoulou, I Pernice, JHH Weiler (eds), *Legitimacy Issues of the European Union in the Face of Crisis. Dimitris Tsatsos in Memoriam*, European Constitutional Law Network-Series vol 9, 2nd edn (Baden Baden, Nomos, 2018) 25.

P Gérard and W Verrijdt, 'Belgian Constitutional Court Adopts National Identity Discourse: Belgian Constitutional Court No 62/2016, 28 April 2016' (2017) 13 *European Constitutional Law Review* 182.

DJ Gerber, 'Economic Constitutionalism and the Challenge of Globalization: The Enemy is Gone? Long Live the Enemy: Comment' (2001) 1571 *Journal of Institutional and Theoretical Economics* 14.

M Giannacopoulos, 'Sovereign Debt Crises, Referendums and the Changing Face of Colonial Power' (2017) 31 *Continuum: Journal of Media and Cultural Studies* 21.

N Gibbs, 'Post-Sovereignty and the European Legal Space' (2017) 80 *The Modern Law Review* 812.

S Gill, 'New Constitutionalism, Democratisation and Global Political Economy' (1998) 10 *Global Change, Peace & Security* 23.

E de Giorgi and C Moury, 'Conclusions: Great Recession, Great Co-operation?' in E de Giorgi and C Moury (eds), *Government-Opposition in Southern European Countries during the Economic Crisis: Great Recession, Great Cooperation?* (Abingdon, Routledge 2017).

C Ginter, 'Constitutionality of the European Stability Mechanism in Estonia: Applying Proportionality to Sovereignty' (2013) 9 *European Constitutional Law Review* 335.

J Giotaki, 'The Cypriot "Bail-In Litigation": A First Assessment of the Ruling of the Supreme Court of Cyprus' (2013) 28 *Journal of International Banking and Financial Law* 485.

A Glencross and AH Trechsel, *EU Federalism and Constitutionalism – The Legacy of Altiero Spinelli* (Lanham, Lexington, 2010).

C Glinski and Ch Joerges, 'European Unity in Diversity?! A Conflicts-Law Re-construction of Controversial Current Developments' in K Purnhagen and P Rott (eds), *Varieties of European Economic Law and Regulation. Liber Amicorum for Hans Micklitz* (Cham, Springer, 2014) 285.

A Golub, M Mahoney and J Harlow, 'Sustainability and Intergenerational Equity: Do Past Injustices Matter?' (2013) 8 *Sustainability Science* 269.

RE Goodin, 'Democratic Deliberation Within' (2000) 29 *Philosophy and Public Affairs* 81.

R Goodland, 'The Concept of Environmental Sustainability' (1995) 26 *Annual Review of Ecology and Systematics* 1.

M Goodwin, *Right Response Understanding and Countering Populist Extremism in Europe* (London, Chatham House, 2011).

LW Gormley, Ch Hadjiemmanuil and I Harden, *European Economic and Monetary Union: The Institutional Framework* (London, Kluwer Law International, 1997).

ChV Gortsos, *The New EU Directive (2014/49/EU) on Deposit Guarantee Schemes: An Element of the European Banking Union* (Athens, Nomiki Vivliothiki, 2014).

—— 'The Proposed Legal Framework for Establishing a European Monetary Fund (EMF): A Systematic Presentation and a Preliminary Assessment' (2017), available at: ssrn.com/abstract=3090343.

—— 'Deposit Guarantee Schemes: General Aspects and Recent Institutional and Regulatory Developments at International and EU Level' (2016), available at: ssrn.com/abstract=2758635.

—— 'A Poisonous (?) Mix: Bail-Out of Credit Institutions Combined with Bail-In of their Liabilities under the BRRD – The Use of "Government Financial Stabilisation Tools" (GFSTs)' (2016), available at: ssrn.com/abstract=2876508.

—— 'Macro-Prudential Tasks in the Framework of the Single Supervisory Mechanism (SSM): An Analysis of Article 5 of the SSM Regulation' European Center of Economic and Financial law Working Paper Series no 2015/12 (2015), available at: papers.ssrn.com/sol3/papers.cfm?abstract_id=2594714.

—— 'The Single Resolution Mechanism (SRM) and the Single Resolution Fund (SRF): Legal Aspects of the Second Main Pillar of the European Banking Union', 4th edn (2018), available at: ssrn.com/abstract=2668653.

—— 'Legal Aspects of the European Central Bank (ECB) – The ECB within the European System of Central Banks (ESCB) and the European System of Financial Supervision (ESFS)', 2nd edn (2018), available at: ssrn.com/abstract=3162024.

—— 'Financial Engineering Coupled with Regulatory Incentives: Is there a Strong Market Case for Sovereign Bond-Backed Securities (SBBSs) in the Euro-Area? A Brief Analysis of the European Commission's Proposal for a Regulation on SBBSs', available at (2018) ssrn.com/abstract=3244320.

A Gosseries, *Intergenerational Justice: Probing the Assumptions, Exploring the Implications*, PhD thesis (Louvain-la-Neuve, Université Catholique de Louvain, 2000).

CC Gould, *Globalizing Democracy and Human Rights* (Cambridge, Cambridge University Press, 2004).

P de Grauwe, *Economics of Monetary Union*, 12th edn (Oxford, Oxford University Press 2018).

D Gros and N Thygesen, *European Monetary Integration: From the European Monetary System to Economic and Monetary*, 2nd edn (New York, Financial Times Prentice Hall, 1998).

G Gunther, 'The Supreme Court, 1971 Term' (1972) 86 *Harvard Law Review* 8.

A Gutmann and D Thompson, *Democracy and Disagreement* (Cambridge, MA, Harvard University Press, 1996).

—— *Why deliberative democracy?* (Princeton, Princeton University Press, 2004).

D Gwynn Morgan, 'The Constitution and the Financial Crisis in Ireland' in X Contiades (ed), *Constitutions in the Global Financial Crisis: A Comparative Analysis* (Farnham, Ashgate, 2013) 63.

J Habermas, *The Crisis of the European Union: A Response* (Cambridge, Polity Press, 2013).

—— *Between Facts and Norms* (Cambridge, MA, Massachusetts Institute of Technology Press, 1996).

—— *Strukturwandel der Öffentlichkeit. Untersuchungen zu einer Kategorie der bürgerlichen Gesellschaft*, 5 Auflage (Darmstadt, Luchterhand, 1962), translated into English: *The Structural Transformation of the Public Sphere: An Inquiry into a Category of Bourgeois Cociety* (Boston, MA, Massachusetts Institute of Technology Press, 1989).

—— 'Justice and Solidarity: On the Discussion Concerning "Stage 6"' (1989) 21 *Philosophical Forum* 32.

—— 'The European Nation-State and the Pressures of Globalization' (1999) 44 *Blätter für Deutsche und Internationale Politik* 425.

—— *The Lure of Technocracy* (Cambridge, Polity Press, 2015).

—— 'The European Nation-State: On the Past and Future of Sovereignty and Citizenship' in CP Cronin and P de Greiff, *The Inclusion of the Other* (Cambridge, MA, Massachusetts Institute of Technology Press, 1999) 105.

M Haentjens, 'Selected Commentary on the Bank Recovery and Resolution Directive' in G Moss QC, B Wessels and M Haentjens (eds), *EU Banking and Insurance Insolvency*, 2nd edn (Oxford, Oxford University Press, 2017) 177.

S Hagemann and B Høyland, 'Bicameral Politics in the European Union' (2010) 48 *Journal of Common Market Studies* 811.

DA Halikiopoulou, 'Right-Wing Populist Momentum? A Review of 2017 Elections across Europe' (2018) 56 *Journal of Common Market Studies* 63.

M Hallerberg, B Marzinotto and GB Wolff, 'How Effective and Legitimate is the European Semester? Increasing the Role of the European Parliament' Bruegel Working Paper no 2011/09 (Brussels, 2011).

WH Hamilton, 'Property – According to Locke' (1932) 41 *Yale Law Journal* 864.

F Hartleb, 'A Thorn in the Side of European Elites: The New Euroscepticism' (2011) 10 *European View* 265.

D Harvey, *The Condition of Post-Modernity: An Enquiry into the Origins of Cultural Change* (Cambridge, Wiley-Blackwell, 1989).

—— 'Between Space and Time: Reflections on the Geographical Imagination' (1990) 80 *Annals of the Association of American Geographers* 418.

K Hassett, 'Does Economic Success Require Democracy? Does Economic Success Require Democracy?' *The American Magazine*, May–June 2007.

D Held, *Models of Democracy*, 3rd edn (Cambridge, Polity Press, 2006).

C Herrmann, 'Pringle v Ireland. Case C-370/12' (2013) 107 *American Journal of International Law* 410.

CA Hill, 'Why did Anyone Listen to the Rating Aagencies after Enron?' (2009) 4 *Journal of Business and Technology Law* 283.

—— 'Regulating the Rating Agencies' (2004) 82 *Washington University Law Quarterly* 43.

A Hinarejos, *The Euro Area Crisis in Constitutional Perspective* (Oxford, Oxord University Press, 2015).

—— 'Gauweiler and the Outright Monetary Transactions Programme: The Mandate of the European Central Bank and the Changing Nature of Economic and Monetary Union' (2015) 11 *European Constitutional Law Review* 563.

S Hix, A Noury and G Roland, 'Power to the Parties: Cohesion and Competition in the European Parliament, 1979–2001' (2005) 35 *British Journal of Political Science* 209.

S Hix, *What's Wrong with the European Union and how to Fix it?* (Cambridge, Polity Press, 2008).

—— 'Elections, Parties, and Institutional Design. A Comparative Perspective on European Union Democracy' (1998) 21 *West European Politics* 19.

Th Hobbes, *De Cive* (1642).

L Hooghe and G Marks, 'A Postfunctionalist Theory of European Integration: From Permissive Consensus to Constraining Dissensus' (2009) 39 *British Journal of Political Science* 1.

PM Huber, 'The Rescue of the Euro and its Constitutionality' in W-G Ringe and PM Huber (eds), *Legal Challenges in the Global Financial Crisis: Bail-Outs, the Euro and Regulation* (Oxford, Hart Publishing, 2015) 9.

J Huber and J Robertson, *Creating New Money – A Monetary Reform for the Information Age* (London, New Economics Foundation, 2000).

ThO Hueglin and A Fenna, *Comparative Federalism: A Systematic Inquiry*, 2nd edn (Toronto, University of Toronto Press, 2015).

M Ioannidis, 'Europe's New Tranformations: How the EU Economic Constitution has Changed during the Eurozone Crisis' (2013) 53 *Common Market Law Review* 1237.

K Jaklic, *Constitutional Pluralism in the EU* (Oxford, Oxford University Press, 2014).

K Jayasuriya, 'Globalization, Sovereignty, and the Rule of Law: From Political to Economic Constitutionalism?' (2001) 8 *Constellations* 442.

B Jessop, 'The Rise of Governance and the Risk of Failure' (1998) 50 *International Social Science Journal* 29.

Ch Joerges, 'Unity in Diversity as Europe's Vocation and Conflict's Law as Europe's Constitutional Form', London School of Economics Europe in Question Discussion paper Series, LEQS paper no 28/2010 (revised version 2013).

—— 'The Idea of a Three-Dimensional Conflicts Law as Constitutional Form' RECON Online Working Paper 2010/05 (2010), available at: www.reconproject.eu/projectweb/portalproject/RECONWorkingPapers.html.

—— 'Conflicts-Law Constitutionalism: Ambitions and Problems' ZenTra Working Paper in Transnational Studies No 10/2012 (2012), available at: ssrn.com/abstract=2182092.

KM Johansson and P Zervakis, 'Historical-Institutional Framework' in K Johansson and P Zervakis (eds), *European Political Parties* (Baden-Baden, Nomos, 2002) 11.

J Jupille, JA Caporaso and JT Checkel, 'Intergration Institutions: Rationalism, Constructivism, and the Study of the European Union' (2003) 36 *Comparative Political Studies* 7.

I Kant, *Perpetual Peace: A Philosophical Essay 1795* (Charleston, Nabu Press, 2013).

R Kardasheva, 'The Power to Delay: The European Parliament's Influence in the Consultation Procedure' (2009) 47 *Journal of Common Market Studies* 385.

RD Kelemen, *The Rules of Federalism: Institutions and Regulatory Politics in the EU and Beyond* (Cambridge, MA, Harvard University Press, 2004).

PB Kenen, *Economic and Monetary Union in Europe: Moving beyond Maastricht* (Cambridge, Cambridge University Press, 1995).

DM Kennedy, *Freedom from Fear: The American People in Depression and War 1929–1945* (Oxford, Oxford University Press, 1999).

P Kenway, *From Keynesianism to Monetarism: The Evolution of UK Macroeconometric Models* (London, Routledge, 1994).

R Keohane and J Nye, 'Power and Interdependence' in RK Betts (ed), *Conflict after the Cold War: Arguments on Causes of War and Peace*, 4th edn (Abingdon, Routledge, 2012).

P Kiiver, 'The Early-Warning System for the Principle of Subsidiarity: The National Parliament as a Conseil d'Etat for Europe' (2011) 36 *European Law Review* 98.

—— 'The Treaty of Lisbon, the National Parliaments and the Principle of Subsidiarity' (2008) 15 *Maastricht Journal of European and Comparative Law* 77.

C Kilpatrick, 'Constitutions, Social Rights and Sovereign Debt States in Europe: A Challenging New Area of Constitutional Inquiry' in T Beukers, B de Witte and C Kilpatrick (eds), *Constitutional Change through Euro-Crisis Law* (Cambridge, Cambridge University Press, 2017) 279.

PF Kjaer, *Constitutionalism in the Global Realm. A Sociological Approach* (Abingdon, Routledge, 2014).

N Kleftouri, *Deposit Protection and Bank Resolution* (Oxford, Oxford University Press, 2015).

N Klein, *The Shock Doctrine. The Rise of Disaster Capitalism* (London, Penguin, 2008).

Ch Koedooder, 'The Pringle Judgment: Economic and/or Monetary Union?' (2013) 37 *Fordham International Law Journal* 110.

B Kohler-Koch and B Rittberger, 'The "Governance Turn" in EU Studies' (2006) 44 *Journal of Common Market Studies* 27.

J Komárek, 'National Constitutional Courts in the European Constitutional Democracy' (2014) 12 *International Journal of Constitutional Law* 525.

R Koslowski, 'Understanding the European Union as a Federal Polity' in T Christiansen, KE Jørgensen and A Wiener (eds), *The Social Construction of Europe* (London, Sage, 2001).

—— 'A Constructivist approach to Understanding the European Union as a Federal Polity' (1999) 6 *Journal of European Public Policy* 561.

LD Kramer, *The People Themselves: Popular Constitutionalism and Judicial Review* (Oxford, Oxford University Press, 2004).

MH Kramer, *John Locke and the Origins of Private Property: Philosophical Explorations of Individuals, Community, and Equality* (Cambridge, Cambridge University Press, 1997).

B Kushman, *Rethinking the New Deal Court. The Structure of a Constitutional Revolution* (Oxford, Oxford University Press, 1998).

A Kyriakidis, 'EU Institutions after the Eurozone Crisis: What has Changed?' (2017) *Hellenic Review of European Law* 19.

J Lacroix, *Communautarisme versus Libéralisme: quel Modèle d'Intégration Politique? Les Présupposés Normatifs d'une Union Politique Européenne à la Lumière des Débats Intellectuels Contemporains*, PhD Thesis (Université de Bruxelles, 2003).

K-H Ladeur, 'The Financial Market Crisis – a Case of Network Failure?' in PF Kjaer, G Teubner and A Febbrajo (eds), *The Financial Crisis in Constitutional Perspective. The Dark Side of Functional Differentiation* (Oxford, Hart Publishing, 2011).

A Lang, *World Trade Law after Neoliberalism: Reimagining the Global Economic Order* (Oxford, Oxford University Press, 2011).

K Lenaerts and J Gutiérrez-Fons, 'The European Court of Justice as the Guardian of the Rule of EU Social Law' in F Vandenbroucke, C Barnardm and G de Baere (eds), *A European Social Union after the Crisis* (Cambridge, Cambridge University Press, 2017) 407.

K Lenaerts and A Verhoeven, 'Institutional Balance as a Guarantee for Democracy' in Ch Joerges and R Dehousse (eds), *Good Governance in Europe's Integrated Market* (Oxford, Oxford University Press, 2002) 35.

P Lindseth, *Power and Legitimacy. Reconciling Europe and the Nation-State* (Oxford, Oxford University Press, 2010).

—— 'Reflections on the "Administrative, not Constitutional" Character of EU Law in Times of Crisis' (2017) 9 *Perspectives on Federalism* 1.

J Locke, *Second Treatise of Civil Government* (originally published 1690, Indianapolis, Hackett 1980).

M Longo and Ph Murray, *Europe's Legitimacy Crisis: From Causes to Solutions* (Basingstoke, Palgrave Macmillan, 2015).

L de Lucia, 'The Rationale of Economics and Law in the Aftermath of the Crisis: A Lesson from Michel Foucault' (2016) 12 *European Constitutional Law Review* 445.

S Lucchini, J Moscianese, I de Angelis and F di Benedetto, 'State Aid and the Banking System in the Financial Crisis: From Bail-out to Bail-in' (2016) *Journal of European Competition Law and Practice* 1.

N Luhmann, *Soziale Systeme: Grundriß einer allgemeinen Theorie* (Frankfurt, Suhrkamp, 1987).

—— 'Die Weltgesellschaft' (1971) 57 *Archiv für Rechts- und Sozialphilosophie* 1.

N MacCormick, *Questioning Sovereignty: Law, State, and Nation in the European Commonwealth, Law, State, and Practical Reason Series* (Oxford, Oxford University Press, 1997).

—— 'Beyond the Sovereign State' (1993) 56 *The Modern Law Review* 1.

JEM Machado, 'The Sovereign Debt Crisis and the Constitution's Negative Outlook: A Portuguese Preliminary Assessment' in X Contiades (ed), *Constitutions in the Global Financial Crisis. A Comparative Analysis* (Farnham, Ashgate, 2013) 219.

M Maduro, 'Contrapunctual Law: Europe's Constitutional Pluralism in Action' in N Walker (ed), *Sovereignty in Transition* (Oxford, Hart Publishing, 2003) 501.

X Magnon, 'Décision n° 2012-653 DC du 9 août 2012, Traité sur la Stabilité, la Coordination et la Gouvernance au sein de l'Union Economique et Monétaire' (2012) 92 *Revue Française de Droit Constitutionnel* 860.

G Majone, *Dilemmas of European Integration: The Ambiguities and Pitfalls of Integration by Stealth* (Oxford, Oxford University Press, 2005).

—— 'Europe's "Democratic Deficit": The Question of Standards' (1998) 4 *European Law Journal* 5.

P-A van Malleghem, 'Pringle: A Paradigm Shift in the European Union's Monetary Constitution' (2013) 14 *German Law Journal* 141.

GF Mancini, *Democracy and Constitutionalism in the European Union: Collected Essays* (Oxford, Hart Publishing, 2000).

J Manolopoulos, *Greece's 'Odious' Debt: The Looting of the Hellenic Republic by the Euro, the Political Elite and the Investment Community* (London, Anthem Press, 2011).

J Mansbridge, 'The Place of Self-Interest and the Role of Power in Deliberative Democracy' (2010) 18 *Journal of Political Philosophy* 64.

M Markakis and P Dermine, 'Bailouts, the Legal Status of Memoranda of Understanding, and the Scope of application of the EU Charter: Florescu' (2018) 55 *Common Market Law Review* 643.

A Marketou, 'Greece: Constitutional Deconstruction and the Loss of National Sovereignty' in T Beukers, B.de Witte and C Kilpatrick (eds), *Constitutional Change through Euro-Crisis Law* (Cambridge, Cambridge University Press, 2017) 179.

G Marks, 'Structural Policy and Multi-level Governance in the EC' in A Cafruny and G Rosenthal (eds), *The State of the European Community: The Maastricht Debate and beyond* (Boulder, Lynne Rienner, 1993) 391.

G Marks and L Hooghe, (2004) 'Contrasting Visions of Multi-level Governance' in I Bache and M Flinders (eds), *Multi-level Governance* (Oxford, Oxford University Press) 15.

JR May and E Daly, *Global Environmental Constitutionalism* (New York, Cambridge University Press, 2015).

FC Mayer, 'Rebels without a Cause? A Critical Analysis of the German Constitutional Court's OMT Reference' (2014) 15 *German Law Journal* 111.

AG Merino, 'Legal Developments in the Economic and Monetary Union during the Debt Crisis: The Mechanisms of Financial Assistance' (2012) 49 *Common Market Law Review* 1613.

A Michaelides and A Orphanides (eds), *The Cyprus Bail-in: Policy Lessons from the Cyprus Economic Crisis* (London, Imperial College Press, 2016).

A Michaelides, 'Cyprus: From Boom to Bail-in' (2014) 29 *Economic Policy* 639.

J Milios and D Sotiropoulos, 'Crisis of Greece or Crisis of the Euro? A View from the "Periphery"' (2010) 12 *Journal of Balkan and Near Eastern Studies* 223.

A Moravcsik, 'Preferences and Power in the European Community: A Liberal Intergovernmentalist Approach' (1993) 31 *Journal of Common Market Studies* 473.

—— 'Is Something Rotten in the State of Denmark? Constructivism and European Integration.' (1999) 6 *Journal of European Public Policy* 669.

K Nicolaïdis, 'Our European Demoi-cracy: Is this Constitution a Third Way for Europe?' in K Nicolaïdis and S Weatherill (eds), *Whose Europe? National Models and the Constitution of the European Union* (Oxford, Oxford University Press, 2003) 137.

P Niesen, 'Volk-von-Teufeln-Republikanismus: Zur Frage nach den Moralischen Ressourcen der Liberalen Demokratie' in K Günther and L Wingert (eds), *Die Öffentlichkeit der Vernunft und die Vernunft der Öffentlichkeit. Festschrift für J Habermas* (Frankfurt, Suhrkamp, 2001) 568.

L Oberndorfer, 'A New Economic Governance through Secondary Legislation? Analysis and Constitutional Assessment: From New Constitutionalism, via Authoritarian Constitutionalism to Progressive Constitutionalism' in N Bruun, K Lörcher and I Schömann (eds), *The Economic and Financial Crisis and Collective Labour Law in Europe* (Oxford, Hart Publishing, 2014) 25.

C Offe and U Preuss, 'Democracy Institutions and Moral Resources' in D Held (ed), *Political Theory Today* (Cambridge, Polity, 1991) 156.

C Ostrom, M Tiebout and R Warren, 'The Organization of Government in Metropolitan Areas: A Theoretical Inquiry' (1961) 55 *The American Political Science Review* 831.

KPV O'Sullivan and T Kennedy, 'What Caused the Irish Banking Crisis? (2010) 18 *Journal of Financial Regulation and Compliance* 224.

J van Overtveldt, *The End of the Euro: The Uneasy Future of the European Union* (Berkeley, Agate Publishing, 2011).

E Padilla, 'Intergenerational Equity and Sustainability' (2002) 41 *Ecological Economics* 69.

G Pagoulatos, 'Greece after the Bailouts: Assessment of a Qualified Failure', GreeSE Paper no 130, Hellenic Observatory, European Institute, LSE (2018), available at: http://eprints.lse.ac.uk/91957.

G Pagoulatos, 'State-driven in Boom and in Bust: Structural limitations of Financial Power in Greece' (2014) 49 *Government and Opposition* 452.

G Pagoulatos and L Tsoukalis 'Multilevel Governance in the European Union' in E Jones, A Menon and S Weatherill (eds), *Handbook on the European Union* (Oxford, Oxford University Press, 2012) 62.

K Palonen and C Wiesner 'Second Chamber, "Congress of Ambassadors" or Federal Presidency. Parliamentary and Non-parliamentary Aspects in the European Council's Rules of Procedure' (2016) 36 *Parliaments, Estates and Representation* 71.

ChF Parker and Ch Karlsson, 'The UN Climate Change Negotiations and the Role of the United States: Assessing American Leadership from Copenhagen to Paris' (2018) 27 *Environmental Politics* 519.

P Pavlopoulos, *An Enemy of Representative Democracy. The Predominance of "Economics" over "Public Institutions"* (Athens, Gutenberg, 2018).

L Pech and S Platon, 'Judicial Independence under Threat: The Court of Justice to the Rescue in the *ASJP* Case' (2018) 55 *Common Market Law Review* 1827.

S Peers, 'The Stability Treaty: Permanent Austerity or Gesture Politics?' (2012) 8 *European Constitutional Law Review* 404.

T Pelagidis and M Mitsopoulos, *Understanding the Crisis in Greece: From Boom to Bust*, 2nd edn (New York, Palgrave Macmillan, 2011).

E-U Petersmann, *International Economic Law in the 21st Century. Constitutional Pluralism and Multilevel Governance of Interdependent Public Goods* (Oxford, Hart Publishing, 2012).

J Peterson, 'Juncker's Political European Commission and an EU in Crisis' (2017) 55 *Journal of Common Market Studies* 349.

—— 'Subsidiarity: A Definition to Suit any Vision?' (1994) 47 *Parliamentary Affairs* 116.

S Piattoni, 'Multi-level Governance: a Historical and Conceptual Analysis' (2009) 31 *Journal of European Public Policy* 163.

S Pierré-Caps, 'Le Conseil Constitutionnel et la Stabilité Economico-Financière' (2013) 30 *Civitas Europa* 145.

P Pikramenos, 'Public Law in Extraordinary Circumstances from the Point of View of the Annulment of the Administrative Procedure' (2012) 44 *Theory and Practice of Administrative Law* 97 (in Greek).

K Polanyi, 'Our Obsolete Market Mentality. Civilization must find a New Thought Pattern' (1947) 3 *Commentary* 109.

—— 'The Economy as Instituted Process' in K Polanyi, CM Arensberg and HW Pearson (eds), *Trade and Market in the Early Empires: Economies in History and Theory* (New York, The Free Press, 1957) 243.

D Popovic, *Protecting Property in European Human Rights Law* (Utrecht, Eleven International, 2009).

K Popper, 'The Logic of the Social Sciences' in T Adorno (ed), *The Positivist Dispute in German Sociology* (New York, Harper and Row, 1976) 87.

D della Porta, 'Late Neoliberalism and its Discontents: A Comparative Conclusion' in D della Porta et als (eds), *Late Neoliberalism and its Discontents in the Economic Crisis: Comparing Social Movements in the European Periphery* (London, Palgrave Macmillan, 2017) 261.

RA Posner, 'The Constitution as an Economic Document' (1987) 56 *George Washington Law Review* 4.

N Poulatzas, *Clashes in Contemporary Capitalism* (London, New Left Books, 1975).

U Puetter, *The European Council and the Council: New Intergovernmentalism and Institutional Change* (Oxford, Oxford University Press, 2014).

A Psygkas, *From the 'Democratic Deficit' to a 'Democratic Surplus': Constructing Administrative Democracy in Europe* (New York, Oxford University Press, 2017).

Ch Rauh and M Zürn, 'Zur Politisierung der EU in der Krise' in M Heidenreich (ed), *Krise der europäischen Vergesellschaftung?* (Wiesbaden, Springer VS, 2014).

J Rawls, *The Law of Peoples with the Idea of Public Reason Revisited* (Cambridge, MA, Harvard University Press, 1999).

—— *A Theory of Justice* (Cambridge, MA, Harvard University Press, 1971).

V Reding, 'Mit einer Vision aus der Krise finden' *Frankfurter Allgemeine Zeitung*, 9 March 2012, *Die Europäische Union: Zukunft, Chancen, Risiken* (Frankfurter Allgemeine Archiv, Frankfurt am Main, 2013).

M Renner, 'Death by Complexity. The Financial Crisis and the Crisis of Law in World Society' in PF Kjaer, G Teubner and A Febbrajo (eds), *The Financial Crisis in Constitutional Perspective. The Dark Side of Functional Differentiation* (Oxford, Hart Publishing, 2011) 93.

WH Riker and PC Ordeshook, 'A Theory of the Calculus of Voting' (1968) 62 *The American Political Science Review* 25.

J Rodrigues and J Reis, 'The Asymmetries of European Integration and the Crisis of Capitalism in Portugal' (2012) 16 *Competition and Change* 188.

B Rosamond, *Theories of European Union Integration* (Basingstoke, Macmillan 2000).

A Rosas and L Armati, *EU Constitutional Law: An Introduction*, 2nd edn (Oxford, Hart Publishing, 2012).

S Royo, *Lessons from the Economic Crisis in Spain*, Europe in Transition -- The NYU European Studies Series (New York, Palgrave Macmillan, 2013).

A Ruiz Robledo, 'The Spanish Constitution in the Turmoil of the Global Financial Crisis' in X Contiades, (ed), *Constitutions in the Global Financial Crisis: A Comparative Analysis* (Farnham, Ashgate, 2013) 141.

L Sanchez, 'Spain: Dealing with the Economic Emergency through Constitutional Reform and Limited Parliamentary Intervention' in T Beukers, B de Witte and C Kilpatrick (eds), *Constitutional Change through Euro-Crisis Law* (Cambridge, Cambridge University Press, 2017) 199.

H Sauer, 'Doubtful it Stood …: Competence and Power in European Monetary and Constitutional Law in the Aftermath of the CJEU's OMT Judgment' (2015) 16 *German Law Journal* 971.

JD Savage and A Verdun, 'Strengthening the European Commission's Budgetary and Economic Surveillance Capacity since Greece and the Euro Area Crisis: A Study of Five Directorates-General' (2016) 23 *Journal of European Public Policy* 101.

JD Savage and D Howarth 'Enforcing the European Semester: The Politics of Asymmetric Information in the Excessive Deficit and Macroeconomic Imbalance Procedures' (2018) 25 *Journal of European Public Policy* 212.

F Scarpf, *Governing in Europe: Effective and Democratic?* (Oxford, Oxford University Press, 1999).

V Schmidt, 'The "New" EU Governance: "New" Intergovernmentalism Versus "New" Supranationalism plus "New" Parliamentarism" in *Cahiers du CEVIPOL* 5/2016 (Bruxelles, Université Libre de Bruxelles, 2016) 5.

SJ Scholz, *Political Solidarity* (Pennsylvania, Penn State University Press, 2012).

S Schonberg and SJ Schonberg, *Legitimate Expectations in Administrative Law* (Oxford, Oxford University Press, 2000).

M Schwarz, 'A Memorandum of Misunderstanding. The Doomed Road of the European Stability Mechanism and a Possible Way Out: Enhanced Cooperation' (2014) 51 *Common Market Law Review* 389.

Ch Schweiger, *Exploring the EU's Legitimacy Crisis. The Dark Heart of Europe*, New Horizons in European Politics Series (Cheltenham, Elgar, 2016).

B Selejan-Gutan, 'Social and Economic Rights in the Context of the Economic Crisis' (2013) 4 *Romanian Journal of Comparative Law* 139.

A Sen, 'The Crisis of European Democracy' *New York Times*, 22 May 2012.

V de Serière, 'Recovery and Resolution Plans of Banks in the Context of the BRRD and the SRM: Some Fundamental Issues, in D Busch and G Ferrarini (eds), *European Banking Union* (Oxford, Oxford University Press, 2015) 10.01.

L Sermet, *The European Convention on Human Rights and Property Rights*, Human Rights Files No 11 rev (Strasbourg, Council of Europe, 1998).

JC Shambaugh, R Reis and H Rey, 'The Euro's Three Crises' (2012) 1 *Brookings Papers on Economic Activity* 157.

I Shapiro, 'Optimal Deliberation?' (2002) 10 *Journal of Political Philosophy* 196.

RJ Shiller, *The New Financial Order. Risk in the 21st Century* (Princeton, Princeton University Press, 2004).

O Shy, R Stenbacka and V Yankov, 'Limited Deposit Insurance Coverage and Bank Competition', FEDS Working Paper no 2014-53 (2014).

M Sigron, *Legitimate Expectations under Article 1 of Protocol No. 1 to the European Convention on Human Rights* (Cambridge, Intersentia, 2014).

S Simon, 'Direct Cooperation has begun: Some Remarks on the Judgment of the ECJ on the OMT Decision of the ECB in Response to the German Federal Constitutional Court's First Request for a Preliminary Ruling' (2015) 16 *German Law Journal* 1025.

A Spinelli and E Rossi, *The Ventotene Manifest* (Verona, The Altiero Spinelli Institute for Federalist Studies, 1988).

M Stallechner and D Kolb, *The European Financial Stability Facility (EFSF) and the European Stability Mechanism (ESM)* (Munich, Grin, 2013).

P Statham and H-J Trenz, 'Understanding the Mechanisms of EU Politicization: Lessons from the Eurozone Crisis' (2015) 13 *Comparative European Politics* 287.

P Stephenson, 'Twenty Years of Multi-level Governance: Where does it come from? What is it? Where is it going?' (2013) 20:6 *Journal of European Public Policy* 817.

A de Streel, 'EU Fiscal Governance and the Effectiveness of its Reform' in M Adams, F Fabbrini and P Larouche (eds), *Constitutionalization of European budgetary Constraints: Comparative and Interdisciplinary Perspectives* (Oxford, Hart Publishing, 2014) 85.

CF Strong, *A History of Modern Political Constitutions* (London, Sidgwick and Jackson, 1930).

Z Szente, 'Breaking and Making Constitutional Rules: The Constitutional Effects of the Financial Crisis in Hungary' in X Contiades (ed), *Constitutions in the Global Financial Crisis. A Comparative Analysis* (Farnham, Ashgate, 2013) 245.

HWV Temperley, *The Congress of Vienna 1814–15 and the Conference of Paris 1919* (London, Historical Association, 1923).

G Teubner, *Constitutional Fragments. Societal Constitutionalism and Globalization* (Oxford, Oxford University Press, 2012).

—— 'A Constitutional Moment? The Logics of "Hitting the Bottom"' in PF Kjaer, G Teubner and A Febbrajo (eds), *The Financial Crisis in Constitutional Perspective. The Dark Side of Functional Differentiation* (Oxford, Hart Publishing, 2011) 3.

J Theodore and J Theodore, *Cyprus and the Financial Crisis: The Controversial Bail-out and what it Means for the Eurozone* (London, Palgrave Macmillan, 2015).

R Thomas, *Legitimate Expectations and Proportionality in Administrative Law* (Oxford, Hart Publishing, 2000).

A Tomkins, *Our Republican Constitution* (Oxford, Hart Publishing, 2005).

A Torres Pérez, 'Melloni in Three Acts: From Dialogue to Monologue' (2014) 10 *European Constitutional Law Review* 308.

J Tremmel, 'Establishment of the Rights of Future Generations in National Constitutions' in J Tremmel (ed), *Handbook of Intergenerational Justice* (Cheltenham, Elgar, 2006) 187.

T Tridimas, *The General Principles of EU Law*, 2nd edn (Oxford, Oxford University Press, 2006).

—— 'The ECJ and the National Courts: Dialogue, Cooperation, and Instability' in D Chalmers and A Arnull (eds), *The Oxford Handbook of European Union Law* (Oxford, Oxford University Press, 2015) 403.

T Tridimas and N Xanthoulis, 'A Legal Analysis of the Gauweiler Case' (2016) 23 *Maastricht Journal of European & Comparative Law* 1.

Y Tsirbas and DA Sotiropoulos, 'Europe at the Epicenter of National Politics: The Attitudes of Greek Political Elites towards the European Union and the Economic Crisis' (2016) 41 *Historical Social Research* 86.

K Tuori and K Tuori, *The Eurozone Crisis. A Constitutional Analysis, Cambridge Studies in European Law and Policy* (Cambridge, Cambridge University Press, 2014).

DW Urwin, *The Community of Europe: A History of European Integration since 1945*, 2nd edn (Abingdon, Routledge, 1995).

S Vallance, HC Perkins and J Dixon, 'What is Social Sustainability? A Clarification of Concepts' (2011) 42 *Geoforum* 342.

A Verdun and J Zeitlin 'Introduction: The European Semester as a new Architecture of EU Socioeconomic Governance in Theory and Practice' (2018) 25 *Journal of European Public Policy* 137.

S Verhelst, 'Assessing the Single Supervisory Mechanism: Passing the Point of No Return for Europe's Banking Union' Egmont Paper no 58 (2013), available at: www.egmontinstitute.be/content/uploads/2013/07/Egmont-papers-58.pdf?type=pdf.

G Verhofstadt, *Verenigde Staten van Europa* (Antwerpen, Uitgeverij Houtekiet, 2006), translated into Engish, *The United States of Europe* (London, The Federal Trust, 2006).

C de Waal, *Beyond the Bail-outs: The Anthropology and History of the Greek Crisis* (London, Tauris, 2018).

KA Wade-Benzoni and LP Tost, 'The Egoism and Altruism of Intergenerational Behavior' (2009) 13 *Personality and Social Psychology Review* 165.

N Walker, 'The Idea of Constitutional Pluralism' (2002) 65 *The Modern Law Review* 317.

—— 'Late Sovereignty in the European Union' in N Walker (ed), *Sovereignty in Transition* (Oxford, Hart Publishing, 2003) 3.

FM Watkins, *The Political Tradition of the West: A Study in the Development of Modern Liberalism* (Cambridge, MA, Harvard University Press, 1948).

JHH Weiler, *The Constitution of Europe: 'Do the New Clothes have an Emperor?' and Other Essays on European Integration* (Cambridge, Cambridge University Press, 1999).

—— 'The Community System: The Dual Character of Supranationalism' (1981) 1 *Yearbook of European Law* 257.

—— 'Transformation of Europe" (1991) 100 *Yale Law Journal* 2403.

—— '60 Years since the First European Community – Reflections on Political Messianism' (2011) 22 *European Journal of International Law* 303.

—— 'The Political and Legal Culture of European Integration: An Exploratory Essay' (2011) 9 *International Journal of Constitutional Law* 678.

WW van der Werf, *Democracy in the European Union: An Analysis of the Democratic Deficit in the European Union* (Saarbrücken, Lap Lambert Academic Publishing, 2010).

M Wendel 'Exceeding Judicial Competence in the Name of Democracy: The German Federal Constitutional Court's OMT Reference' (2014) 10 *European Constitutional Law Review* 263.

—— 'Judicial Restraint and the Return to Openness: The Decision of the German Federal Constitutional Court on the ESM and the Fiscal Treaty of 12 September 2012' (2013) 14 *German Law Journal* 22.

CE White, *The Constitution and the New Deal* (Cambridge, MA, Harvard University Press, 2000).

E Wymeersch, 'The Single Supervisory Mechanism: Institutional aspects' in D Busch and G Ferrarini (eds), *European Banking Union* (Oxford, Oxford University Press 2015) 4.04.

N Xanthoulis, 'ESM, Union Institutions and EU Treaties: A Symbiotic Relationship' (2017) 1 *International Journal for Financial Services* 23.

GS Zavvos and S Kaltsouni, 'The Single Resolution Mechanism in the European Banking Union: Legal Foundation, Governance, Structure and Financing' in M Haentjens and B Wessels (eds), *Research Handbook on Crisis Management in the Banking Sector* (Cheltenham, Edward Elgar Publishing, 2015) 117.

SA Zenios, 'Fairness and Reflexivity in the Cyprus Bail-in' (2016) 43 *Empirica* 579.

INDEX

Lightning Source UK Ltd.
Milton Keynes UK
UKHW020700210521
384111UK00003B/54